This is the story of
how we came to be.
Of what happened to us,
and to those we knew,
and loved, and fought.
Where it went right...
and where it went wrong.

Sixty years.

One-hundred and thirteen people,
born with the power.

The story of the
world we touched.
And all places where
the world touched us.

And the terror
and the beauty
and the death
that happened in
the spaces in-between

RISING
STARS

B O R N   I N   F I R E

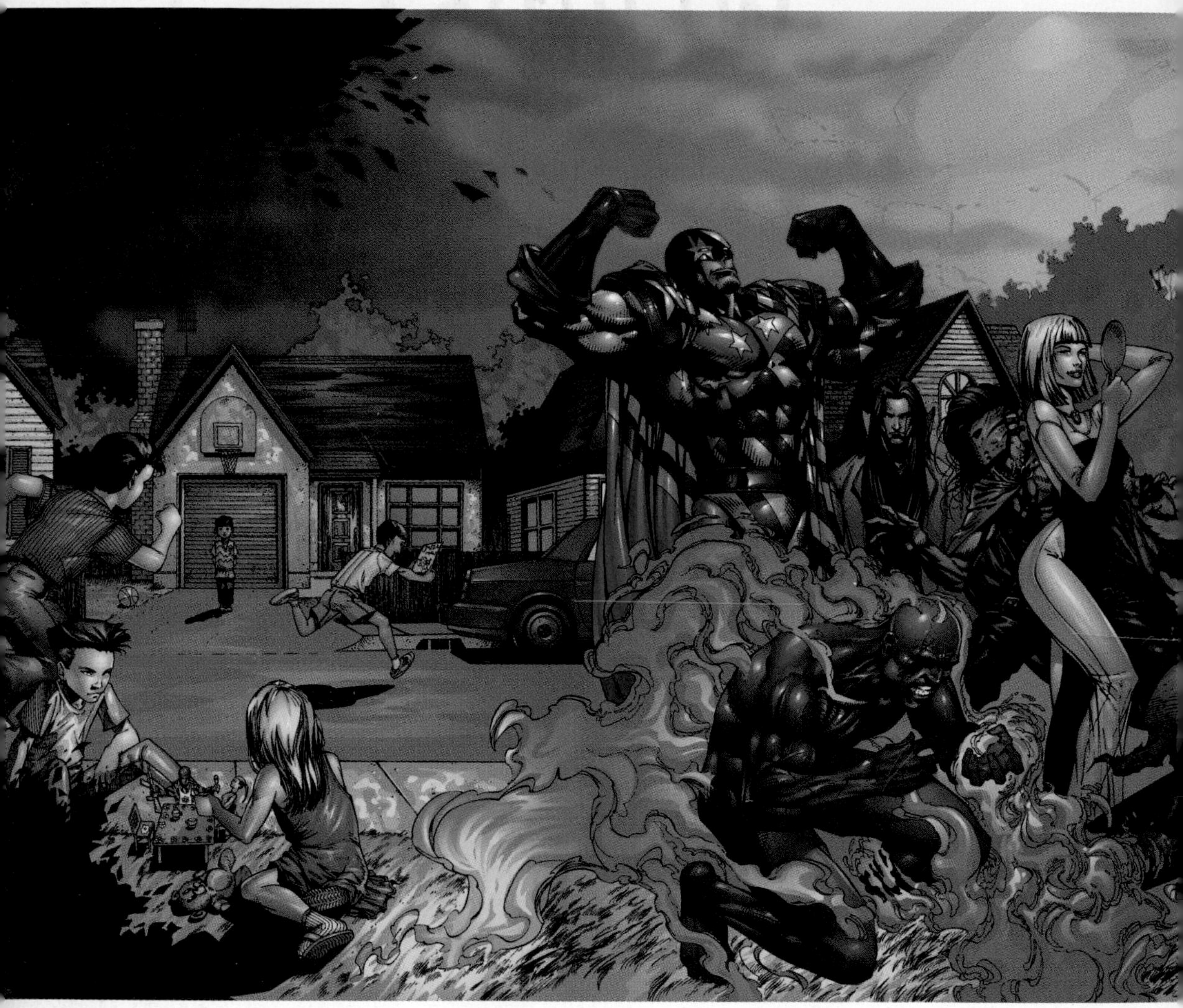

Cover to issue one

FOREWORD

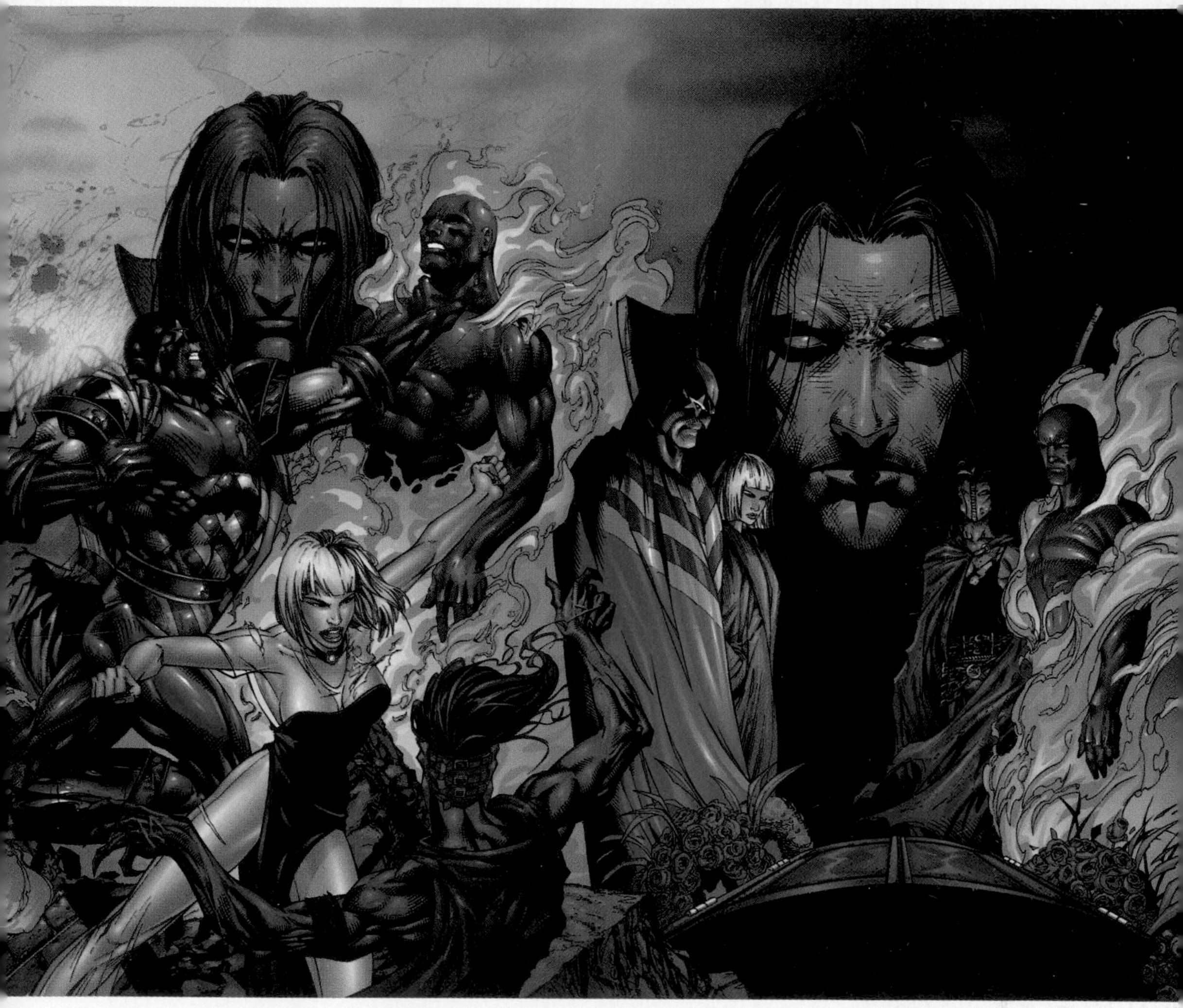

There's a fine and wonderful moment near the end of THE PHANTOM TOLLBOOTH, that rich, wise children's book by Norton Juster, where Milo, the hero, having succeeded in a mighty quest is told the one piece of important information he was denied at the start of his journey.

He's told that the task he has just accomplished was impossible.

When he asks why they hadn't told him that before, it is pointed out to him that, had he known it was impossible, he wouldn't have done it.

Which brings us to J. Michael Straczynski. Joe, as he is known to his friends.

Eight years ago, Joe sent me the 'bible' and some preliminary material for a television series he intended to make, to be called Babylon 5. It was to be a five year long story that would be the episodic televisual equivalent of a novel, with a beginning, a middle and an end. This was his plan, in the world of American television that cancels series in a heartbeat, based on the whim of executives or the fickle nature of the viewing public.

I refrained from pointing out the obvious: that what he was planning to do was, entirely and in every way, impossible.

It's probably a good thing that I didn't mention this because, five years later, he had accomplished what he set out to do, and delivered what he had promised. Babylon 5 existed, a whole huge story which began and middled and stopped. He wrote all of the last three seasons (except for one episode in season 5, written by some other bloke), and most of the first two seasons. It was his story, his vision, his characters.

It was impossible. He did it, and it was impossible. He won Hugo Awards, and Nebula Awards, and special awards they invented just to give to him, because it was good, often *really* good, and because he had genuinely done something no-one had done before. They knew it was impossible and they didn't bother. Joe didn't. Faith, as he once pointed out, prevails.

Now, he's taken the things he learned and, proving something about the nature of the man and his vision — I'm damned if I know what — he's setting out to do it again.

Only this time in comics, and in the field of Superhero comics at that. He's setting out to tell a huge story, a *real* story, teeming with a multitude of characters, good, bad and otherwise. He knows how his story begins, and how it ends, and (if he's anything like me) some, but not all, of how it middles. The material he has sent me so far is fascinating and intriguing (to talk more about the premise would be doing Joe's work a disservice — just keep reading), and is, I have no doubt, going to be much-talked-about.

It's good to welcome Joe to the world of serial comics. I dearly hope he gets to tell his tale, his way, to the end of the road, and see no reason why he shouldn't. What he's doing here, after all, isn't even impossible. It's just very, very unlikely.

But then, that's never stopped him before.

Hush, now. The lights are going down. They are starting to play the overture.

And, one by one, the stars are beginning to rise...

—NEIL GAIMAN

page 6

Nova Placenta
RISING STARS
Created by: J. Michael Straczynski
story: J. Michael Straczynski
pencils: Keu Cha, inks: Jason Gorder,
colors: Liquid!, letters: Dennis Heisler
editor: David Wohl, associate editor: Sonia Im
Cover by: Keu Cha, Jason Gorder & Liquid!

page 31

can't touch this
specials

page 54

page 77

page 100

page 123

THINGS FALL APART

page 146

THINGS FALL APART

page 169

THINGS FALL APART

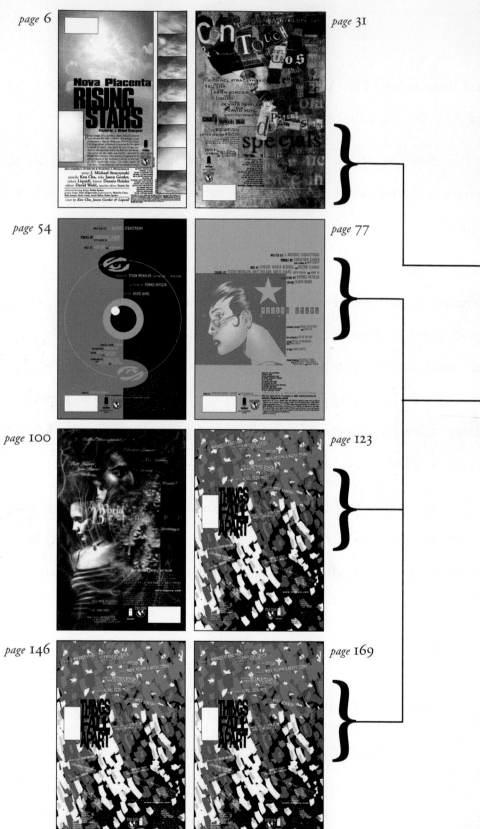

Rising Stars Created by: J Michael Straczynski

Writer: J Michael Straczynski

(chapters 1 & 2)
Penciler: Keu Cha
Inker: Jason Gorder
Colorist: Liquid!
Letterer: Dennis Heisler
Covers: Keu Cha, Jason Gorder and Liquid!

(chapters 3 through 8)
Pencilers: Christian Zanier with layouts by Ken Lashley
Inkers: Livesay with Edwin Rosell *(3)*, Victor Llamas *(4)*, Marlo Alquiza *(4)*
Colorists: Matt Nelson*(4-7)*, Brett Evans*(4,6,8)* and Tyson Wengler*(3,4)* with
            John Starr*(3,5,7)*, Drew Pasada*(4)*, Jimmy Yu*(4)*, Steve Firchow*(5)*, Nathan Cabrera*(7)* and Sonia Im*(7)*
Letterer: Dennis Heisler*(3-5)* and Dreamer Design's Robin Spehar *and* Dennis Heisler*(6-8)*
Covers: Peter Steigerwald*(3)*
            Christian Zanier, Livesay *and* Tyson Wengler*(4)*
            Christian Zanier, Livesay *and* Matt Nelson*(5,6)*
            Christian Zanier, Livesay *and* Steve Firchow*(7,8)*

Original Series Editors: David Wohl*(1-4) and* Renae Geerlings*(5-8)*
Original Series Associate Editors: Sonia Im*(1-4) and* Renae Geerlings*(4)*
Inkers Assitant: Steve Nelson*(3-8)*

(For Rising Stars: Born in Fire)
Design: Peter Steigerwald
Collected Editions Editor: Peter Steigerwald
Managing Editor: Renae Geerlings
Editorial Assistant: Mike Salter
Editor In Chief: Matt Hawkins
Production: Nick Chun, Annie Skiles, *Alvin Coats, Rafael Duffie and Beth Sotelo*
Cover: Gary Frank *and* Peter Steigerwald

(For Top Cow)
MARC SILVESTRI_chief executive officer
DAVID WOHL_president of creative affairs
MATT HAWKINS_president of publishing/editor in chief
PETER STEIGERWALD_vp of publishing and design/art director
RENAE GEERLINGS_managing editor

SONIA IM_director of licensing and public relations
FRANK MASTROMAURO_director of sales and marketing
VINCE HERNANDEZ_direct sales manager
NICHOLAS CHUN_production manager
ALVIN COATS_special projects coordinator

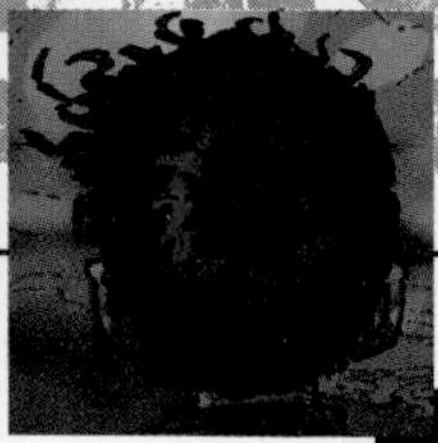

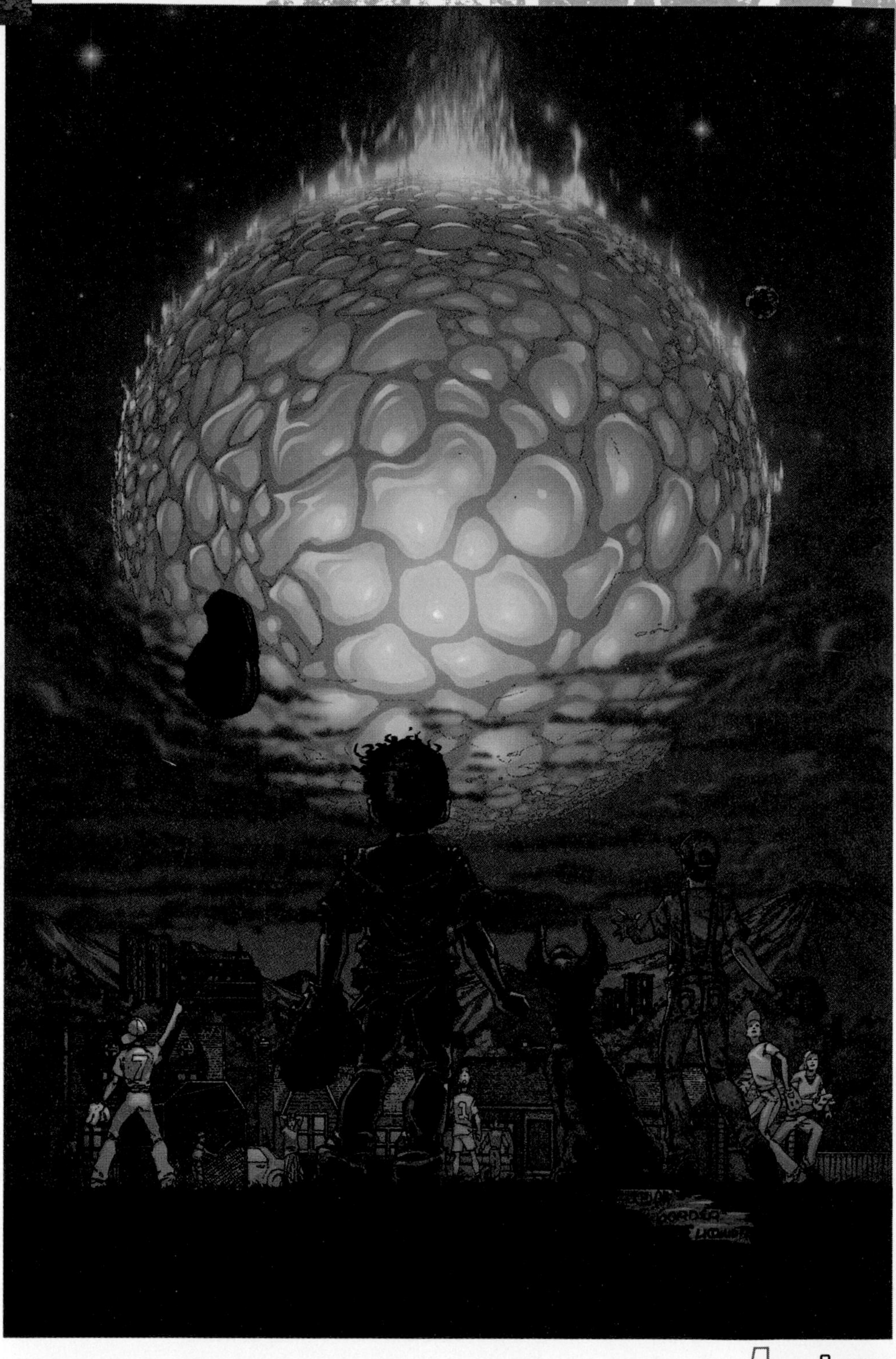

Chapter 1
Nova Placenta

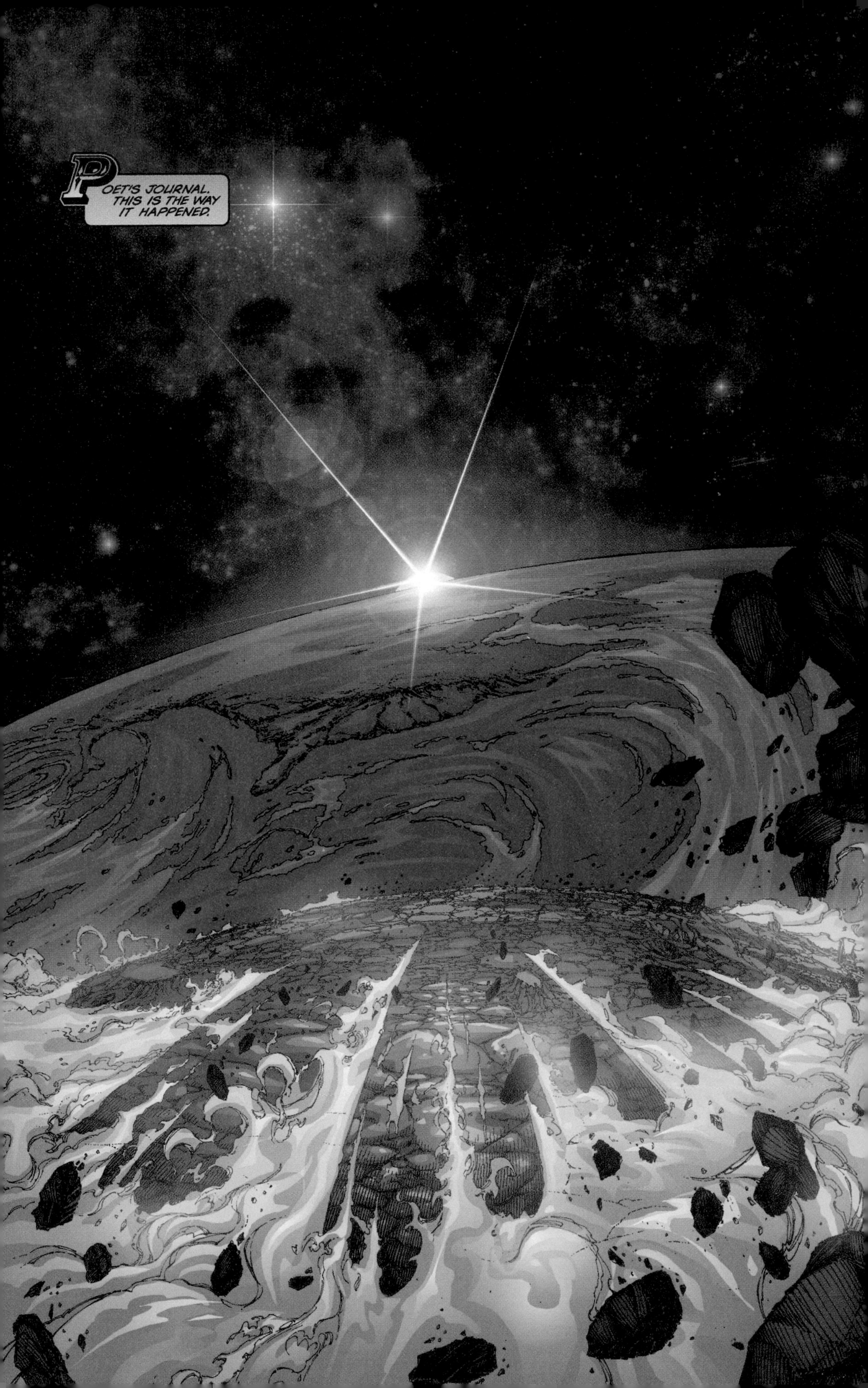
POET'S JOURNAL. THIS IS THE WAY IT HAPPENED.

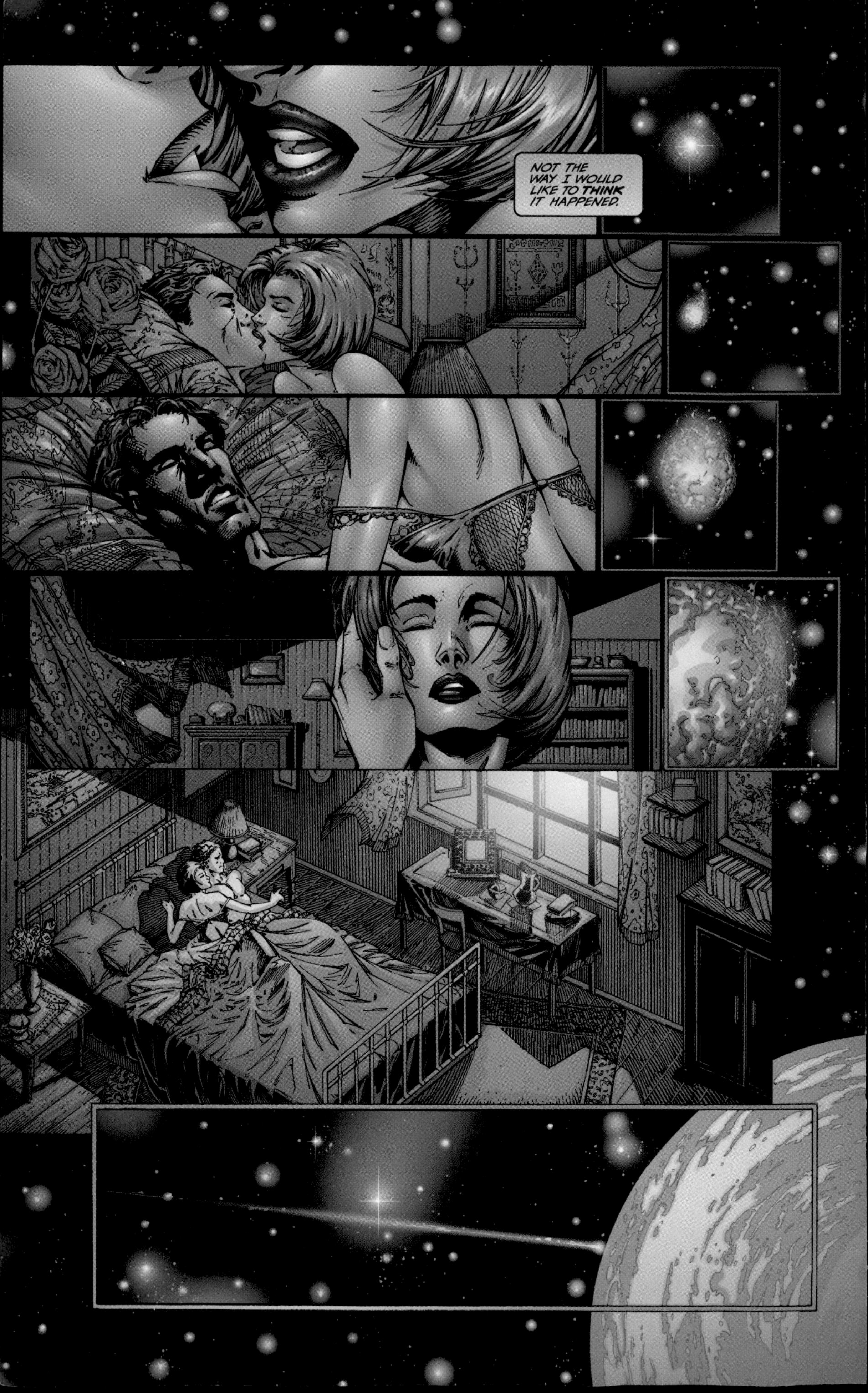
NOT THE WAY I WOULD LIKE TO THINK IT HAPPENED.

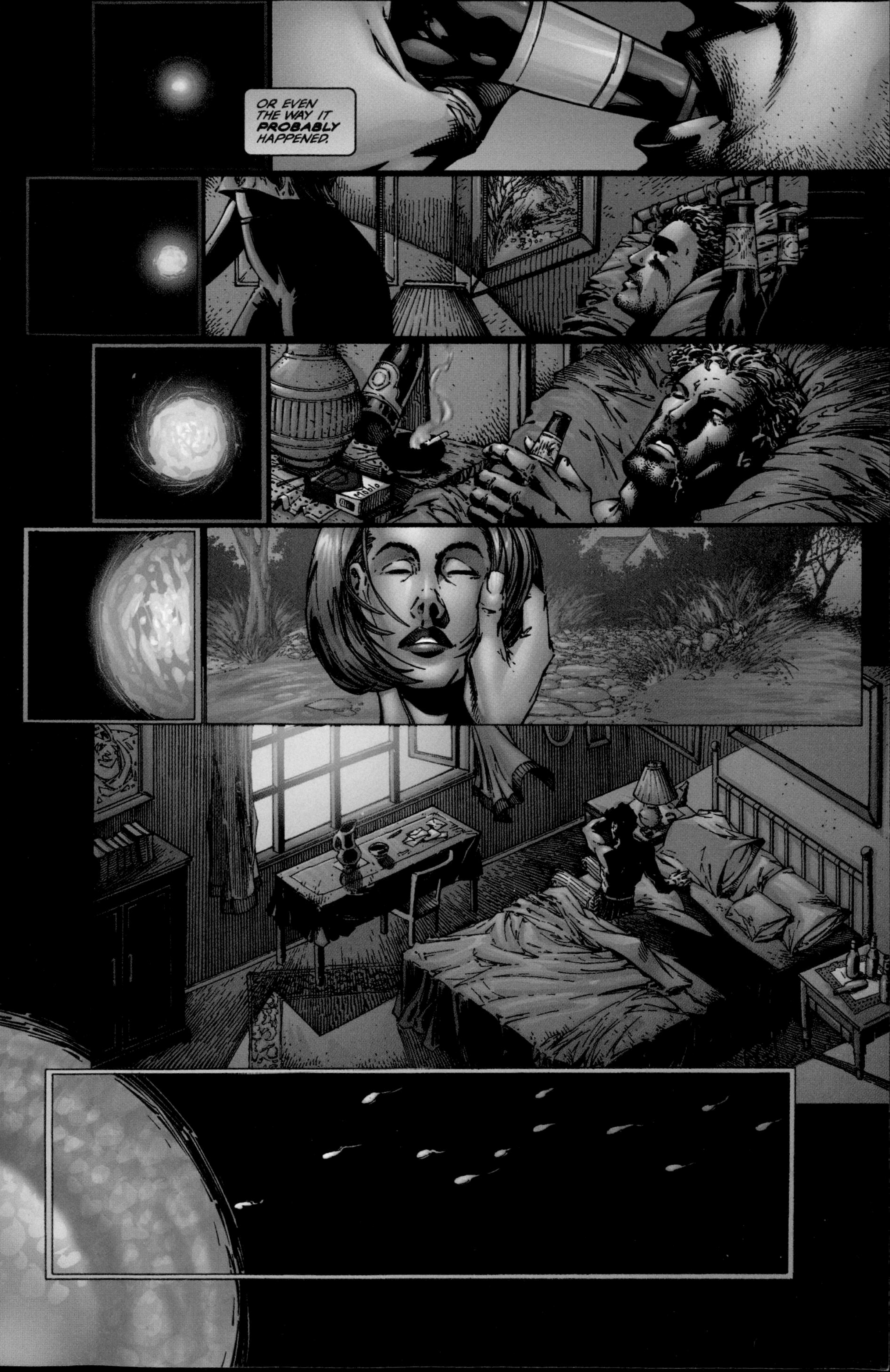
OR EVEN THE WAY IT **PROBABLY** HAPPENED.

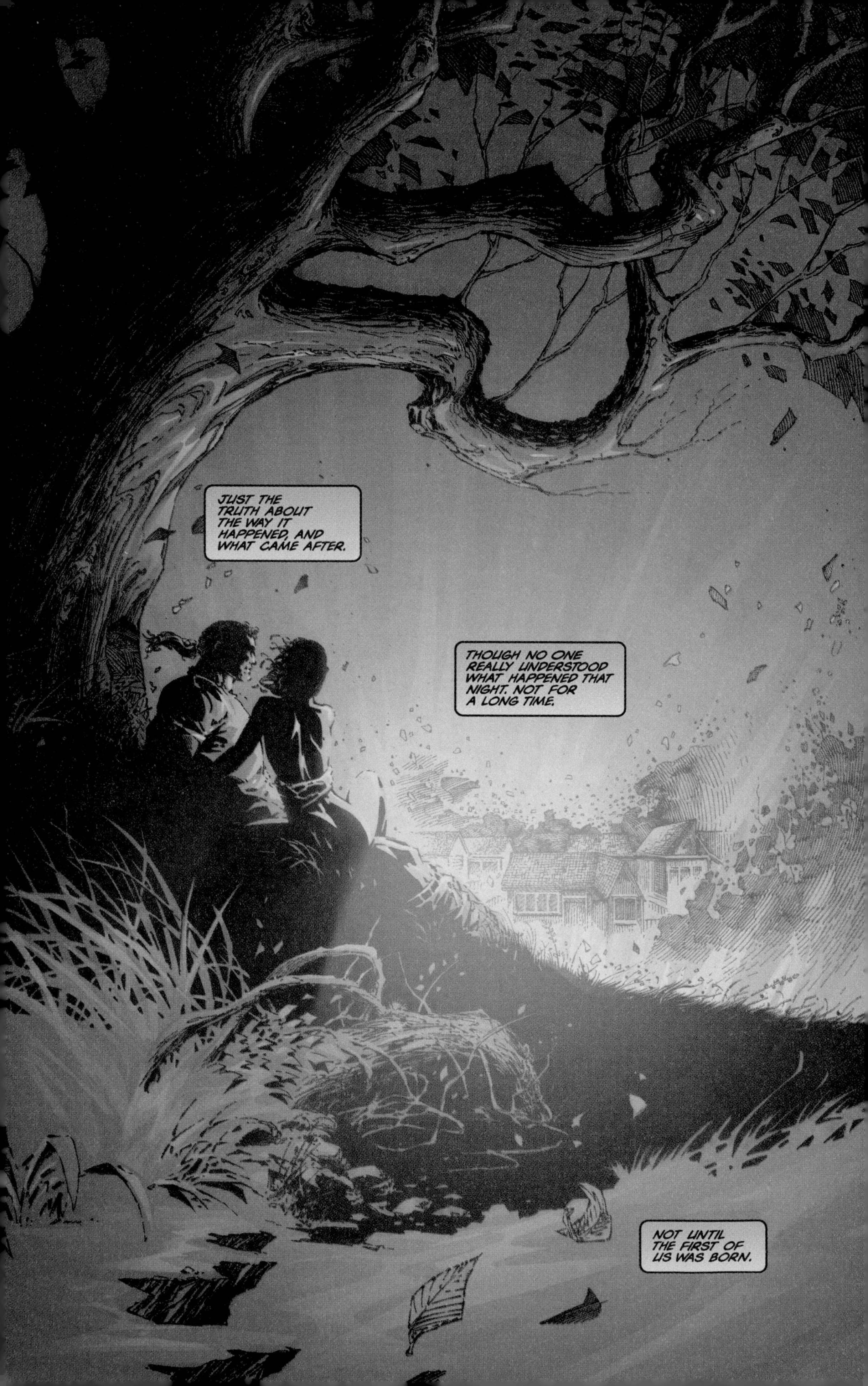
JUST THE TRUTH ABOUT THE WAY IT HAPPENED, AND WHAT CAME AFTER.
THOUGH NO ONE REALLY UNDERSTOOD WHAT HAPPENED THAT NIGHT. NOT FOR A LONG TIME.
NOT UNTIL THE FIRST OF US WAS BORN.

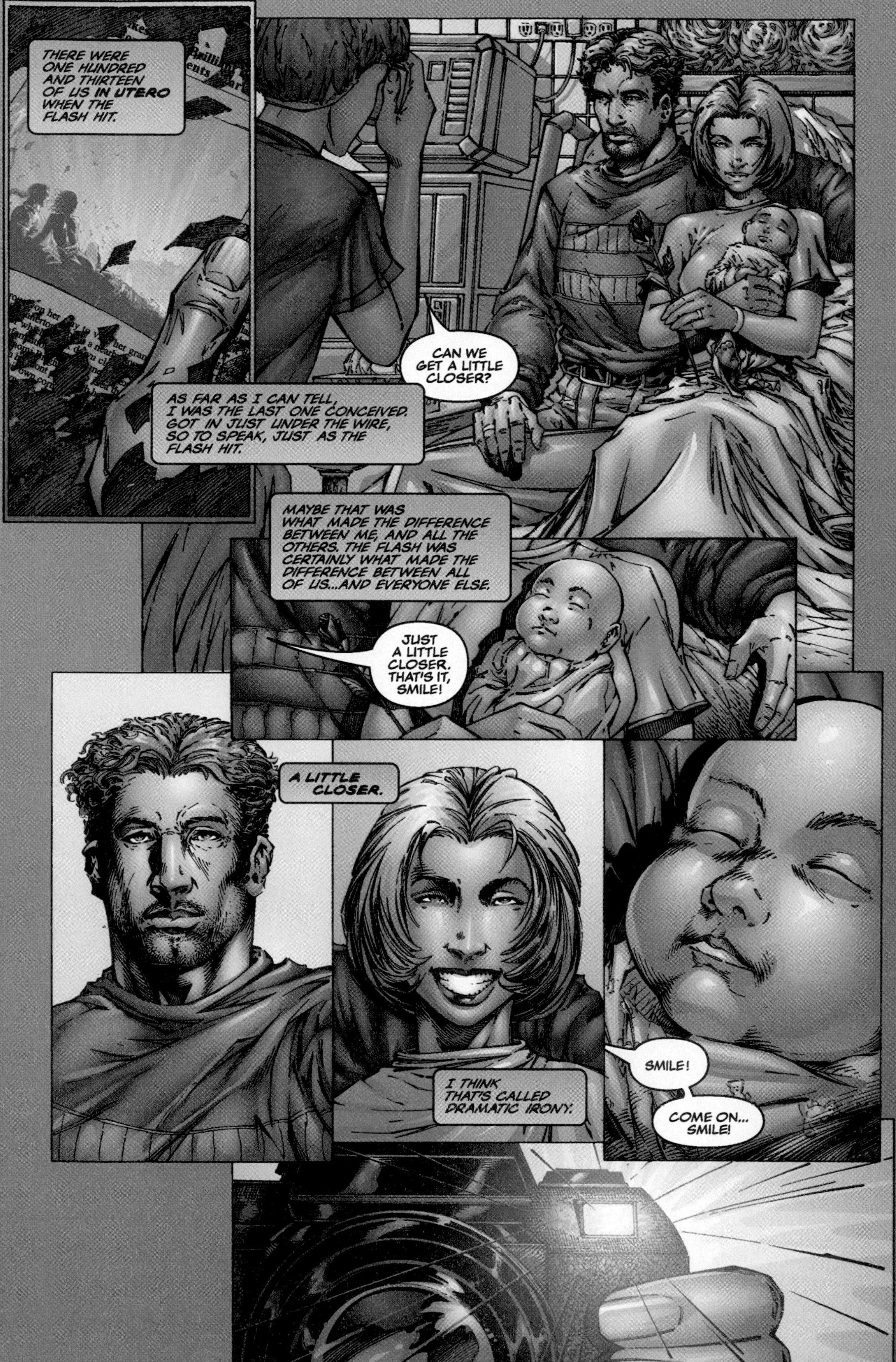
THERE WERE ONE HUNDRED AND THIRTEEN OF US IN UTERO WHEN THE FLASH HIT.
CAN WE GET A LITTLE CLOSER?
AS FAR AS I CAN TELL, I WAS THE LAST ONE CONCEIVED. GOT IN JUST UNDER THE WIRE, SO TO SPEAK, JUST AS THE FLASH HIT.
MAYBE THAT WAS WHAT MADE THE DIFFERENCE BETWEEN ME, AND ALL THE OTHERS. THE FLASH WAS CERTAINLY WHAT MADE THE DIFFERENCE BETWEEN ALL OF US...AND EVERYONE ELSE.
JUST A LITTLE CLOSER. THAT'S IT, SMILE!
A LITTLE CLOSER.
I THINK THAT'S CALLED DRAMATIC IRONY.
SMILE!
COME ON... SMILE!

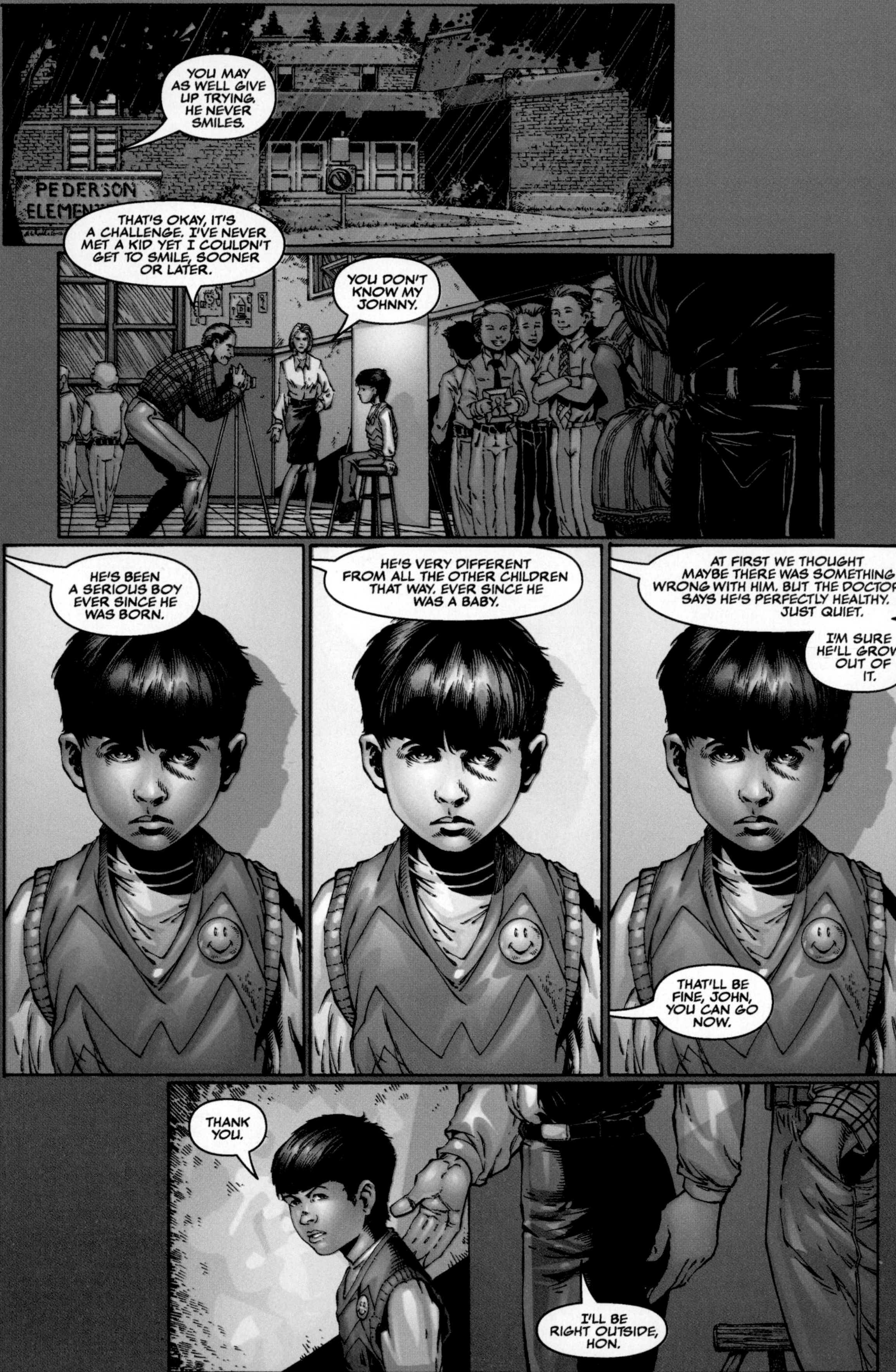

YOU MAY AS WELL GIVE UP TRYING. HE NEVER SMILES.
PEDERSON ELEMEN
THAT'S OKAY, IT'S A CHALLENGE. I'VE NEVER MET A KID YET I COULDN'T GET TO SMILE, SOONER OR LATER.
YOU DON'T KNOW MY JOHNNY.
HE'S BEEN A SERIOUS BOY EVER SINCE HE WAS BORN.
HE'S VERY DIFFERENT FROM ALL THE OTHER CHILDREN THAT WAY. EVER SINCE HE WAS A BABY.
AT FIRST WE THOUGHT MAYBE THERE WAS SOMETHING WRONG WITH HIM. BUT THE DOCTOR SAYS HE'S PERFECTLY HEALTHY. JUST QUIET.
I'M SURE HE'LL GROW OUT OF IT.
THAT'LL BE FINE, JOHN, YOU CAN GO NOW.
THANK YOU.
I'LL BE RIGHT OUTSIDE, HON.

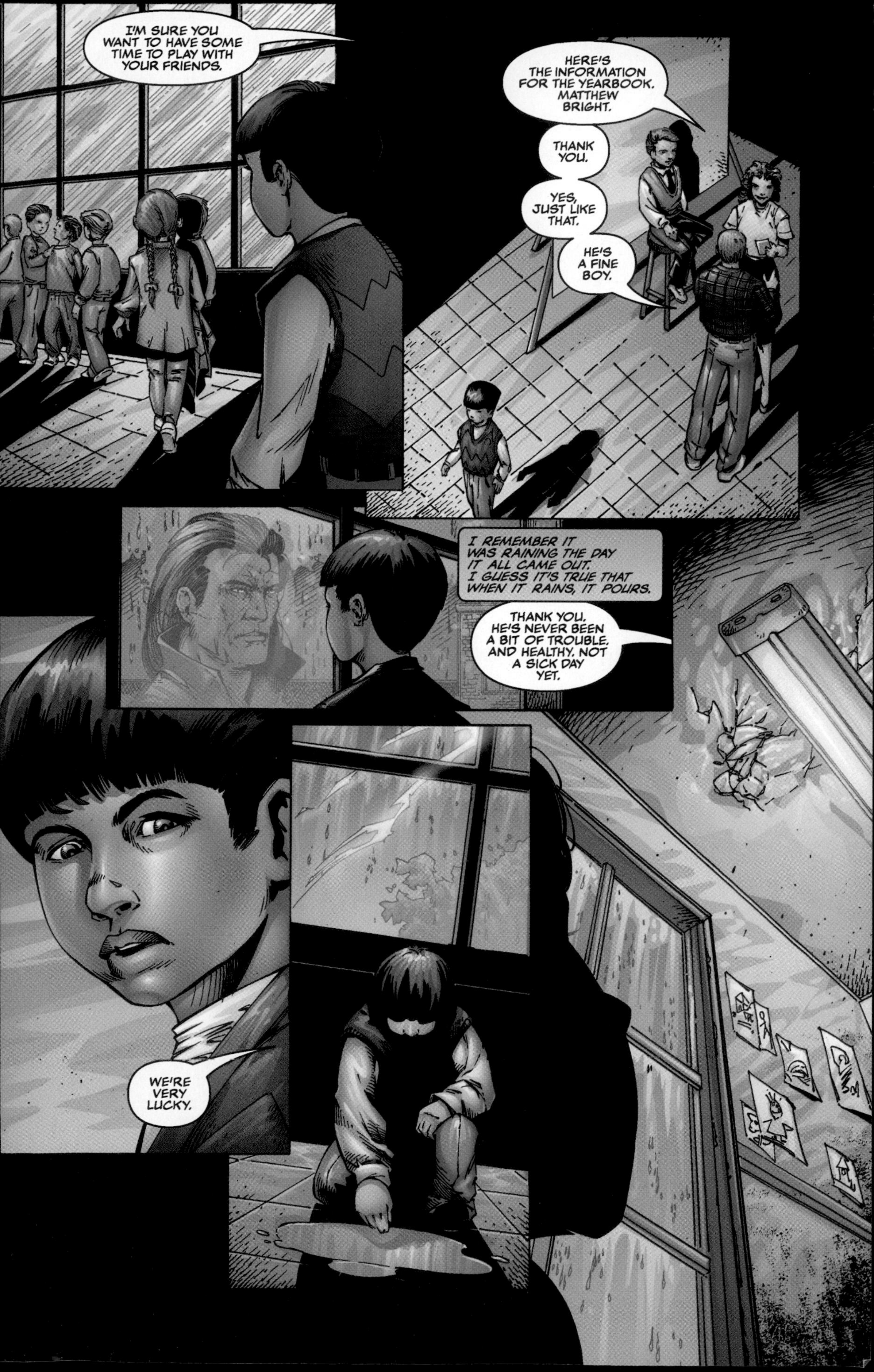
I'M SURE YOU WANT TO HAVE SOME TIME TO PLAY WITH YOUR FRIENDS.
HERE'S THE INFORMATION FOR THE YEARBOOK. MATTHEW BRIGHT.
THANK YOU.
YES, JUST LIKE THAT.
HE'S A FINE BOY.
I REMEMBER IT WAS RAINING THE DAY IT ALL CAME OUT. I GUESS IT'S TRUE THAT WHEN IT RAINS, IT POURS.
THANK YOU. HE'S NEVER BEEN A BIT OF TROUBLE. AND HEALTHY. NOT A SICK DAY YET.
WE'RE VERY LUCKY.

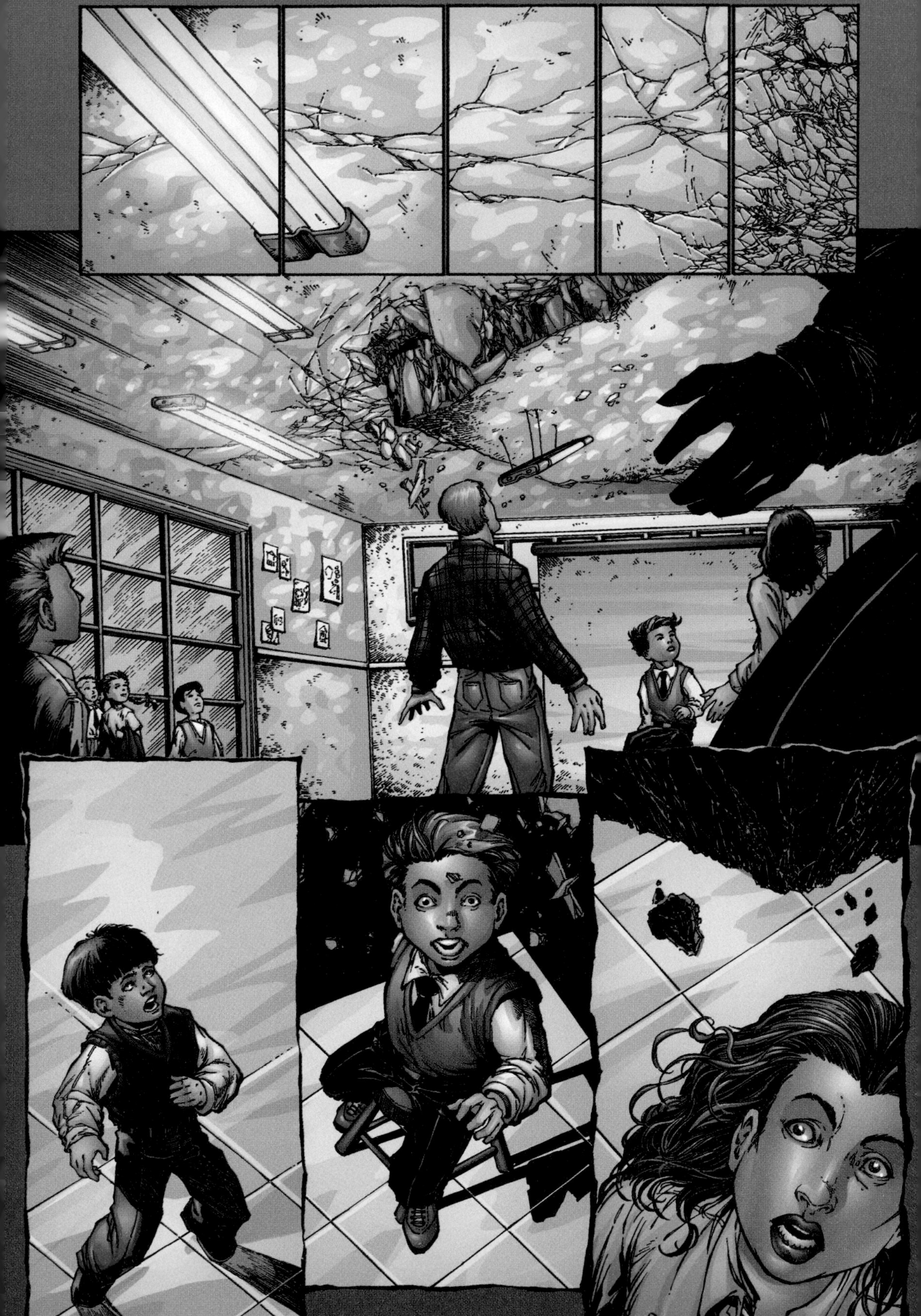

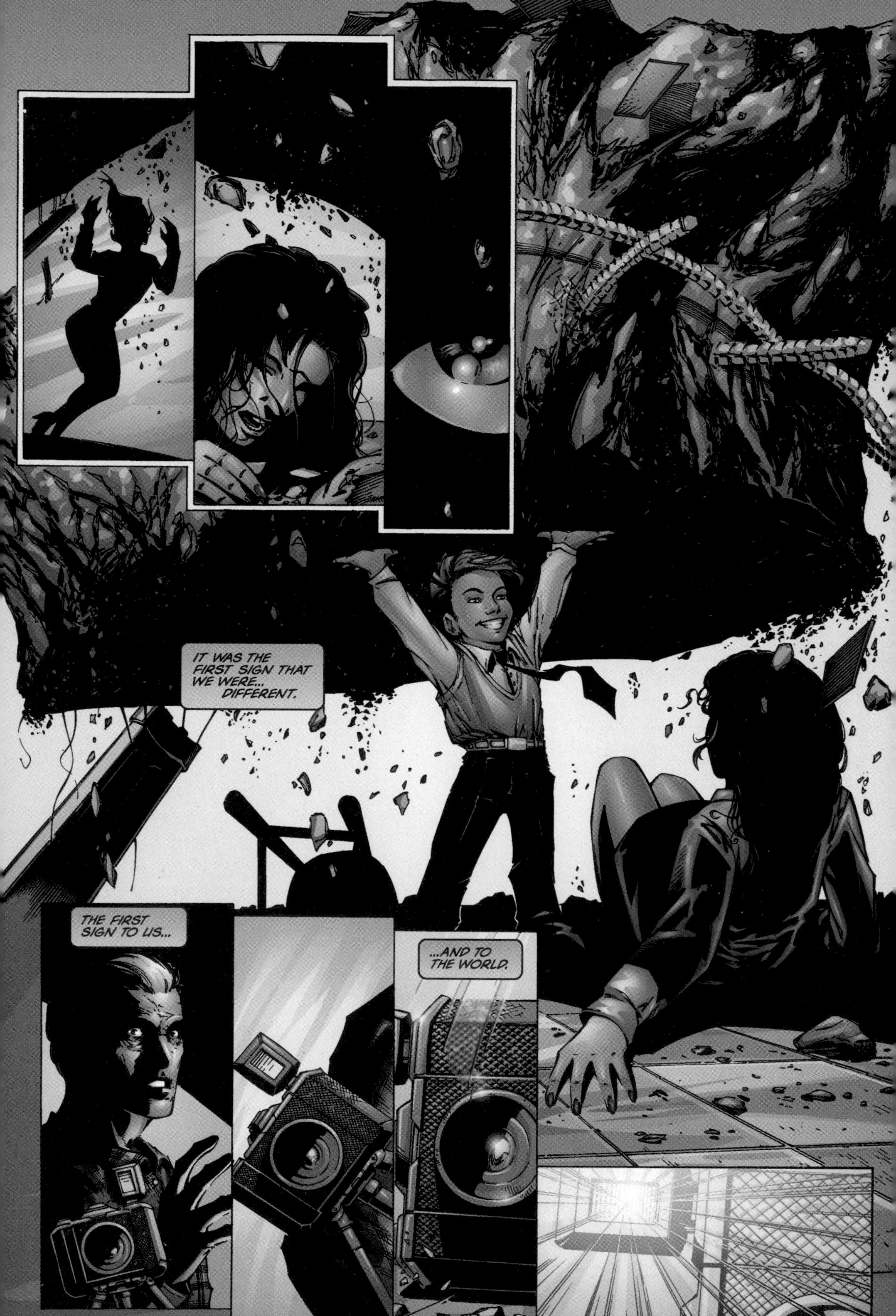
IT WAS THE FIRST SIGN THAT WE WERE... DIFFERENT.
THE FIRST SIGN TO US...
...AND TO THE WORLD.

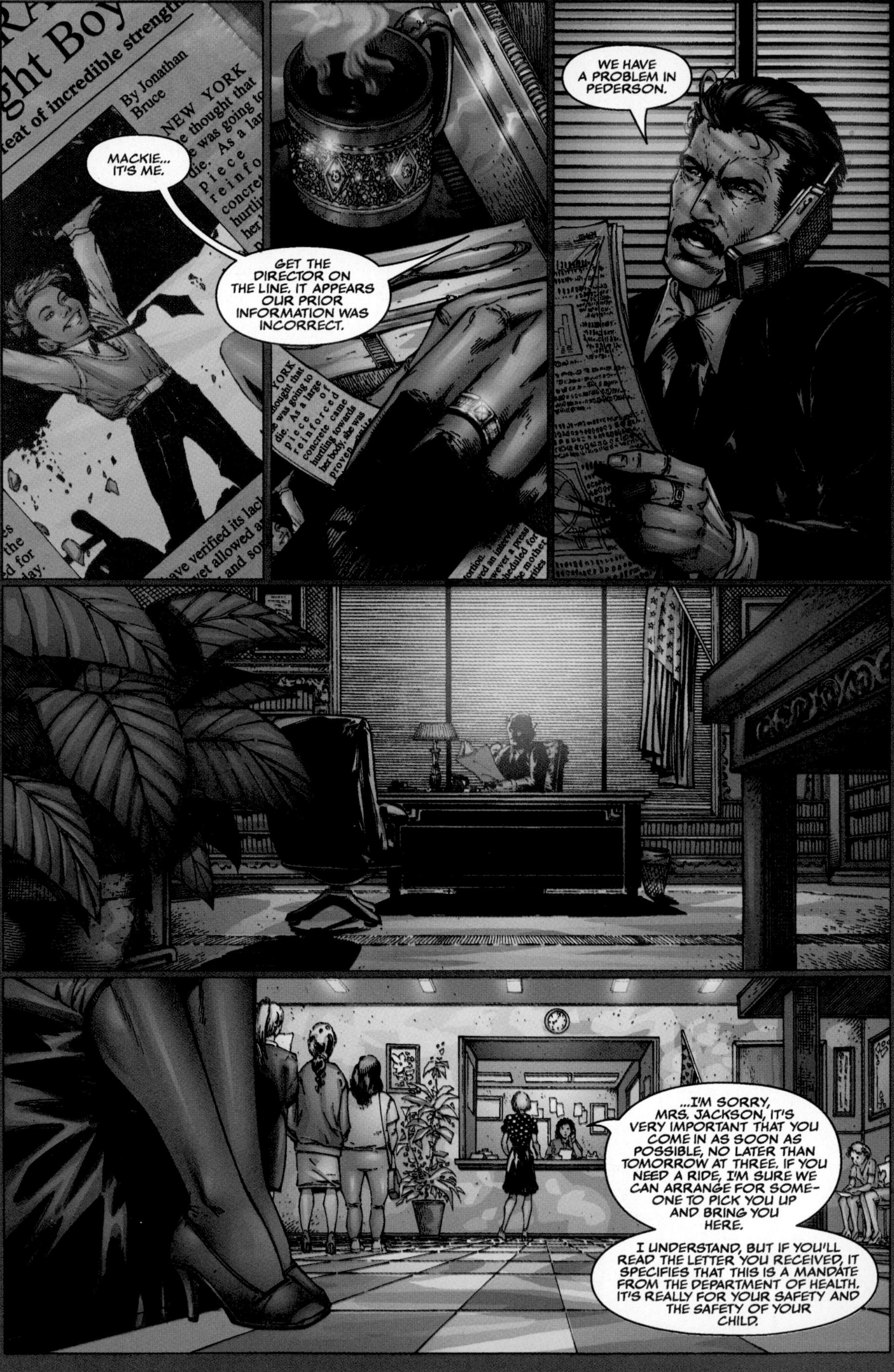

By Jonathan Bruce
NEW YORK
MACKIE... IT'S ME.
GET THE DIRECTOR ON THE LINE. IT APPEARS OUR PRIOR INFORMATION WAS INCORRECT.
WE HAVE A PROBLEM IN PEDERSON.
...I'M SORRY, MRS. JACKSON, IT'S VERY IMPORTANT THAT YOU COME IN AS SOON AS POSSIBLE, NO LATER THAN TOMORROW AT THREE. IF YOU NEED A RIDE, I'M SURE WE CAN ARRANGE FOR SOME-ONE TO PICK YOU UP AND BRING YOU HERE.
I UNDERSTAND, BUT IF YOU'LL READ THE LETTER YOU RECEIVED, IT SPECIFIES THAT THIS IS A MANDATE FROM THE DEPARTMENT OF HEALTH. IT'S REALLY FOR YOUR SAFETY AND THE SAFETY OF YOUR CHILD.

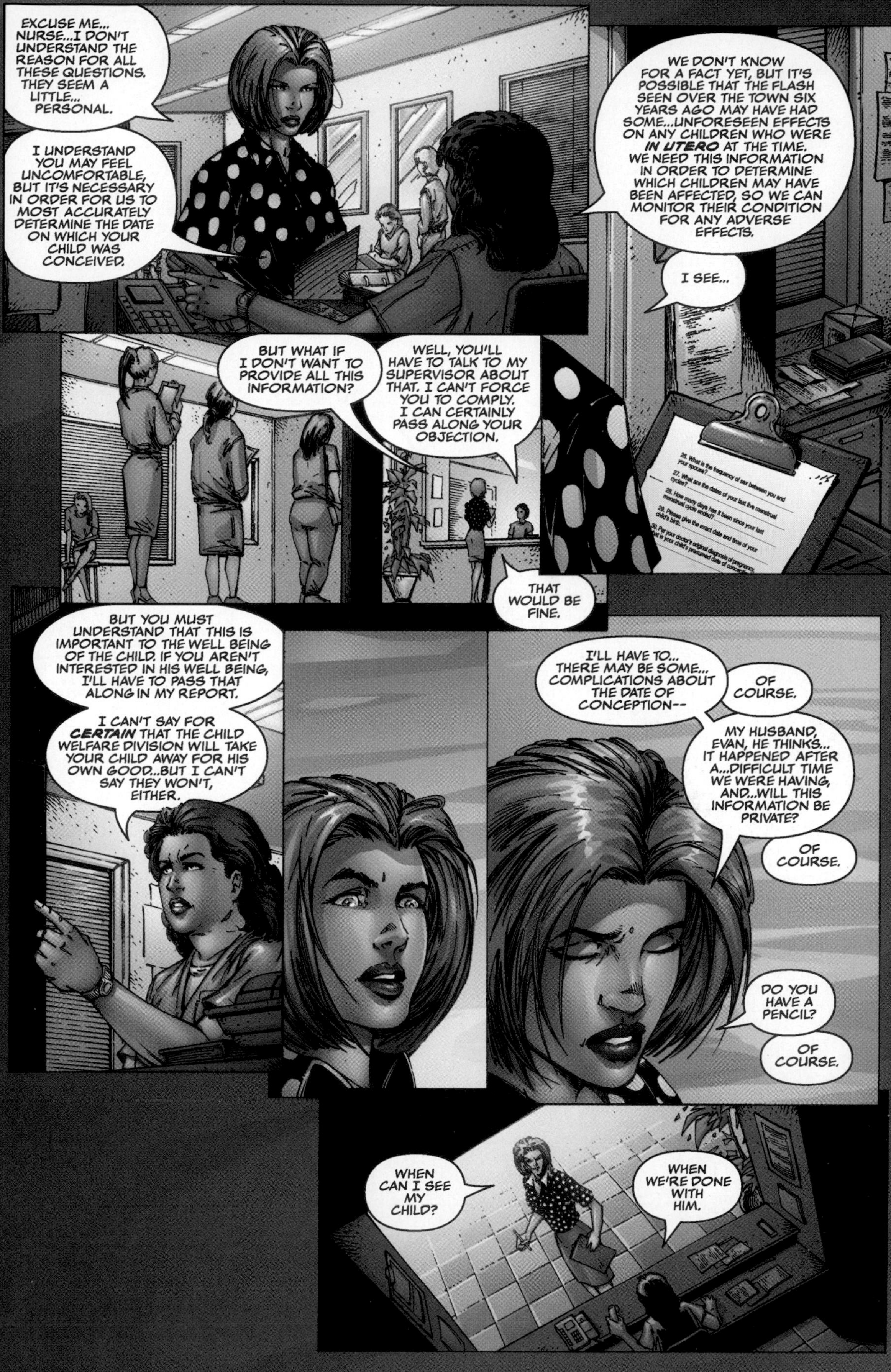
EXCUSE ME... NURSE...I DON'T UNDERSTAND THE REASON FOR ALL THESE QUESTIONS. THEY SEEM A LITTLE... PERSONAL.
I UNDERSTAND YOU MAY FEEL UNCOMFORTABLE, BUT IT'S NECESSARY IN ORDER FOR US TO MOST ACCURATELY DETERMINE THE DATE ON WHICH YOUR CHILD WAS CONCEIVED.
WE DON'T KNOW FOR A FACT YET, BUT IT'S POSSIBLE THAT THE FLASH SEEN OVER THE TOWN SIX YEARS AGO MAY HAVE HAD SOME...UNFORESEEN EFFECTS ON ANY CHILDREN WHO WERE IN UTERO AT THE TIME. WE NEED THIS INFORMATION IN ORDER TO DETERMINE WHICH CHILDREN MAY HAVE BEEN AFFECTED, SO WE CAN MONITOR THEIR CONDITION FOR ANY ADVERSE EFFECTS.
I SEE...
BUT WHAT IF I DON'T WANT TO PROVIDE ALL THIS INFORMATION?
WELL, YOU'LL HAVE TO TALK TO MY SUPERVISOR ABOUT THAT. I CAN'T FORCE YOU TO COMPLY. I CAN CERTAINLY PASS ALONG YOUR OBJECTION.
26. What is the frequency of sex between you and your spouse?
27. What are the dates of your last five menstrual cycles?
28. How many days has it been since your last menstrual cycle ended?
29. Please give the exact date and time of your child's birth.
30. Per your doctor's original diagnosis of pregnancy
THAT WOULD BE FINE.
BUT YOU MUST UNDERSTAND THAT THIS IS IMPORTANT TO THE WELL BEING OF THE CHILD. IF YOU AREN'T INTERESTED IN HIS WELL BEING, I'LL HAVE TO PASS THAT ALONG IN MY REPORT.
I CAN'T SAY FOR CERTAIN THAT THE CHILD WELFARE DIVISION WILL TAKE YOUR CHILD AWAY FOR HIS OWN GOOD...BUT I CAN'T SAY THEY WON'T, EITHER.
I'LL HAVE TO... THERE MAY BE SOME... COMPLICATIONS ABOUT THE DATE OF CONCEPTION--
OF COURSE.
MY HUSBAND, EVAN, HE THINKS... IT HAPPENED AFTER A...DIFFICULT TIME WE WERE HAVING, AND...WILL THIS INFORMATION BE PRIVATE?
OF COURSE.
DO YOU HAVE A PENCIL?
OF COURSE.
WHEN CAN I SEE MY CHILD?
WHEN WE'RE DONE WITH HIM.

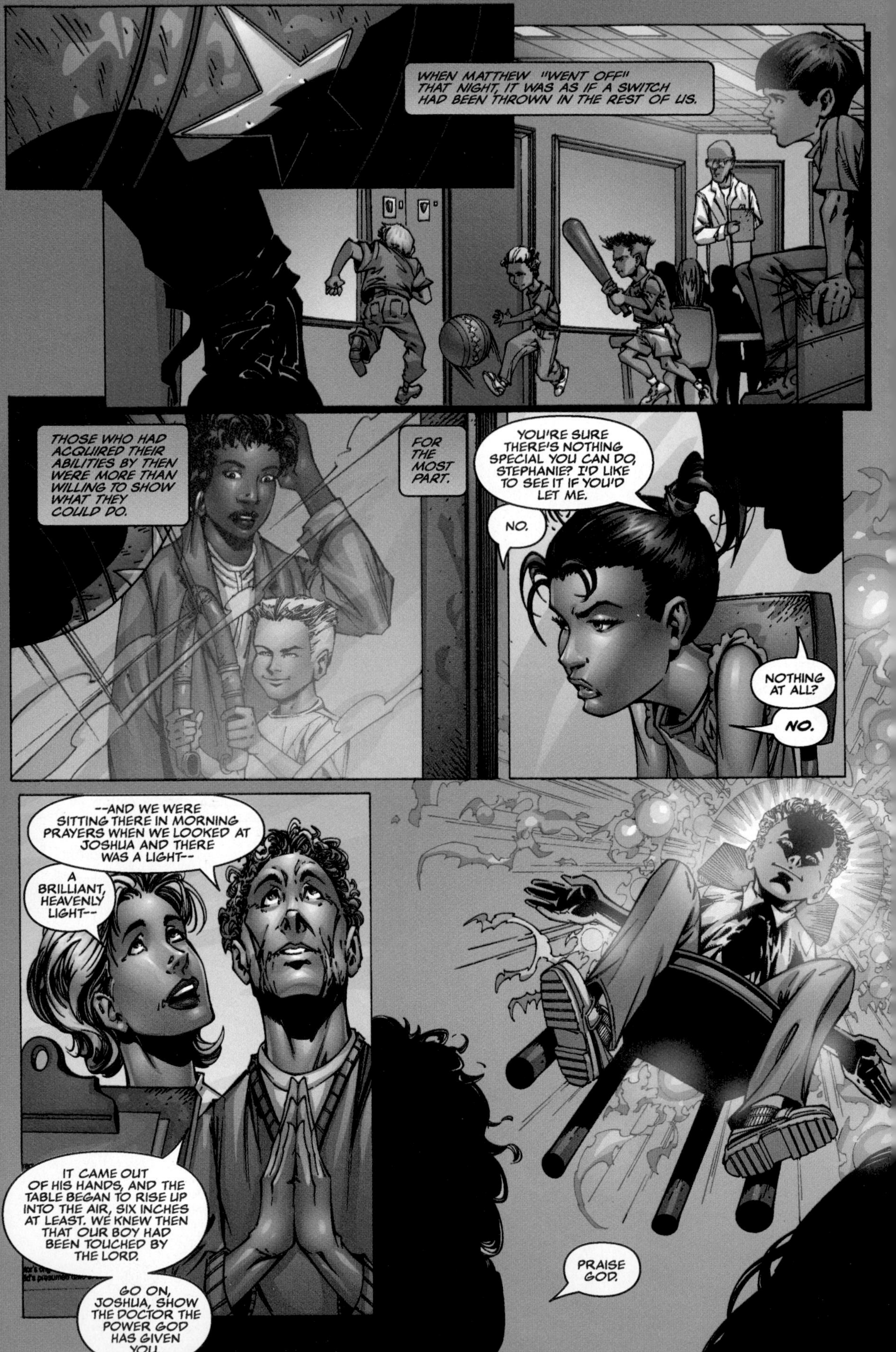

WHEN MATTHEW "WENT OFF" THAT NIGHT, IT WAS AS IF A SWITCH HAD BEEN THROWN IN THE REST OF US.
THOSE WHO HAD ACQUIRED THEIR ABILITIES BY THEN WERE MORE THAN WILLING TO SHOW WHAT THEY COULD DO.
FOR THE MOST PART.
YOU'RE SURE THERE'S NOTHING SPECIAL YOU CAN DO, STEPHANIE? I'D LIKE TO SEE IT IF YOU'D LET ME.
NO.
NOTHING AT ALL?
NO.
--AND WE WERE SITTING THERE IN MORNING PRAYERS WHEN WE LOOKED AT JOSHUA AND THERE WAS A LIGHT--
A BRILLIANT, HEAVENLY LIGHT--
IT CAME OUT OF HIS HANDS, AND THE TABLE BEGAN TO RISE UP INTO THE AIR, SIX INCHES AT LEAST. WE KNEW THEN THAT OUR BOY HAD BEEN TOUCHED BY THE LORD.
GO ON, JOSHUA, SHOW THE DOCTOR THE POWER GOD HAS GIVEN YOU.
PRAISE GOD.

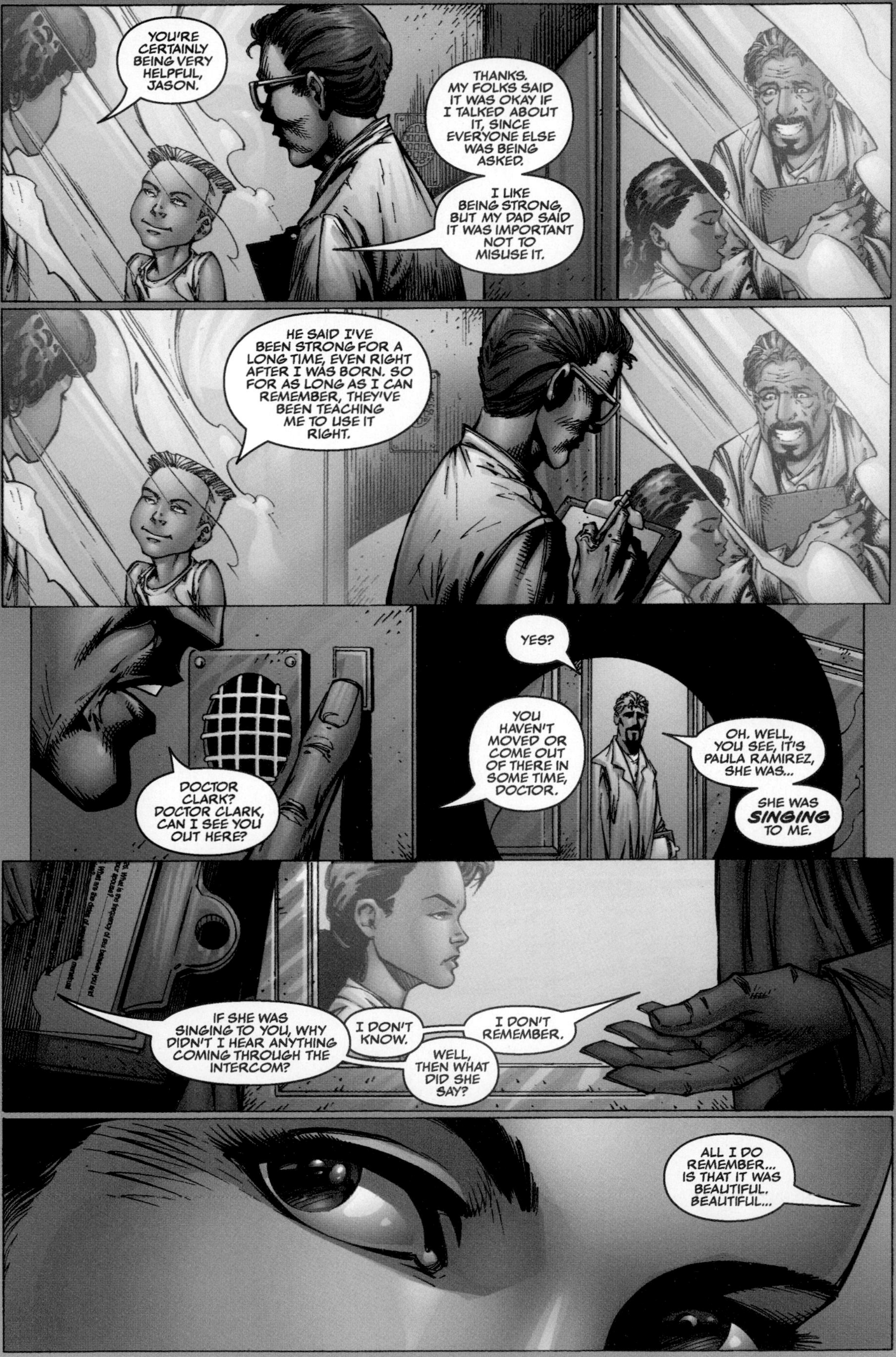

YOU'RE CERTAINLY BEING VERY HELPFUL, JASON.
THANKS. MY FOLKS SAID IT WAS OKAY IF I TALKED ABOUT IT, SINCE EVERYONE ELSE WAS BEING ASKED.
I LIKE BEING STRONG, BUT MY DAD SAID IT WAS IMPORTANT NOT TO MISUSE IT.
HE SAID I'VE BEEN STRONG FOR A LONG TIME, EVEN RIGHT AFTER I WAS BORN. SO FOR AS LONG AS I CAN REMEMBER, THEY'VE BEEN TEACHING ME TO USE IT RIGHT.
DOCTOR CLARK? DOCTOR CLARK, CAN I SEE YOU OUT HERE?
YES?
YOU HAVEN'T MOVED OR COME OUT OF THERE IN SOME TIME, DOCTOR.
OH. WELL, YOU SEE, IT'S PAULA RAMIREZ, SHE WAS...
SHE WAS ***SINGING*** TO ME.
IF SHE WAS SINGING TO YOU, WHY DIDN'T I HEAR ANYTHING COMING THROUGH THE INTERCOM?
I DON'T KNOW.
WELL, THEN WHAT DID SHE SAY?
I DON'T REMEMBER.
ALL I DO REMEMBER... IS THAT IT WAS BEAUTIFUL. BEAUTIFUL...

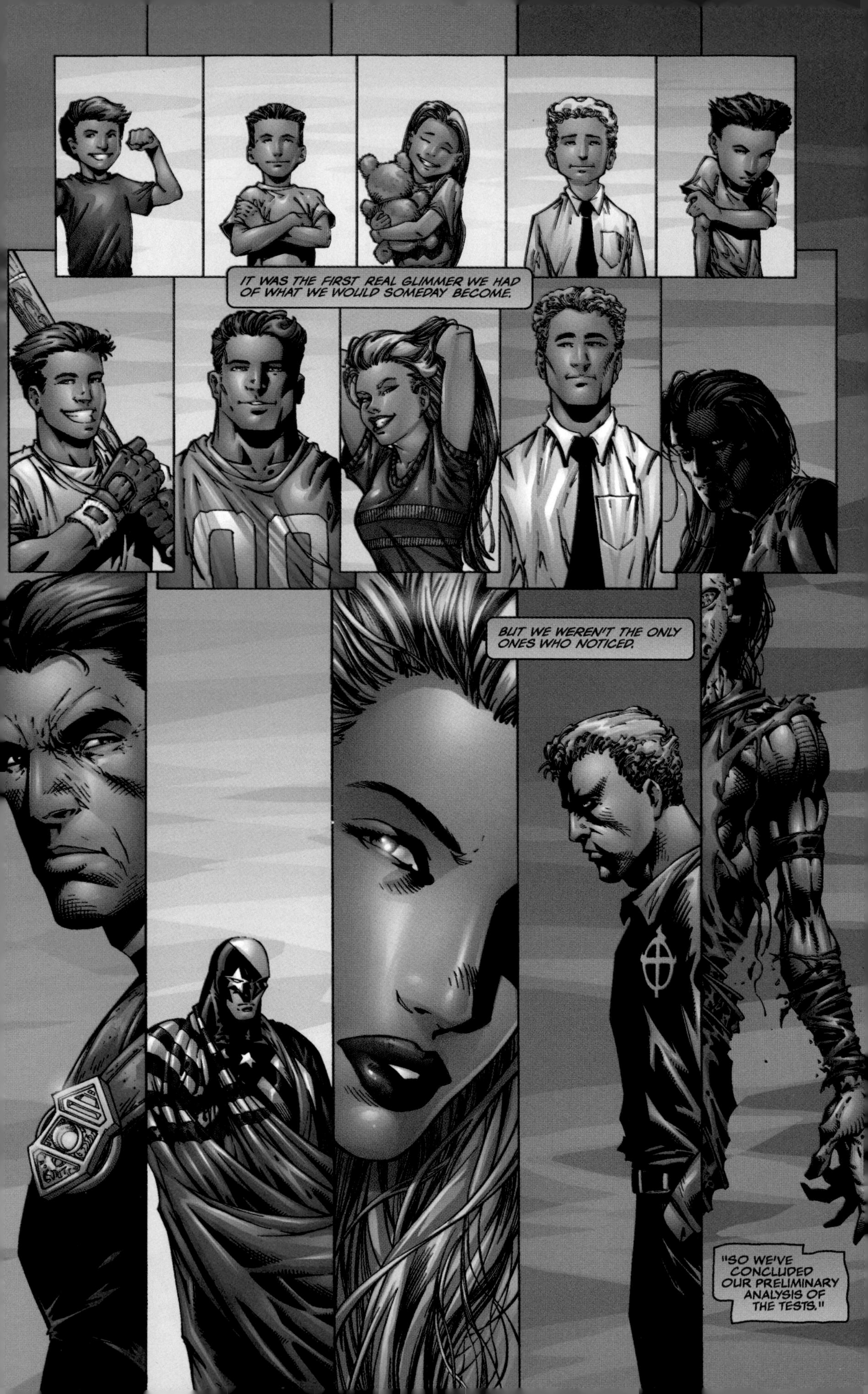
IT WAS THE FIRST REAL GLIMMER WE HAD OF WHAT WE WOULD SOMEDAY BECOME.
BUT WE WEREN'T THE ONLY ONES WHO NOTICED.
"SO WE'VE CONCLUDED OUR PRELIMINARY ANALYSIS OF THE TESTS."

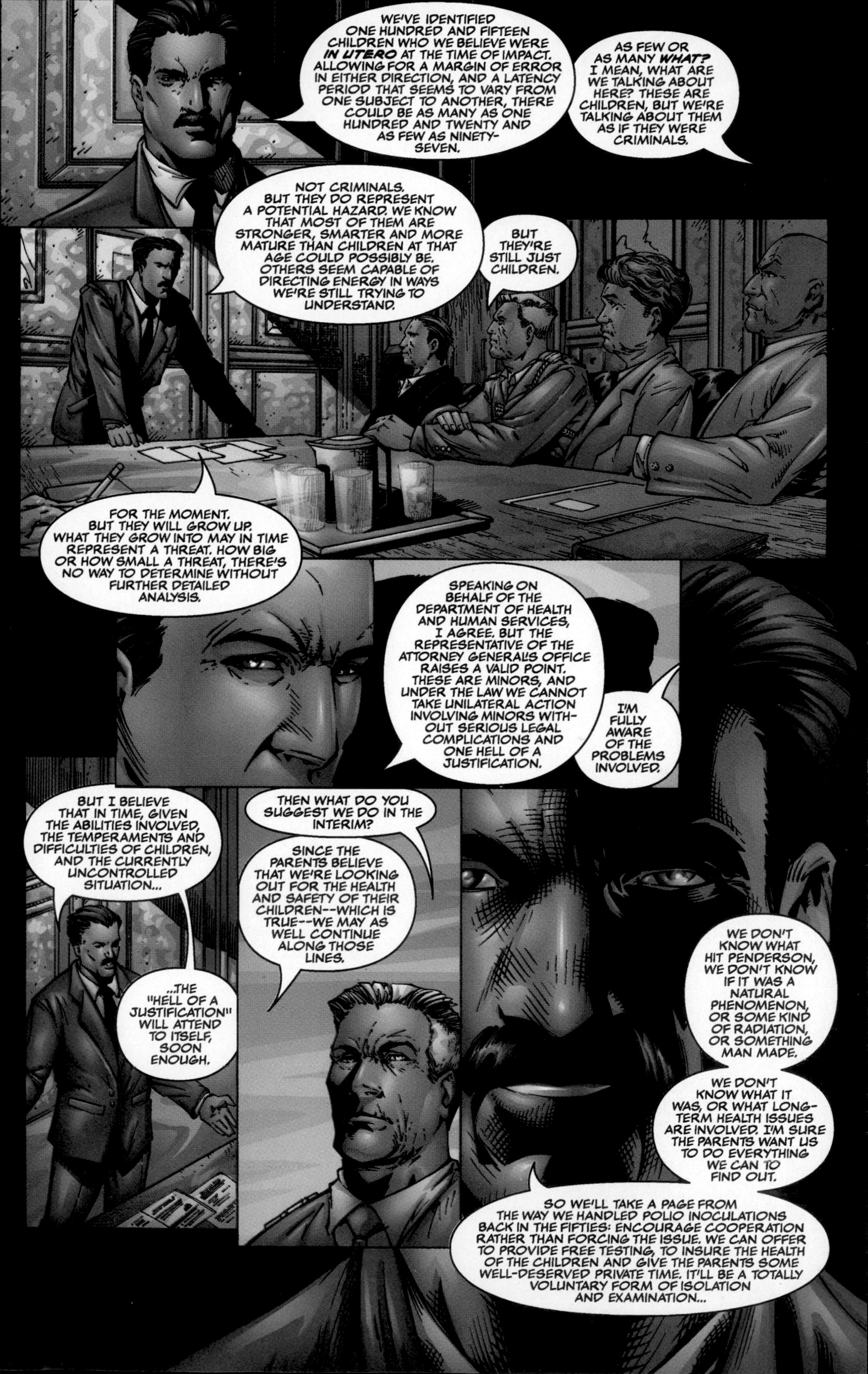
WE'VE IDENTIFIED ONE HUNDRED AND FIFTEEN CHILDREN WHO WE BELIEVE WERE *IN UTERO* AT THE TIME OF IMPACT. ALLOWING FOR A MARGIN OF ERROR IN EITHER DIRECTION, AND A LATENCY PERIOD THAT SEEMS TO VARY FROM ONE SUBJECT TO ANOTHER, THERE COULD BE AS MANY AS ONE HUNDRED AND TWENTY AND AS FEW AS NINETY-SEVEN.
AS FEW OR AS MANY *WHAT?* I MEAN, WHAT ARE WE TALKING ABOUT HERE? THESE ARE CHILDREN, BUT WE'RE TALKING ABOUT THEM AS IF THEY WERE CRIMINALS.
NOT CRIMINALS. BUT THEY DO REPRESENT A POTENTIAL HAZARD. WE KNOW THAT MOST OF THEM ARE STRONGER, SMARTER AND MORE MATURE THAN CHILDREN AT THAT AGE COULD POSSIBLY BE. OTHERS SEEM CAPABLE OF DIRECTING ENERGY IN WAYS WE'RE STILL TRYING TO UNDERSTAND.
BUT THEY'RE STILL JUST CHILDREN.
FOR THE MOMENT. BUT THEY WILL GROW UP. WHAT THEY GROW INTO MAY IN TIME REPRESENT A THREAT. HOW BIG OR HOW SMALL A THREAT, THERE'S NO WAY TO DETERMINE WITHOUT FURTHER DETAILED ANALYSIS.
SPEAKING ON BEHALF OF THE DEPARTMENT OF HEALTH AND HUMAN SERVICES, I AGREE. BUT THE REPRESENTATIVE OF THE ATTORNEY GENERAL'S OFFICE RAISES A VALID POINT. THESE ARE MINORS, AND UNDER THE LAW WE CANNOT TAKE UNILATERAL ACTION INVOLVING MINORS WITHOUT SERIOUS LEGAL COMPLICATIONS AND ONE HELL OF A JUSTIFICATION.
I'M FULLY AWARE OF THE PROBLEMS INVOLVED.
BUT I BELIEVE THAT IN TIME, GIVEN THE ABILITIES INVOLVED, THE TEMPERAMENTS AND DIFFICULTIES OF CHILDREN, AND THE CURRENTLY UNCONTROLLED SITUATION...
...THE "HELL OF A JUSTIFICATION" WILL ATTEND TO ITSELF, SOON ENOUGH.
THEN WHAT DO YOU SUGGEST WE DO IN THE INTERIM?
SINCE THE PARENTS BELIEVE THAT WE'RE LOOKING OUT FOR THE HEALTH AND SAFETY OF THEIR CHILDREN--WHICH IS TRUE--WE MAY AS WELL CONTINUE ALONG THOSE LINES.
WE DON'T KNOW WHAT HIT PENDERSON, WE DON'T KNOW IF IT WAS A NATURAL PHENOMENON, OR SOME KIND OF RADIATION, OR SOMETHING MAN MADE.
WE DON'T KNOW WHAT IT WAS, OR WHAT LONG-TERM HEALTH ISSUES ARE INVOLVED. I'M SURE THE PARENTS WANT US TO DO EVERYTHING WE CAN TO FIND OUT.
SO WE'LL TAKE A PAGE FROM THE WAY WE HANDLED POLIO INOCULATIONS BACK IN THE FIFTIES: ENCOURAGE COOPERATION RATHER THAN FORCING THE ISSUE. WE CAN OFFER TO PROVIDE FREE TESTING, TO INSURE THE HEALTH OF THE CHILDREN AND GIVE THE PARENTS SOME WELL-DESERVED PRIVATE TIME. IT'LL BE A TOTALLY VOLUNTARY FORM OF ISOLATION AND EXAMINATION...

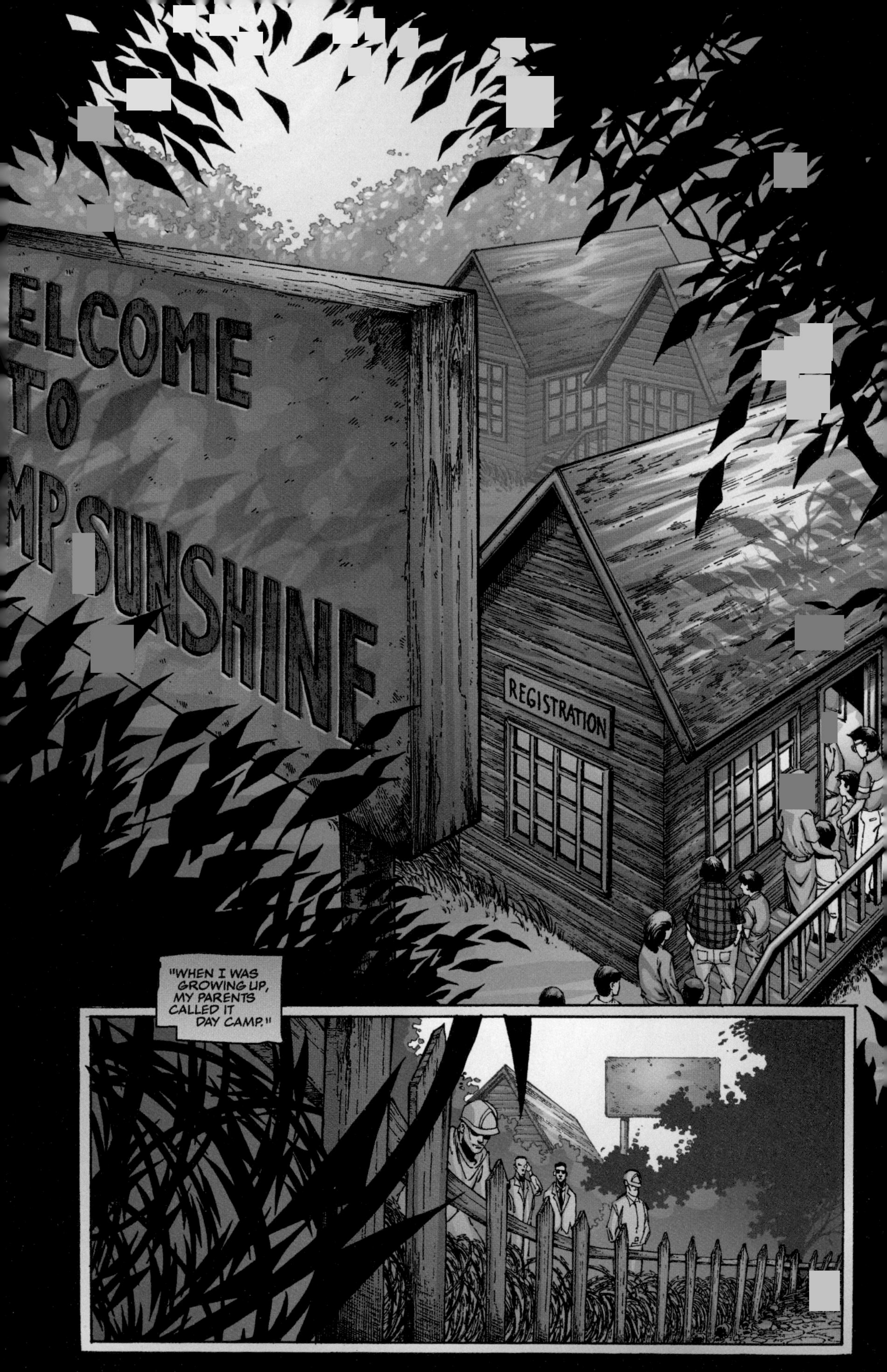
ELCOME
TO
MP SUNSHINE
REGISTRATION
"WHEN I WAS GROWING UP, MY PARENTS CALLED IT DAY CAMP."

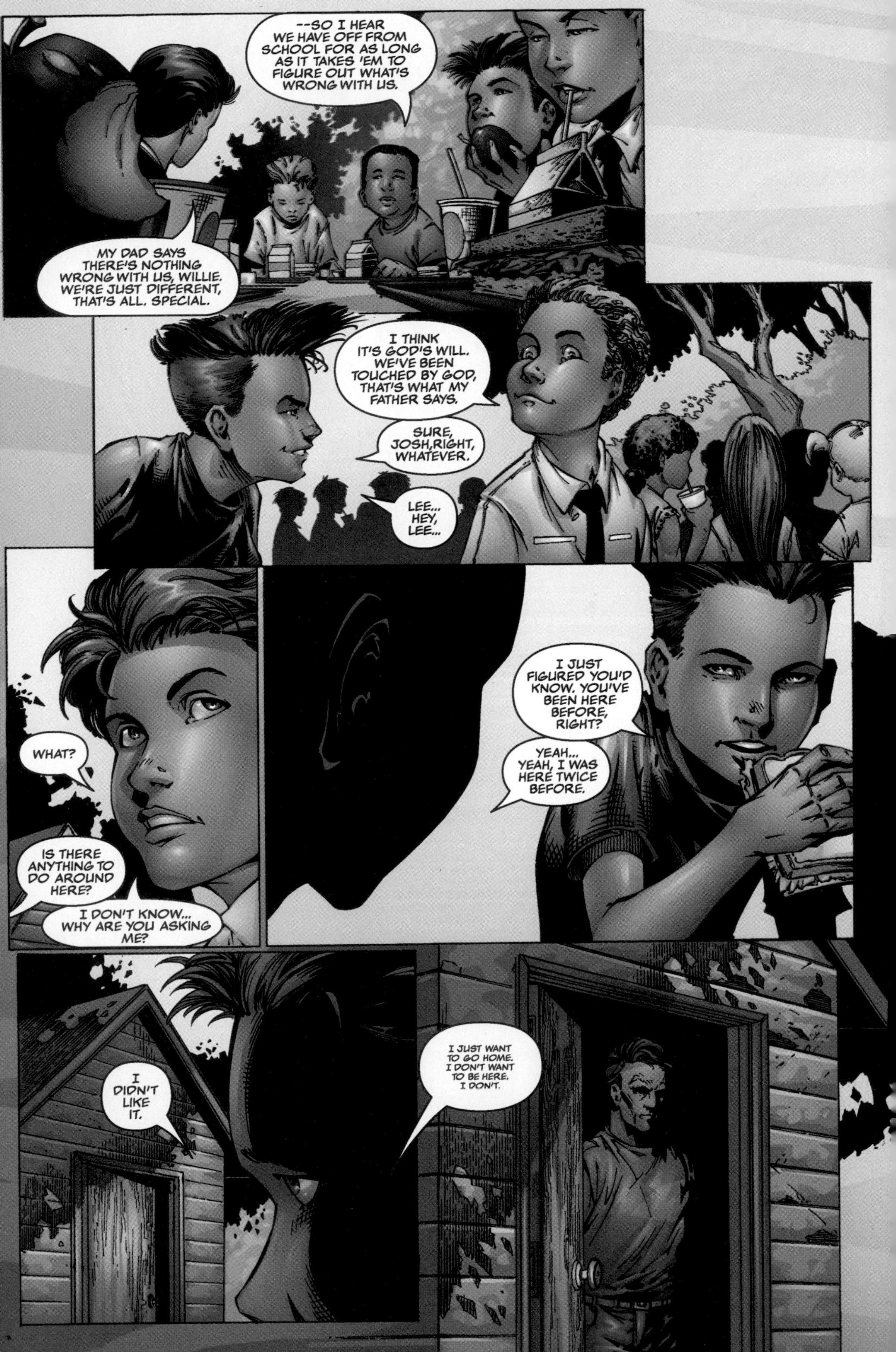
--SO I HEAR WE HAVE OFF FROM SCHOOL FOR AS LONG AS IT TAKES 'EM TO FIGURE OUT WHAT'S WRONG WITH US.
MY DAD SAYS THERE'S NOTHING WRONG WITH US, WILLIE. WE'RE JUST DIFFERENT, THAT'S ALL. SPECIAL.
I THINK IT'S GOD'S WILL. WE'VE BEEN TOUCHED BY GOD, THAT'S WHAT MY FATHER SAYS.
SURE, JOSH,RIGHT, WHATEVER.
LEE... HEY, LEE...
WHAT?
IS THERE ANYTHING TO DO AROUND HERE?
I DON'T KNOW... WHY ARE YOU ASKING ME?
I JUST FIGURED YOU'D KNOW. YOU'VE BEEN HERE BEFORE, RIGHT?
YEAH... YEAH, I WAS HERE TWICE BEFORE.
I DIDN'T LIKE IT.
I JUST WANT TO GO HOME. I DON'T WANT TO BE HERE. I DON'T.

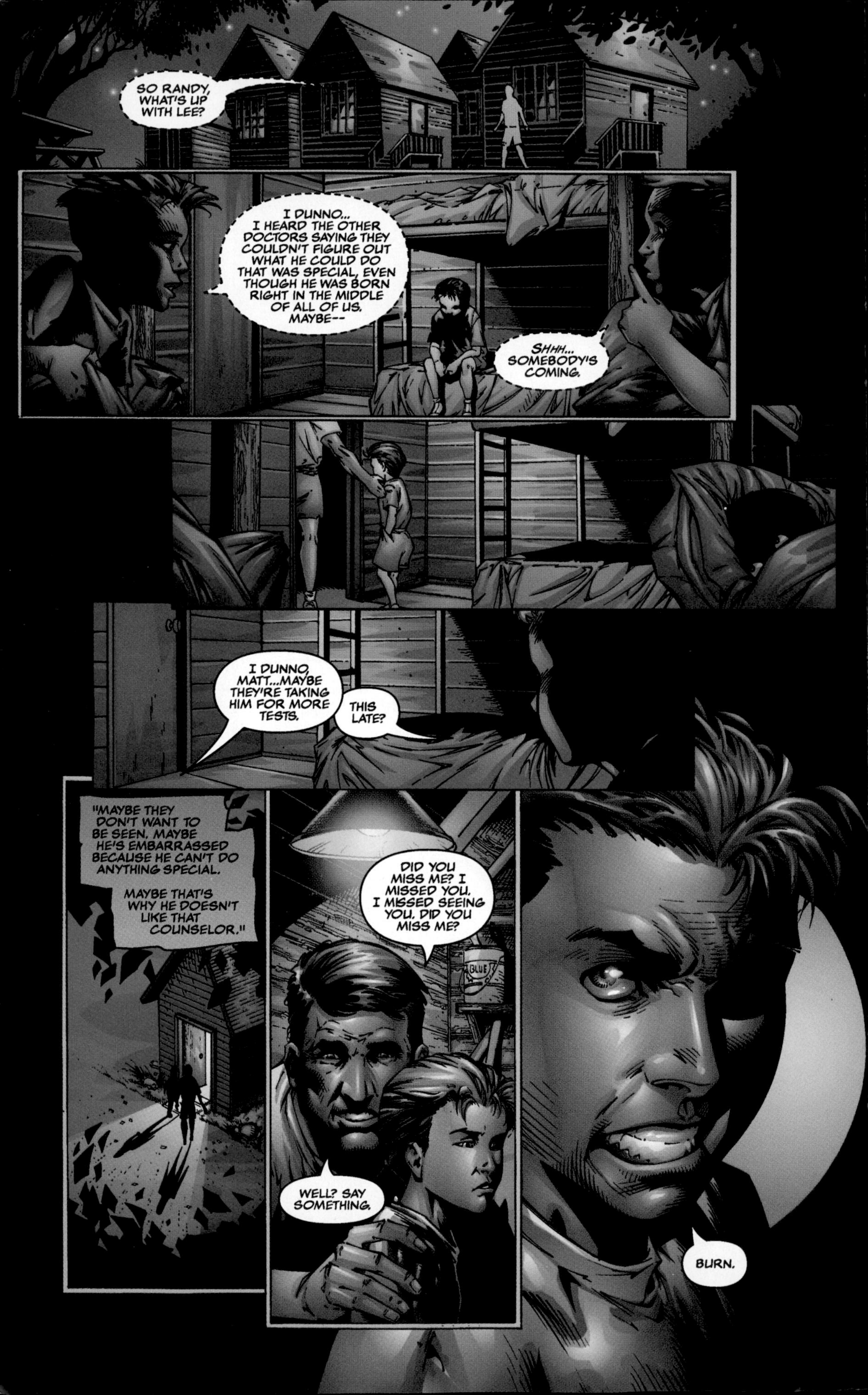
SO RANDY, WHAT'S UP WITH LEE?
I DUNNO... I HEARD THE OTHER DOCTORS SAYING THEY COULDN'T FIGURE OUT WHAT HE COULD DO THAT WAS SPECIAL, EVEN THOUGH HE WAS BORN RIGHT IN THE MIDDLE OF ALL OF US. MAYBE--
SHHH... SOMEBODY'S COMING.
I DUNNO, MATT...MAYBE THEY'RE TAKING HIM FOR MORE TESTS.
THIS LATE?
"MAYBE THEY DON'T WANT TO BE SEEN. MAYBE HE'S EMBARRASSED BECAUSE HE CAN'T DO ANYTHING SPECIAL.
MAYBE THAT'S WHY HE DOESN'T LIKE THAT COUNSELOR."
DID YOU MISS ME? I MISSED YOU. I MISSED SEEING YOU. DID YOU MISS ME?
WELL? SAY SOMETHING.
BURN.

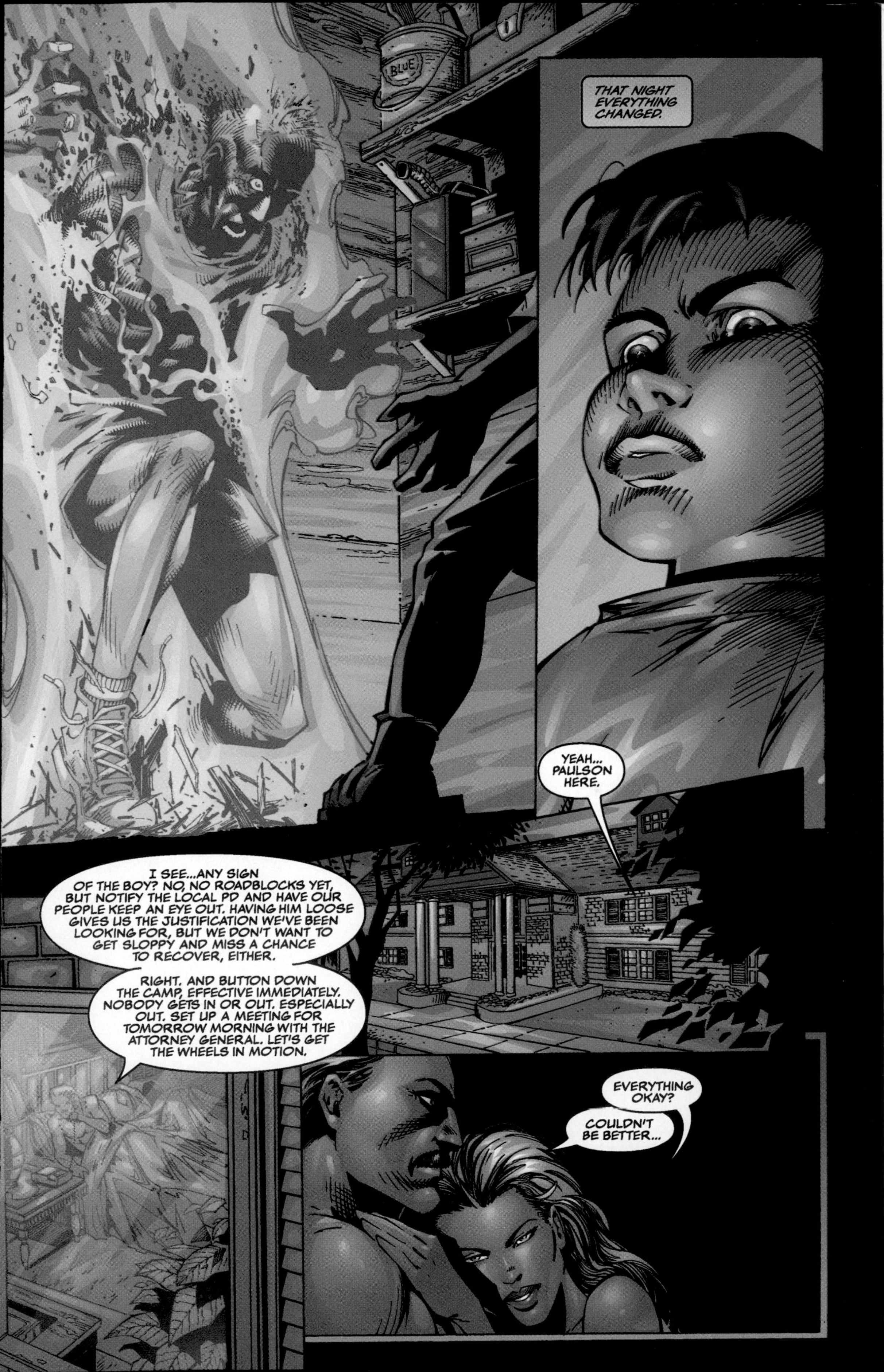
THAT NIGHT EVERYTHING CHANGED.
YEAH... PAULSON HERE.
I SEE...ANY SIGN OF THE BOY? NO, NO ROADBLOCKS YET, BUT NOTIFY THE LOCAL PD AND HAVE OUR PEOPLE KEEP AN EYE OUT. HAVING HIM LOOSE GIVES US THE JUSTIFICATION WE'VE BEEN LOOKING FOR, BUT WE DON'T WANT TO GET SLOPPY AND MISS A CHANCE TO RECOVER, EITHER.
RIGHT. AND BUTTON DOWN THE CAMP, EFFECTIVE IMMEDIATELY. NOBODY GETS IN OR OUT. ESPECIALLY OUT. SET UP A MEETING FOR TOMORROW MORNING WITH THE ATTORNEY GENERAL. LET'S GET THE WHEELS IN MOTION.
EVERYTHING OKAY?
COULDN'T BE BETTER...

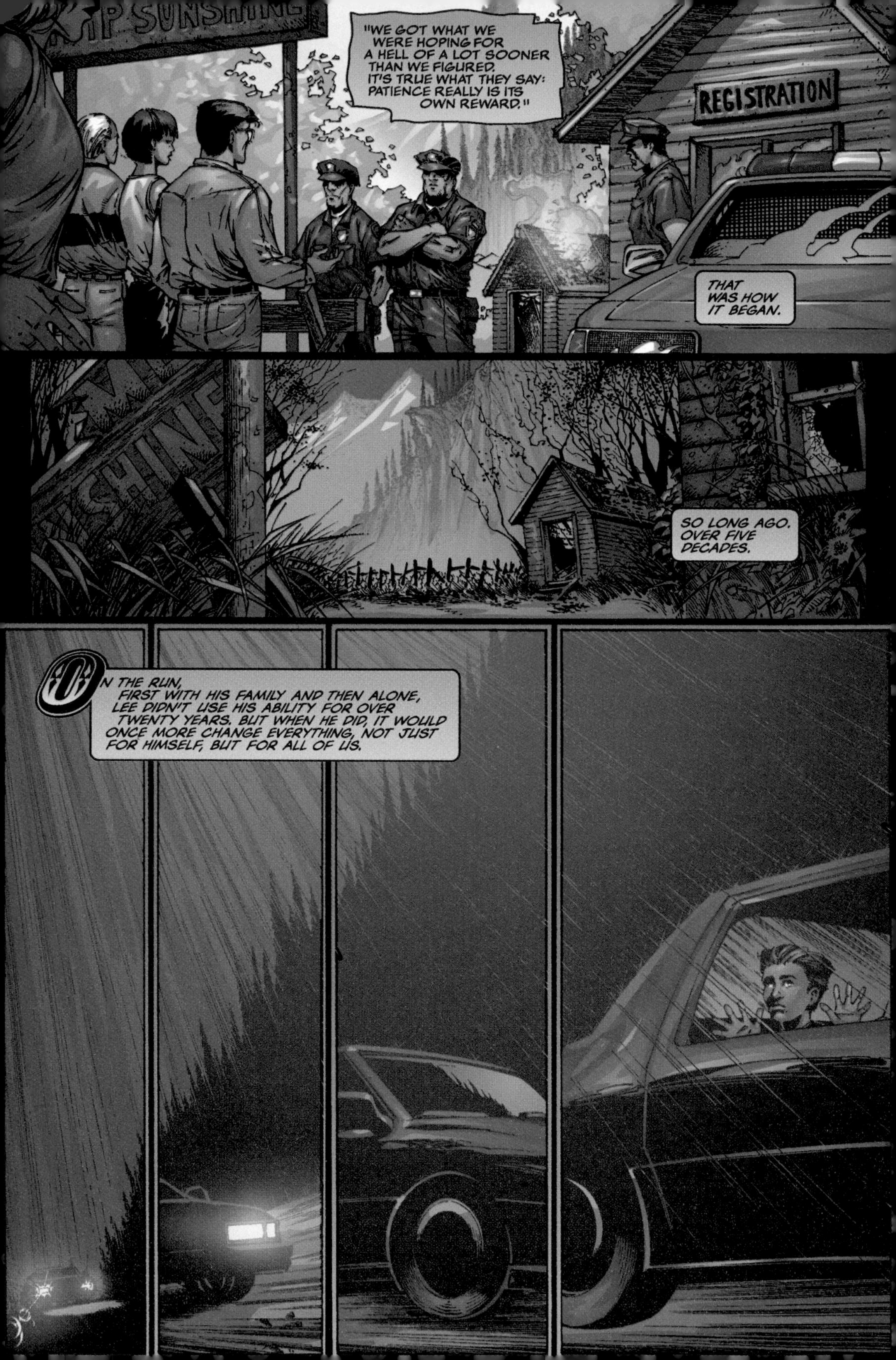
"WE GOT WHAT WE WERE HOPING FOR A HELL OF A LOT SOONER THAN WE FIGURED. IT'S TRUE WHAT THEY SAY: PATIENCE REALLY IS ITS OWN REWARD."
REGISTRATION
THAT WAS HOW IT BEGAN.
SO LONG AGO. OVER FIVE DECADES.
ON THE RUN, FIRST WITH HIS FAMILY AND THEN ALONE, LEE DIDN'T USE HIS ABILITY FOR OVER TWENTY YEARS. BUT WHEN HE DID, IT WOULD ONCE MORE CHANGE EVERYTHING, NOT JUST FOR HIMSELF, BUT FOR ALL OF US.

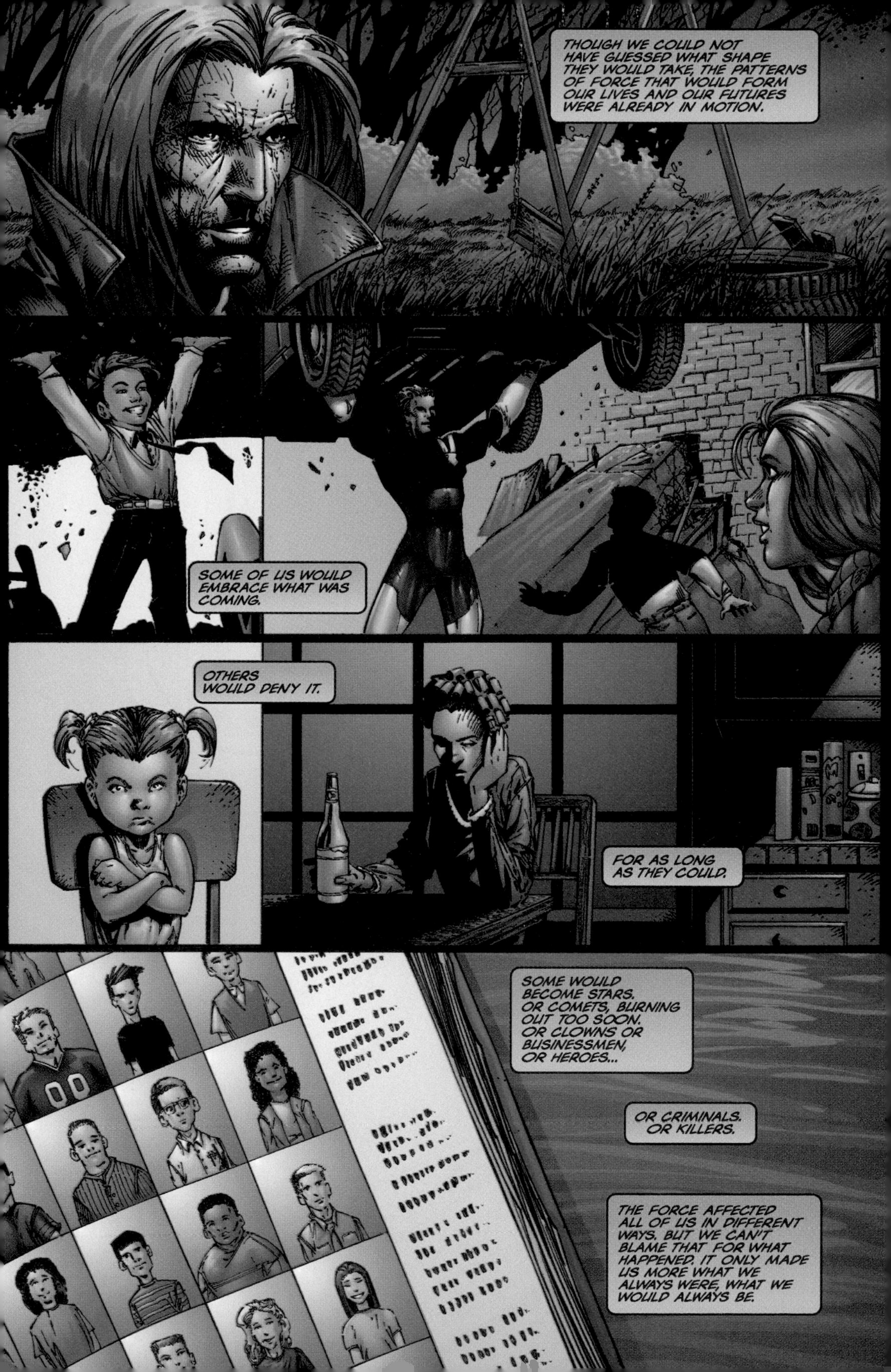
THOUGH WE COULD NOT HAVE GUESSED WHAT SHAPE THEY WOULD TAKE, THE PATTERNS OF FORCE THAT WOULD FORM OUR LIVES AND OUR FUTURES WERE ALREADY IN MOTION.
SOME OF US WOULD EMBRACE WHAT WAS COMING.
OTHERS WOULD DENY IT.
FOR AS LONG AS THEY COULD.
SOME WOULD BECOME STARS. OR COMETS, BURNING OUT TOO SOON. OR CLOWNS OR BUSINESSMEN, OR HEROES...
OR CRIMINALS. OR KILLERS.
THE FORCE AFFECTED ALL OF US IN DIFFERENT WAYS. BUT WE CAN'T BLAME THAT FOR WHAT HAPPENED. IT ONLY MADE US MORE WHAT WE ALWAYS WERE, WHAT WE WOULD ALWAYS BE.

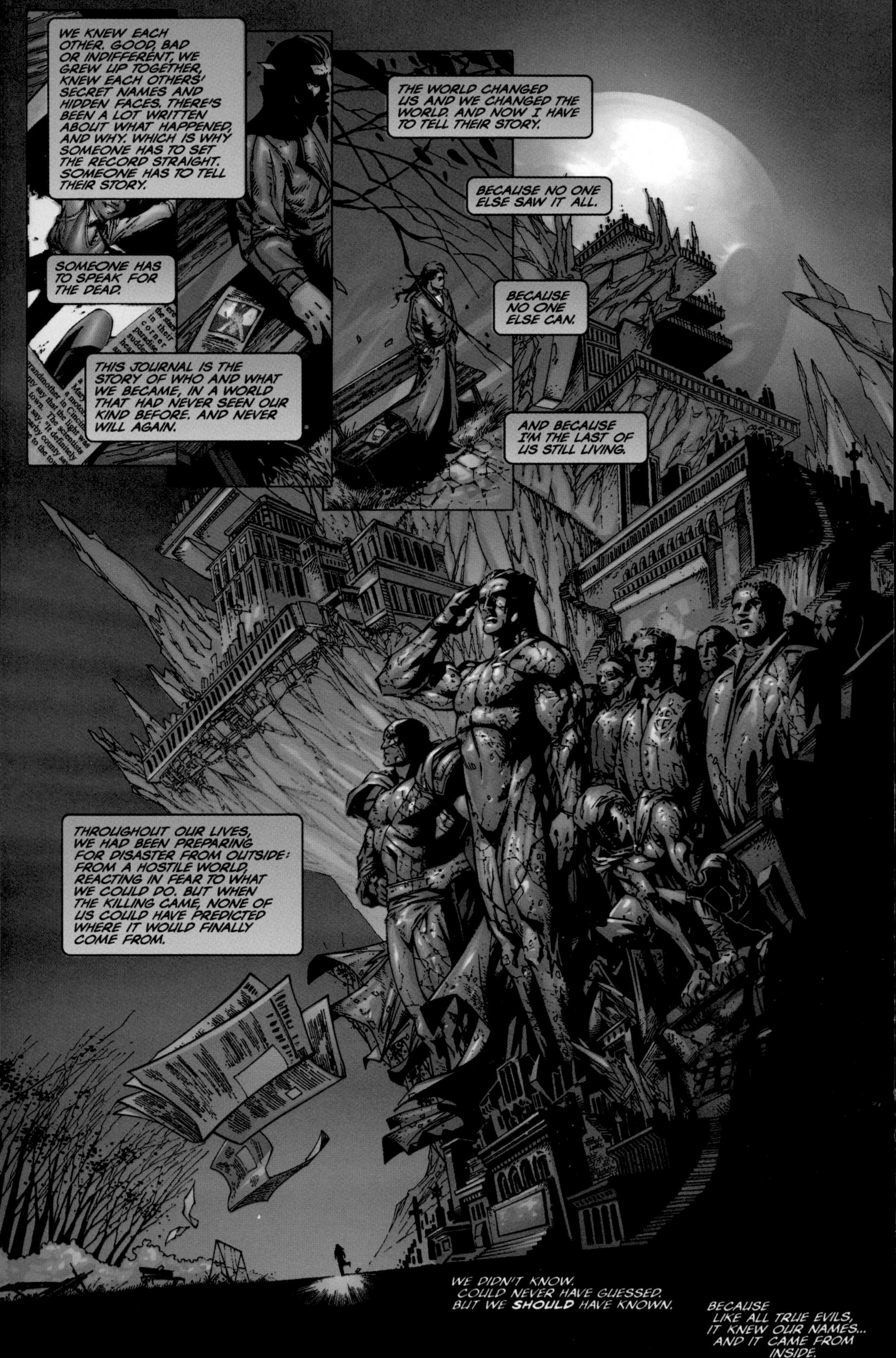
WE KNEW EACH OTHER. GOOD, BAD OR INDIFFERENT, WE GREW UP TOGETHER, KNEW EACH OTHERS' SECRET NAMES AND HIDDEN FACES. THERE'S BEEN A LOT WRITTEN ABOUT WHAT HAPPENED, AND WHY. WHICH IS WHY SOMEONE HAS TO SET THE RECORD STRAIGHT. SOMEONE HAS TO TELL THEIR STORY.
SOMEONE HAS TO SPEAK FOR THE DEAD.
THIS JOURNAL IS THE STORY OF WHO AND WHAT WE BECAME, IN A WORLD THAT HAD NEVER SEEN OUR KIND BEFORE. AND NEVER WILL AGAIN.
THE WORLD CHANGED US AND WE CHANGED THE WORLD. AND NOW I HAVE TO TELL THEIR STORY.
BECAUSE NO ONE ELSE SAW IT ALL.
BECAUSE NO ONE ELSE CAN.
AND BECAUSE I'M THE LAST OF US STILL LIVING.
THROUGHOUT OUR LIVES, WE HAD BEEN PREPARING FOR DISASTER FROM OUTSIDE: FROM A HOSTILE WORLD, REACTING IN FEAR TO WHAT WE COULD DO. BUT WHEN THE KILLING CAME, NONE OF US COULD HAVE PREDICTED WHERE IT WOULD FINALLY COME FROM.
WE DIDN'T KNOW. COULD NEVER HAVE GUESSED. BUT WE **SHOULD** HAVE KNOWN.
BECAUSE LIKE ALL TRUE EVILS, IT KNEW OUR NAMES... AND IT CAME FROM INSIDE.

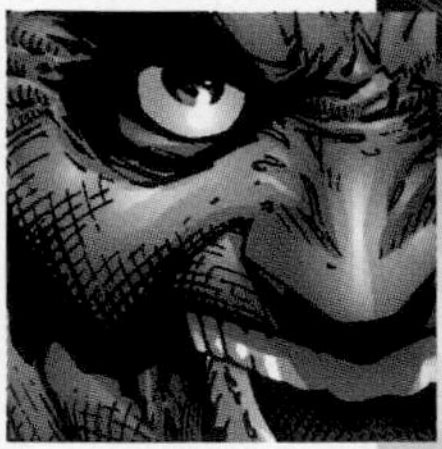

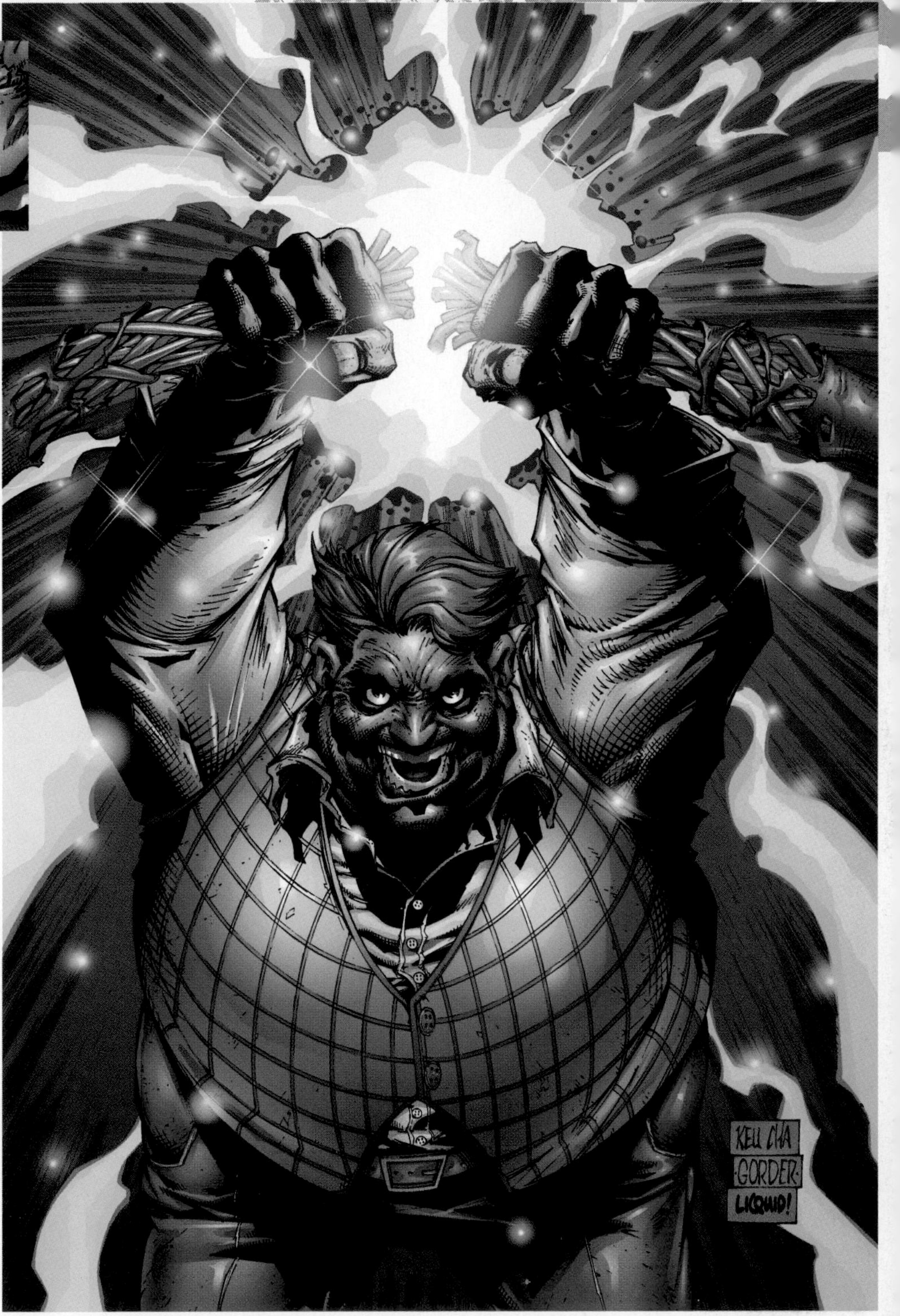

Chapter 2
Can't Touch This

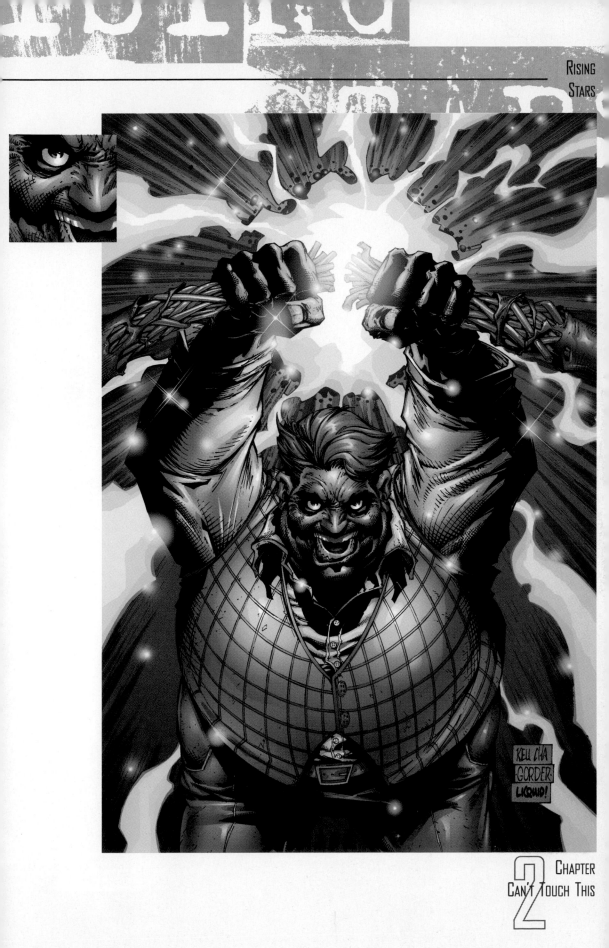

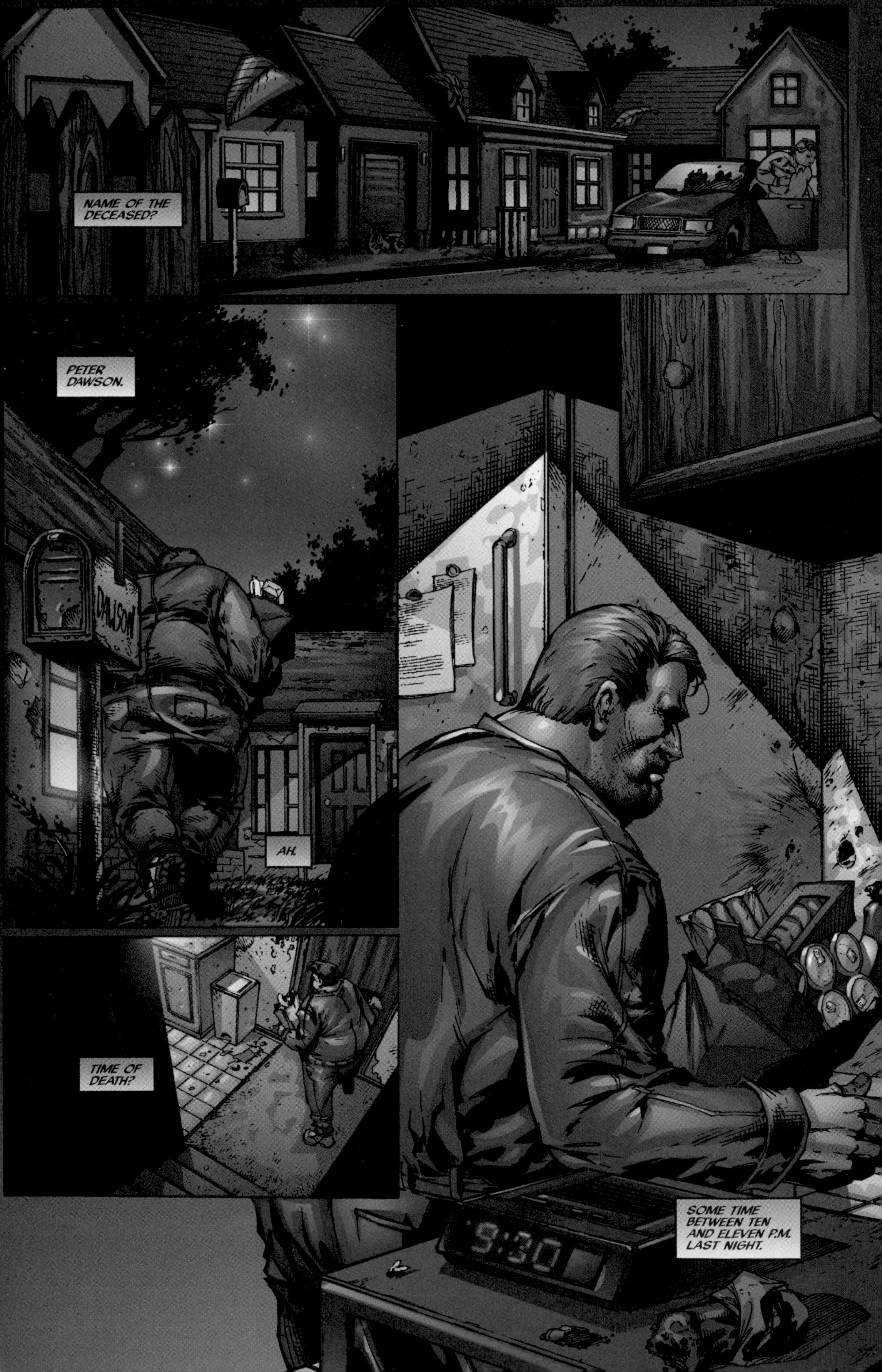
NAME OF THE DECEASED?
PETER DAWSON.
DAWSON
AH.
TIME OF DEATH?
SOME TIME BETWEEN TEN AND ELEVEN P.M. LAST NIGHT.
9:30

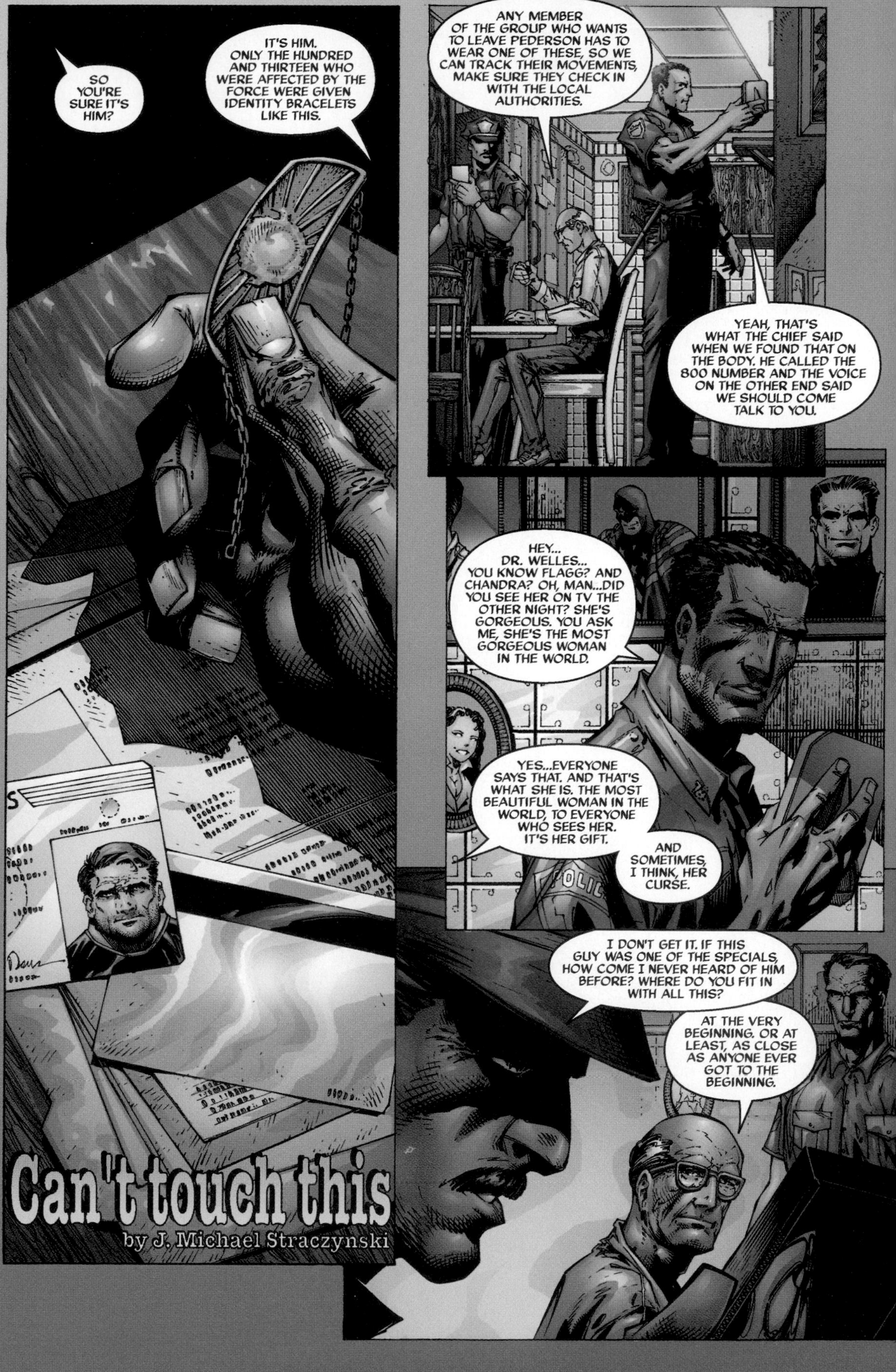
SO YOU'RE SURE IT'S HIM?
IT'S HIM. ONLY THE HUNDRED AND THIRTEEN WHO WERE AFFECTED BY THE FORCE WERE GIVEN IDENTITY BRACELETS LIKE THIS.
ANY MEMBER OF THE GROUP WHO WANTS TO LEAVE PEDERSON HAS TO WEAR ONE OF THESE, SO WE CAN TRACK THEIR MOVEMENTS, MAKE SURE THEY CHECK IN WITH THE LOCAL AUTHORITIES.
YEAH, THAT'S WHAT THE CHIEF SAID WHEN WE FOUND THAT ON THE BODY. HE CALLED THE 800 NUMBER AND THE VOICE ON THE OTHER END SAID WE SHOULD COME TALK TO YOU.
HEY... DR. WELLES... YOU KNOW FLAGG? AND CHANDRA? OH, MAN...DID YOU SEE HER ON TV THE OTHER NIGHT? SHE'S GORGEOUS. YOU ASK ME, SHE'S THE MOST GORGEOUS WOMAN IN THE WORLD.
YES...EVERYONE SAYS THAT. AND THAT'S WHAT SHE IS. THE MOST BEAUTIFUL WOMAN IN THE WORLD, TO EVERYONE WHO SEES HER. IT'S HER GIFT.
AND SOMETIMES, I THINK, HER CURSE.
I DON'T GET IT. IF THIS GUY WAS ONE OF THE SPECIALS, HOW COME I NEVER HEARD OF HIM BEFORE? WHERE DO YOU FIT IN WITH ALL THIS?
AT THE VERY BEGINNING. OR AT LEAST, AS CLOSE AS ANYONE EVER GOT TO THE BEGINNING.
Can't touch this
by J. Michael Straczynski

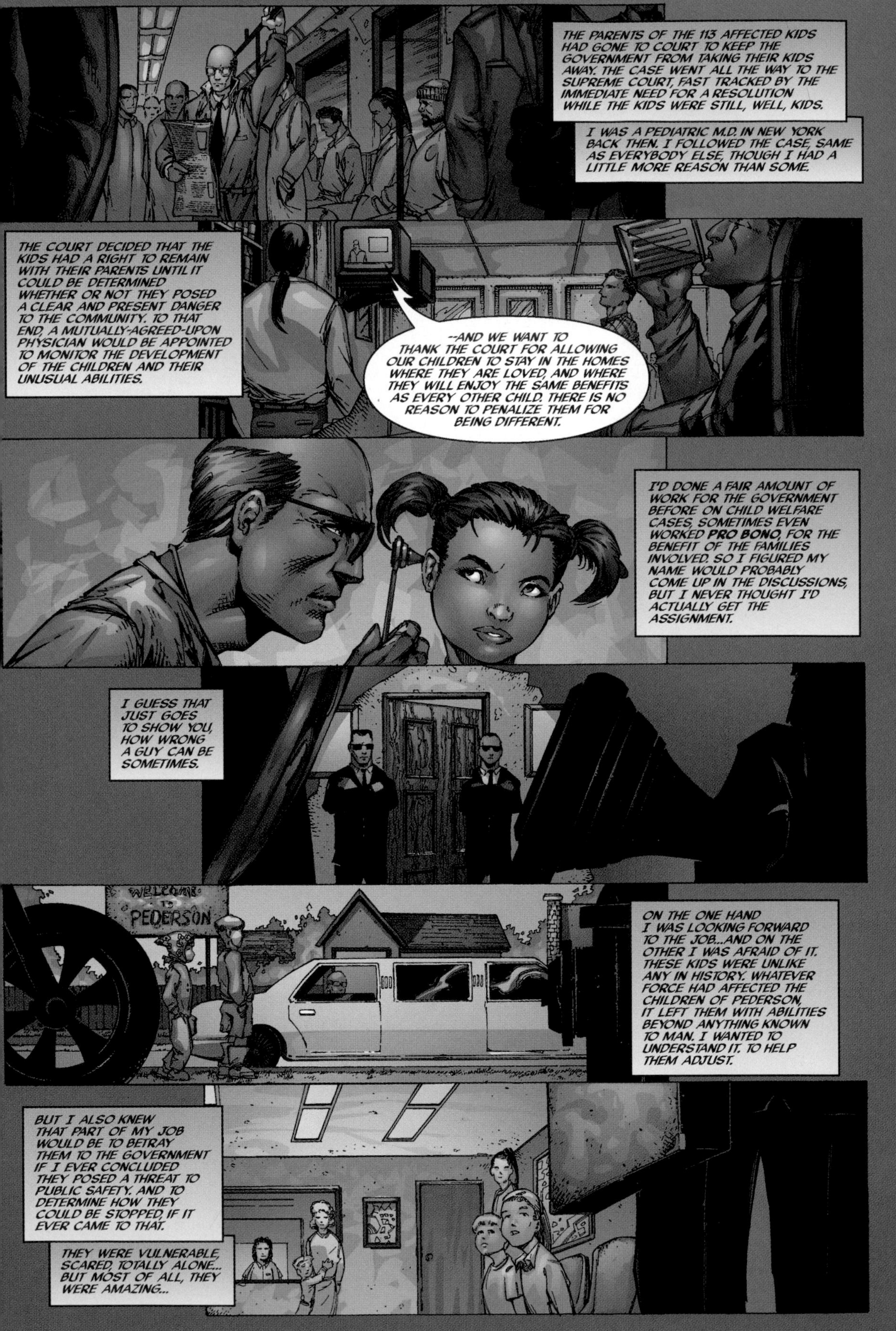
THE PARENTS OF THE 113 AFFECTED KIDS HAD GONE TO COURT TO KEEP THE GOVERNMENT FROM TAKING THEIR KIDS AWAY. THE CASE WENT ALL THE WAY TO THE SUPREME COURT, FAST TRACKED BY THE IMMEDIATE NEED FOR A RESOLUTION WHILE THE KIDS WERE STILL, WELL, KIDS.
I WAS A PEDIATRIC M.D. IN NEW YORK BACK THEN. I FOLLOWED THE CASE, SAME AS EVERYBODY ELSE, THOUGH I HAD A LITTLE MORE REASON THAN SOME.
THE COURT DECIDED THAT THE KIDS HAD A RIGHT TO REMAIN WITH THEIR PARENTS UNTIL IT COULD BE DETERMINED WHETHER OR NOT THEY POSED A CLEAR AND PRESENT DANGER TO THE COMMUNITY. TO THAT END, A MUTUALLY-AGREED-UPON PHYSICIAN WOULD BE APPOINTED TO MONITOR THE DEVELOPMENT OF THE CHILDREN AND THEIR UNUSUAL ABILITIES.
--AND WE WANT TO THANK THE COURT FOR ALLOWING OUR CHILDREN TO STAY IN THE HOMES WHERE THEY ARE LOVED, AND WHERE THEY WILL ENJOY THE SAME BENEFITS AS EVERY OTHER CHILD. THERE IS NO REASON TO PENALIZE THEM FOR BEING DIFFERENT.
I'D DONE A FAIR AMOUNT OF WORK FOR THE GOVERNMENT BEFORE ON CHILD WELFARE CASES, SOMETIMES EVEN WORKED **PRO BONO**, FOR THE BENEFIT OF THE FAMILIES INVOLVED. SO I FIGURED MY NAME WOULD PROBABLY COME UP IN THE DISCUSSIONS, BUT I NEVER THOUGHT I'D ACTUALLY GET THE ASSIGNMENT.
I GUESS THAT JUST GOES TO SHOW YOU, HOW WRONG A GUY CAN BE SOMETIMES.
WELCOME TO PEDERSON
ON THE ONE HAND I WAS LOOKING FORWARD TO THE JOB...AND ON THE OTHER I WAS AFRAID OF IT. THESE KIDS WERE UNLIKE ANY IN HISTORY. WHATEVER FORCE HAD AFFECTED THE CHILDREN OF PEDERSON, IT LEFT THEM WITH ABILITIES BEYOND ANYTHING KNOWN TO MAN. I WANTED TO UNDERSTAND IT. TO HELP THEM ADJUST.
BUT I ALSO KNEW THAT PART OF MY JOB WOULD BE TO BETRAY THEM TO THE GOVERNMENT IF I EVER CONCLUDED THEY POSED A THREAT TO PUBLIC SAFETY. AND TO DETERMINE HOW THEY COULD BE STOPPED, IF IT EVER CAME TO THAT.
THEY WERE VULNERABLE, SCARED, TOTALLY ALONE... BUT MOST OF ALL, THEY WERE AMAZING...

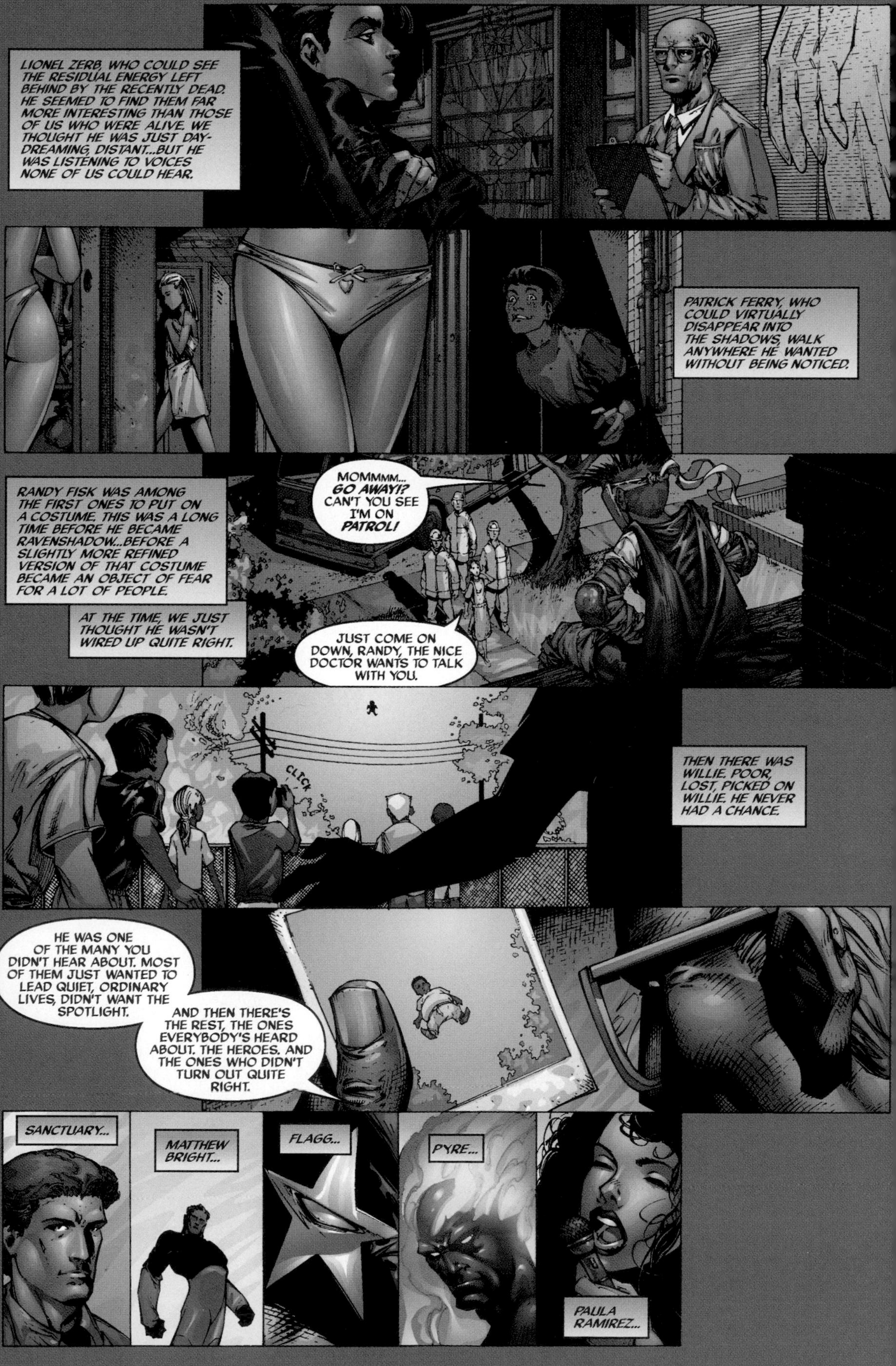

LIONEL ZERB, WHO COULD SEE THE RESIDUAL ENERGY LEFT BEHIND BY THE RECENTLY DEAD. HE SEEMED TO FIND THEM FAR MORE INTERESTING THAN THOSE OF US WHO WERE ALIVE. WE THOUGHT HE WAS JUST DAY-DREAMING, DISTANT...BUT HE WAS LISTENING TO VOICES NONE OF US COULD HEAR.
PATRICK FERRY, WHO COULD VIRTUALLY DISAPPEAR INTO THE SHADOWS, WALK ANYWHERE HE WANTED WITHOUT BEING NOTICED.
RANDY FISK WAS AMONG THE FIRST ONES TO PUT ON A COSTUME. THIS WAS A LONG TIME BEFORE HE BECAME RAVENSHADOW...BEFORE A SLIGHTLY MORE REFINED VERSION OF THAT COSTUME BECAME AN OBJECT OF FEAR FOR A LOT OF PEOPLE.
MOMMMM... GO AWAY!? CAN'T YOU SEE I'M ON PATROL!
AT THE TIME, WE JUST THOUGHT HE WASN'T WIRED UP QUITE RIGHT.
JUST COME ON DOWN, RANDY, THE NICE DOCTOR WANTS TO TALK WITH YOU.
CLICK
THEN THERE WAS WILLIE. POOR, LOST, PICKED ON WILLIE. HE NEVER HAD A CHANCE.
HE WAS ONE OF THE MANY YOU DIDN'T HEAR ABOUT. MOST OF THEM JUST WANTED TO LEAD QUIET, ORDINARY LIVES, DIDN'T WANT THE SPOTLIGHT.
AND THEN THERE'S THE REST, THE ONES EVERYBODY'S HEARD ABOUT. THE HEROES. AND THE ONES WHO DIDN'T TURN OUT QUITE RIGHT.
SANCTUARY...
MATTHEW BRIGHT...
FLAGG...
PYRE...
PAULA RAMIREZ...

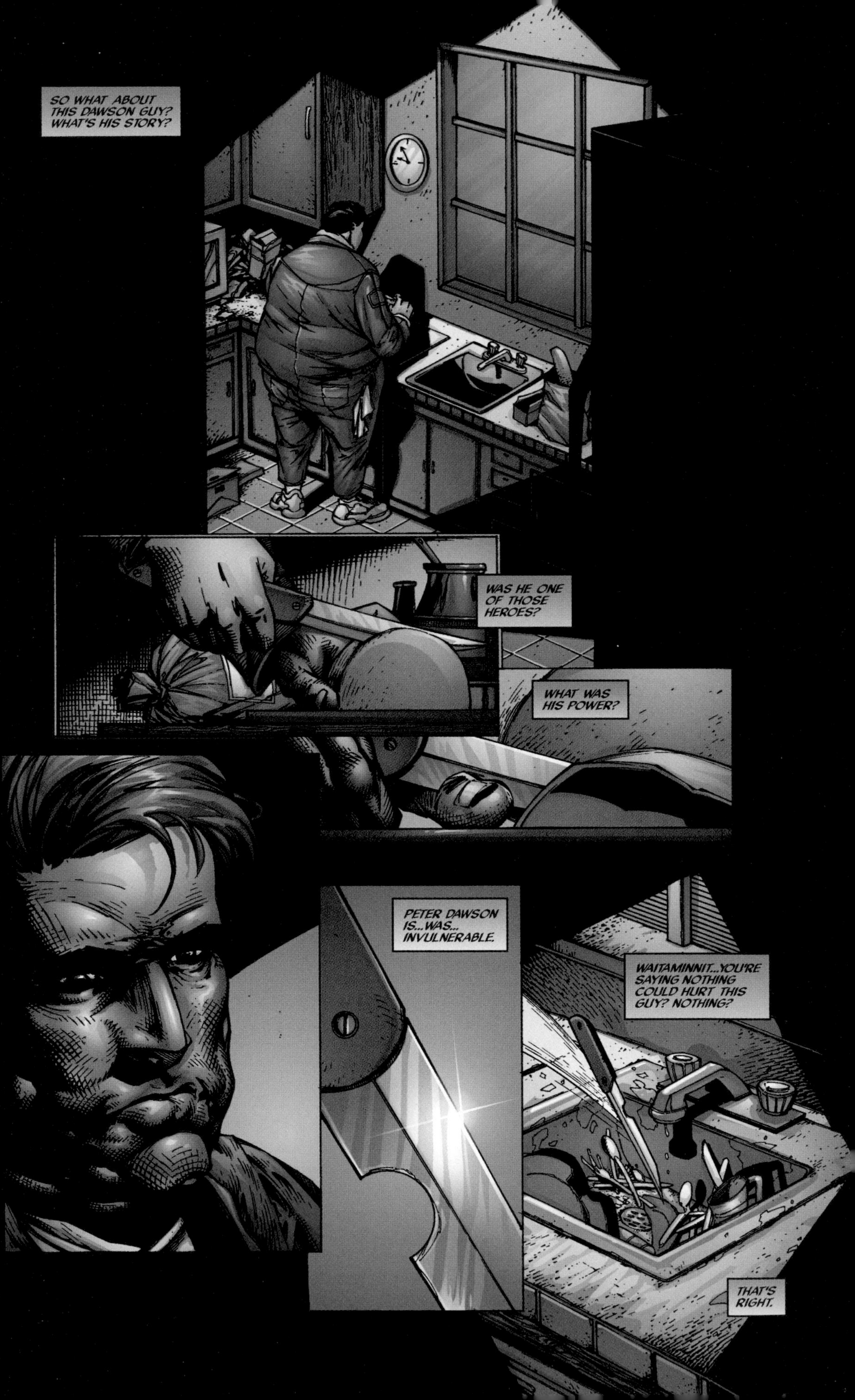
SO WHAT ABOUT THIS DAWSON GUY? WHAT'S HIS STORY?
WAS HE ONE OF THOSE HEROES?
WHAT WAS HIS POWER?
PETER DAWSON IS...WAS... INVULNERABLE.
WAITAMINNIT...YOU'RE SAYING NOTHING COULD HURT THIS GUY? NOTHING?
THAT'S RIGHT.

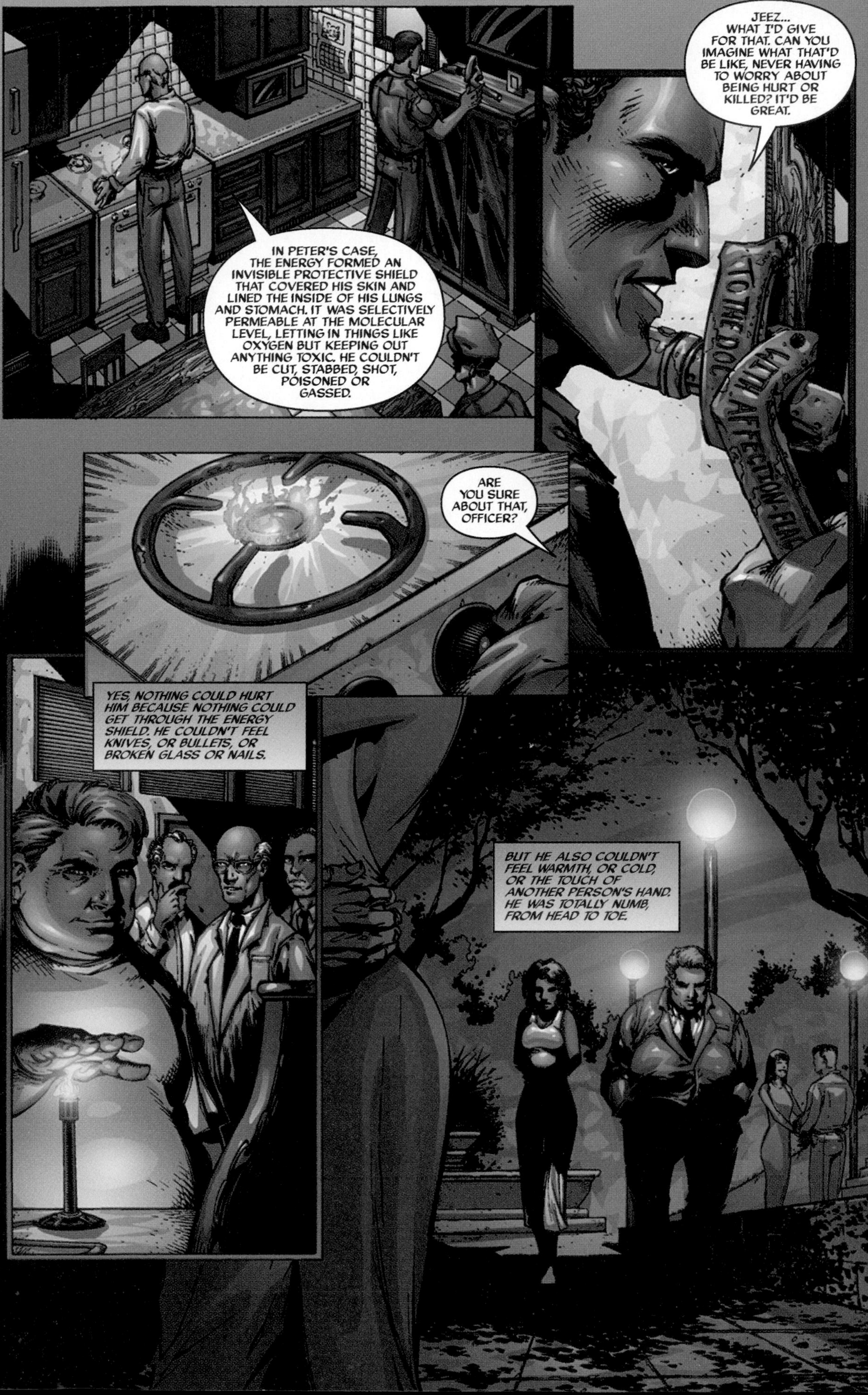
IN PETER'S CASE, THE ENERGY FORMED AN INVISIBLE PROTECTIVE SHIELD THAT COVERED HIS SKIN AND LINED THE INSIDE OF HIS LUNGS AND STOMACH. IT WAS SELECTIVELY PERMEABLE AT THE MOLECULAR LEVEL, LETTING IN THINGS LIKE OXYGEN BUT KEEPING OUT ANYTHING TOXIC. HE COULDN'T BE CUT, STABBED, SHOT, POISONED OR GASSED.
JEEZ... WHAT I'D GIVE FOR THAT. CAN YOU IMAGINE WHAT THAT'D BE LIKE, NEVER HAVING TO WORRY ABOUT BEING HURT OR KILLED? IT'D BE GREAT.
TO THE DOC
WITH AFFECTION
ARE YOU SURE ABOUT THAT, OFFICER?
YES, NOTHING COULD HURT HIM BECAUSE NOTHING COULD GET THROUGH THE ENERGY SHIELD. HE COULDN'T FEEL KNIVES, OR BULLETS, OR BROKEN GLASS OR NAILS.
BUT HE ALSO COULDN'T FEEL WARMTH, OR COLD, OR THE TOUCH OF ANOTHER PERSON'S HAND. HE WAS TOTALLY NUMB, FROM HEAD TO TOE.

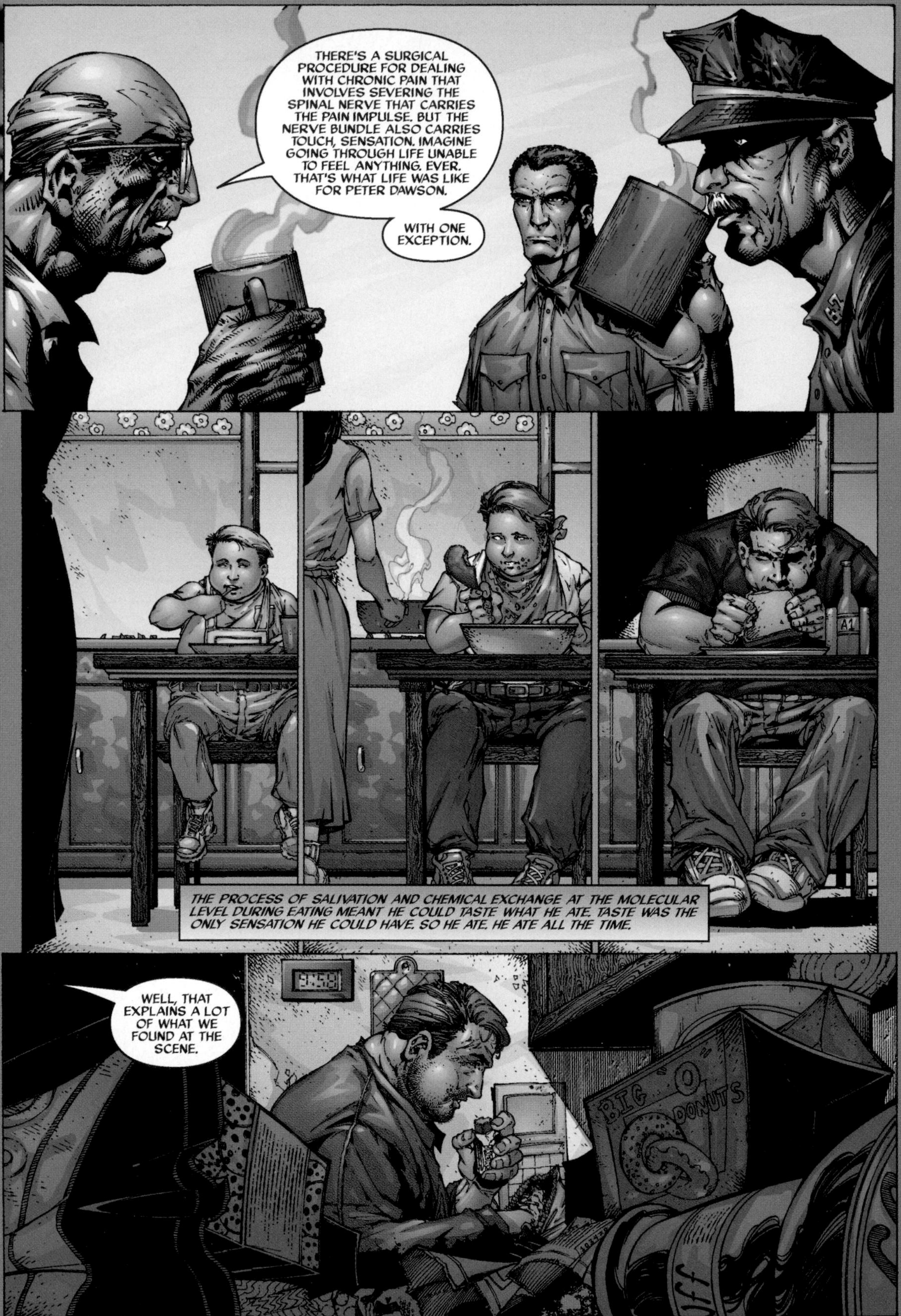
THERE'S A SURGICAL PROCEDURE FOR DEALING WITH CHRONIC PAIN THAT INVOLVES SEVERING THE SPINAL NERVE THAT CARRIES THE PAIN IMPULSE. BUT THE NERVE BUNDLE ALSO CARRIES TOUCH, SENSATION. IMAGINE GOING THROUGH LIFE UNABLE TO FEEL ANYTHING. EVER. THAT'S WHAT LIFE WAS LIKE FOR PETER DAWSON.
WITH ONE EXCEPTION.
A1
THE PROCESS OF SALIVATION AND CHEMICAL EXCHANGE AT THE MOLECULAR LEVEL DURING EATING MEANT HE COULD TASTE WHAT HE ATE. TASTE WAS THE ONLY SENSATION HE COULD HAVE. SO HE ATE. HE ATE ALL THE TIME.
WELL, THAT EXPLAINS A LOT OF WHAT WE FOUND AT THE SCENE.
BIG "O" DONUTS

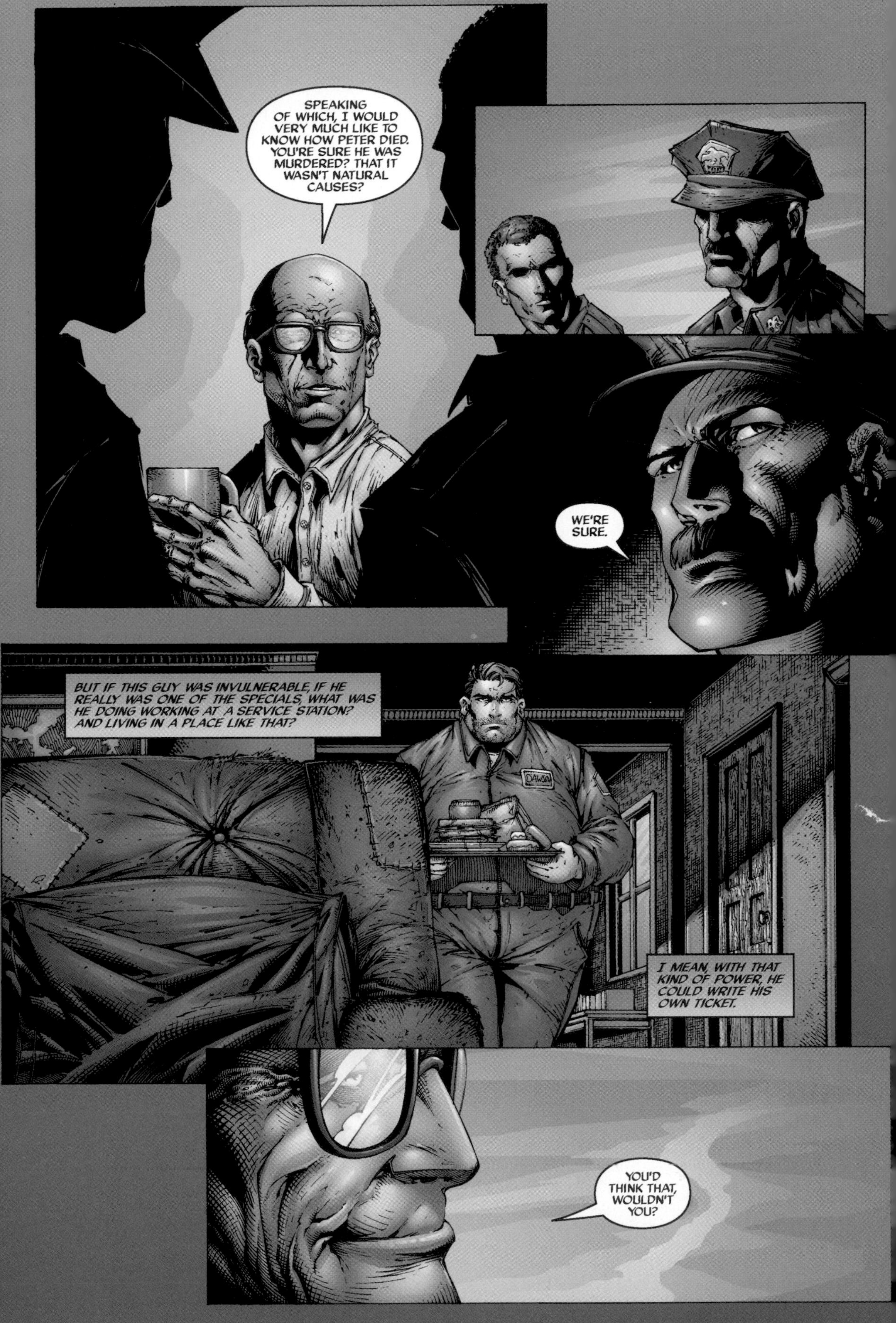
SPEAKING OF WHICH, I WOULD VERY MUCH LIKE TO KNOW HOW PETER DIED. YOU'RE SURE HE WAS MURDERED? THAT IT WASN'T NATURAL CAUSES?
WE'RE SURE.
BUT IF THIS GUY WAS INVULNERABLE, IF HE REALLY WAS ONE OF THE SPECIALS, WHAT WAS HE DOING WORKING AT A SERVICE STATION? AND LIVING IN A PLACE LIKE THAT?
I MEAN, WITH THAT KIND OF POWER, HE COULD WRITE HIS OWN TICKET.
YOU'D THINK THAT, WOULDN'T YOU?

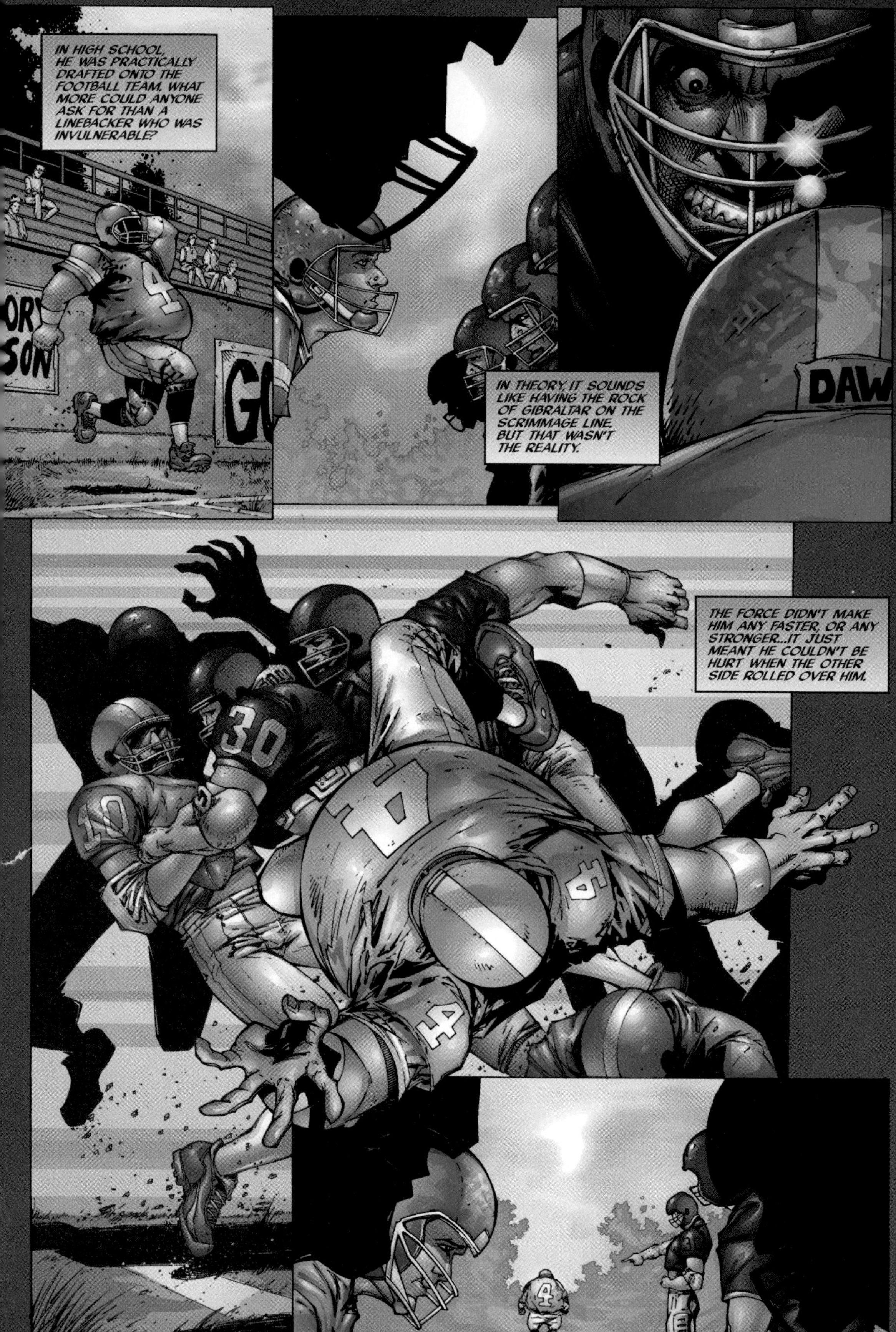
IN HIGH SCHOOL, HE WAS PRACTICALLY DRAFTED ONTO THE FOOTBALL TEAM. WHAT MORE COULD ANYONE ASK FOR THAN A LINEBACKER WHO WAS INVULNERABLE?
IN THEORY, IT SOUNDS LIKE HAVING THE ROCK OF GIBRALTAR ON THE SCRIMMAGE LINE. BUT THAT WASN'T THE REALITY.
THE FORCE DIDN'T MAKE HIM ANY FASTER, OR ANY STRONGER...IT JUST MEANT HE COULDN'T BE HURT WHEN THE OTHER SIDE ROLLED OVER HIM.

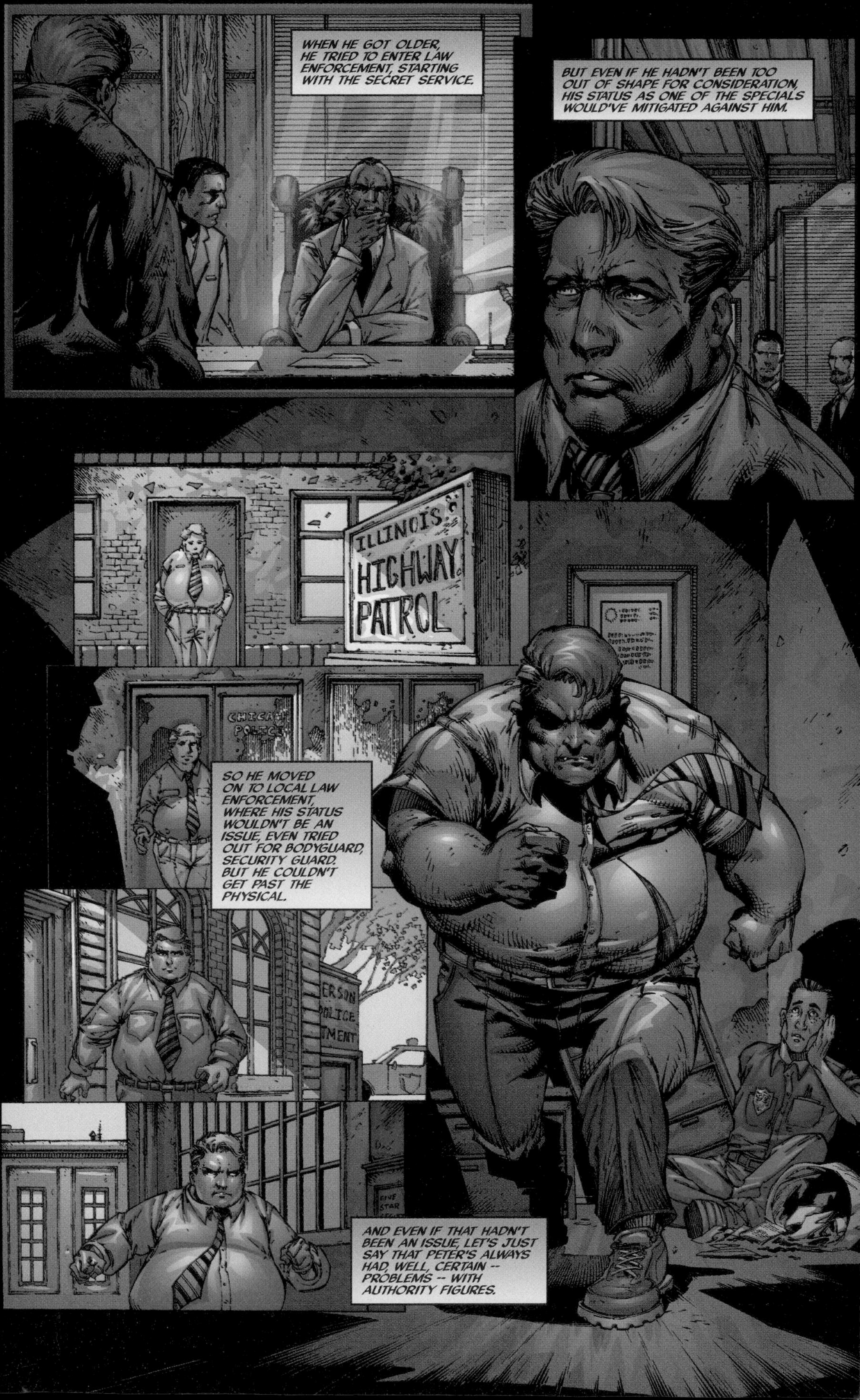
WHEN HE GOT OLDER, HE TRIED TO ENTER LAW ENFORCEMENT, STARTING WITH THE SECRET SERVICE.
BUT EVEN IF HE HADN'T BEEN TOO OUT OF SHAPE FOR CONSIDERATION, HIS STATUS AS ONE OF THE SPECIALS WOULD'VE MITIGATED AGAINST HIM.
ILLINOIS HIGHWAY PATROL
SO HE MOVED ON TO LOCAL LAW ENFORCEMENT, WHERE HIS STATUS WOULDN'T BE AN ISSUE, EVEN TRIED OUT FOR BODYGUARD, SECURITY GUARD. BUT HE COULDN'T GET PAST THE PHYSICAL.
AND EVEN IF THAT HADN'T BEEN AN ISSUE, LET'S JUST SAY THAT PETER'S ALWAYS HAD, WELL, CERTAIN -- PROBLEMS -- WITH AUTHORITY FIGURES.

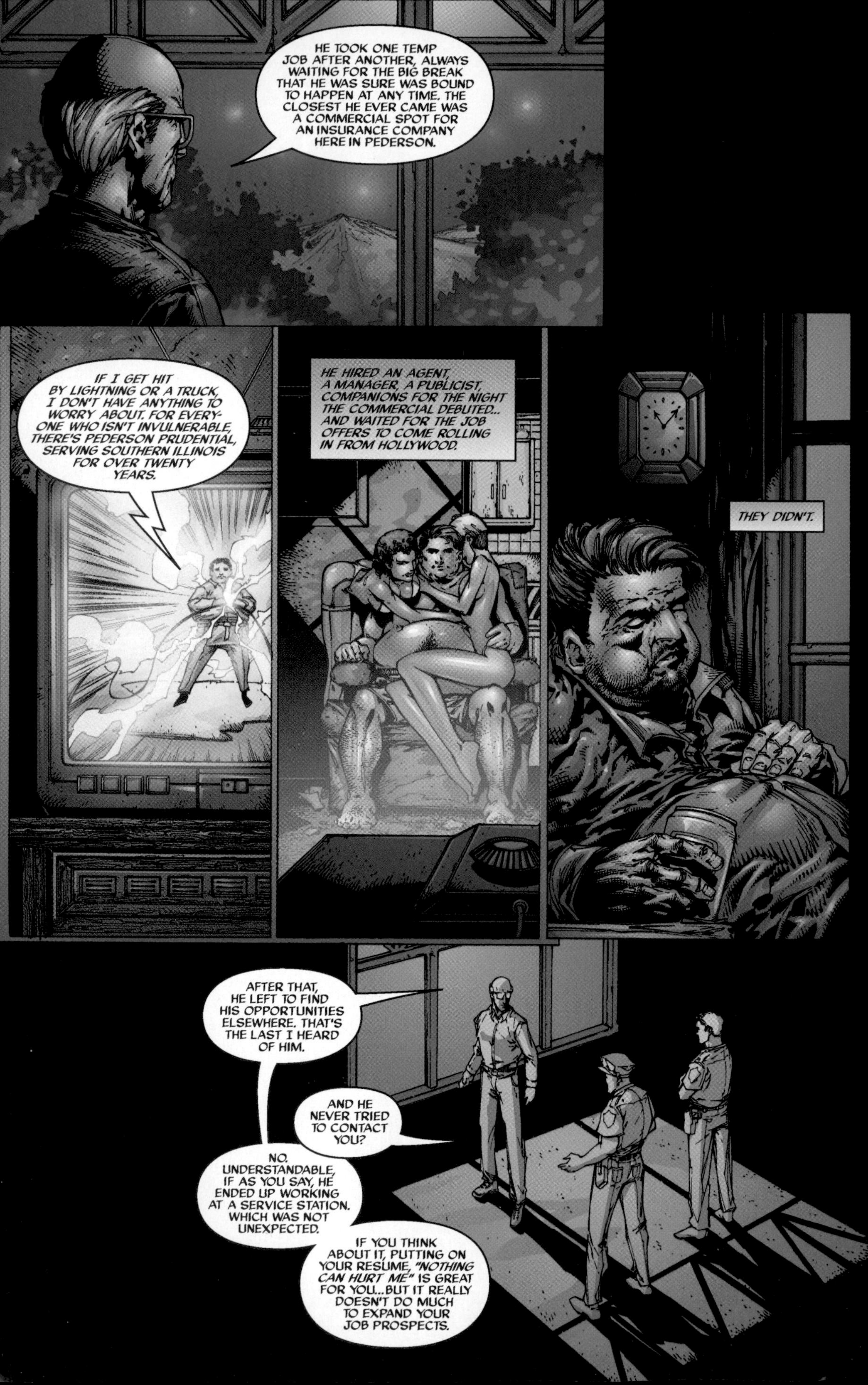
HE TOOK ONE TEMP JOB AFTER ANOTHER, ALWAYS WAITING FOR THE BIG BREAK THAT HE WAS SURE WAS BOUND TO HAPPEN AT ANY TIME. THE CLOSEST HE EVER CAME WAS A COMMERCIAL SPOT FOR AN INSURANCE COMPANY HERE IN PEDERSON.
IF I GET HIT BY LIGHTNING OR A TRUCK, I DON'T HAVE ANYTHING TO WORRY ABOUT. FOR EVERY-ONE WHO ISN'T INVULNERABLE, THERE'S PEDERSON PRUDENTIAL, SERVING SOUTHERN ILLINOIS FOR OVER TWENTY YEARS.
HE HIRED AN AGENT, A MANAGER, A PUBLICIST, COMPANIONS FOR THE NIGHT THE COMMERCIAL DEBUTED... AND WAITED FOR THE JOB OFFERS TO COME ROLLING IN FROM HOLLYWOOD.
THEY DIDN'T.
AFTER THAT, HE LEFT TO FIND HIS OPPORTUNITIES ELSEWHERE. THAT'S THE LAST I HEARD OF HIM.
AND HE NEVER TRIED TO CONTACT YOU?
NO. UNDERSTANDABLE, IF AS YOU SAY, HE ENDED UP WORKING AT A SERVICE STATION. WHICH WAS NOT UNEXPECTED.
IF YOU THINK ABOUT IT, PUTTING ON YOUR RESUME, "NOTHING CAN HURT ME" IS GREAT FOR YOU...BUT IT REALLY DOESN'T DO MUCH TO EXPAND YOUR JOB PROSPECTS.

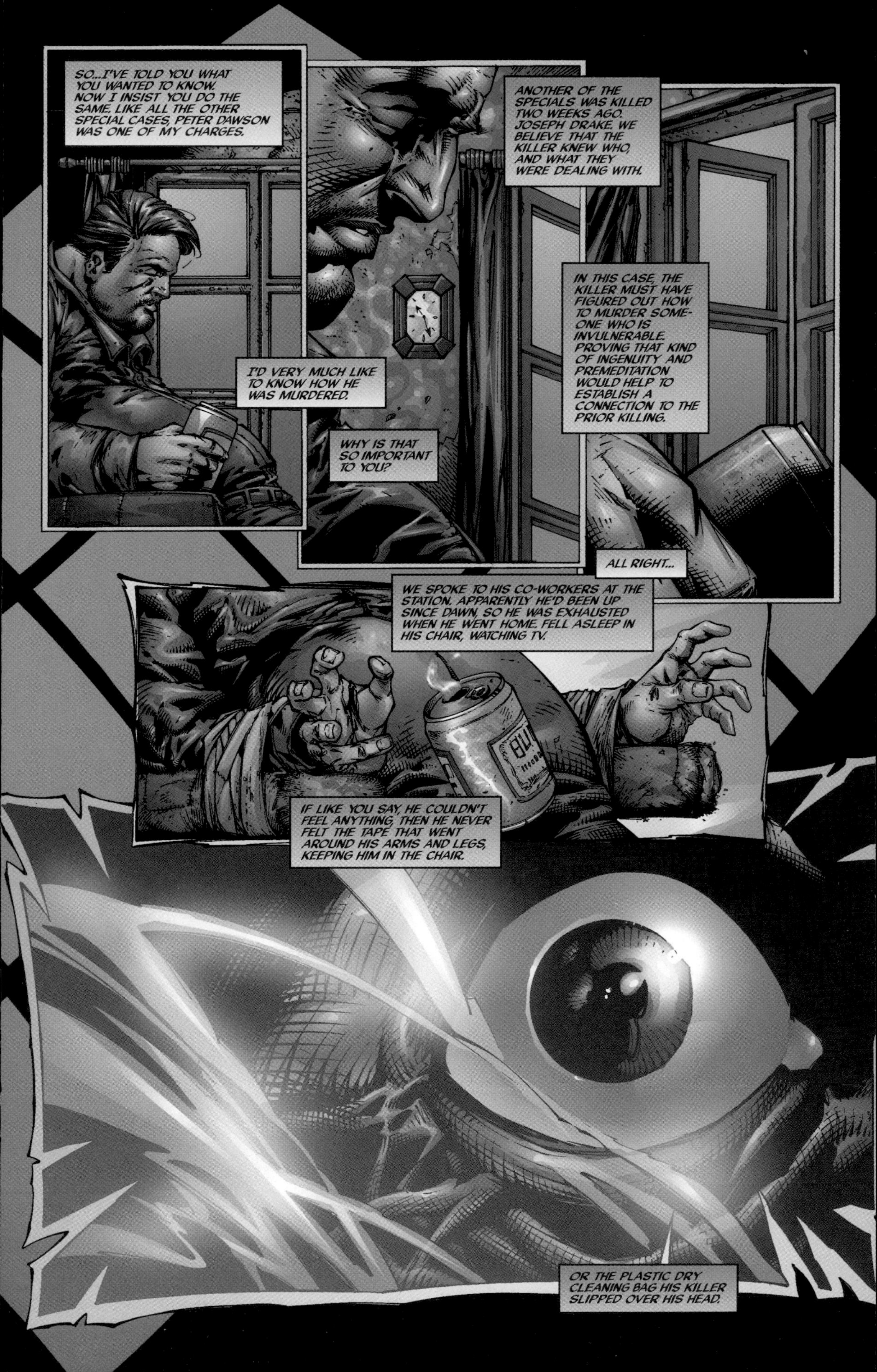
SO...I'VE TOLD YOU WHAT YOU WANTED TO KNOW. NOW I INSIST YOU DO THE SAME. LIKE ALL THE OTHER SPECIAL CASES, PETER DAWSON WAS ONE OF MY CHARGES.
I'D VERY MUCH LIKE TO KNOW HOW HE WAS MURDERED.
WHY IS THAT SO IMPORTANT TO YOU?
ANOTHER OF THE SPECIALS WAS KILLED TWO WEEKS AGO. JOSEPH DRAKE. WE BELIEVE THAT THE KILLER KNEW WHO, AND WHAT THEY WERE DEALING WITH.
IN THIS CASE, THE KILLER MUST HAVE FIGURED OUT HOW TO MURDER SOME-ONE WHO IS INVULNERABLE. PROVING THAT KIND OF INGENUITY AND PREMEDITATION WOULD HELP TO ESTABLISH A CONNECTION TO THE PRIOR KILLING.
ALL RIGHT...
WE SPOKE TO HIS CO-WORKERS AT THE STATION. APPARENTLY HE'D BEEN UP SINCE DAWN, SO HE WAS EXHAUSTED WHEN HE WENT HOME. FELL ASLEEP IN HIS CHAIR, WATCHING TV.
IF LIKE YOU SAY, HE COULDN'T FEEL ANYTHING, THEN HE NEVER FELT THE TAPE THAT WENT AROUND HIS ARMS AND LEGS, KEEPING HIM IN THE CHAIR.
OR THE PLASTIC DRY CLEANING BAG HIS KILLER SLIPPED OVER HIS HEAD.

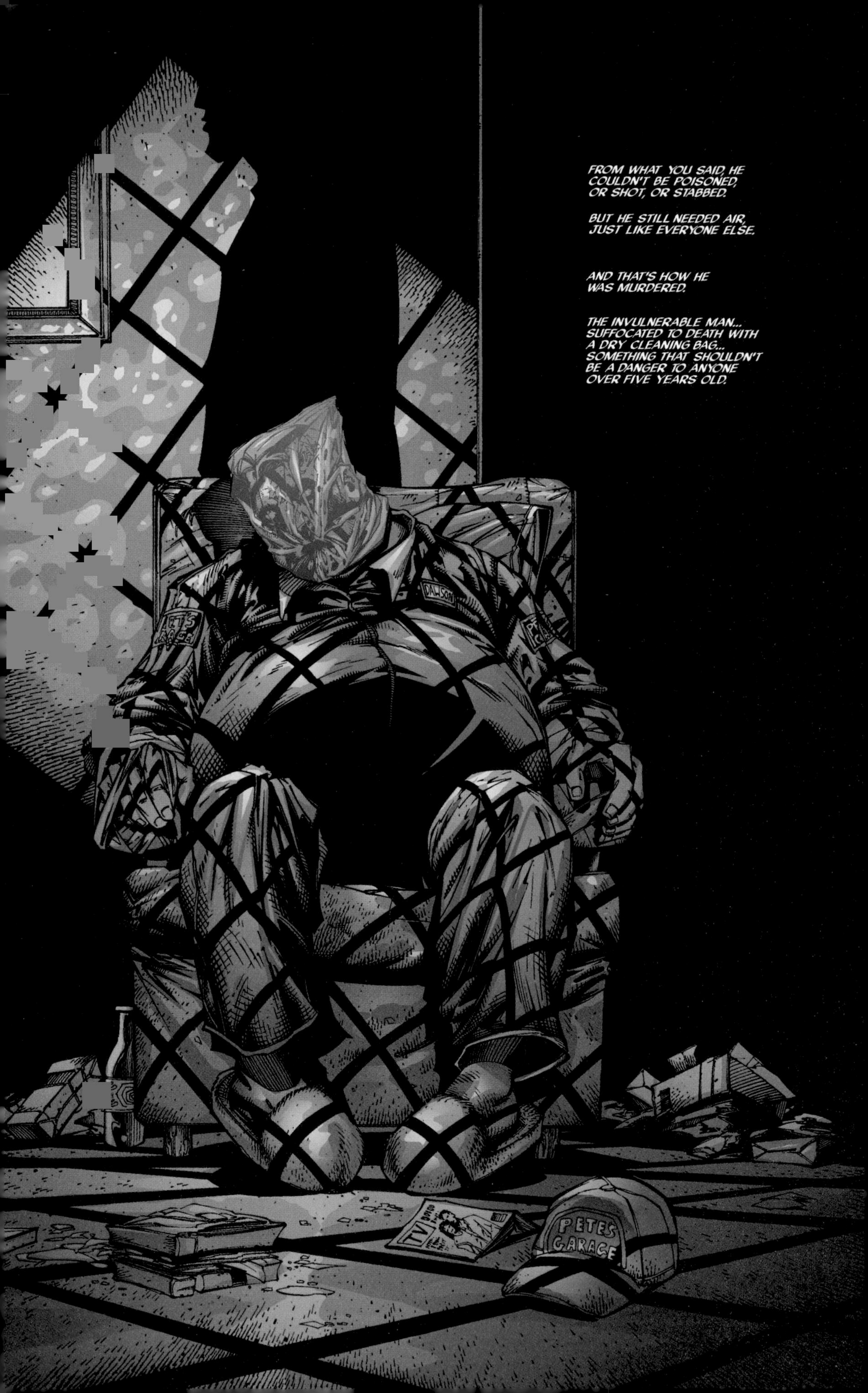
FROM WHAT YOU SAID, HE COULDN'T BE POISONED, OR SHOT, OR STABBED.
BUT HE STILL NEEDED AIR, JUST LIKE EVERYONE ELSE.
AND THAT'S HOW HE WAS MURDERED.
THE INVULNERABLE MAN... SUFFOCATED TO DEATH WITH A DRY CLEANING BAG... SOMETHING THAT SHOULDN'T BE A DANGER TO ANYONE OVER FIVE YEARS OLD.
PETES GARAGE

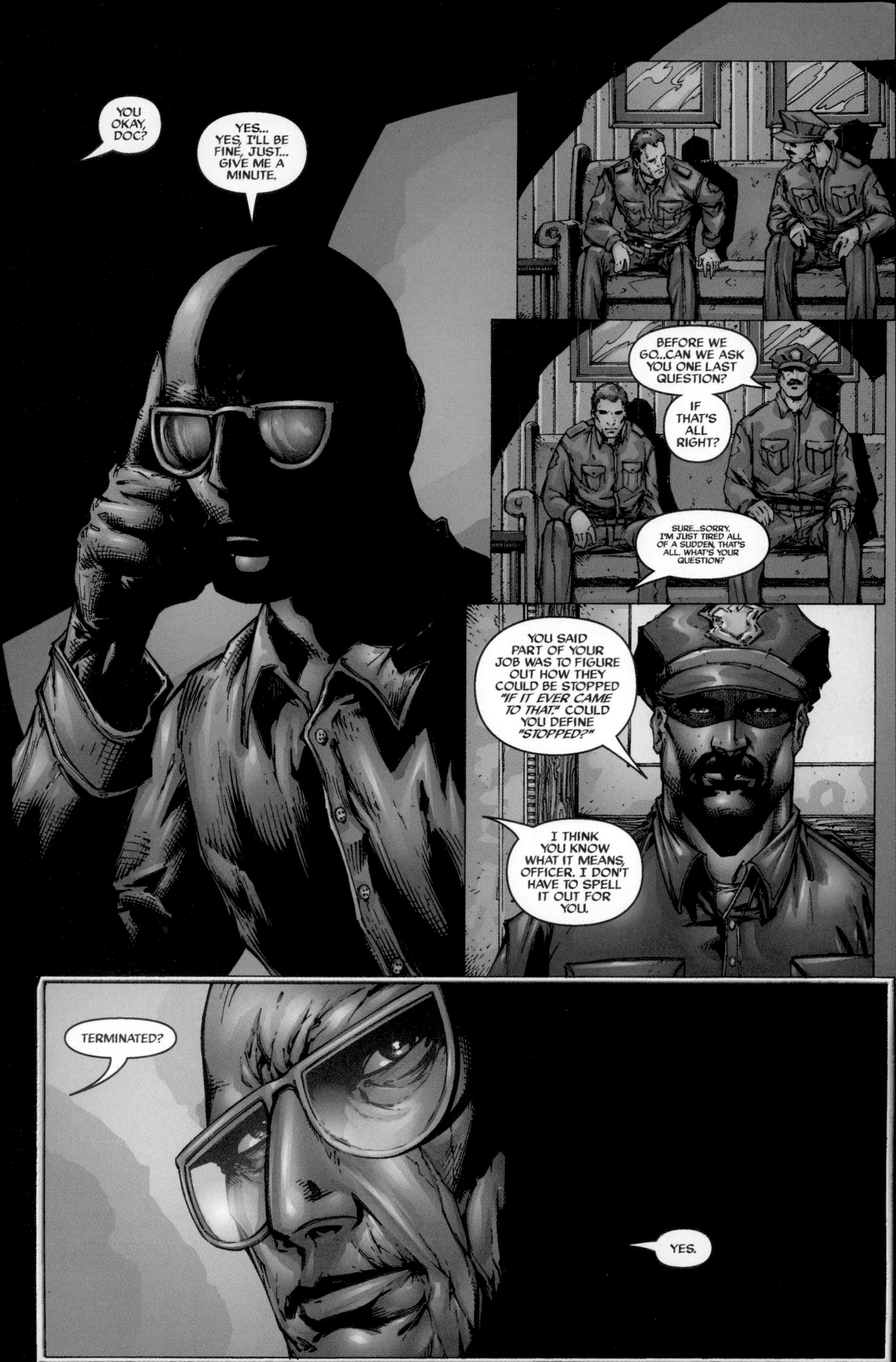

YOU OKAY, DOC?
YES... YES, I'LL BE FINE, JUST... GIVE ME A MINUTE.
BEFORE WE GO...CAN WE ASK YOU ONE LAST QUESTION?
IF THAT'S ALL RIGHT?
SURE...SORRY. I'M JUST TIRED ALL OF A SUDDEN, THAT'S ALL. WHAT'S YOUR QUESTION?
YOU SAID PART OF YOUR JOB WAS TO FIGURE OUT HOW THEY COULD BE STOPPED *"IF IT EVER CAME TO THAT."* COULD YOU DEFINE *"STOPPED?"*
I THINK YOU KNOW WHAT IT MEANS, OFFICER. I DON'T HAVE TO SPELL IT OUT FOR YOU.
TERMINATED?
YES.

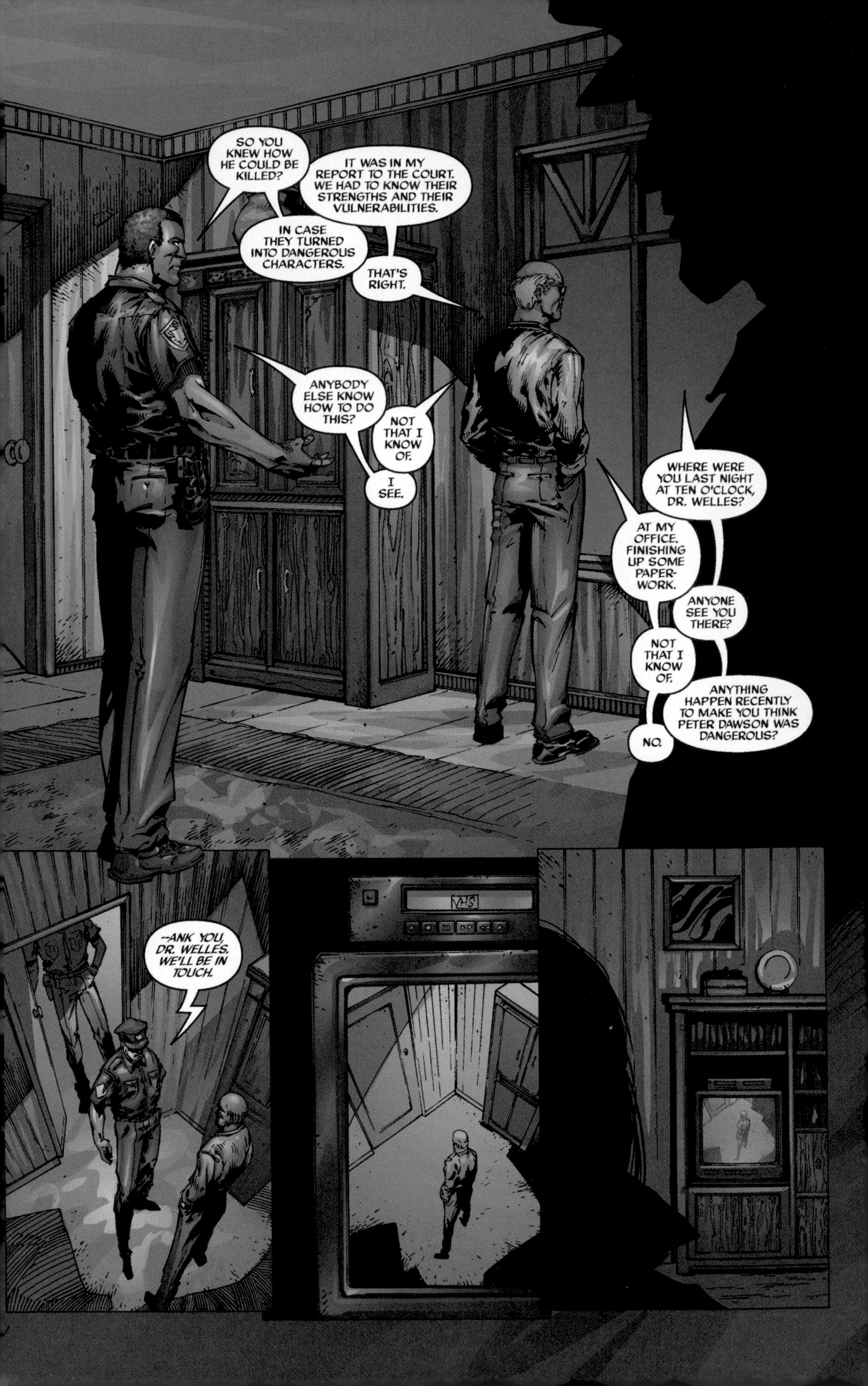
SO YOU KNEW HOW HE COULD BE KILLED?
IT WAS IN MY REPORT TO THE COURT. WE HAD TO KNOW THEIR STRENGTHS AND THEIR VULNERABILITIES.
IN CASE THEY TURNED INTO DANGEROUS CHARACTERS.
THAT'S RIGHT.
ANYBODY ELSE KNOW HOW TO DO THIS?
NOT THAT I KNOW OF.
I SEE.
WHERE WERE YOU LAST NIGHT AT TEN O'CLOCK, DR. WELLES?
AT MY OFFICE. FINISHING UP SOME PAPER-WORK.
ANYONE SEE YOU THERE?
NOT THAT I KNOW OF.
ANYTHING HAPPEN RECENTLY TO MAKE YOU THINK PETER DAWSON WAS DANGEROUS?
NO.
--ANK YOU, DR. WELLES. WE'LL BE IN TOUCH.
VHS

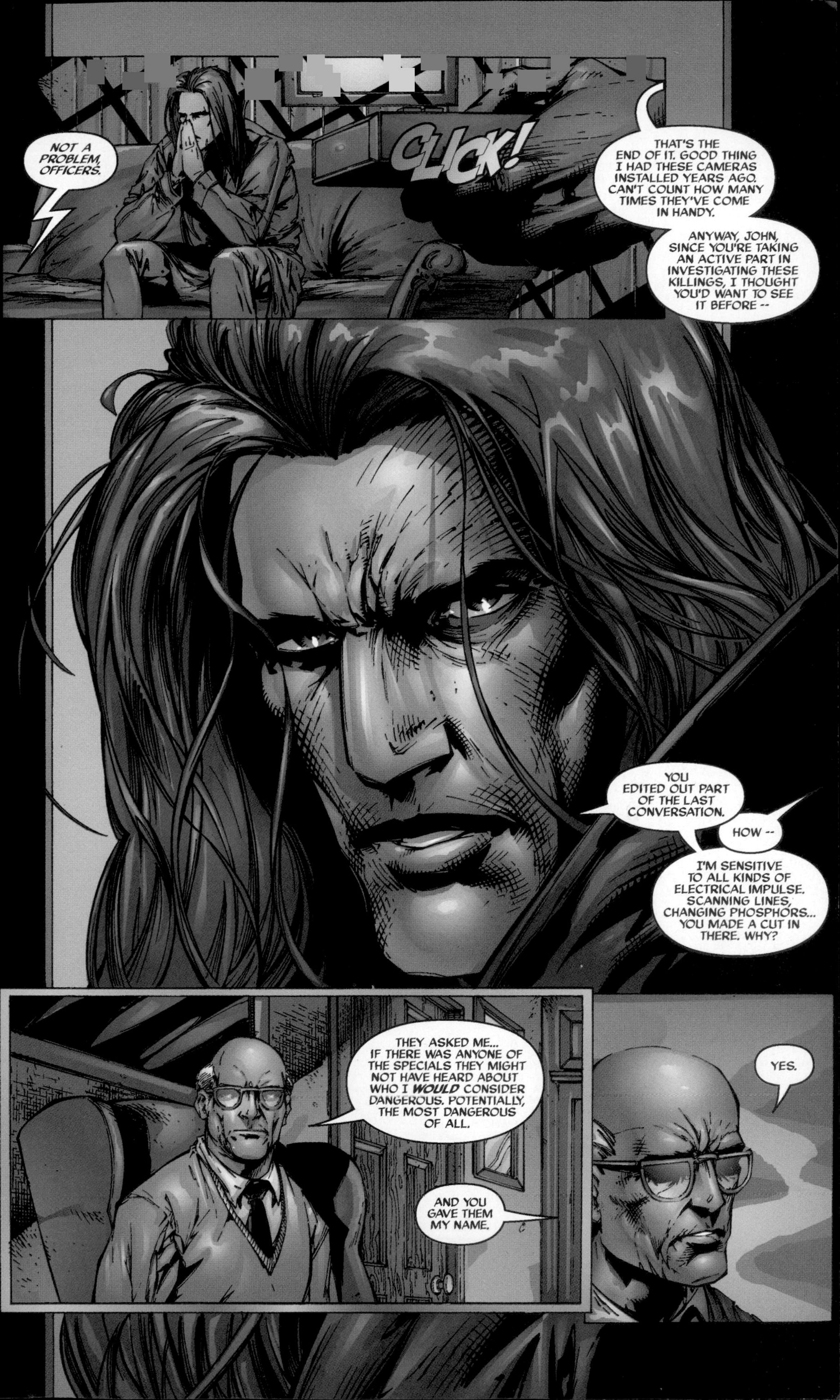
NOT A PROBLEM, OFFICERS.
CLICK!
THAT'S THE END OF IT. GOOD THING I HAD THESE CAMERAS INSTALLED YEARS AGO. CAN'T COUNT HOW MANY TIMES THEY'VE COME IN HANDY.
ANYWAY, JOHN, SINCE YOU'RE TAKING AN ACTIVE PART IN INVESTIGATING THESE KILLINGS, I THOUGHT YOU'D WANT TO SEE IT BEFORE --
YOU EDITED OUT PART OF THE LAST CONVERSATION.
HOW --
I'M SENSITIVE TO ALL KINDS OF ELECTRICAL IMPULSE. SCANNING LINES, CHANGING PHOSPHORS... YOU MADE A CUT IN THERE. WHY?
THEY ASKED ME... IF THERE WAS ANYONE OF THE SPECIALS THEY MIGHT NOT HAVE HEARD ABOUT WHO I *WOULD* CONSIDER DANGEROUS. POTENTIALLY, THE MOST DANGEROUS OF ALL.
AND YOU GAVE THEM MY NAME.
YES.

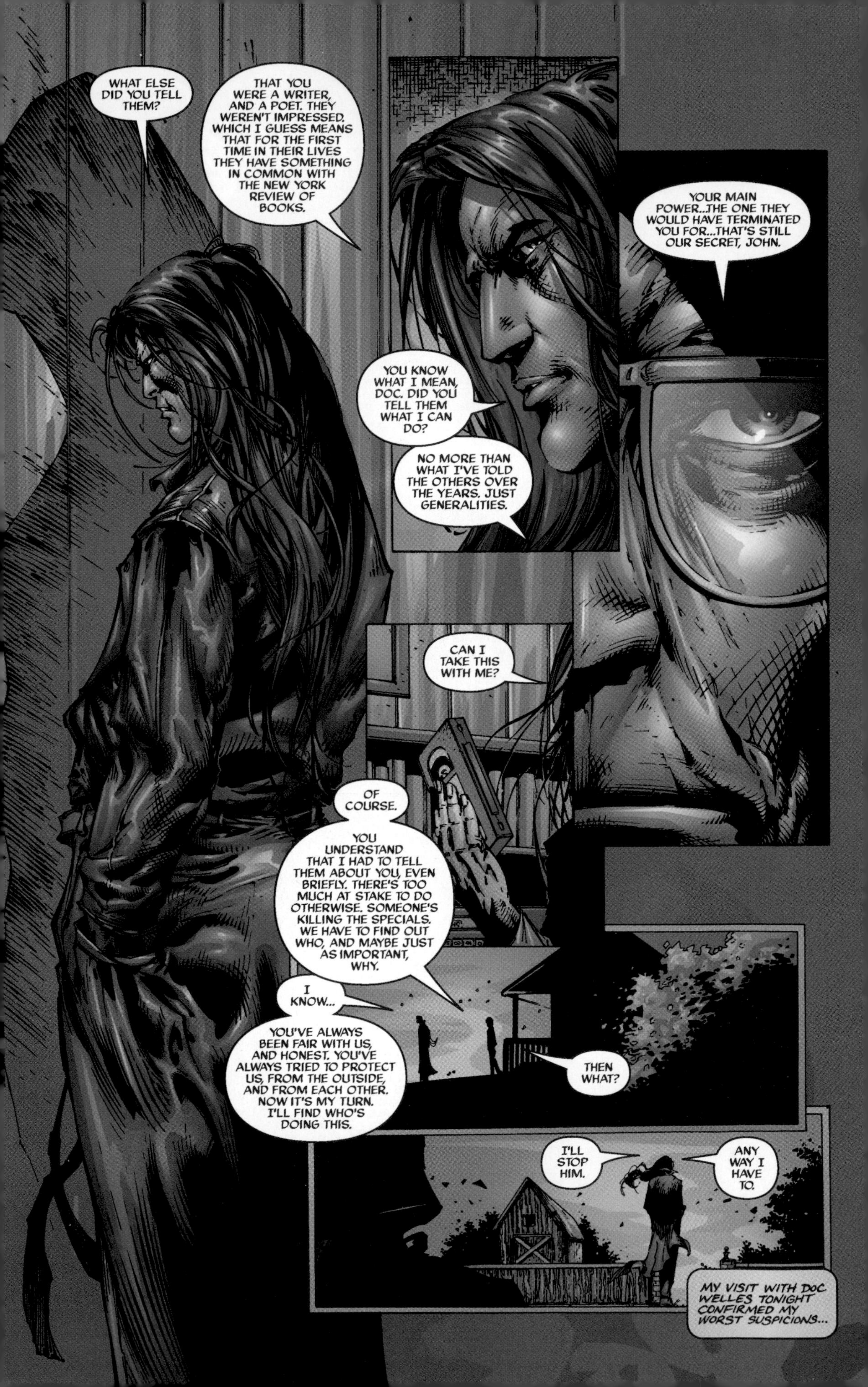
WHAT ELSE DID YOU TELL THEM?
THAT YOU WERE A WRITER, AND A POET. THEY WEREN'T IMPRESSED. WHICH I GUESS MEANS THAT FOR THE FIRST TIME IN THEIR LIVES THEY HAVE SOMETHING IN COMMON WITH THE NEW YORK REVIEW OF BOOKS.
YOUR MAIN POWER...THE ONE THEY WOULD HAVE TERMINATED YOU FOR...THAT'S STILL OUR SECRET, JOHN.
YOU KNOW WHAT I MEAN, DOC. DID YOU TELL THEM WHAT I CAN DO?
NO MORE THAN WHAT I'VE TOLD THE OTHERS OVER THE YEARS. JUST GENERALITIES.
CAN I TAKE THIS WITH ME?
OF COURSE.
YOU UNDERSTAND THAT I HAD TO TELL THEM ABOUT YOU, EVEN BRIEFLY. THERE'S TOO MUCH AT STAKE TO DO OTHERWISE. SOMEONE'S KILLING THE SPECIALS. WE HAVE TO FIND OUT WHO, AND MAYBE JUST AS IMPORTANT, WHY.
I KNOW...
YOU'VE ALWAYS BEEN FAIR WITH US, AND HONEST. YOU'VE ALWAYS TRIED TO PROTECT US, FROM THE OUTSIDE, AND FROM EACH OTHER. NOW IT'S MY TURN. I'LL FIND WHO'S DOING THIS.
THEN WHAT?
I'LL STOP HIM.
ANY WAY I HAVE TO.
MY VISIT WITH DOC WELLES TONIGHT CONFIRMED MY WORST SUSPICIONS...

The killer is one of us. An outsider would not have known how to find him, or the nature of his power, or how he could be killed. We all talked about it as we were growing up, even though we weren't supposed to. Each time one of us discovered we had a new ability, or a new variation on an ability that had already manifested itself, we showed it to the others. In a way, it was a high-powered case of

"You show me yours and I'll show you mine."

But it was also a way of figuring out what the possibilities were. Until Matthew discovered he could fly, it hadn't occured to some of the others. Then we all tried it and sure enough, some of us found that they could fly as well. The rest of us ended up bruised, banged and occasionally fractured. But it never stopped us from trying again when another new power was discovered. Even now, there are some who were born in the window of the force who haven't shown any unusual abilities. The abilities probably exist, but they haven't been confronted by the right circumstance yet to find out what they are. Unfortunately, these powers didn't come with a driver's manual.

So we all knew what Peter could do, and what he couldn't do, and probably some of us had figured out how he could be killed. That was another, darker game we played, late at night, when the adults weren't around. "If Matt and Joshua got in a fight to the death, who would win?" I think that even then, on some level, we all knew that if some of us went bad, they could only be stopped by others like us. We would have the power, and the knowledge, and ultimately the responsibility.

And now it seems as if one of us is, indeed, trying to stop the rest. To hunt us down, using the secrets that only we know about one another. Of course that assumes that we're talking about just one person, but I think we have to believe that for now. The alternative is something I don't like to think about.

The question is who, and why? Followed shortly by, who's next?

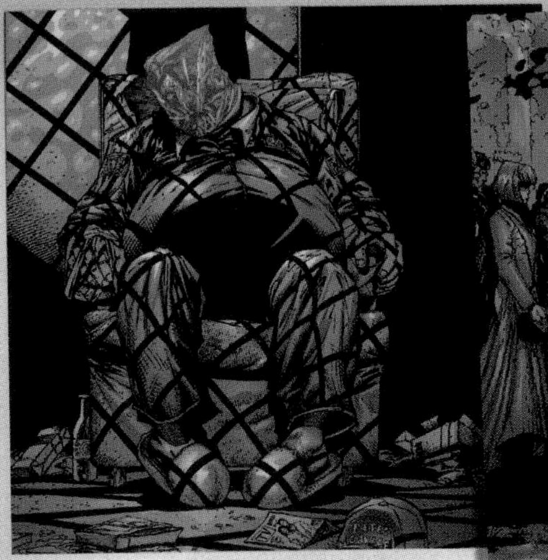

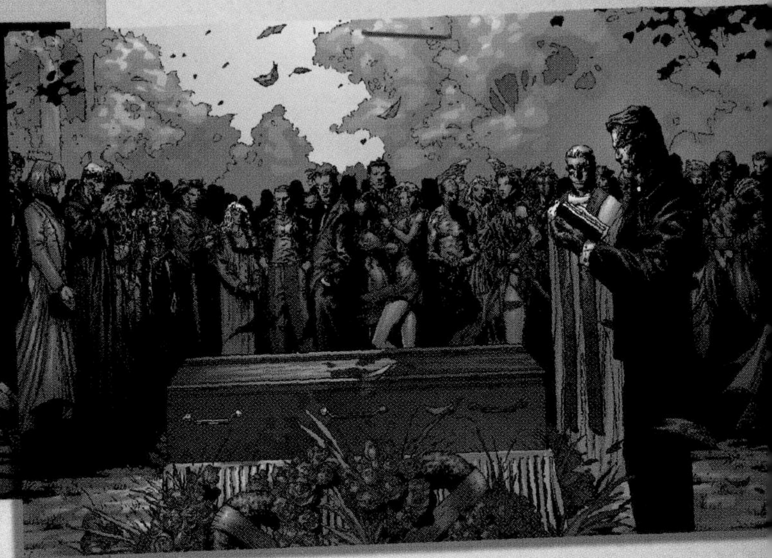

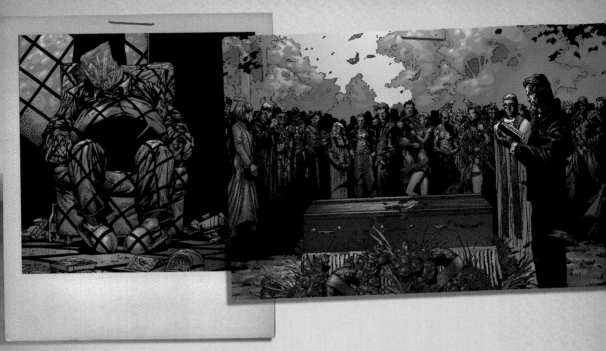

THAT'S THE PART THAT DOESN'T MAKE SENSE. PETER AND JOEY DRAKE WERE BOTTOM-RUNGERS, POSSESSING LIMITED ABILITIES THAT THEY WEREN'T ABLE TO USE TO GREAT ADVANTAGE. THEY DIDN'T POSE A THREAT TO ANYONE. THEY HAD NOTHING IN COMMON OTHER THAN THEIR LIMITED ABILITIES.

MAYBE THAT'S PART OF IT. MAYBE WHOEVER'S DOING THIS IS STARTING WITH THE LESSER-POWERED CASES FIRST, THE ONES THAT WOULD BE EASIEST TO KILL. IF THAT'S TRUE, THEN WE NEED TO WARN THE OTHERS AT SIMILAR POWER-LEVELS THAT THE KILLER MIGHT BE COMING AFTER THEM NEXT. BUT THAT'S AN AWFULLY BIG "IF", AND THERE'S SOMETHING TO BE SAID FOR NOT PANICKING THE OTHERS WITHOUT CAUSE. ON THE OTHER HAND, IF WHAT I SAW ON THAT TAPE DOESN'T CONSTITUTE SUFFICIENT CAUSE, I DON'T KNOW WHAT DOES.

IF STARTING WITH THE VICTIMS DOESN'T GO ANYWHERE, MAYBE WE SHOULD START WITH THE LIST OF POSSIBLE KILLERS, SINCE IT'S SHORTER. MOST OF US ARE PRETTY WELL ACCOUNTED FOR, OUR MOVEMENTS COVERED BY THE PRESS, OR THE GOVERNMENT, OR BOTH. SLIPPING AWAY FOR AN OCCASIONAL MURDER WOULD BE ALMOST IMPOSSIBLE FOR SOMEONE LIKE SANCTUARY, OR CHANDRA, FOR INSTANCE. RAVENSHADOW COULD DO IT, HE GOES AND COMES AS HE WANTS, WITHOUT BEING SEEN, BUT I KNOW RANDY, AND AS ODD AS HE IS, WHICH IS PLENTY, I CAN'T SEE HIM DOING THIS.

THE LOWER-POWER CASES DON'T DRAW THE SAME KIND OF ATTENTION, SO IN THEORY ONE OF THEM COULD DO IT. THE KILLINGS DIDN'T REQUIRE SPECIAL SKILLS, ONLY SPECIAL KNOWLEDGE. MAYBE SOMEONE'S UPSET ABOUT NOT HAVING MORE POWER? OR MAYBE SOMEONE  DISCOVERED ABILITIES HE DIDN'T KNOW HE HAD, A POWER THAT MATURED LATE IN LIFE, AND NOW HE'S TAKING OUT SOME OLD RESENTMENTS ON THE OTHERS.

THERE HAVE ONLY BEEN A FEW OF US TO TOTALLY SLIP THROUGH THE NET. LIKE WILLIE SMITH.

THERE ISN'T ONE OF US WHO DOESN'T STILL FEEL BAD ABOUT WHAT HAPPENED TO WILLIE. HE COULD FLY, THAT WAS HIS POWER, BUT HE WAS NEVER ABLE TO GET MORE THAN A FEW FEET OFF THE GROUND. THE DOC FIGURED THE PROBLEM WAS PSYCHOLOGICAL, A POOR SELF IMAGE. THE OTHER KIDS JOKED THAT HE WAS TOO FAT TO FLY HIGH, AND MAYBE HE BELIEVED THAT. CERTAINLY THE WAY WE THINK ABOUT THE POWERS SEEMS TO HAVE AN EFFECT ON THEM.

EITHER WAY, MOST OF THE OTHER KIDS WERE PRETTY CRUEL TO HIM. ALL KIDS HAVE THE POTENTIAL TO BE CRUEL IF THEY THINK THEY HAVE AN ADVANTAGE OVER SOMEONE, AND BECAUSE OF WHAT WE COULD DO, WE HAD A LOT OF ADVANTAGES... AND THE POTENTIAL FOR A LOT OF CRUELTY. I USED TO WONDER WHY THEY COULDN'T HAVE PUT HIM IN WITH NORMAL KIDS, BUT IT WASN'T PRACTICAL. THEY WOULD HAVE TORN HIM APART, BECAUSE HE WAS DIFFERENT.

SO HE STAYED WITH US. AND PUT UP WITH THE INSULTS, AND THE SLIGHTS, AND THE JOKES AT HIS EXPENSE, THE RANDOM CRUELTIES. THEN ONE DAY, A REALLY BAD DAY FOR WILLIE, THEY JUST WOULDN'T GIVE HIM A BREAK, IT WAS AS IF SOMETHING FINALLY SNAPPED INSIDE HIM. HE JUST STOOD THERE, GLARING AT THE BUNCH OF US, ARMS FLAT AT HIS SIDE... AND THEN HE STARTED RISING INTO THE AIR. HE ROSE HIGHER, AND HIGHER, STRAIGHT UP, NEVER TAKING HIS EYES OFF US. WE WERE TOO STUNNED TO REACT, EVEN THE ONES WHO COULD'VE FLOWN AFTER HIM WERE TOO ASTONISHED TO DO ANYTHING.

HE KEPT ON GOING UP, AND UP, UNTIL HE DISAPPEARED INTO THE CLOUDS. MATT WAS THE FIRST ONE TO COME TO HIS SENSES AND FLY AFTER HIM, BUT BY THEN WILLIE WAS LONG GONE. THAT NIGHT THE CAMP TEACHERS CLAMPED DOWN, AND NOBODY WAS ALLOWED TO GO FLYING FOR ALMOST A MONTH AFTERWARD. I GUESS THEY NEVER REALLY THOUGHT MUCH ABOUT US ESCAPING THAT WAY UNTIL WILLIE DID IT.

WE NEVER FOUND OUT WHAT HAPPENED TO HIM. SOME OF US CHOSE TO BELIEVE THAT HE KEPT ON GOING UNTIL HE FOUND A PLACE WHERE HE COULD BE ACCEPTED. OTHERS FIGURED HE KEPT RISING UNTIL HE HIT THE STRATOSPHERE, RAN OUT OF AIR, AND DIED UP THERE, THAT MAYBE HIS BODY IS STILL IN ORBIT SOMEWHERE.

AND MAYBE HE'S BEEN WAITING AROUND FOR A CHANCE TO GET BACK AT US, WHEN NO ONE WOULD BE LOOKING.

AND THEN THERE'S LEE. BUT WE ALL KNOW WHAT HAPPENED TO LEE, SINCE IT HAPPENED ON NATIONAL TELEVISION.

IN SOME WAYS, IT FEELS LIKE ALL THIS TROUBLE STARTED AFTER LEE WAS KILLED, EVEN THOUGH THAT WASN'T A MURDER. IT WAS A DIFFICULT DECISION AND A TRAGIC ENDING TO AN EVEN MORE TRAGIC LIFE.

BUT IT WASN'T MURDER.

IT'S LATE NOW. I HAVE TO SLEEP. MORE ON LEE NEXT TIME.

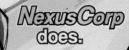

It's not enough to plan for today. It takes a special kind of company to plan for tomorrow...and protect the future. *NexusCorp* is leading the way, with a hero for today preserving the peace and prosperity of tomorrow.

FLAGG! ©™

SEE OUR NEW NAME SOON!

Does a big company really care about heroes?

NexusCorp does.

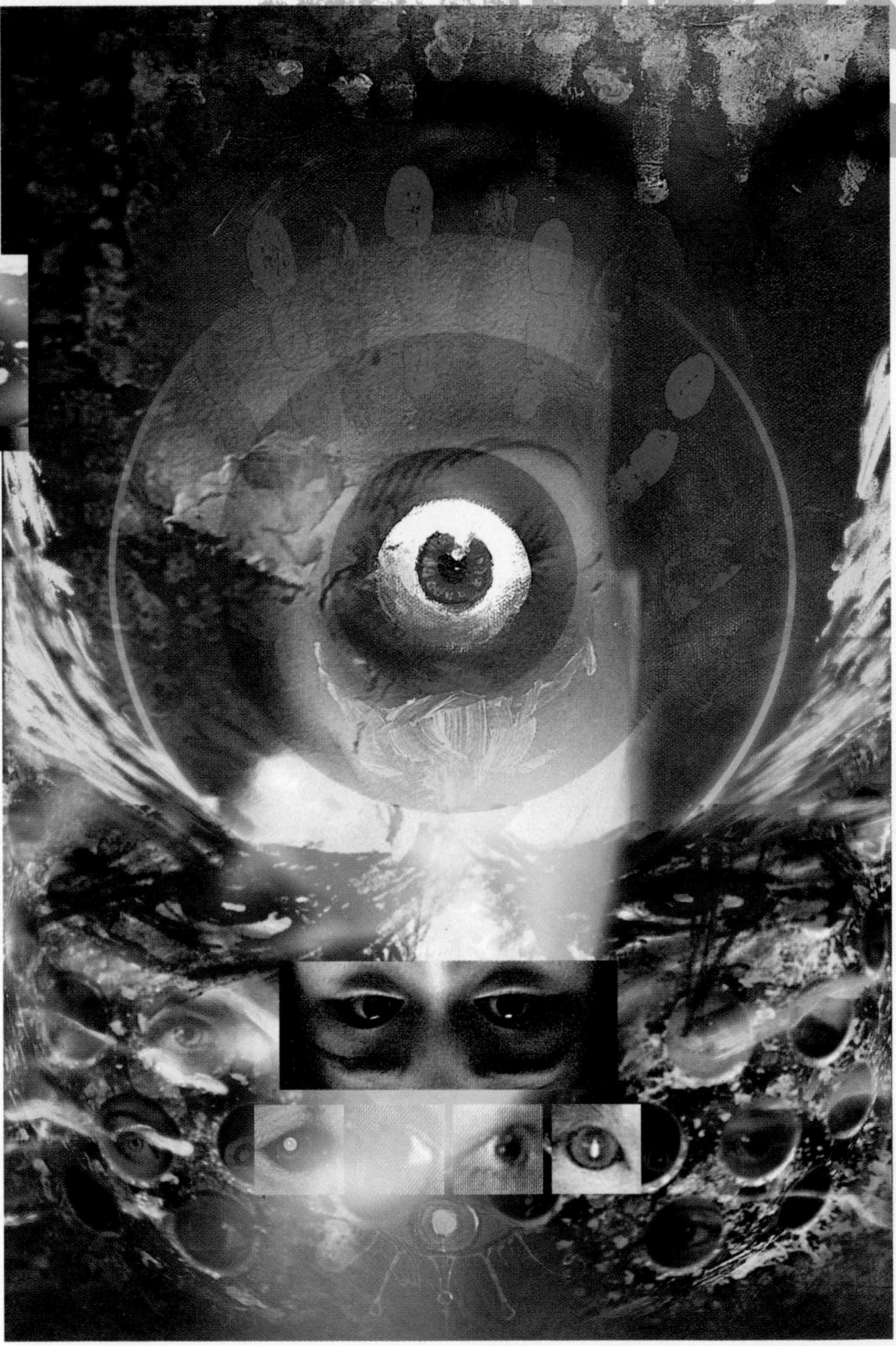

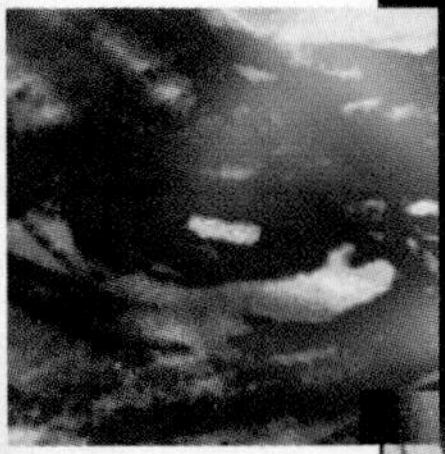

Chapter 3
Whatever Happened to Lee Jackson?

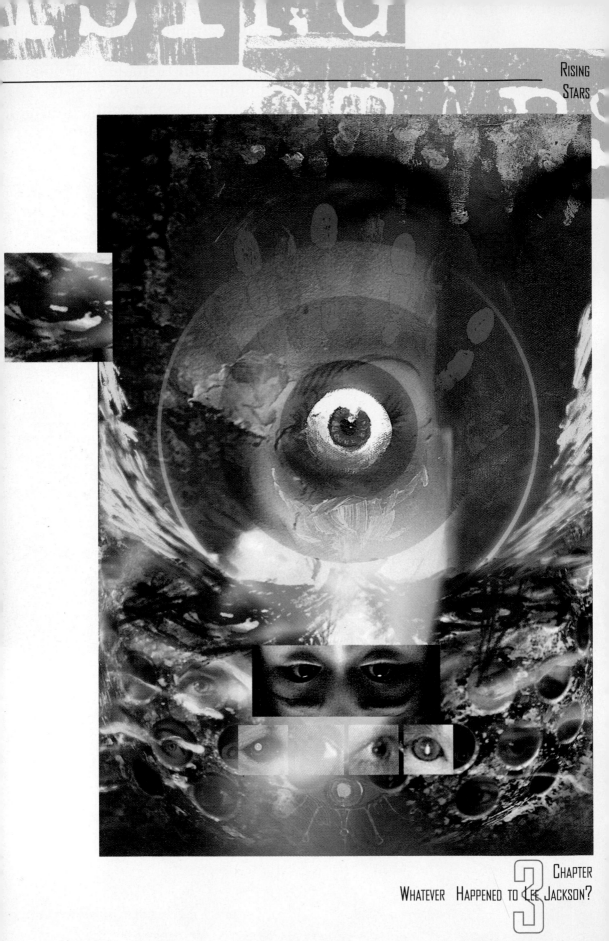

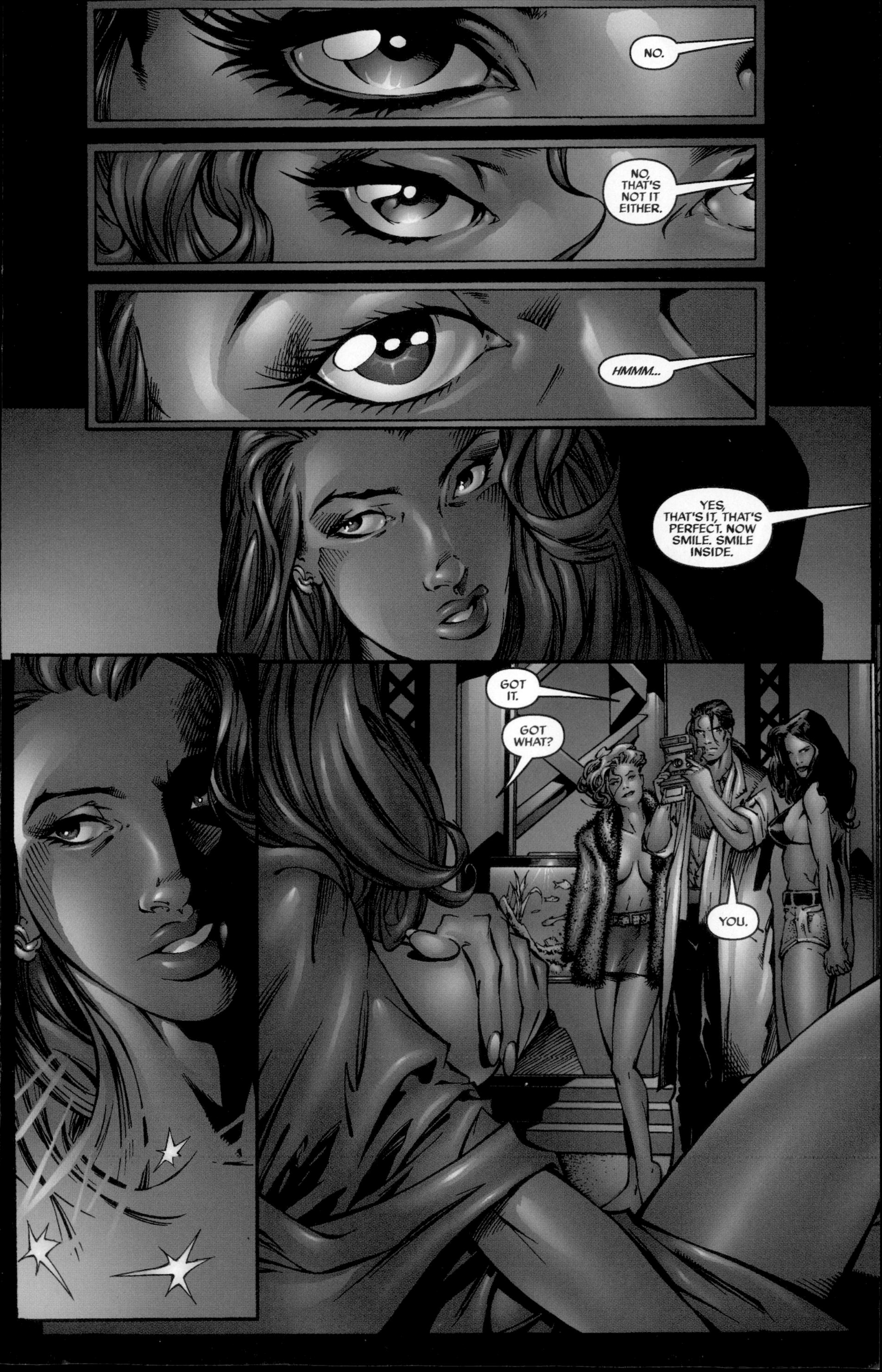
NO.
NO, THAT'S NOT IT EITHER.
HMMM...
YES, THAT'S IT, THAT'S PERFECT. NOW SMILE. SMILE INSIDE.
GOT IT.
GOT WHAT?
YOU.

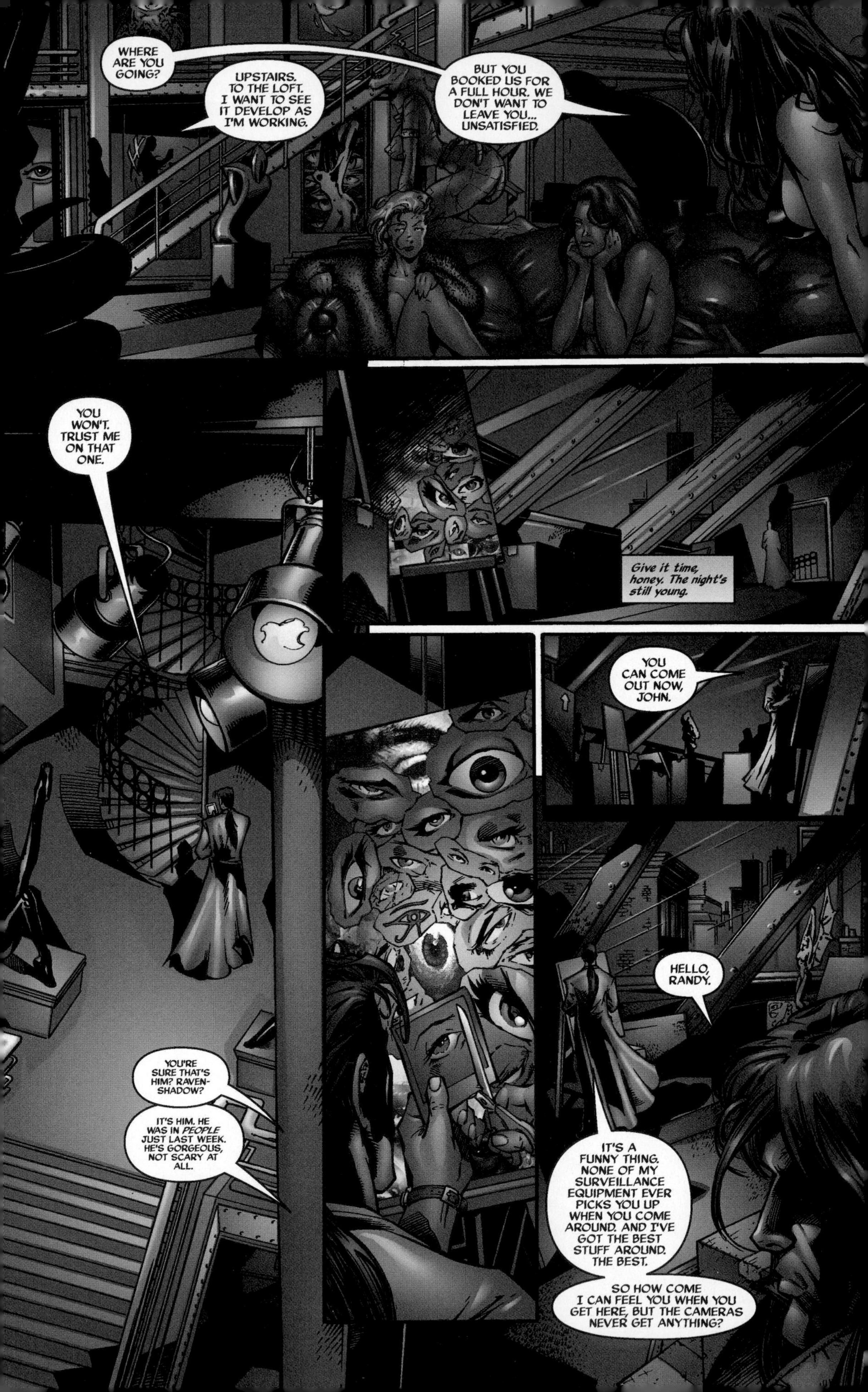
WHERE ARE YOU GOING?
UPSTAIRS. TO THE LOFT. I WANT TO SEE IT DEVELOP AS I'M WORKING.
BUT YOU BOOKED US FOR A FULL HOUR. WE DON'T WANT TO LEAVE YOU... UNSATISFIED.
YOU WON'T. TRUST ME ON THAT ONE.
Give it time, honey. The night's still young.
YOU'RE SURE THAT'S HIM? RAVEN-SHADOW?
IT'S HIM. HE WAS IN PEOPLE JUST LAST WEEK. HE'S GORGEOUS, NOT SCARY AT ALL.
YOU CAN COME OUT NOW, JOHN.
HELLO, RANDY.
IT'S A FUNNY THING. NONE OF MY SURVEILLANCE EQUIPMENT EVER PICKS YOU UP WHEN YOU COME AROUND. AND I'VE GOT THE BEST STUFF AROUND. THE BEST.
SO HOW COME I CAN FEEL YOU WHEN YOU GET HERE, BUT THE CAMERAS NEVER GET ANYTHING?

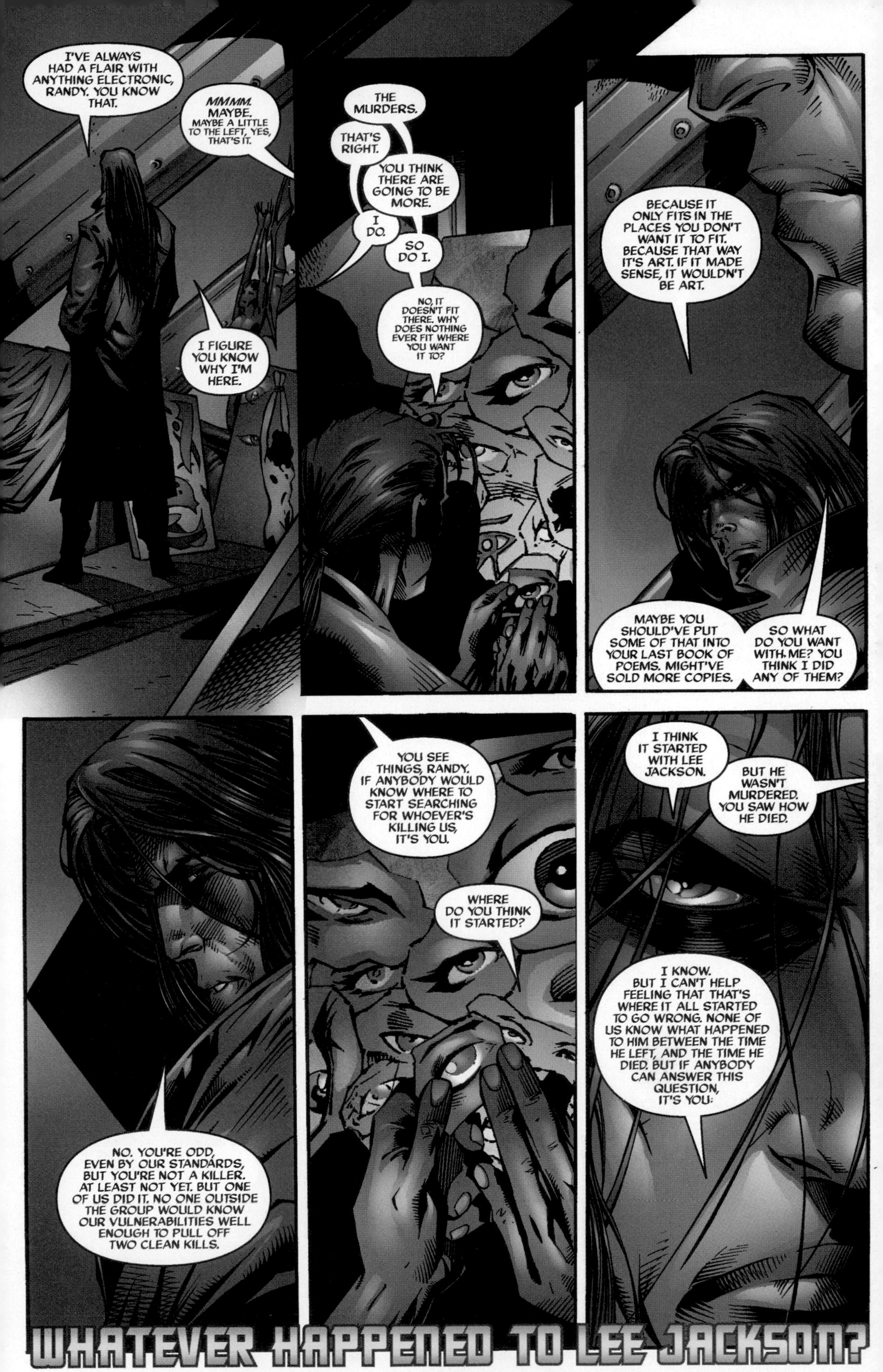
I'VE ALWAYS HAD A FLAIR WITH ANYTHING ELECTRONIC, RANDY. YOU KNOW THAT.
MMMM. MAYBE. MAYBE A LITTLE TO THE LEFT, YES, THAT'S IT.
I FIGURE YOU KNOW WHY I'M HERE.
THE MURDERS.
THAT'S RIGHT.
YOU THINK THERE ARE GOING TO BE MORE.
I DO.
SO DO I.
NO, IT DOESN'T FIT THERE. WHY DOES NOTHING EVER FIT WHERE YOU WANT IT TO?
BECAUSE IT ONLY FITS IN THE PLACES YOU DON'T WANT IT TO FIT. BECAUSE THAT WAY IT'S ART. IF IT MADE SENSE, IT WOULDN'T BE ART.
MAYBE YOU SHOULD'VE PUT SOME OF THAT INTO YOUR LAST BOOK OF POEMS. MIGHT'VE SOLD MORE COPIES.
SO WHAT DO YOU WANT WITH ME? YOU THINK I DID ANY OF THEM?
NO. YOU'RE ODD, EVEN BY OUR STANDARDS, BUT YOU'RE NOT A KILLER. AT LEAST NOT YET. BUT ONE OF US DID IT. NO ONE OUTSIDE THE GROUP WOULD KNOW OUR VULNERABILITIES WELL ENOUGH TO PULL OFF TWO CLEAN KILLS.
YOU SEE THINGS, RANDY. IF ANYBODY WOULD KNOW WHERE TO START SEARCHING FOR WHOEVER'S KILLING US, IT'S YOU.
WHERE DO YOU THINK IT STARTED?
I THINK IT STARTED WITH LEE JACKSON.
BUT HE WASN'T MURDERED. YOU SAW HOW HE DIED.
I KNOW. BUT I CAN'T HELP FEELING THAT THAT'S WHERE IT ALL STARTED TO GO WRONG. NONE OF US KNOW WHAT HAPPENED TO HIM BETWEEN THE TIME HE LEFT, AND THE TIME HE DIED. BUT IF ANYBODY CAN ANSWER THIS QUESTION, IT'S YOU:
WHATEVER HAPPENED TO LEE JACKSON?

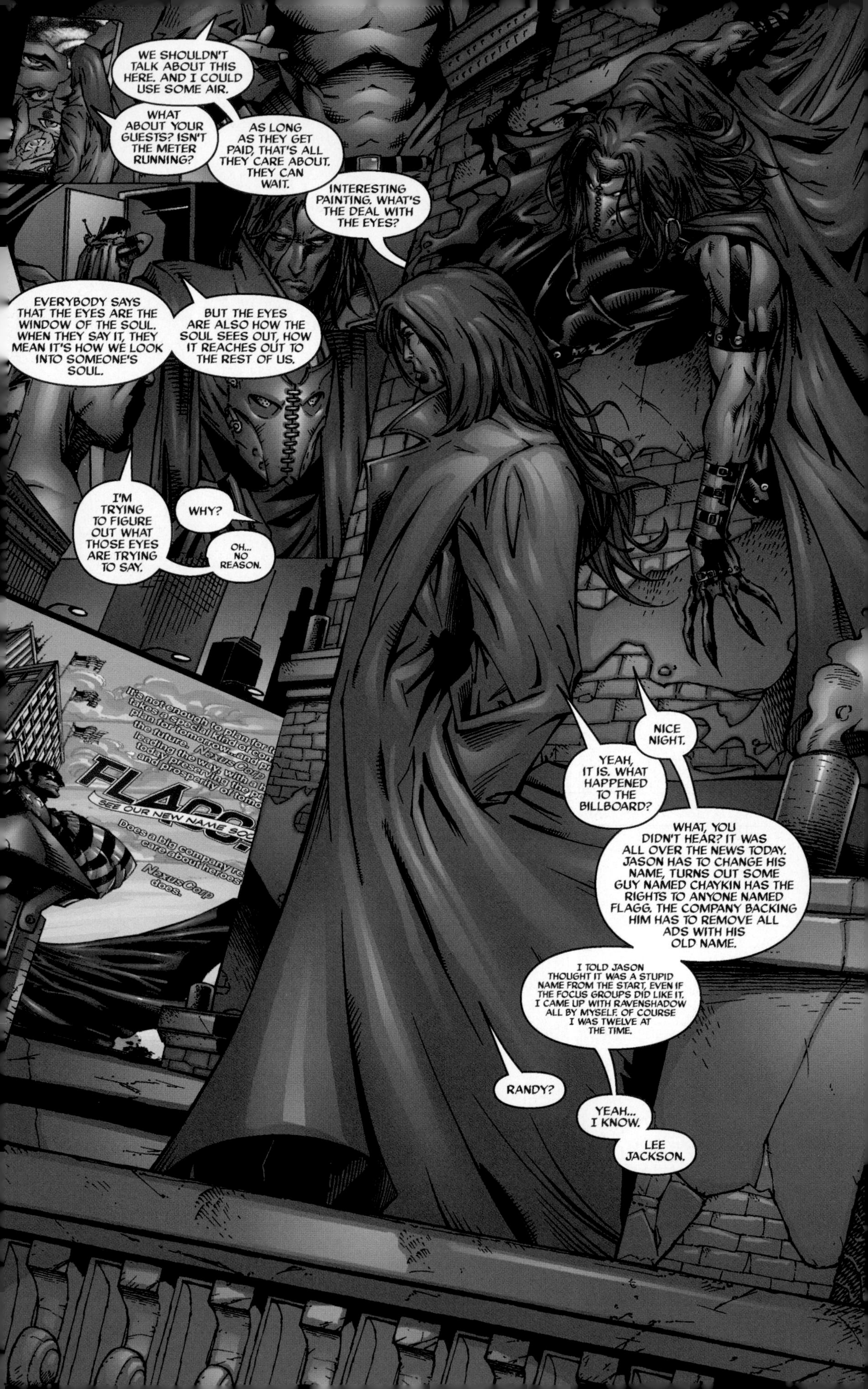
WE SHOULDN'T TALK ABOUT THIS HERE. AND I COULD USE SOME AIR.
WHAT ABOUT YOUR GUESTS? ISN'T THE METER RUNNING?
AS LONG AS THEY GET PAID, THAT'S ALL THEY CARE ABOUT. THEY CAN WAIT.
INTERESTING PAINTING. WHAT'S THE DEAL WITH THE EYES?
EVERYBODY SAYS THAT THE EYES ARE THE WINDOW OF THE SOUL. WHEN THEY SAY IT, THEY MEAN IT'S HOW WE LOOK INTO SOMEONE'S SOUL.
BUT THE EYES ARE ALSO HOW THE SOUL SEES OUT, HOW IT REACHES OUT TO THE REST OF US.
I'M TRYING TO FIGURE OUT WHAT THOSE EYES ARE TRYING TO SAY.
WHY?
OH... NO REASON.
NICE NIGHT.
YEAH, IT IS. WHAT HAPPENED TO THE BILLBOARD?
WHAT, YOU DIDN'T HEAR? IT WAS ALL OVER THE NEWS TODAY. JASON HAS TO CHANGE HIS NAME, TURNS OUT SOME GUY NAMED CHAYKIN HAS THE RIGHTS TO ANYONE NAMED FLAGG. THE COMPANY BACKING HIM HAS TO REMOVE ALL ADS WITH HIS OLD NAME.
I TOLD JASON I THOUGHT IT WAS A STUPID NAME FROM THE START, EVEN IF THE FOCUS GROUPS DID LIKE IT. I CAME UP WITH RAVENSHADOW ALL BY MYSELF. OF COURSE I WAS TWELVE AT THE TIME.
RANDY?
YEAH... I KNOW.
LEE JACKSON.

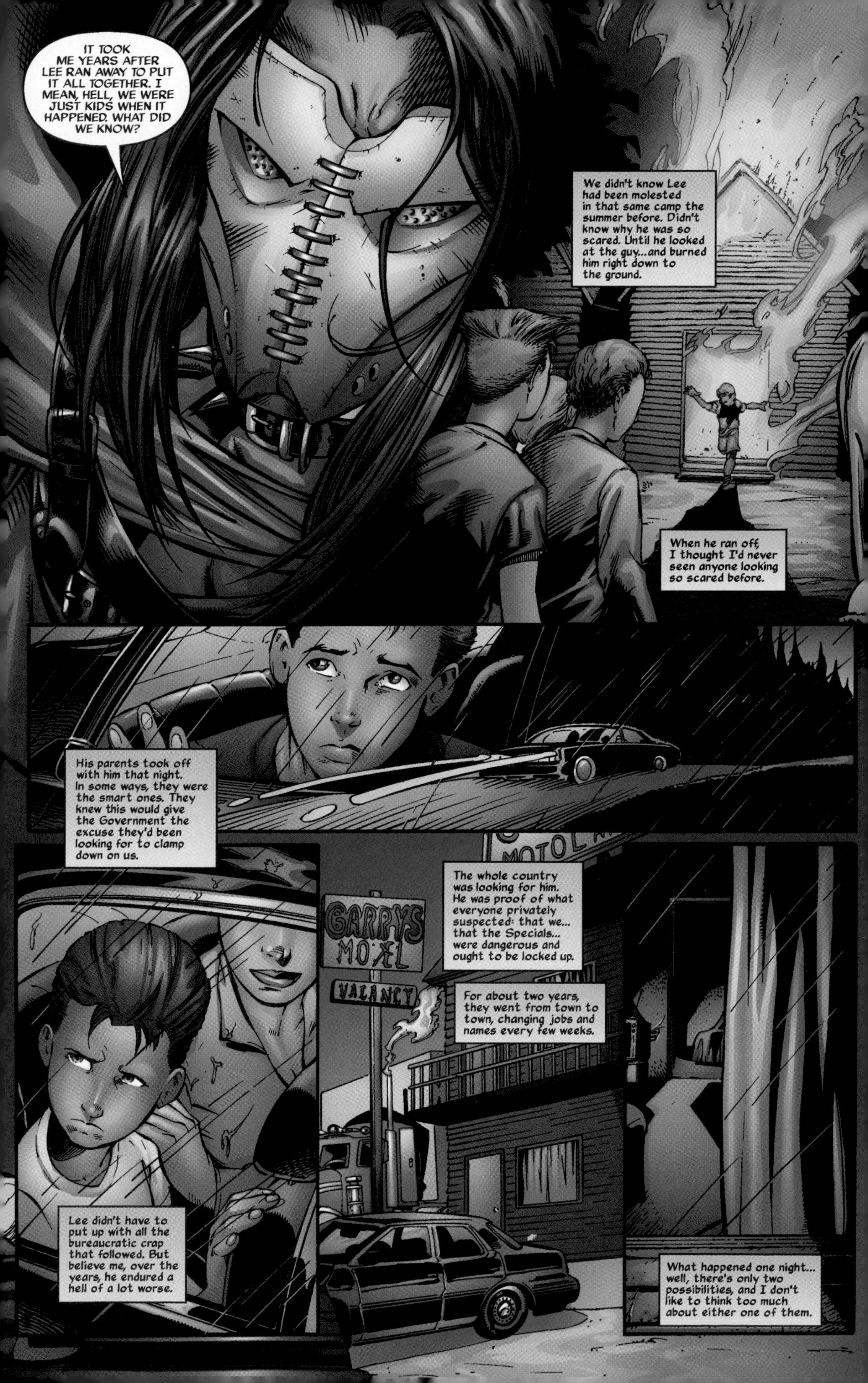
IT TOOK ME YEARS AFTER LEE RAN AWAY TO PUT IT ALL TOGETHER. I MEAN, HELL, WE WERE JUST KIDS WHEN IT HAPPENED. WHAT DID WE KNOW?
We didn't know Lee had been molested in that same camp the summer before. Didn't know why he was so scared. Until he looked at the guy...and burned him right down to the ground.
When he ran off, I thought I'd never seen anyone looking so scared before.
His parents took off with him that night. In some ways, they were the smart ones. They knew this would give the Government the excuse they'd been looking for to clamp down on us.
Lee didn't have to put up with all the bureaucratic crap that followed. But believe me, over the years, he endured a hell of a lot worse.
GARRYS MO EL
VACANCY
The whole country was looking for him. He was proof of what everyone privately suspected: that we... that the Specials... were dangerous and ought to be locked up.
For about two years, they went from town to town, changing jobs and names every few weeks.
What happened one night... well, there's only two possibilities, and I don't like to think too much about either one of them.

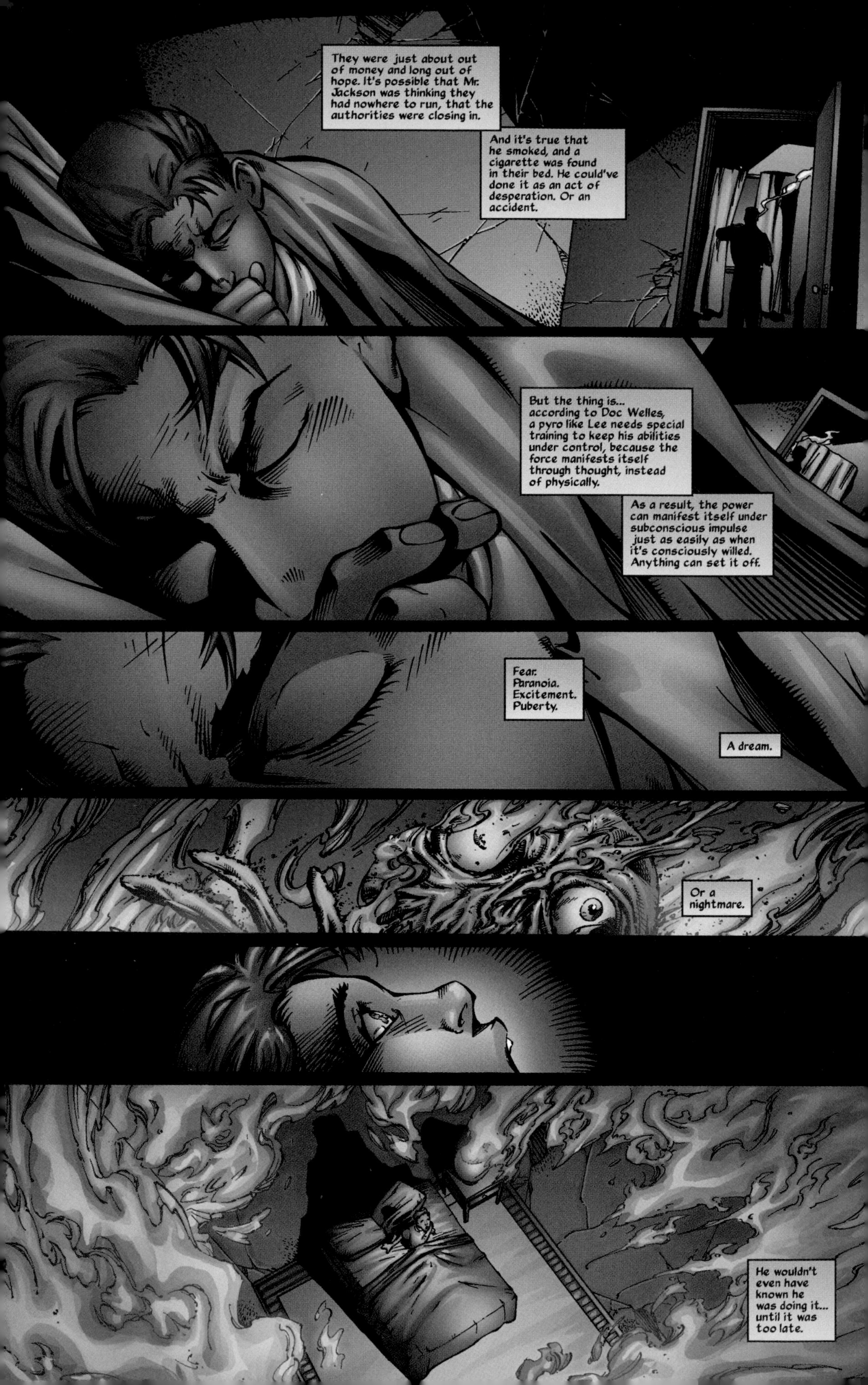
They were just about out of money and long out of hope. It's possible that Mr. Jackson was thinking they had nowhere to run, that the authorities were closing in.
And it's true that he smoked, and a cigarette was found in their bed. He could've done it as an act of desperation. Or an accident.
But the thing is... according to Doc Welles, a pyro like Lee needs special training to keep his abilities under control, because the force manifests itself through thought, instead of physically.
As a result, the power can manifest itself under subconscious impulse just as easily as when it's consciously willed. Anything can set it off.
Fear. Paranoia. Excitement. Puberty.
A dream.
Or a nightmare.
He wouldn't even have known he was doing it... until it was too late.

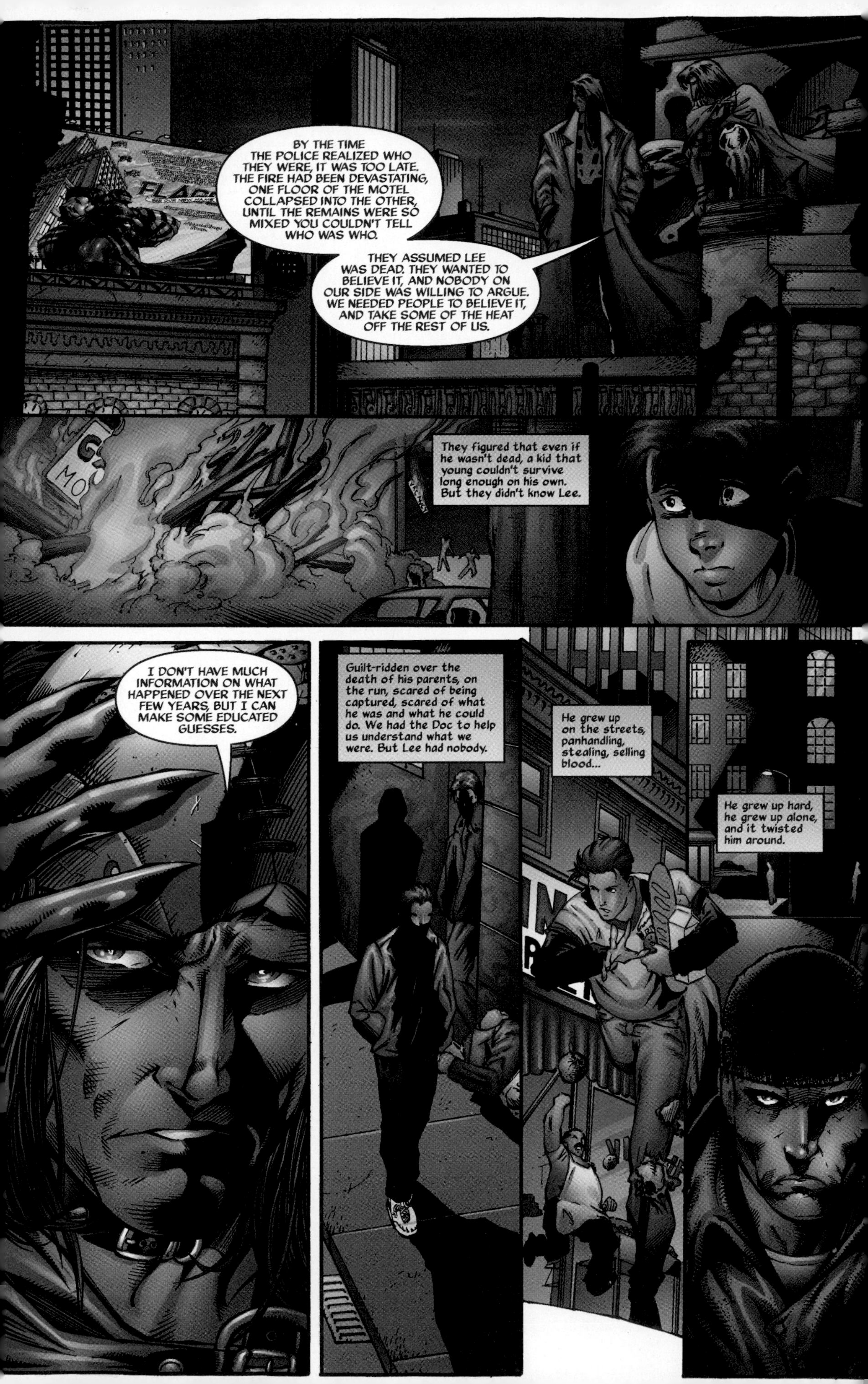
BY THE TIME THE POLICE REALIZED WHO THEY WERE, IT WAS TOO LATE. THE FIRE HAD BEEN DEVASTATING, ONE FLOOR OF THE MOTEL COLLAPSED INTO THE OTHER, UNTIL THE REMAINS WERE SO MIXED YOU COULDN'T TELL WHO WAS WHO.
THEY ASSUMED LEE WAS DEAD. THEY WANTED TO BELIEVE IT, AND NOBODY ON OUR SIDE WAS WILLING TO ARGUE. WE NEEDED PEOPLE TO BELIEVE IT, AND TAKE SOME OF THE HEAT OFF THE REST OF US.
They figured that even if he wasn't dead, a kid that young couldn't survive long enough on his own. But they didn't know Lee.
I DON'T HAVE MUCH INFORMATION ON WHAT HAPPENED OVER THE NEXT FEW YEARS, BUT I CAN MAKE SOME EDUCATED GUESSES.
Guilt-ridden over the death of his parents, on the run, scared of being captured, scared of what he was and what he could do. We had the Doc to help us understand what we were. But Lee had nobody.
He grew up on the streets, panhandling, stealing, selling blood...
He grew up hard, he grew up alone, and it twisted him around.

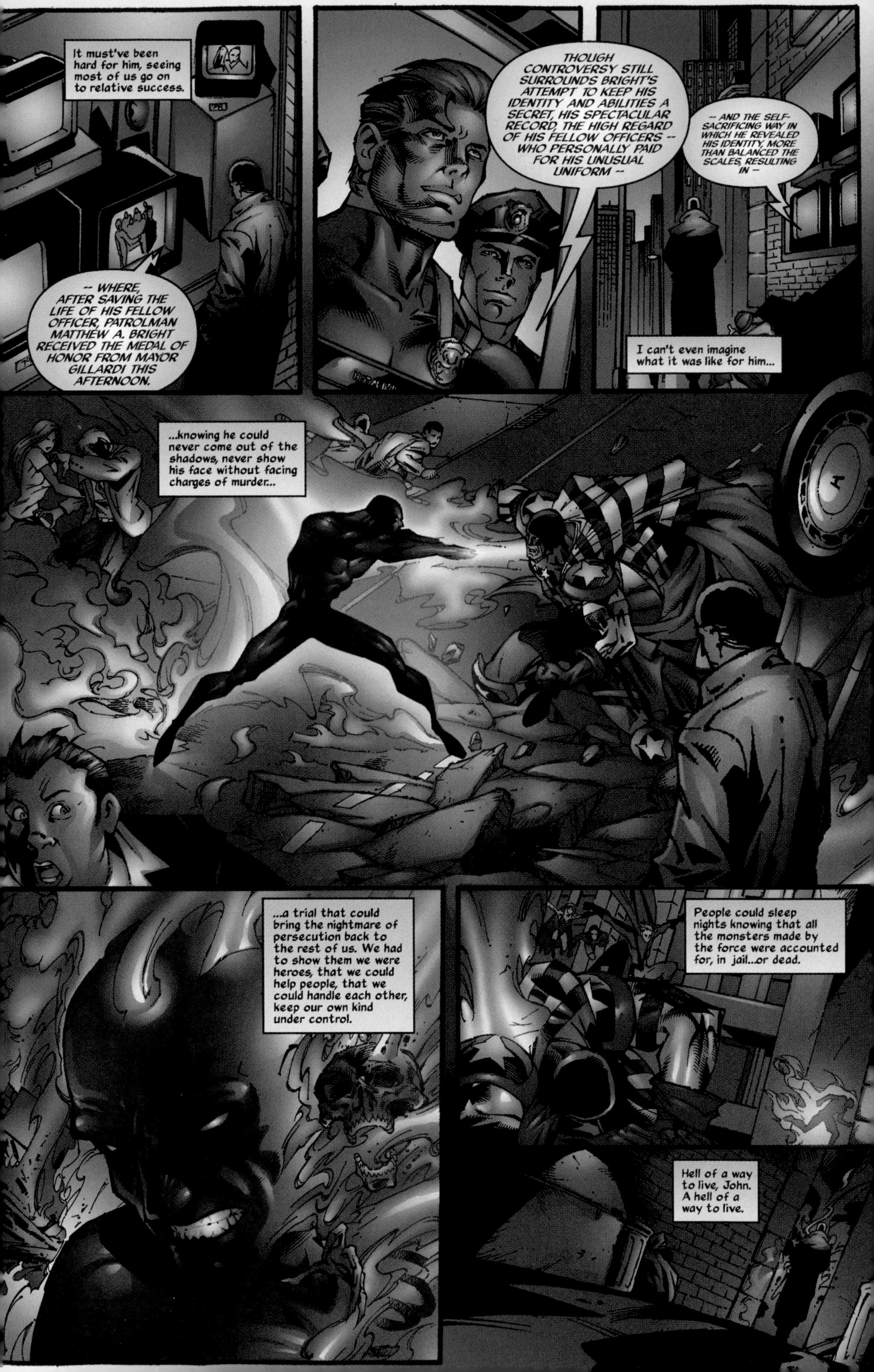
It must've been hard for him, seeing most of us go on to relative success.
-- WHERE, AFTER SAVING THE LIFE OF HIS FELLOW OFFICER, PATROLMAN MATTHEW A. BRIGHT RECEIVED THE MEDAL OF HONOR FROM MAYOR GILLARDI THIS AFTERNOON.
THOUGH CONTROVERSY STILL SURROUNDS BRIGHT'S ATTEMPT TO KEEP HIS IDENTITY AND ABILITIES A SECRET, HIS SPECTACULAR RECORD, THE HIGH REGARD OF HIS FELLOW OFFICERS -- WHO PERSONALLY PAID FOR HIS UNUSUAL UNIFORM --
-- AND THE SELF-SACRIFICING WAY IN WHICH HE REVEALED HIS IDENTITY, MORE THAN BALANCED THE SCALES, RESULTING IN --
I can't even imagine what it was like for him...
...knowing he could never come out of the shadows, never show his face without facing charges of murder...
...a trial that could bring the nightmare of persecution back to the rest of us. We had to show them we were heroes, that we could help people, that we could handle each other, keep our own kind under control.
People could sleep nights knowing that all the monsters made by the force were accounted for, in jail...or dead.
Hell of a way to live, John. A hell of a way to live.

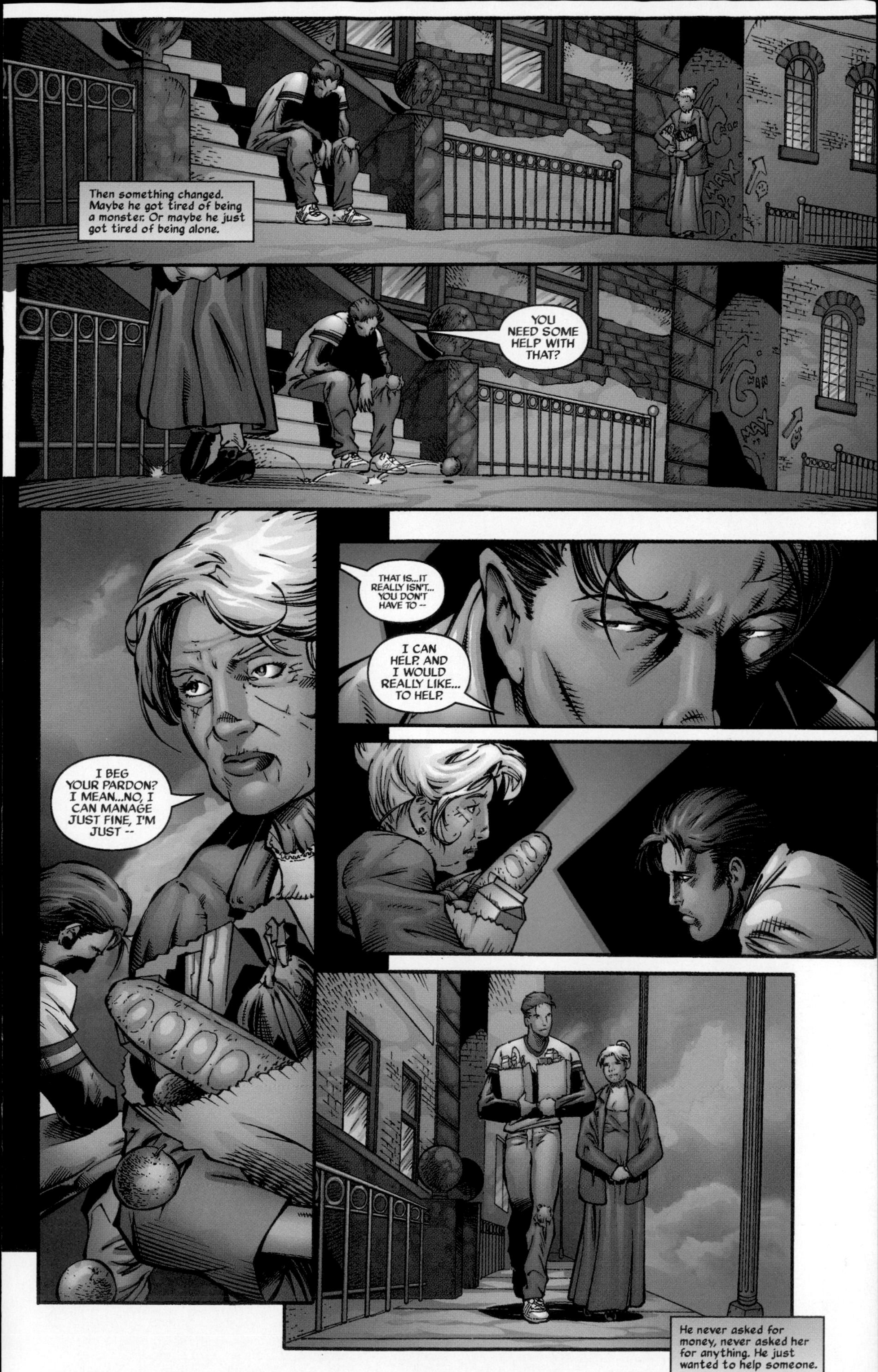
Then something changed. Maybe he got tired of being a monster. Or maybe he just got tired of being alone.
YOU NEED SOME HELP WITH THAT?
I BEG YOUR PARDON? I MEAN...NO, I CAN MANAGE JUST FINE, I'M JUST --
THAT IS...IT REALLY ISN'T... YOU DON'T HAVE TO --
I CAN HELP. AND I WOULD REALLY LIKE... TO HELP.
He never asked for money, never asked her for anything. He just wanted to help someone.

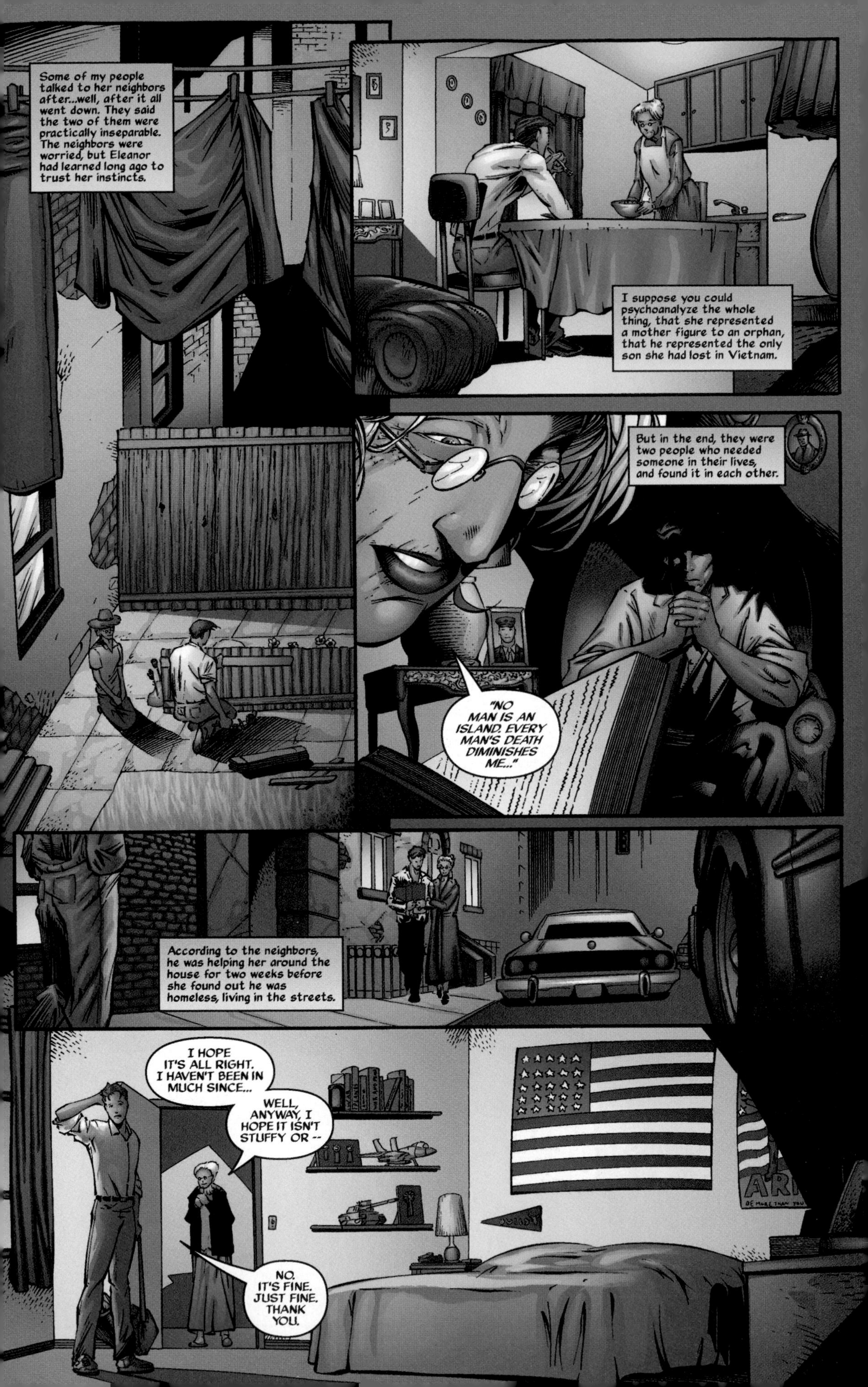
Some of my people talked to her neighbors after...well, after it all went down. They said the two of them were practically inseparable. The neighbors were worried, but Eleanor had learned long ago to trust her instincts.
I suppose you could psychoanalyze the whole thing, that she represented a mother figure to an orphan, that he represented the only son she had lost in Vietnam.
But in the end, they were two people who needed someone in their lives, and found it in each other.
"NO MAN IS AN ISLAND. EVERY MAN'S DEATH DIMINISHES ME..."
According to the neighbors, he was helping her around the house for two weeks before she found out he was homeless, living in the streets.
I HOPE IT'S ALL RIGHT. I HAVEN'T BEEN IN MUCH SINCE...
WELL, ANYWAY, I HOPE IT ISN'T STUFFY OR --
NO. IT'S FINE. JUST FINE. THANK YOU.

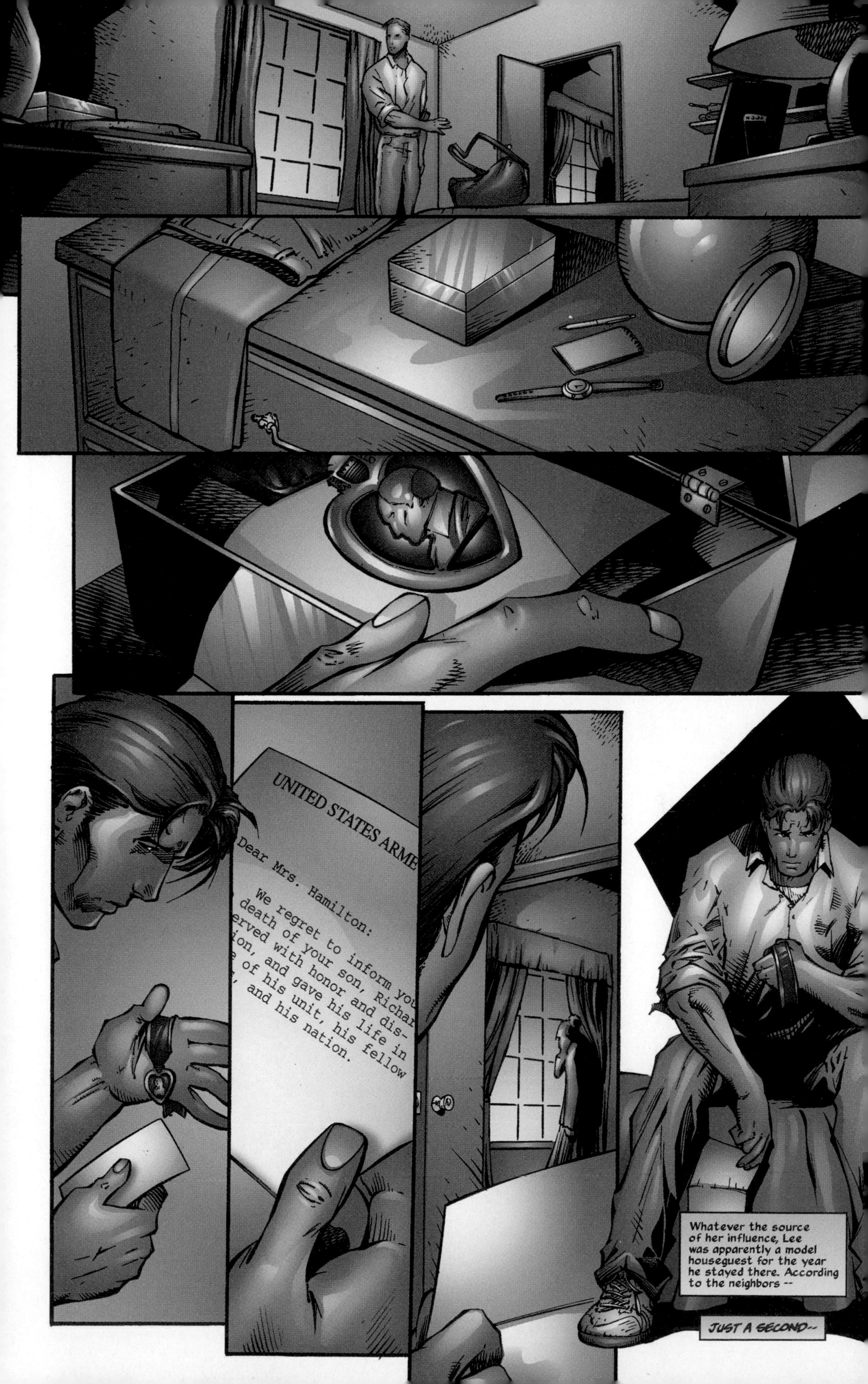
UNITED STATES ARME
Dear Mrs. Hamilton:
We regret to inform you
death of your son, Richar
erved with honor and dis-
ion, and gave his life in
e of his unit, his fellow
, and his nation.
Whatever the source of her influence, Lee was apparently a model houseguest for the year he stayed there. According to the neighbors --
JUST A SECOND--

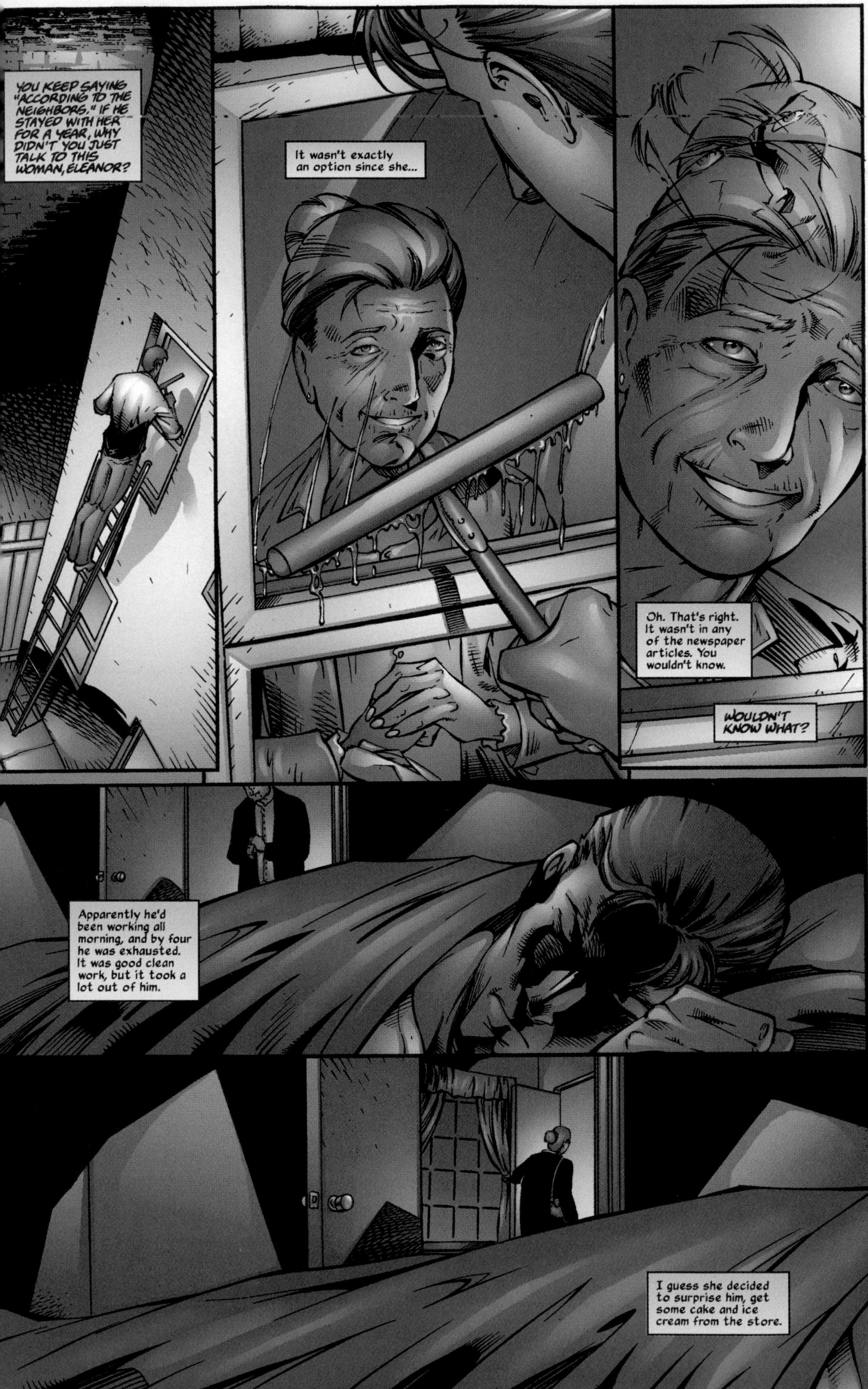
YOU KEEP SAYING "ACCORDING TO THE NEIGHBORS." IF HE STAYED WITH HER FOR A YEAR, WHY DIDN'T YOU JUST TALK TO THIS WOMAN, ELEANOR?
It wasn't exactly an option since she...
Oh. That's right. It wasn't in any of the newspaper articles. You wouldn't know.
WOULDN'T KNOW WHAT?
Apparently he'd been working all morning, and by four he was exhausted. It was good clean work, but it took a lot out of him.
I guess she decided to surprise him, get some cake and ice cream from the store.

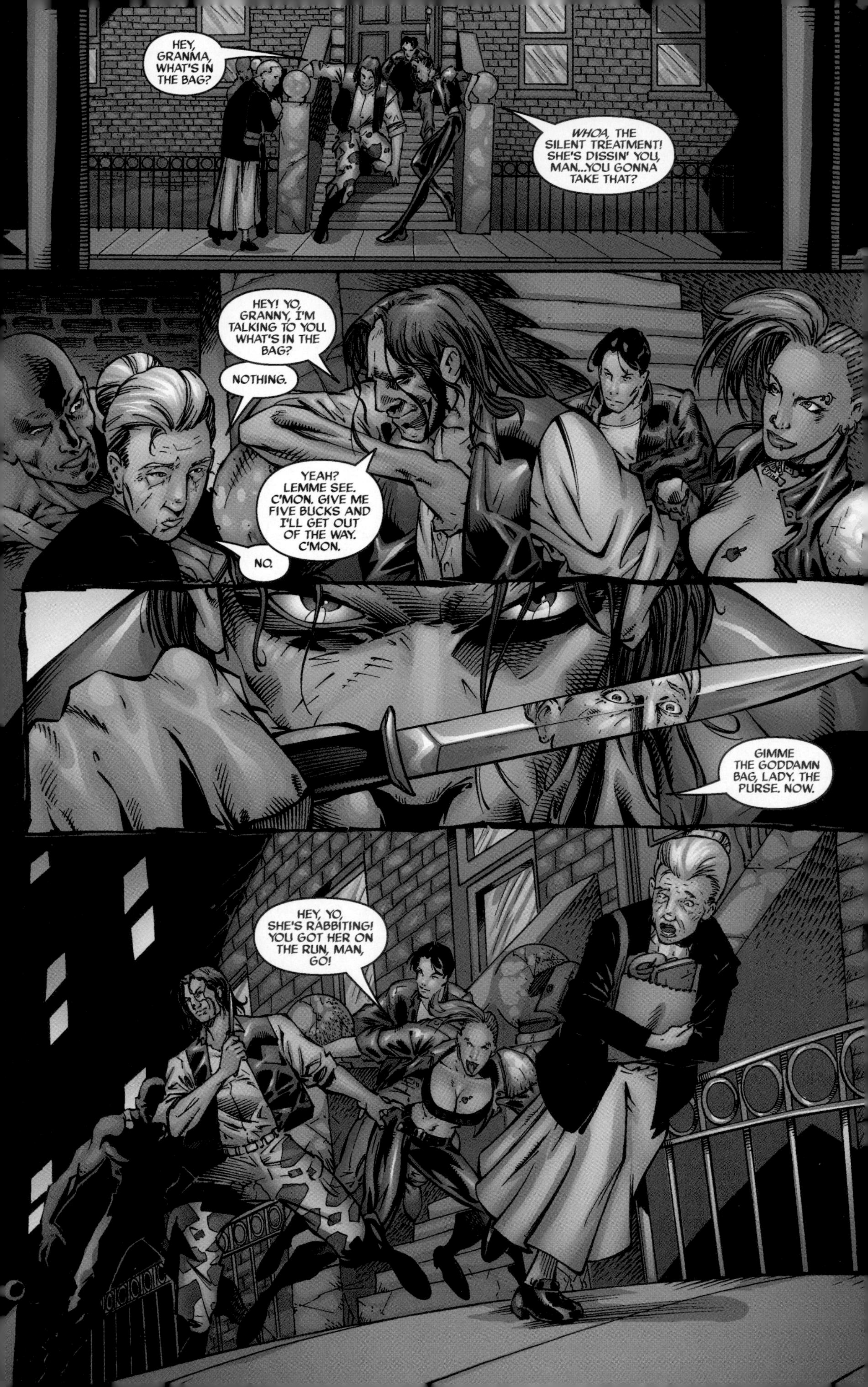
HEY, GRANMA, WHAT'S IN THE BAG?
WHOA, THE SILENT TREATMENT! SHE'S DISSIN' YOU, MAN...YOU GONNA TAKE THAT?
HEY! YO, GRANNY, I'M TALKING TO YOU. WHAT'S IN THE BAG?
NOTHING.
YEAH? LEMME SEE. C'MON. GIVE ME FIVE BUCKS AND I'LL GET OUT OF THE WAY. C'MON.
NO.
GIMME THE GODDAMN BAG, LADY. THE PURSE. NOW.
HEY, YO, SHE'S RABBITING! YOU GOT HER ON THE RUN, MAN, GO!

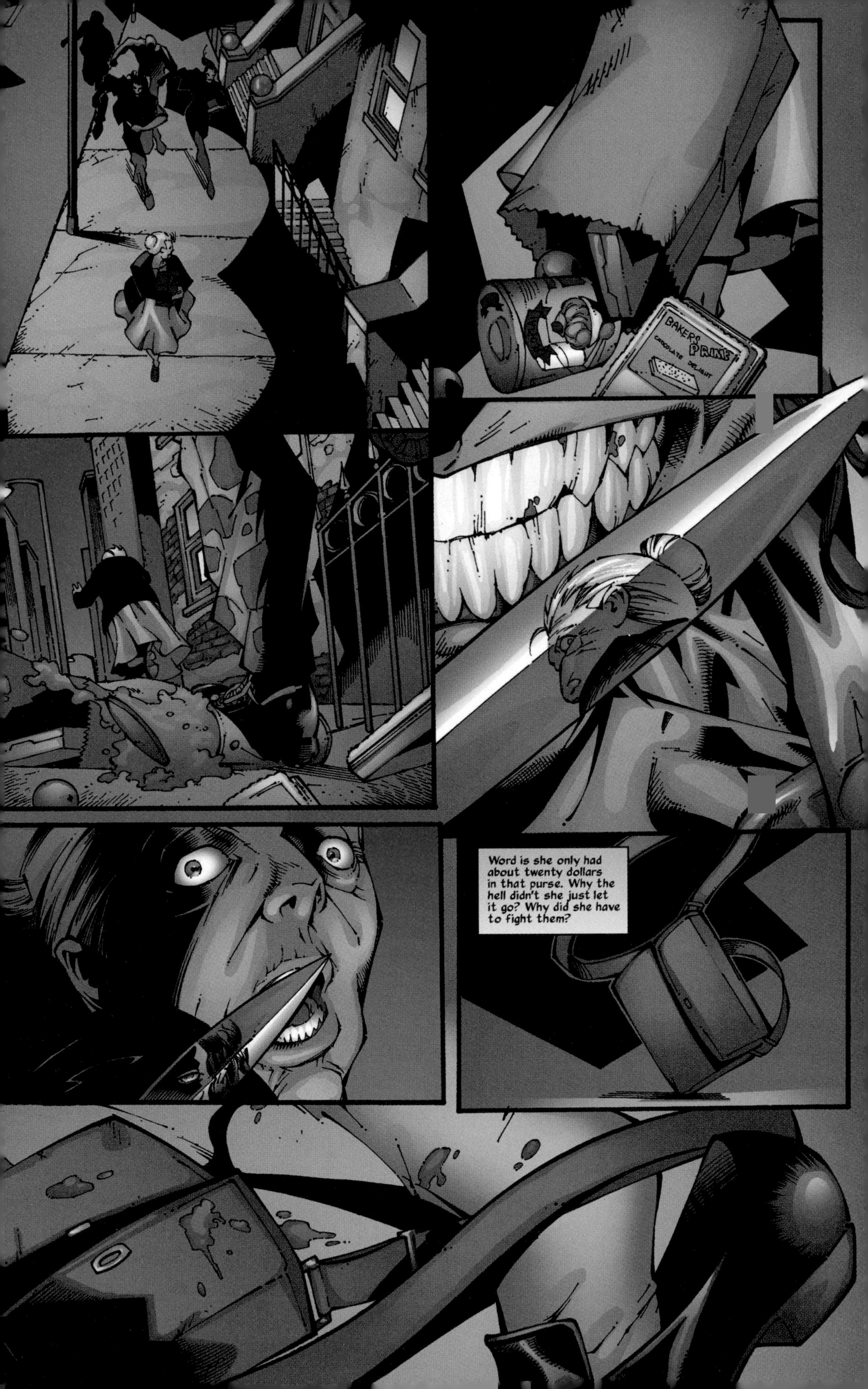
BAKERS PRIME
CHOCOLATE DELIGHT
Word is she only had about twenty dollars in that purse. Why the hell didn't she just let it go? Why did she have to fight them?

EL...?
ELEANOR...?

ELEANOR!

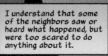

I understand that some
of the neighbors saw or
heard what happened, but
were too scared to do
anything about it.

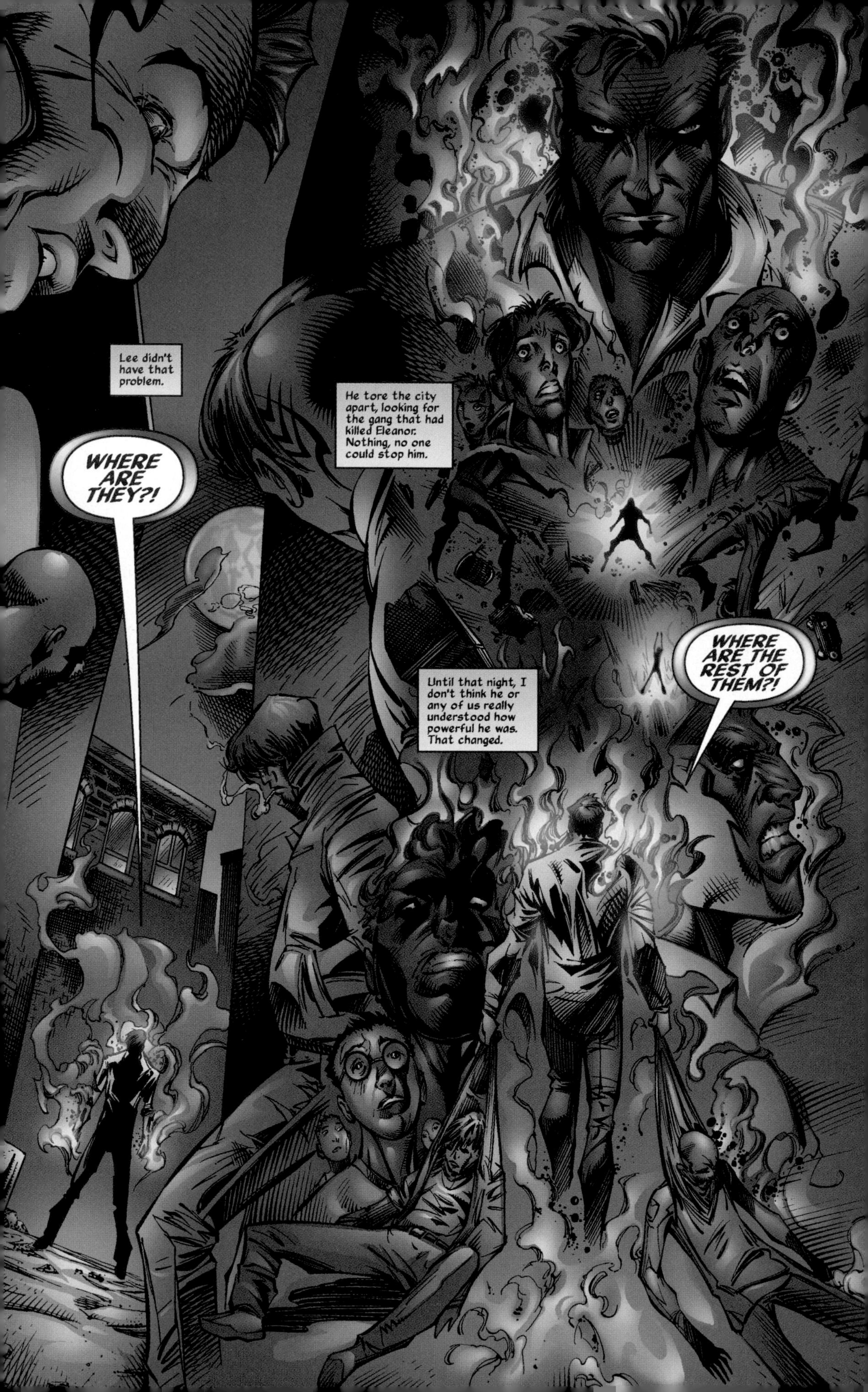
Lee didn't have that problem.
WHERE ARE THEY?!
He tore the city apart, looking for the gang that had killed Eleanor. Nothing, no one could stop him.
Until that night, I don't think he or any of us really understood how powerful he was. That changed.
WHERE ARE THE REST OF THEM?!

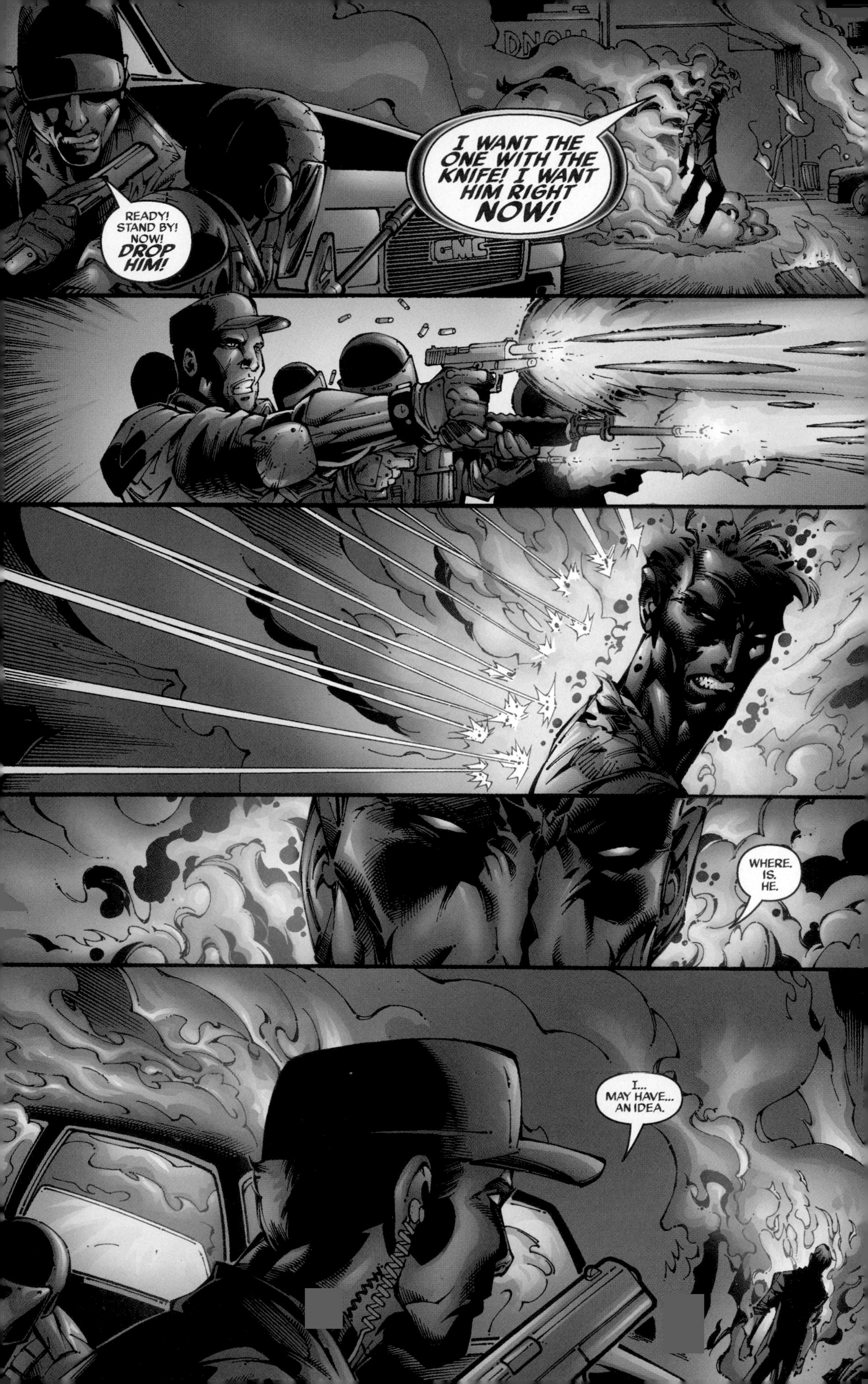
READY! STAND BY! NOW! DROP HIM!
I WANT THE ONE WITH THE KNIFE! I WANT HIM RIGHT NOW!
WHERE. IS. HE.
I... MAY HAVE... AN IDEA.

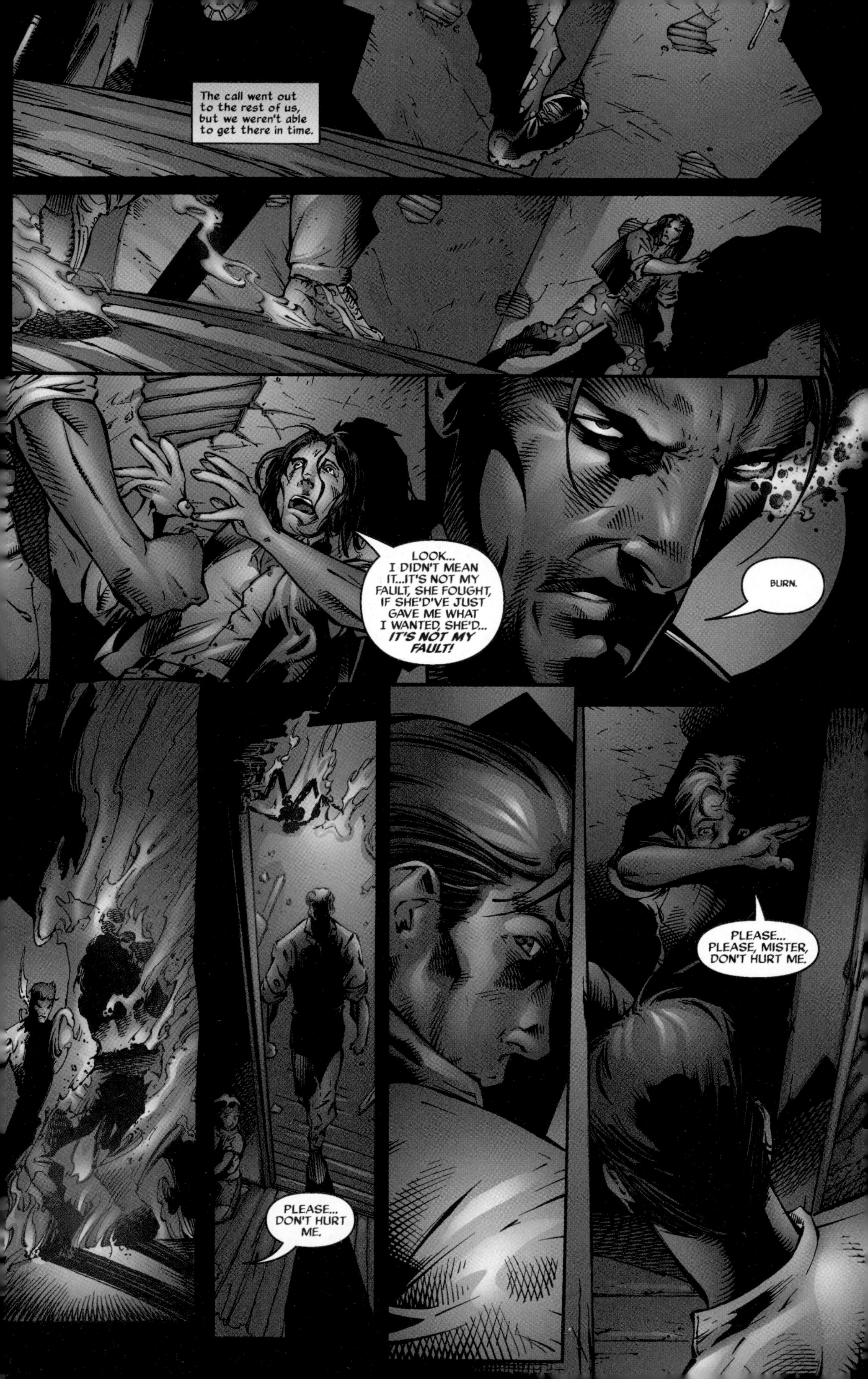

The call went out to the rest of us, but we weren't able to get there in time.
LOOK... I DIDN'T MEAN IT...IT'S NOT MY FAULT, SHE FOUGHT, IF SHE'D'VE JUST GAVE ME WHAT I WANTED, SHE'D... IT'S NOT MY FAULT!
BURN.
PLEASE... DON'T HURT ME.
PLEASE... PLEASE, MISTER, DON'T HURT ME.

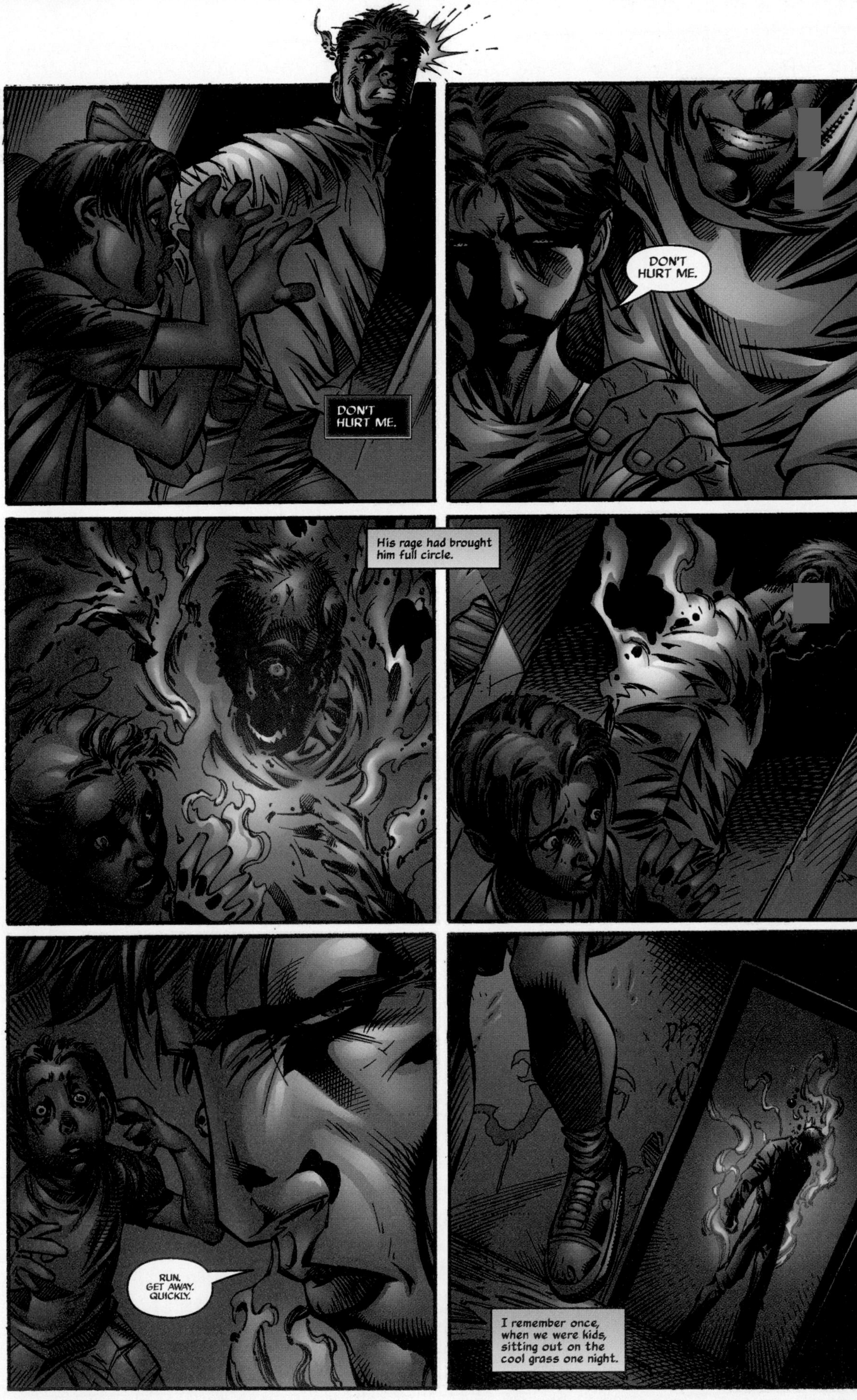
DON'T HURT ME.
DON'T HURT ME.
His rage had brought him full circle.
RUN. GET AWAY. QUICKLY.
I remember once, when we were kids, sitting out on the cool grass one night.

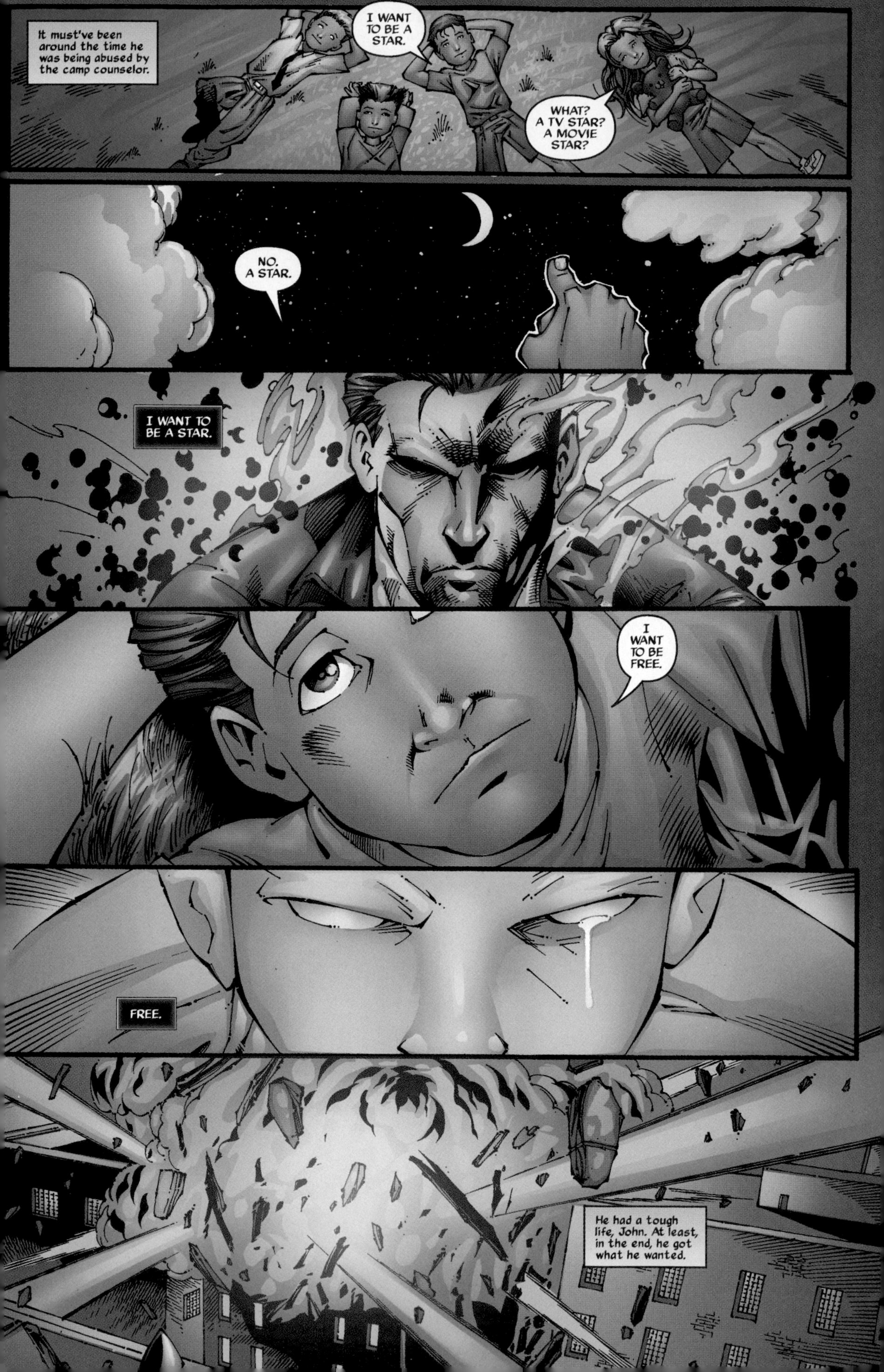
It must've been around the time he was being abused by the camp counselor.
I WANT TO BE A STAR.
WHAT? A TV STAR? A MOVIE STAR?
NO. A STAR.
I WANT TO BE A STAR.
I WANT TO BE FREE.
FREE.
He had a tough life, John. At least, in the end, he got what he wanted.

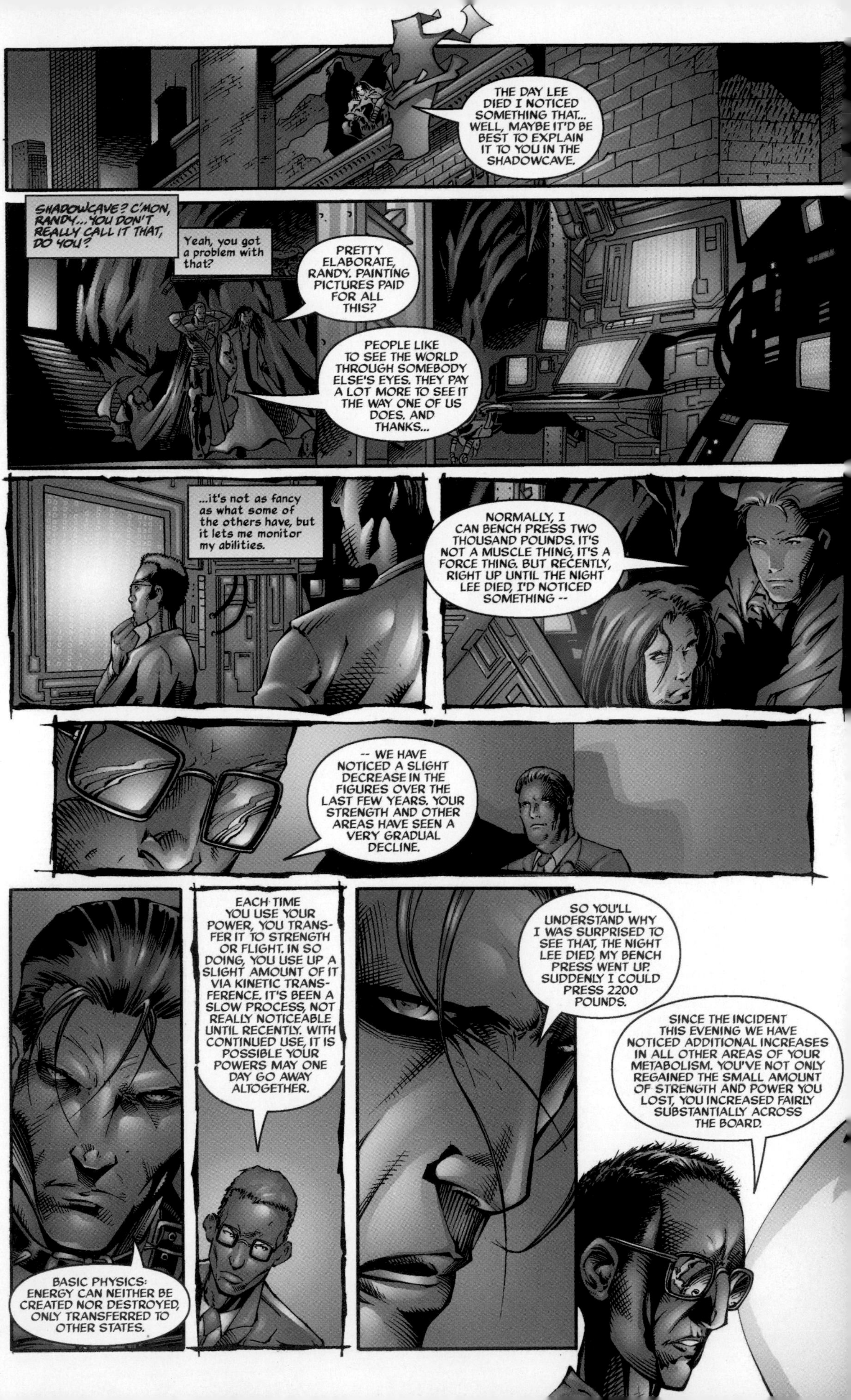
THE DAY LEE DIED I NOTICED SOMETHING THAT... WELL, MAYBE IT'D BE BEST TO EXPLAIN IT TO YOU IN THE SHADOWCAVE.
SHADOWCAVE? C'MON, RANDY... YOU DON'T REALLY CALL IT THAT, DO YOU?
Yeah, you got a problem with that?
PRETTY ELABORATE, RANDY. PAINTING PICTURES PAID FOR ALL THIS?
PEOPLE LIKE TO SEE THE WORLD THROUGH SOMEBODY ELSE'S EYES. THEY PAY A LOT MORE TO SEE IT THE WAY ONE OF US DOES. AND THANKS...
...it's not as fancy as what some of the others have, but it lets me monitor my abilities.
NORMALLY, I CAN BENCH PRESS TWO THOUSAND POUNDS. IT'S NOT A MUSCLE THING, IT'S A FORCE THING. BUT RECENTLY, RIGHT UP UNTIL THE NIGHT LEE DIED, I'D NOTICED SOMETHING --
-- WE HAVE NOTICED A SLIGHT DECREASE IN THE FIGURES OVER THE LAST FEW YEARS. YOUR STRENGTH AND OTHER AREAS HAVE SEEN A VERY GRADUAL DECLINE.
BASIC PHYSICS: ENERGY CAN NEITHER BE CREATED NOR DESTROYED, ONLY TRANSFERRED TO OTHER STATES.
EACH TIME YOU USE YOUR POWER, YOU TRANSFER IT TO STRENGTH OR FLIGHT. IN SO DOING, YOU USE UP A SLIGHT AMOUNT OF IT VIA KINETIC TRANSFERENCE. IT'S BEEN A SLOW PROCESS, NOT REALLY NOTICEABLE UNTIL RECENTLY. WITH CONTINUED USE, IT IS POSSIBLE YOUR POWERS MAY ONE DAY GO AWAY ALTOGETHER.
SO YOU'LL UNDERSTAND WHY I WAS SURPRISED TO SEE THAT, THE NIGHT LEE DIED, MY BENCH PRESS WENT UP. SUDDENLY I COULD PRESS 2200 POUNDS.
SINCE THE INCIDENT THIS EVENING WE HAVE NOTICED ADDITIONAL INCREASES IN ALL OTHER AREAS OF YOUR METABOLISM. YOU'VE NOT ONLY REGAINED THE SMALL AMOUNT OF STRENGTH AND POWER YOU LOST, YOU INCREASED FAIRLY SUBSTANTIALLY ACROSS THE BOARD.

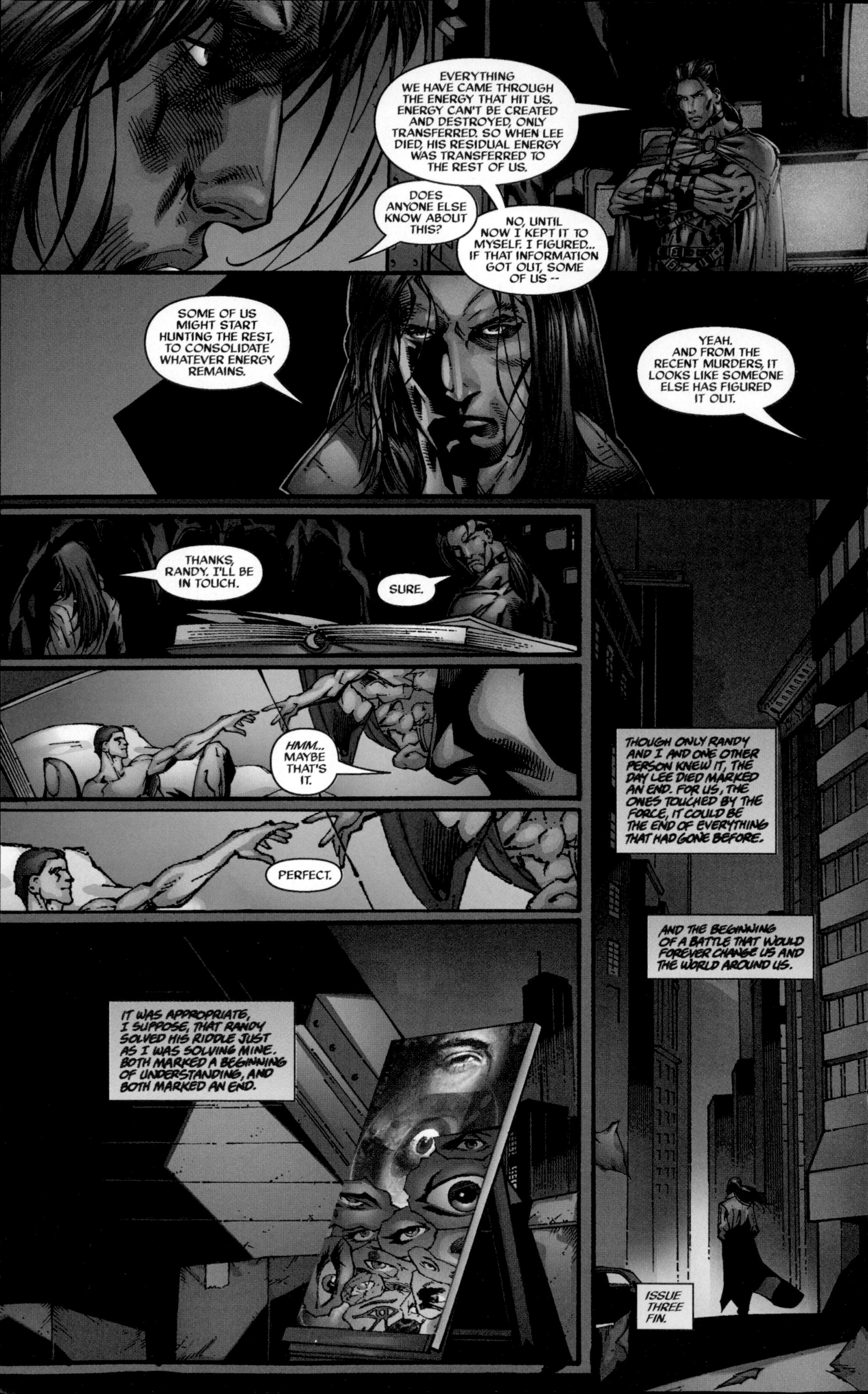
EVERYTHING WE HAVE CAME THROUGH THE ENERGY THAT HIT US. ENERGY CAN'T BE CREATED AND DESTROYED, ONLY TRANSFERRED. SO WHEN LEE DIED, HIS RESIDUAL ENERGY WAS TRANSFERRED TO THE REST OF US.
DOES ANYONE ELSE KNOW ABOUT THIS?
NO, UNTIL NOW I KEPT IT TO MYSELF. I FIGURED... IF THAT INFORMATION GOT OUT, SOME OF US --
SOME OF US MIGHT START HUNTING THE REST, TO CONSOLIDATE WHATEVER ENERGY REMAINS.
YEAH. AND FROM THE RECENT MURDERS, IT LOOKS LIKE SOMEONE ELSE HAS FIGURED IT OUT.
THANKS, RANDY. I'LL BE IN TOUCH.
SURE.
HMM... MAYBE THAT'S IT.
PERFECT.
THOUGH ONLY RANDY AND I AND ONE OTHER PERSON KNEW IT, THE DAY LEE DIED MARKED AN END. FOR US, THE ONES TOUCHED BY THE FORCE, IT COULD BE THE END OF EVERYTHING THAT HAD GONE BEFORE.
AND THE BEGINNING OF A BATTLE THAT WOULD FOREVER CHANGE US AND THE WORLD AROUND US.
IT WAS APPROPRIATE, I SUPPOSE, THAT RANDY SOLVED HIS RIDDLE JUST AS I WAS SOLVING MINE. BOTH MARKED A BEGINNING OF UNDERSTANDING, AND BOTH MARKED AN END.
ISSUE THREE FIN.

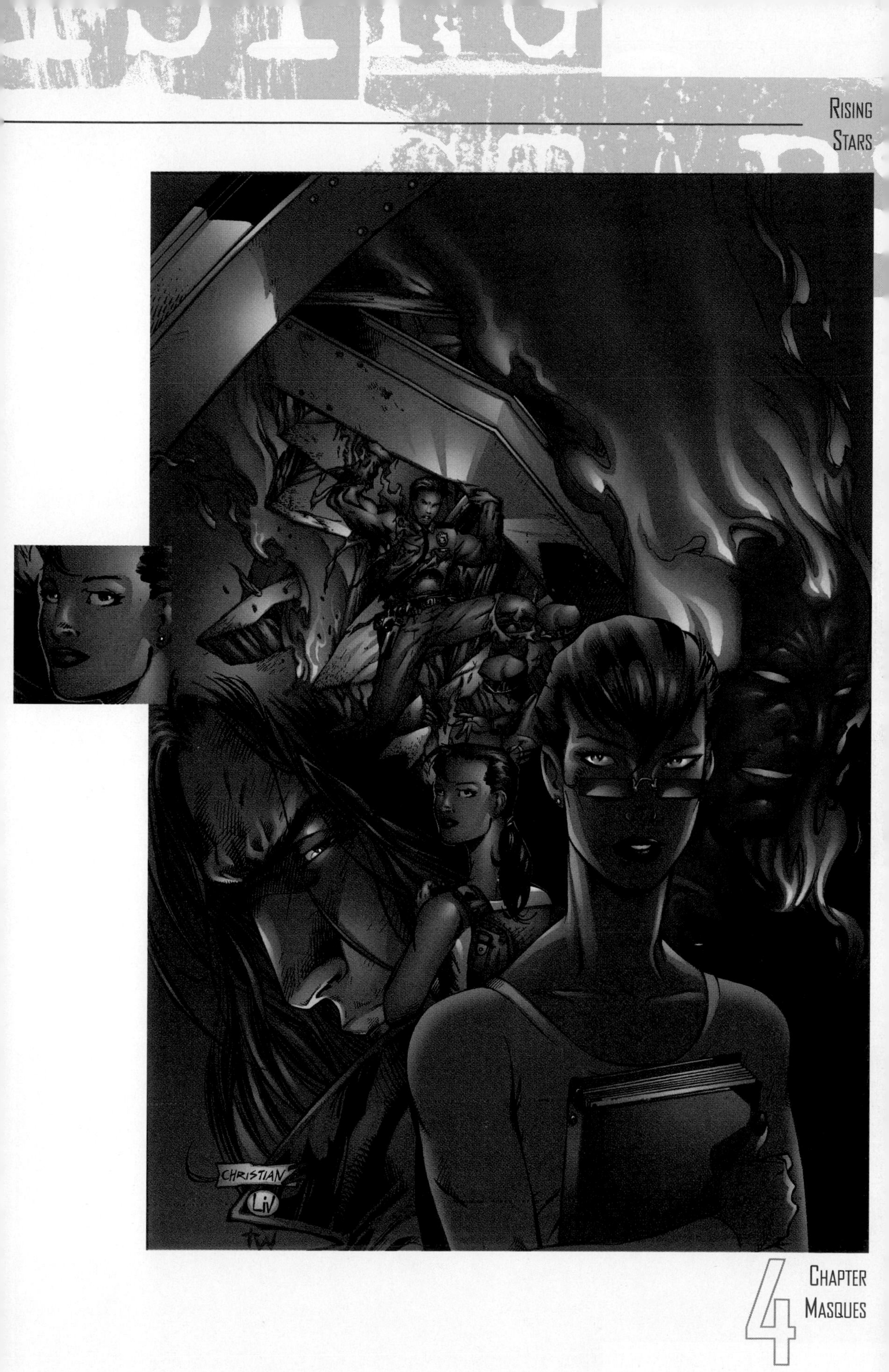
CHRISTIAN
Liv

Chapter 4
Masques

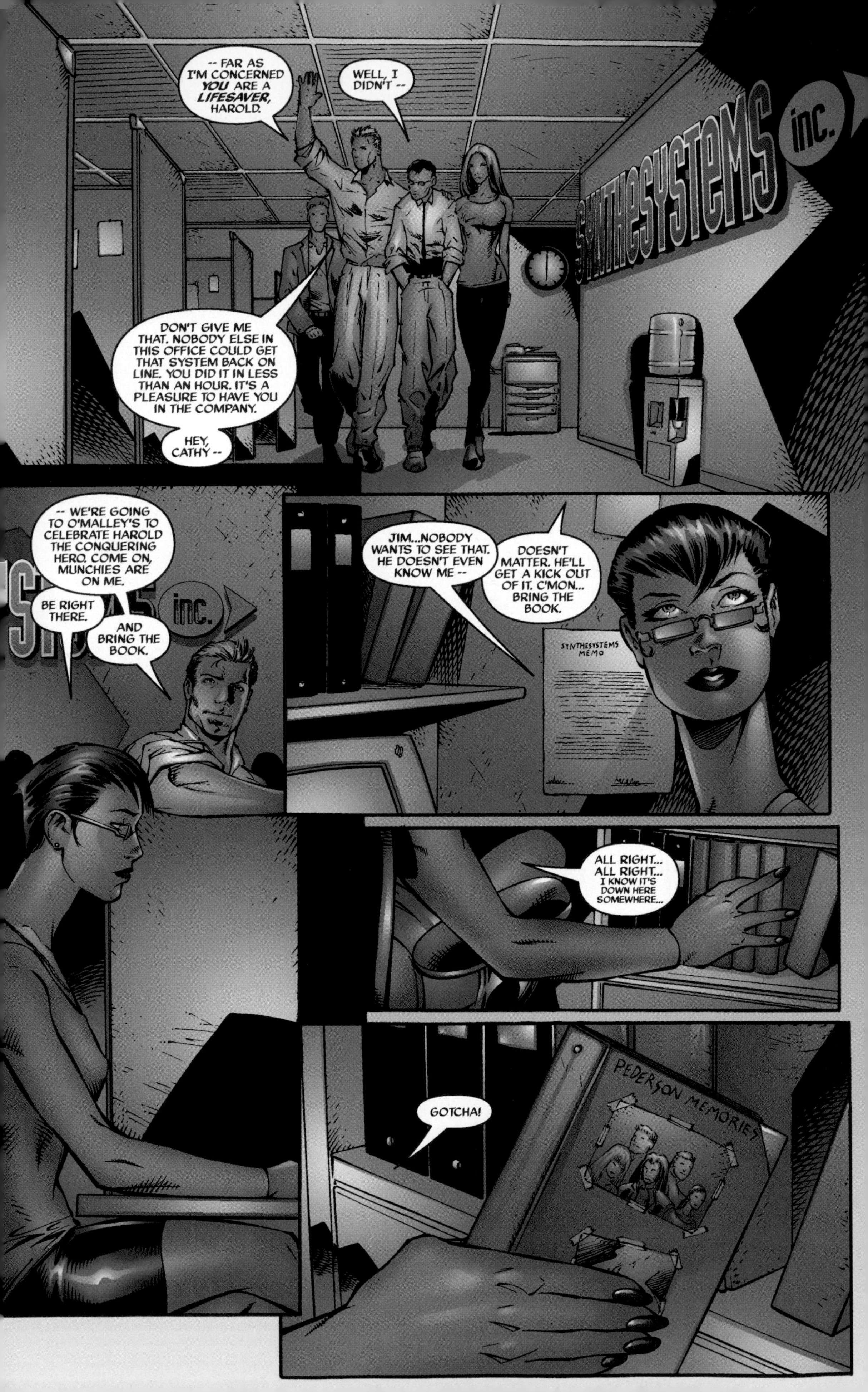
-- FAR AS I'M CONCERNED YOU ARE A LIFESAVER, HAROLD.
WELL, I DIDN'T --
SYNTHESYSTEMS inc.
DON'T GIVE ME THAT. NOBODY ELSE IN THIS OFFICE COULD GET THAT SYSTEM BACK ON LINE. YOU DID IT IN LESS THAN AN HOUR. IT'S A PLEASURE TO HAVE YOU IN THE COMPANY.
HEY, CATHY --
-- WE'RE GOING TO O'MALLEY'S TO CELEBRATE HAROLD THE CONQUERING HERO. COME ON, MUNCHIES ARE ON ME.
BE RIGHT THERE.
AND BRING THE BOOK.
JIM...NOBODY WANTS TO SEE THAT. HE DOESN'T EVEN KNOW ME --
DOESN'T MATTER. HE'LL GET A KICK OUT OF IT. C'MON... BRING THE BOOK.
SYNTHESYSTEMS MEMO
ALL RIGHT... ALL RIGHT... I KNOW IT'S DOWN HERE SOMEWHERE...
GOTCHA!
PEDERSON MEMORIES

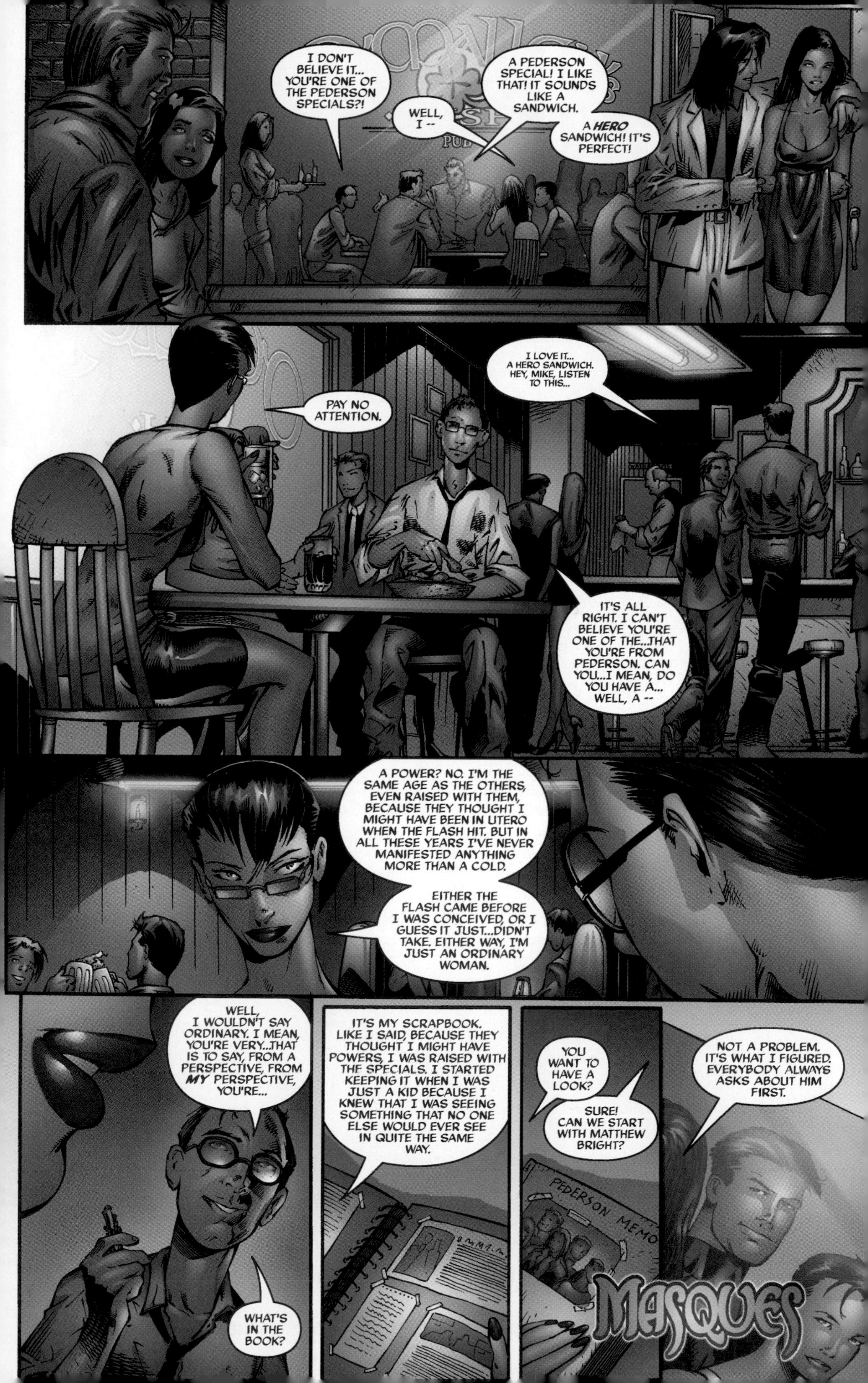
I DON'T BELIEVE IT... YOU'RE ONE OF THE PEDERSON SPECIALS?!
WELL, I --
A PEDERSON SPECIAL! I LIKE THAT! IT SOUNDS LIKE A SANDWICH.
A HERO SANDWICH! IT'S PERFECT!
PUB
PAY NO ATTENTION.
I LOVE IT... A HERO SANDWICH. HEY, MIKE, LISTEN TO THIS...
IT'S ALL RIGHT. I CAN'T BELIEVE YOU'RE ONE OF THE...THAT YOU'RE FROM PEDERSON. CAN YOU...I MEAN, DO YOU HAVE A... WELL, A --
A POWER? NO. I'M THE SAME AGE AS THE OTHERS, EVEN RAISED WITH THEM, BECAUSE THEY THOUGHT I MIGHT HAVE BEEN IN UTERO WHEN THE FLASH HIT. BUT IN ALL THESE YEARS I'VE NEVER MANIFESTED ANYTHING MORE THAN A COLD.
EITHER THE FLASH CAME BEFORE I WAS CONCEIVED, OR I GUESS IT JUST...DIDN'T TAKE. EITHER WAY, I'M JUST AN ORDINARY WOMAN.
WELL, I WOULDN'T SAY ORDINARY. I MEAN, YOU'RE VERY...THAT IS TO SAY, FROM A PERSPECTIVE, FROM MY PERSPECTIVE, YOU'RE...
WHAT'S IN THE BOOK?
IT'S MY SCRAPBOOK. LIKE I SAID, BECAUSE THEY THOUGHT I MIGHT HAVE POWERS, I WAS RAISED WITH THE SPECIALS. I STARTED KEEPING IT WHEN I WAS JUST A KID BECAUSE I KNEW THAT I WAS SEEING SOMETHING THAT NO ONE ELSE WOULD EVER SEE IN QUITE THE SAME WAY.
YOU WANT TO HAVE A LOOK?
SURE! CAN WE START WITH MATTHEW BRIGHT?
PEDERSON MEMO
NOT A PROBLEM. IT'S WHAT I FIGURED. EVERYBODY ALWAYS ASKS ABOUT HIM FIRST.
MASQUES

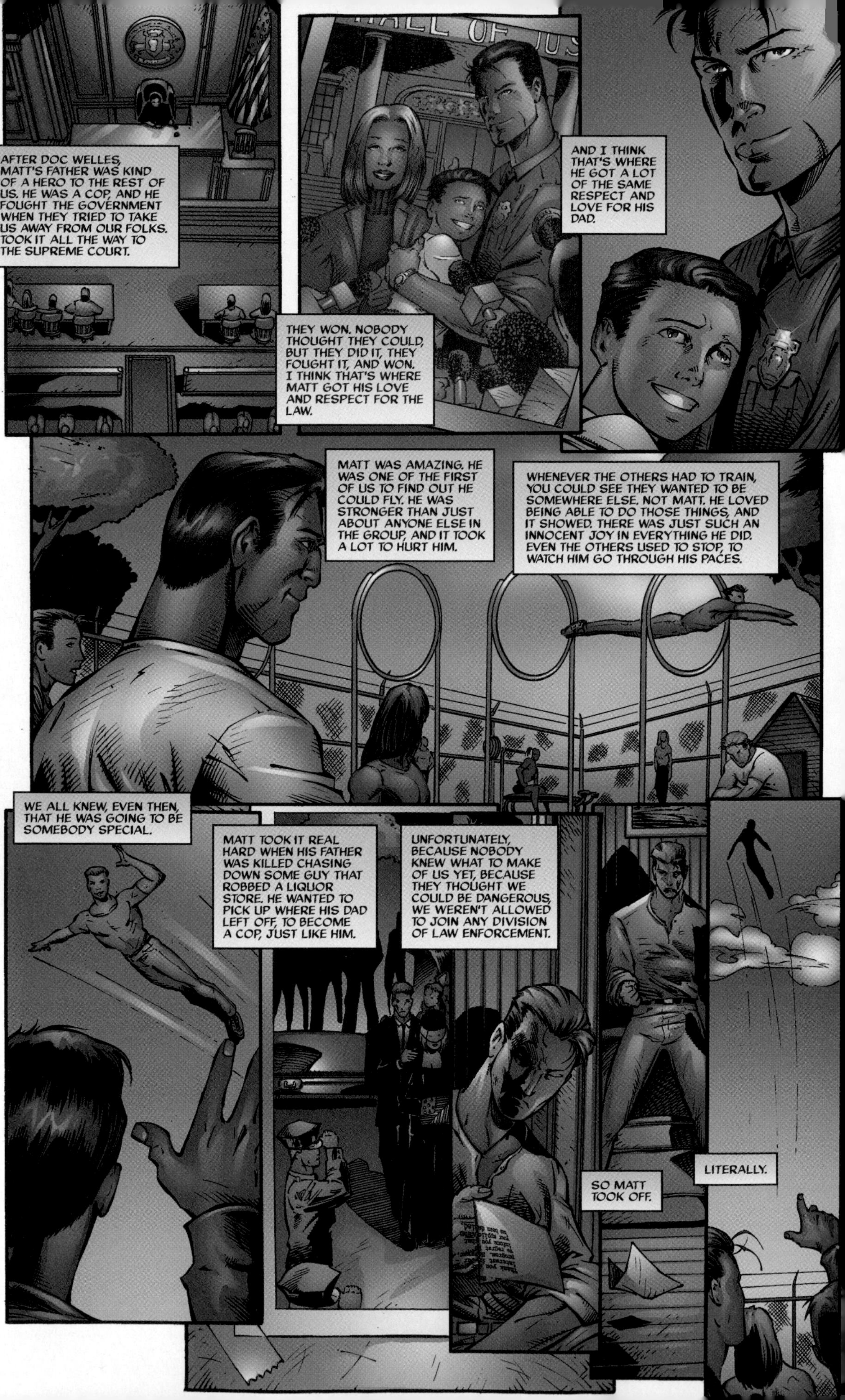
AFTER DOC WELLES, MATT'S FATHER WAS KIND OF A HERO TO THE REST OF US. HE WAS A COP, AND HE FOUGHT THE GOVERNMENT WHEN THEY TRIED TO TAKE US AWAY FROM OUR FOLKS. TOOK IT ALL THE WAY TO THE SUPREME COURT.
THEY WON. NOBODY THOUGHT THEY COULD, BUT THEY DID IT, THEY FOUGHT IT, AND WON. I THINK THAT'S WHERE MATT GOT HIS LOVE AND RESPECT FOR THE LAW.
AND I THINK THAT'S WHERE HE GOT A LOT OF THE SAME RESPECT AND LOVE FOR HIS DAD.
MATT WAS AMAZING. HE WAS ONE OF THE FIRST OF US TO FIND OUT HE COULD FLY. HE WAS STRONGER THAN JUST ABOUT ANYONE ELSE IN THE GROUP, AND IT TOOK A LOT TO HURT HIM.
WHENEVER THE OTHERS HAD TO TRAIN, YOU COULD SEE THEY WANTED TO BE SOMEWHERE ELSE. NOT MATT. HE LOVED BEING ABLE TO DO THOSE THINGS, AND IT SHOWED. THERE WAS JUST SUCH AN INNOCENT JOY IN EVERYTHING HE DID. EVEN THE OTHERS USED TO STOP, TO WATCH HIM GO THROUGH HIS PACES.
WE ALL KNEW, EVEN THEN, THAT HE WAS GOING TO BE SOMEBODY SPECIAL.
MATT TOOK IT REAL HARD WHEN HIS FATHER WAS KILLED CHASING DOWN SOME GUY THAT ROBBED A LIQUOR STORE. HE WANTED TO PICK UP WHERE HIS DAD LEFT OFF, TO BECOME A COP, JUST LIKE HIM.
UNFORTUNATELY, BECAUSE NOBODY KNEW WHAT TO MAKE OF US YET, BECAUSE THEY THOUGHT WE COULD BE DANGEROUS, WE WEREN'T ALLOWED TO JOIN ANY DIVISION OF LAW ENFORCEMENT.
SO MATT TOOK OFF.
LITERALLY.

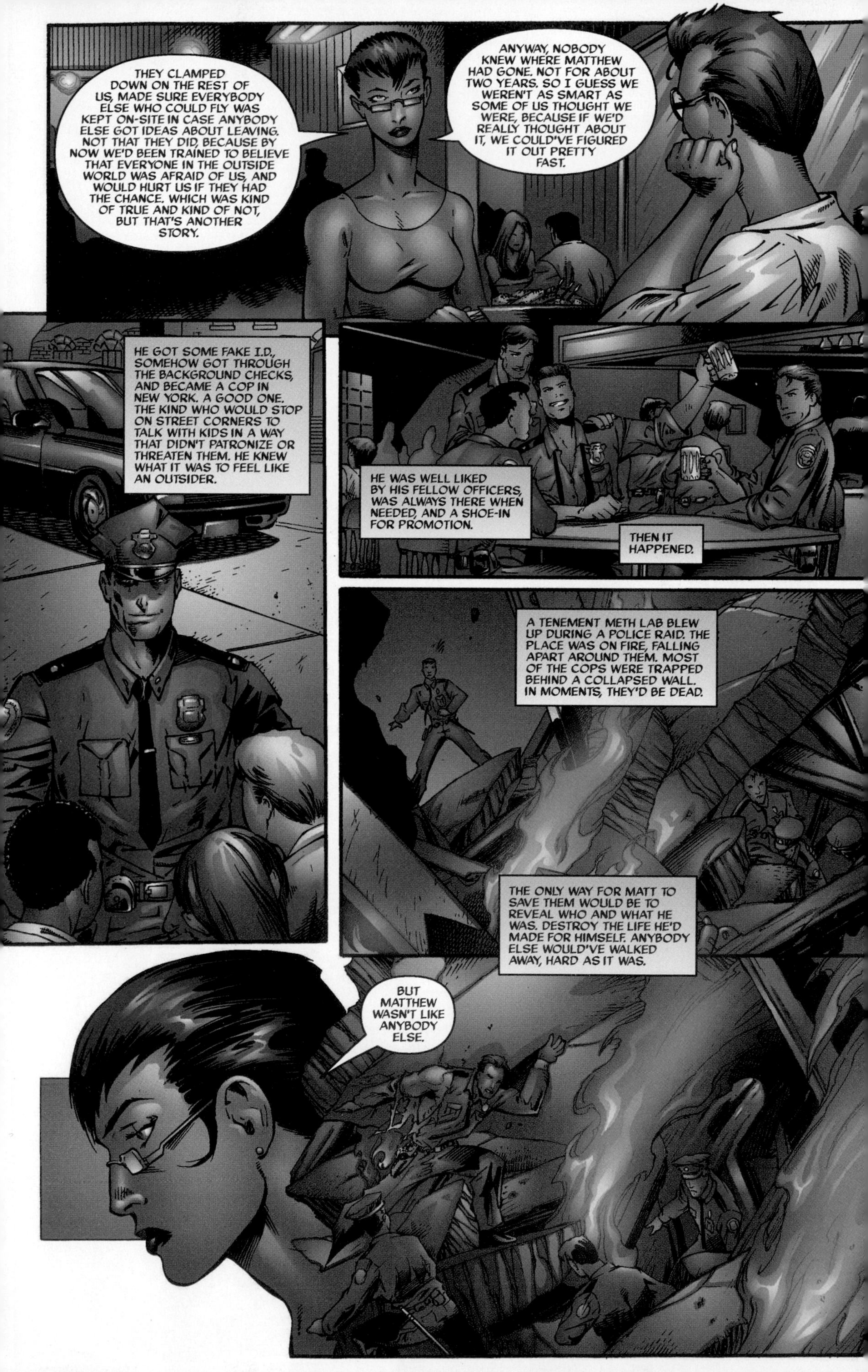
THEY CLAMPED DOWN ON THE REST OF US, MADE SURE EVERYBODY ELSE WHO COULD FLY WAS KEPT ON-SITE IN CASE ANYBODY ELSE GOT IDEAS ABOUT LEAVING. NOT THAT THEY DID, BECAUSE BY NOW WE'D BEEN TRAINED TO BELIEVE THAT EVERYONE IN THE OUTSIDE WORLD WAS AFRAID OF US, AND WOULD HURT US IF THEY HAD THE CHANCE. WHICH WAS KIND OF TRUE AND KIND OF NOT, BUT THAT'S ANOTHER STORY.
ANYWAY, NOBODY KNEW WHERE MATTHEW HAD GONE. NOT FOR ABOUT TWO YEARS. SO I GUESS WE WEREN'T AS SMART AS SOME OF US THOUGHT WE WERE, BECAUSE IF WE'D REALLY THOUGHT ABOUT IT, WE COULD'VE FIGURED IT OUT PRETTY FAST.
HE GOT SOME FAKE I.D., SOMEHOW GOT THROUGH THE BACKGROUND CHECKS, AND BECAME A COP IN NEW YORK. A GOOD ONE. THE KIND WHO WOULD STOP ON STREET CORNERS TO TALK WITH KIDS IN A WAY THAT DIDN'T PATRONIZE OR THREATEN THEM. HE KNEW WHAT IT WAS TO FEEL LIKE AN OUTSIDER.
HE WAS WELL LIKED BY HIS FELLOW OFFICERS, WAS ALWAYS THERE WHEN NEEDED, AND A SHOE-IN FOR PROMOTION.
THEN IT HAPPENED.
A TENEMENT METH LAB BLEW UP DURING A POLICE RAID. THE PLACE WAS ON FIRE, FALLING APART AROUND THEM. MOST OF THE COPS WERE TRAPPED BEHIND A COLLAPSED WALL. IN MOMENTS, THEY'D BE DEAD.
THE ONLY WAY FOR MATT TO SAVE THEM WOULD BE TO REVEAL WHO AND WHAT HE WAS. DESTROY THE LIFE HE'D MADE FOR HIMSELF. ANYBODY ELSE WOULD'VE WALKED AWAY, HARD AS IT WAS.
BUT MATTHEW WASN'T LIKE ANYBODY ELSE.

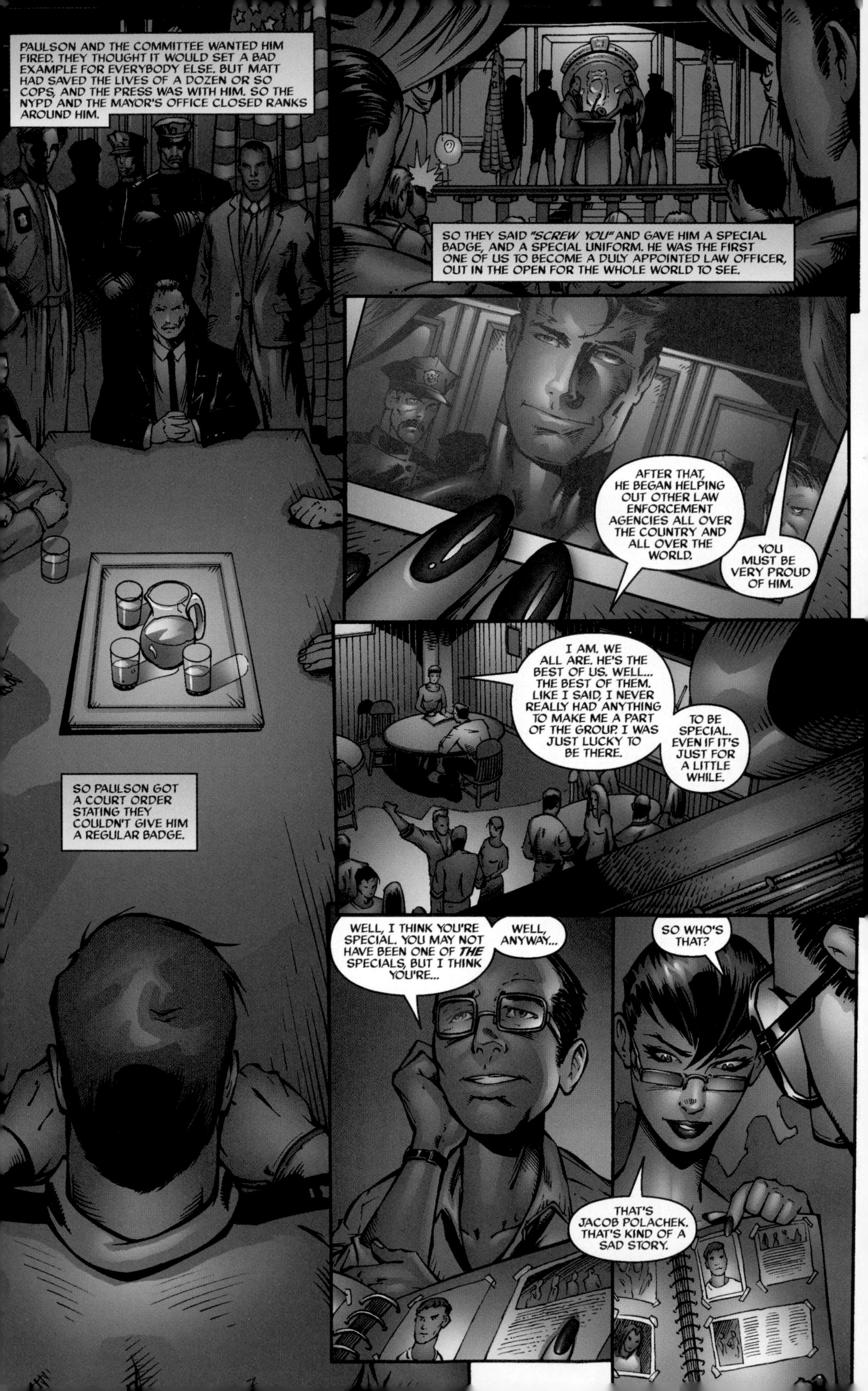
PAULSON AND THE COMMITTEE WANTED HIM FIRED. THEY THOUGHT IT WOULD SET A BAD EXAMPLE FOR EVERYBODY ELSE. BUT MATT HAD SAVED THE LIVES OF A DOZEN OR SO COPS, AND THE PRESS WAS WITH HIM. SO THE NYPD AND THE MAYOR'S OFFICE CLOSED RANKS AROUND HIM.
SO PAULSON GOT A COURT ORDER STATING THEY COULDN'T GIVE HIM A REGULAR BADGE.
SO THEY SAID *"SCREW YOU"* AND GAVE HIM A SPECIAL BADGE, AND A SPECIAL UNIFORM. HE WAS THE FIRST ONE OF US TO BECOME A DULY APPOINTED LAW OFFICER, OUT IN THE OPEN FOR THE WHOLE WORLD TO SEE.
AFTER THAT, HE BEGAN HELPING OUT OTHER LAW ENFORCEMENT AGENCIES ALL OVER THE COUNTRY AND ALL OVER THE WORLD.
YOU MUST BE VERY PROUD OF HIM.
I AM. WE ALL ARE. HE'S THE BEST OF US. WELL... THE BEST OF THEM. LIKE I SAID, I NEVER REALLY HAD ANYTHING TO MAKE ME A PART OF THE GROUP. I WAS JUST LUCKY TO BE THERE.
TO BE SPECIAL. EVEN IF IT'S JUST FOR A LITTLE WHILE.
WELL, I THINK YOU'RE SPECIAL. YOU MAY NOT HAVE BEEN ONE OF ***THE*** SPECIALS, BUT I THINK YOU'RE...
WELL, ANYWAY...
SO WHO'S THAT?
THAT'S JACOB POLACHEK. THAT'S KIND OF A SAD STORY.

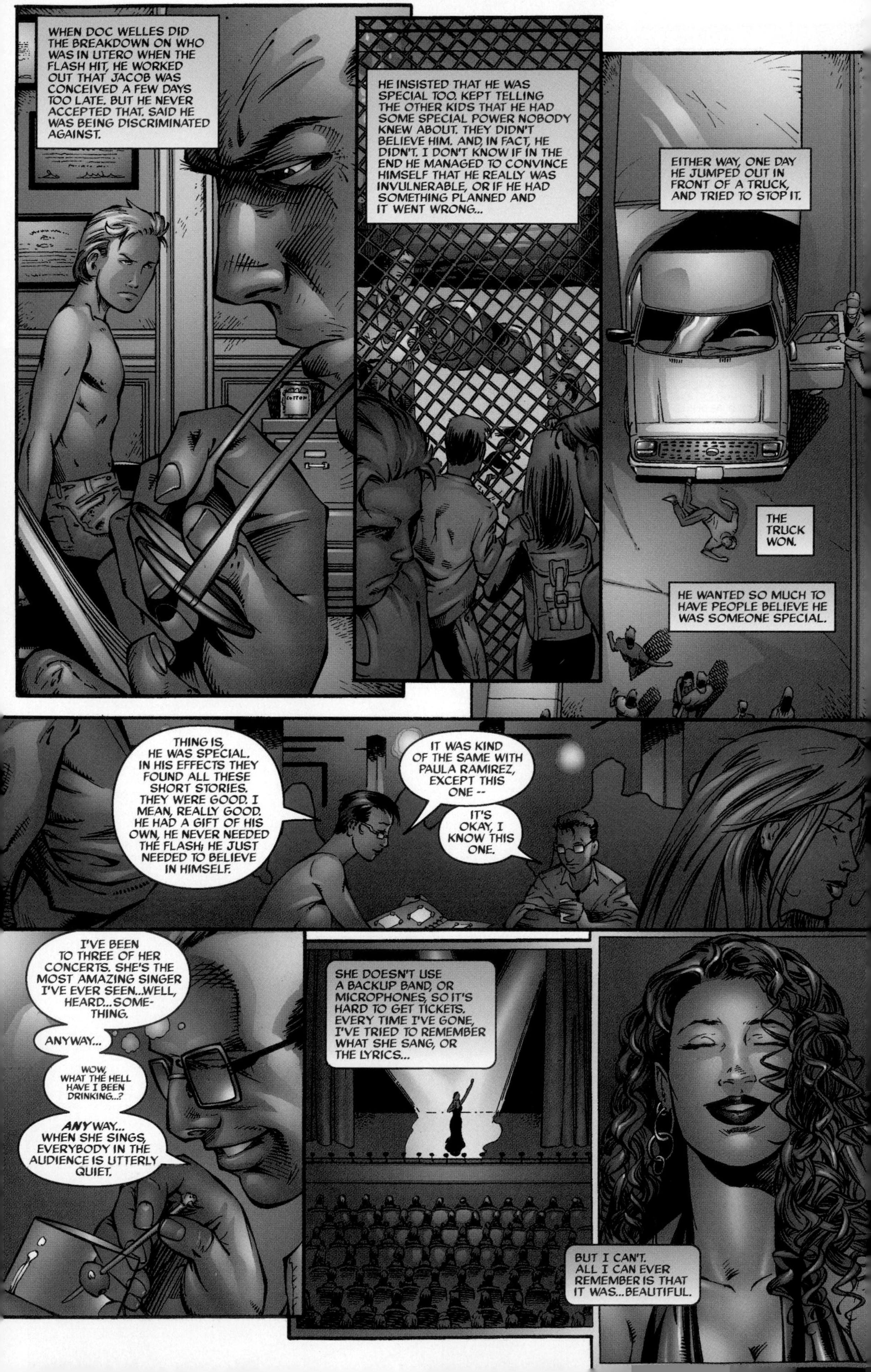
WHEN DOC WELLES DID THE BREAKDOWN ON WHO WAS IN UTERO WHEN THE FLASH HIT, HE WORKED OUT THAT JACOB WAS CONCEIVED A FEW DAYS TOO LATE. BUT HE NEVER ACCEPTED THAT. SAID HE WAS BEING DISCRIMINATED AGAINST.
COTTON
HE INSISTED THAT HE WAS SPECIAL TOO. KEPT TELLING THE OTHER KIDS THAT HE HAD SOME SPECIAL POWER NOBODY KNEW ABOUT. THEY DIDN'T BELIEVE HIM. AND, IN FACT, HE DIDN'T. I DON'T KNOW IF IN THE END HE MANAGED TO CONVINCE HIMSELF THAT HE REALLY WAS INVULNERABLE, OR IF HE HAD SOMETHING PLANNED AND IT WENT WRONG...
EITHER WAY, ONE DAY HE JUMPED OUT IN FRONT OF A TRUCK, AND TRIED TO STOP IT.
THE TRUCK WON.
HE WANTED SO MUCH TO HAVE PEOPLE BELIEVE HE WAS SOMEONE SPECIAL.
THING IS, HE WAS SPECIAL. IN HIS EFFECTS THEY FOUND ALL THESE SHORT STORIES. THEY WERE GOOD. I MEAN, REALLY GOOD. HE HAD A GIFT OF HIS OWN, HE NEVER NEEDED THE FLASH; HE JUST NEEDED TO BELIEVE IN HIMSELF.
IT WAS KIND OF THE SAME WITH PAULA RAMIREZ, EXCEPT THIS ONE --
IT'S OKAY, I KNOW THIS ONE.
I'VE BEEN TO THREE OF HER CONCERTS. SHE'S THE MOST AMAZING SINGER I'VE EVER SEEN...WELL, HEARD...SOME-THING.
ANYWAY...
WOW, WHAT THE HELL HAVE I BEEN DRINKING...?
ANYWAY... WHEN SHE SINGS, EVERYBODY IN THE AUDIENCE IS UTTERLY QUIET.
SHE DOESN'T USE A BACKUP BAND, OR MICROPHONES, SO IT'S HARD TO GET TICKETS. EVERY TIME I'VE GONE, I'VE TRIED TO REMEMBER WHAT SHE SANG, OR THE LYRICS...
BUT I CAN'T. ALL I CAN EVER REMEMBER IS THAT IT WAS...BEAUTIFUL.

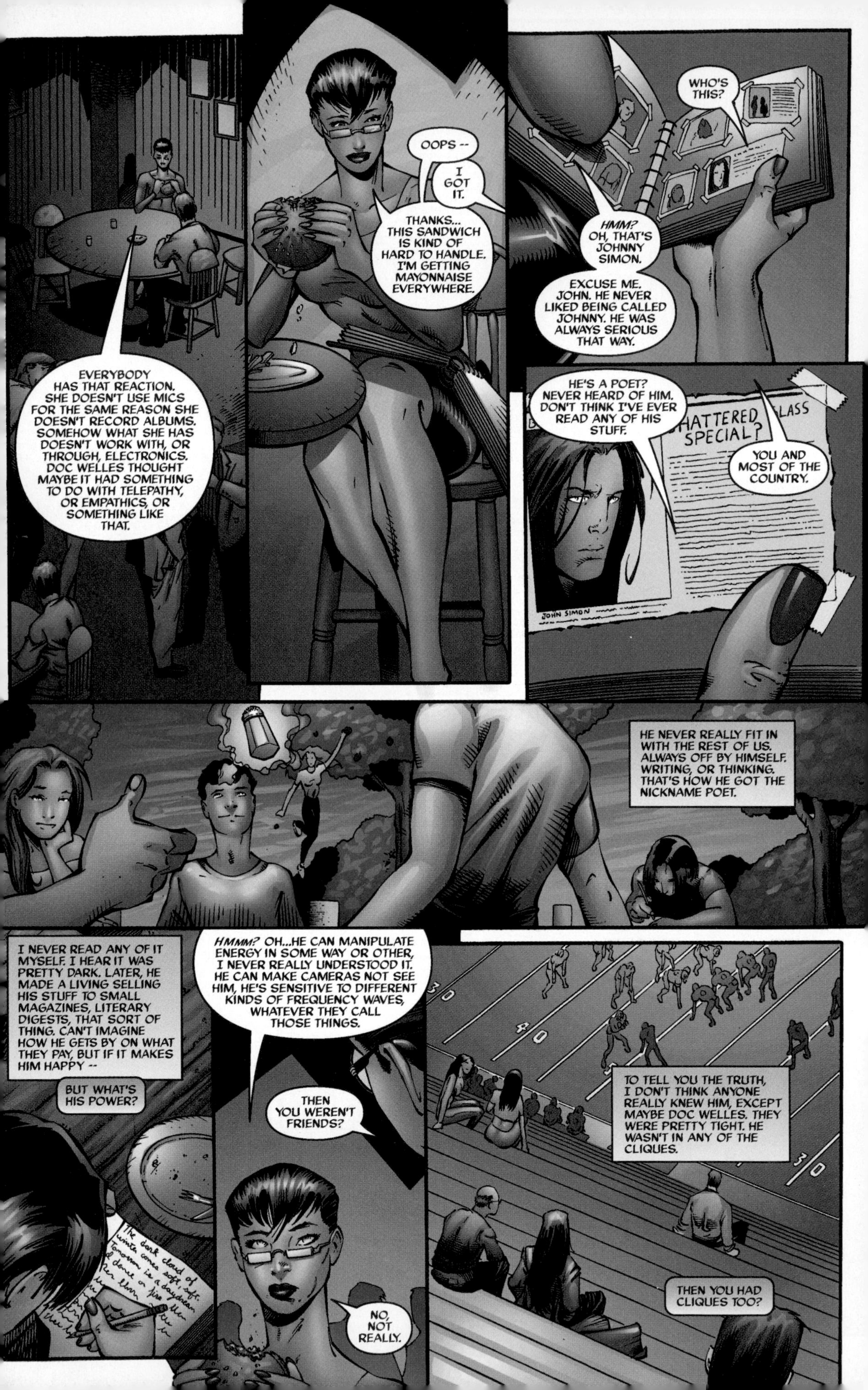

EVERYBODY HAS THAT REACTION. SHE DOESN'T USE MICS FOR THE SAME REASON SHE DOESN'T RECORD ALBUMS. SOMEHOW WHAT SHE HAS DOESN'T WORK WITH, OR THROUGH, ELECTRONICS. DOC WELLES THOUGHT MAYBE IT HAD SOMETHING TO DO WITH TELEPATHY, OR EMPATHICS, OR SOMETHING LIKE THAT.
OOPS --
I GOT IT.
THANKS... THIS SANDWICH IS KIND OF HARD TO HANDLE. I'M GETTING MAYONNAISE EVERYWHERE.
WHO'S THIS?
HMM? OH, THAT'S JOHNNY SIMON.
EXCUSE ME. JOHN. HE NEVER LIKED BEING CALLED JOHNNY. HE WAS ALWAYS SERIOUS THAT WAY.
HE'S A POET? NEVER HEARD OF HIM. DON'T THINK I'VE EVER READ ANY OF HIS STUFF.
SHATTERED GLASS
SPECIAL?
JOHN SIMON
YOU AND MOST OF THE COUNTRY.
HE NEVER REALLY FIT IN WITH THE REST OF US. ALWAYS OFF BY HIMSELF. WRITING, OR THINKING. THAT'S HOW HE GOT THE NICKNAME POET.
I NEVER READ ANY OF IT MYSELF. I HEAR IT WAS PRETTY DARK. LATER, HE MADE A LIVING SELLING HIS STUFF TO SMALL MAGAZINES, LITERARY DIGESTS, THAT SORT OF THING. CAN'T IMAGINE HOW HE GETS BY ON WHAT THEY PAY, BUT IF IT MAKES HIM HAPPY --
BUT WHAT'S HIS POWER?
HMMM? OH...HE CAN MANIPULATE ENERGY IN SOME WAY OR OTHER, I NEVER REALLY UNDERSTOOD IT. HE CAN MAKE CAMERAS NOT SEE HIM, HE'S SENSITIVE TO DIFFERENT KINDS OF FREQUENCY WAVES, WHATEVER THEY CALL THOSE THINGS.
THEN YOU WEREN'T FRIENDS?
NO, NOT REALLY.
TO TELL YOU THE TRUTH, I DON'T THINK ANYONE REALLY KNEW HIM, EXCEPT MAYBE DOC WELLES. THEY WERE PRETTY TIGHT. HE WASN'T IN ANY OF THE CLIQUES.
THEN YOU HAD CLIQUES TOO?

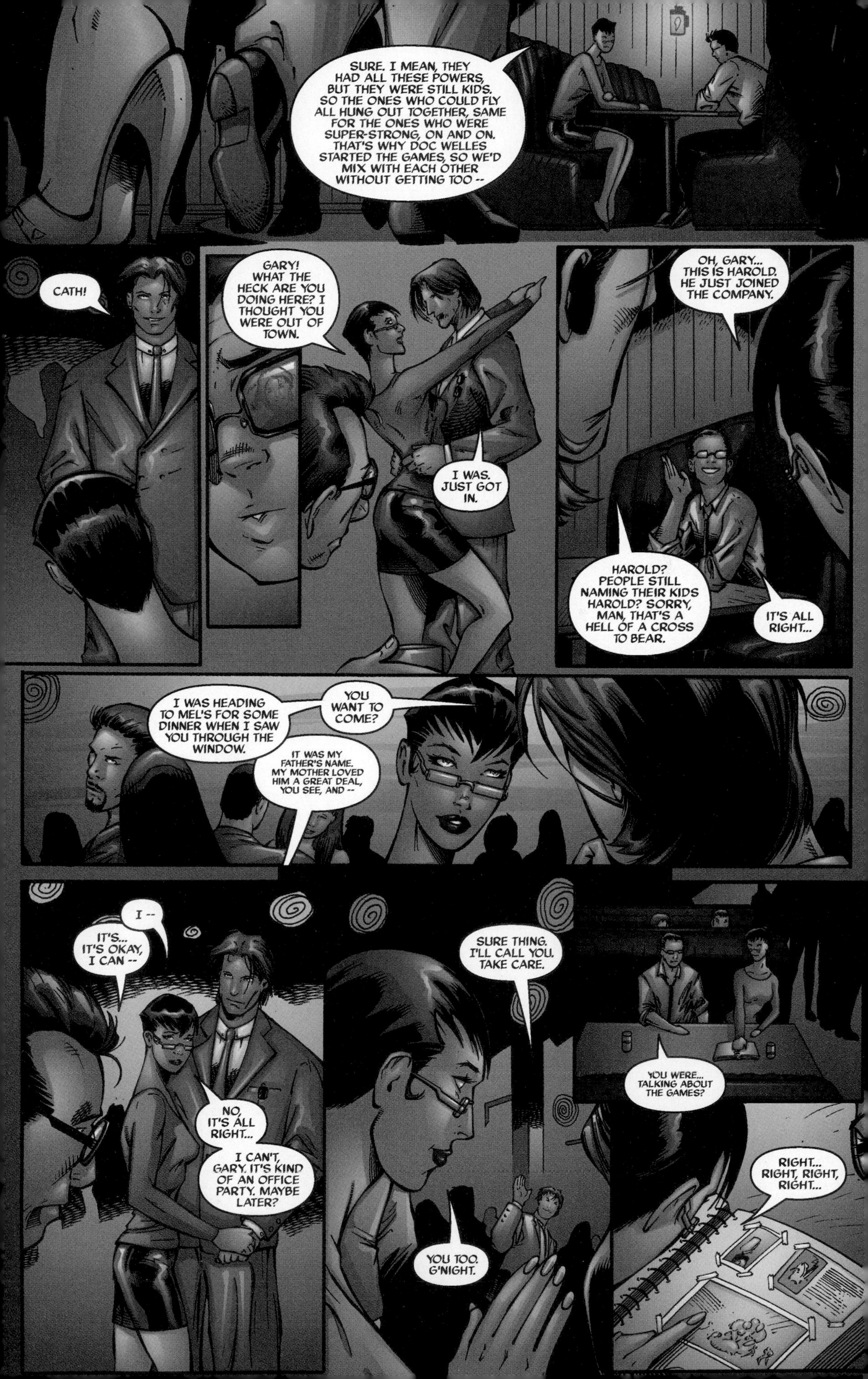
SURE. I MEAN, THEY HAD ALL THESE POWERS, BUT THEY WERE STILL KIDS. SO THE ONES WHO COULD FLY ALL HUNG OUT TOGETHER, SAME FOR THE ONES WHO WERE SUPER-STRONG, ON AND ON. THAT'S WHY DOC WELLES STARTED THE GAMES, SO WE'D MIX WITH EACH OTHER WITHOUT GETTING TOO --
CATH!
GARY! WHAT THE HECK ARE YOU DOING HERE? I THOUGHT YOU WERE OUT OF TOWN.
I WAS. JUST GOT IN.
OH, GARY... THIS IS HAROLD. HE JUST JOINED THE COMPANY.
HAROLD? PEOPLE STILL NAMING THEIR KIDS HAROLD? SORRY, MAN, THAT'S A HELL OF A CROSS TO BEAR.
IT'S ALL RIGHT...
I WAS HEADING TO MEL'S FOR SOME DINNER WHEN I SAW YOU THROUGH THE WINDOW.
YOU WANT TO COME?
IT WAS MY FATHER'S NAME. MY MOTHER LOVED HIM A GREAT DEAL, YOU SEE, AND --
I --
IT'S... IT'S OKAY, I CAN --
NO, IT'S ALL RIGHT...
I CAN'T, GARY. IT'S KIND OF AN OFFICE PARTY. MAYBE LATER?
SURE THING. I'LL CALL YOU. TAKE CARE.
YOU TOO. G'NIGHT.
YOU WERE... TALKING ABOUT THE GAMES?
RIGHT... RIGHT, RIGHT, RIGHT...

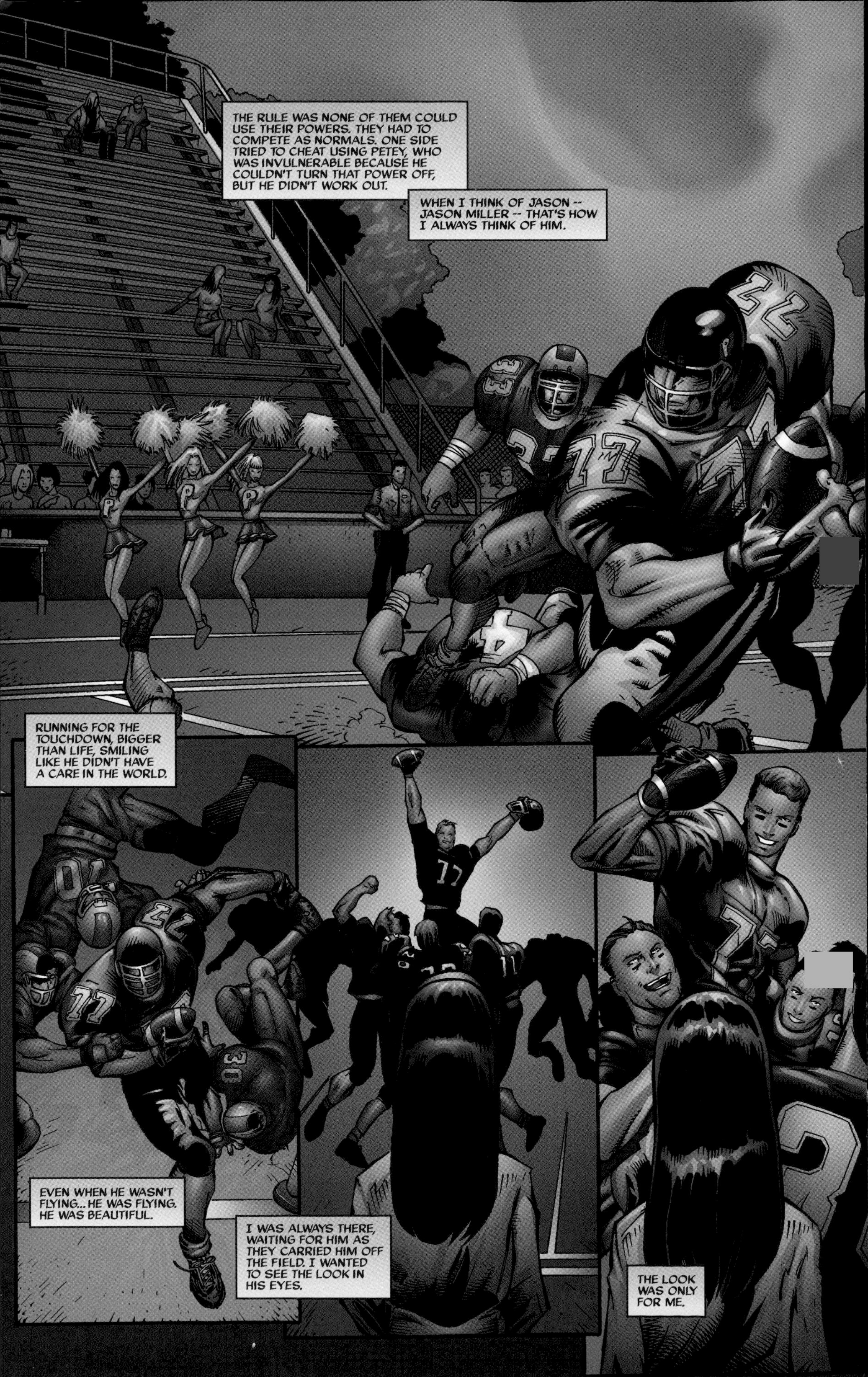
THE RULE WAS NONE OF THEM COULD USE THEIR POWERS. THEY HAD TO COMPETE AS NORMALS. ONE SIDE TRIED TO CHEAT USING PETEY, WHO WAS INVULNERABLE BECAUSE HE COULDN'T TURN THAT POWER OFF, BUT HE DIDN'T WORK OUT.
WHEN I THINK OF JASON -- JASON MILLER -- THAT'S HOW I ALWAYS THINK OF HIM.
RUNNING FOR THE TOUCHDOWN, BIGGER THAN LIFE, SMILING LIKE HE DIDN'T HAVE A CARE IN THE WORLD.
EVEN WHEN HE WASN'T FLYING... HE WAS FLYING. HE WAS BEAUTIFUL.
I WAS ALWAYS THERE, WAITING FOR HIM AS THEY CARRIED HIM OFF THE FIELD. I WANTED TO SEE THE LOOK IN HIS EYES.
THE LOOK WAS ONLY FOR ME.

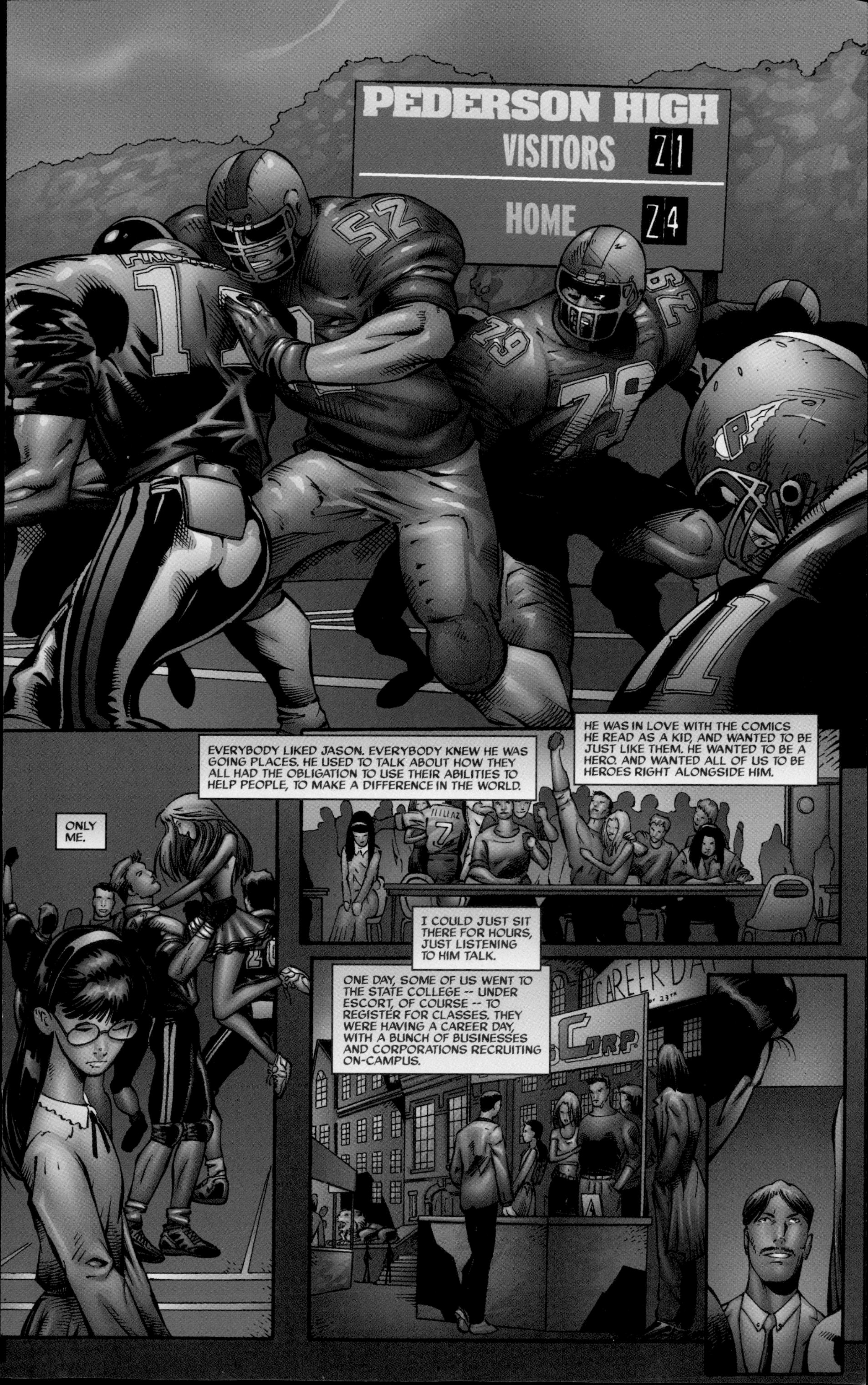
PEDERSON HIGH
VISITORS 21
HOME 24
EVERYBODY LIKED JASON. EVERYBODY KNEW HE WAS GOING PLACES. HE USED TO TALK ABOUT HOW THEY ALL HAD THE OBLIGATION TO USE THEIR ABILITIES TO HELP PEOPLE, TO MAKE A DIFFERENCE IN THE WORLD.
HE WAS IN LOVE WITH THE COMICS HE READ AS A KID, AND WANTED TO BE JUST LIKE THEM. HE WANTED TO BE A HERO. AND WANTED ALL OF US TO BE HEROES RIGHT ALONGSIDE HIM.
ONLY ME.
I COULD JUST SIT THERE FOR HOURS, JUST LISTENING TO HIM TALK.
ONE DAY, SOME OF US WENT TO THE STATE COLLEGE -- UNDER ESCORT, OF COURSE -- TO REGISTER FOR CLASSES. THEY WERE HAVING A CAREER DAY, WITH A BUNCH OF BUSINESSES AND CORPORATIONS RECRUITING ON-CAMPUS.
CAREER DAY
CORP.

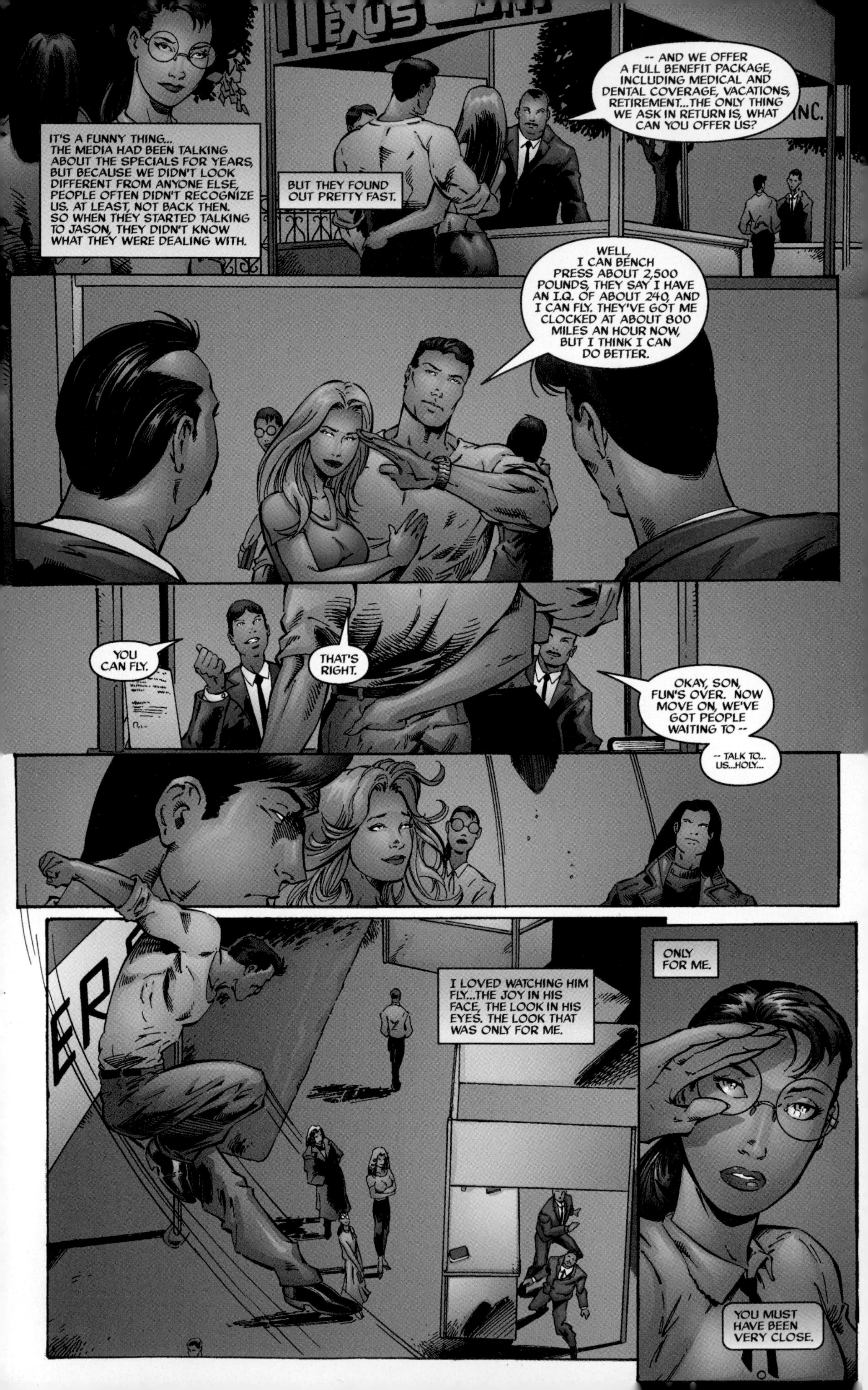
IT'S A FUNNY THING... THE MEDIA HAD BEEN TALKING ABOUT THE SPECIALS FOR YEARS, BUT BECAUSE WE DIDN'T LOOK DIFFERENT FROM ANYONE ELSE, PEOPLE OFTEN DIDN'T RECOGNIZE US. AT LEAST, NOT BACK THEN. SO WHEN THEY STARTED TALKING TO JASON, THEY DIDN'T KNOW WHAT THEY WERE DEALING WITH.
BUT THEY FOUND OUT PRETTY FAST.
-- AND WE OFFER A FULL BENEFIT PACKAGE, INCLUDING MEDICAL AND DENTAL COVERAGE, VACATIONS, RETIREMENT...THE ONLY THING WE ASK IN RETURN IS, WHAT CAN YOU OFFER US?
INC.
WELL, I CAN BENCH PRESS ABOUT 2,500 POUNDS, THEY SAY I HAVE AN I.Q. OF ABOUT 240, AND I CAN FLY. THEY'VE GOT ME CLOCKED AT ABOUT 800 MILES AN HOUR NOW, BUT I THINK I CAN DO BETTER.
YOU CAN FLY.
THAT'S RIGHT.
OKAY, SON, FUN'S OVER. NOW MOVE ON, WE'VE GOT PEOPLE WAITING TO --
-- TALK TO... US...HOLY...
I LOVED WATCHING HIM FLY...THE JOY IN HIS FACE, THE LOOK IN HIS EYES. THE LOOK THAT WAS ONLY FOR ME.
ONLY FOR ME.
YOU MUST HAVE BEEN VERY CLOSE.

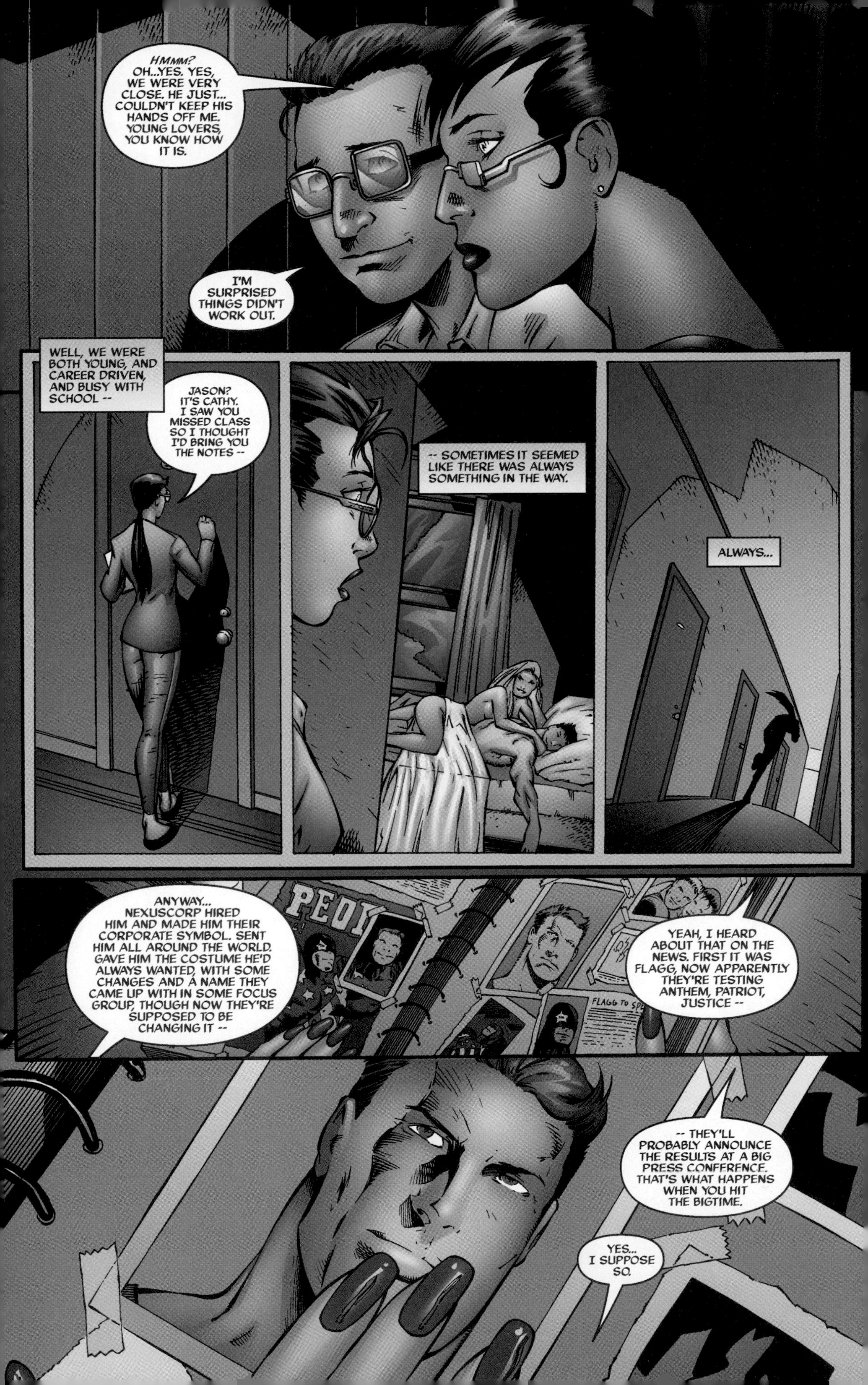
HMMM? OH...YES. YES, WE WERE VERY CLOSE. HE JUST... COULDN'T KEEP HIS HANDS OFF ME. YOUNG LOVERS, YOU KNOW HOW IT IS.
I'M SURPRISED THINGS DIDN'T WORK OUT.
WELL, WE WERE BOTH YOUNG, AND CAREER DRIVEN, AND BUSY WITH SCHOOL --
JASON? IT'S CATHY. I SAW YOU MISSED CLASS SO I THOUGHT I'D BRING YOU THE NOTES --
-- SOMETIMES IT SEEMED LIKE THERE WAS ALWAYS SOMETHING IN THE WAY.
ALWAYS...
ANYWAY... NEXUSCORP HIRED HIM AND MADE HIM THEIR CORPORATE SYMBOL. SENT HIM ALL AROUND THE WORLD. GAVE HIM THE COSTUME HE'D ALWAYS WANTED, WITH SOME CHANGES AND A NAME THEY CAME UP WITH IN SOME FOCUS GROUP, THOUGH NOW THEY'RE SUPPOSED TO BE CHANGING IT --
YEAH, I HEARD ABOUT THAT ON THE NEWS. FIRST IT WAS FLAGG, NOW APPARENTLY THEY'RE TESTING ANTHEM, PATRIOT, JUSTICE --
-- THEY'LL PROBABLY ANNOUNCE THE RESULTS AT A BIG PRESS CONFRENCE. THAT'S WHAT HAPPENS WHEN YOU HIT THE BIGTIME.
YES... I SUPPOSE SO.

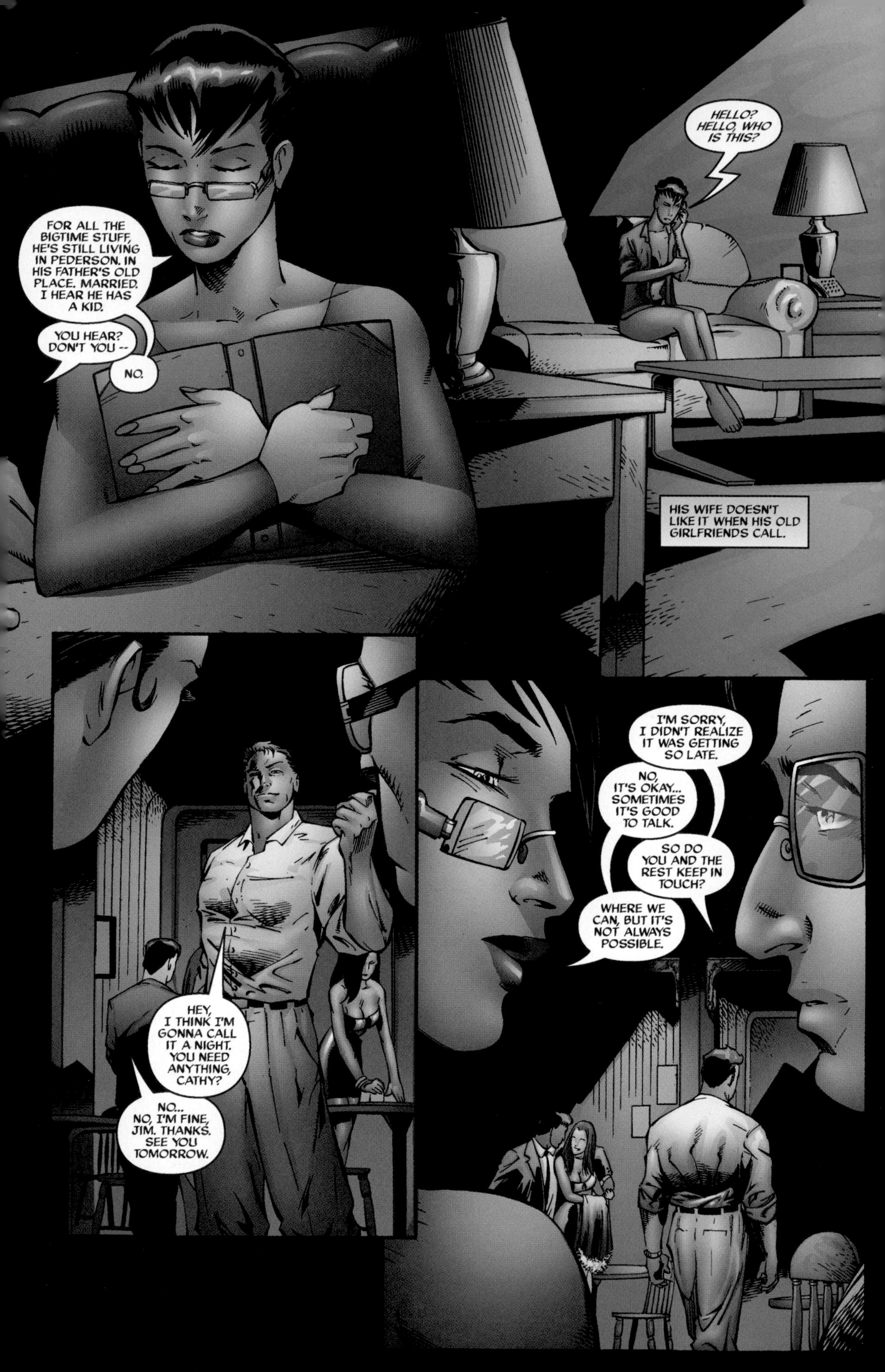
FOR ALL THE BIGTIME STUFF, HE'S STILL LIVING IN PEDERSON. IN HIS FATHER'S OLD PLACE. MARRIED. I HEAR HE HAS A KID.
YOU HEAR? DON'T YOU --
NO.
HELLO? HELLO, WHO IS THIS?
HIS WIFE DOESN'T LIKE IT WHEN HIS OLD GIRLFRIENDS CALL.
HEY, I THINK I'M GONNA CALL IT A NIGHT. YOU NEED ANYTHING, CATHY?
NO... NO, I'M FINE, JIM. THANKS. SEE YOU TOMORROW.
I'M SORRY, I DIDN'T REALIZE IT WAS GETTING SO LATE.
NO, IT'S OKAY... SOMETIMES IT'S GOOD TO TALK.
SO DO YOU AND THE REST KEEP IN TOUCH?
WHERE WE CAN, BUT IT'S NOT ALWAYS POSSIBLE.

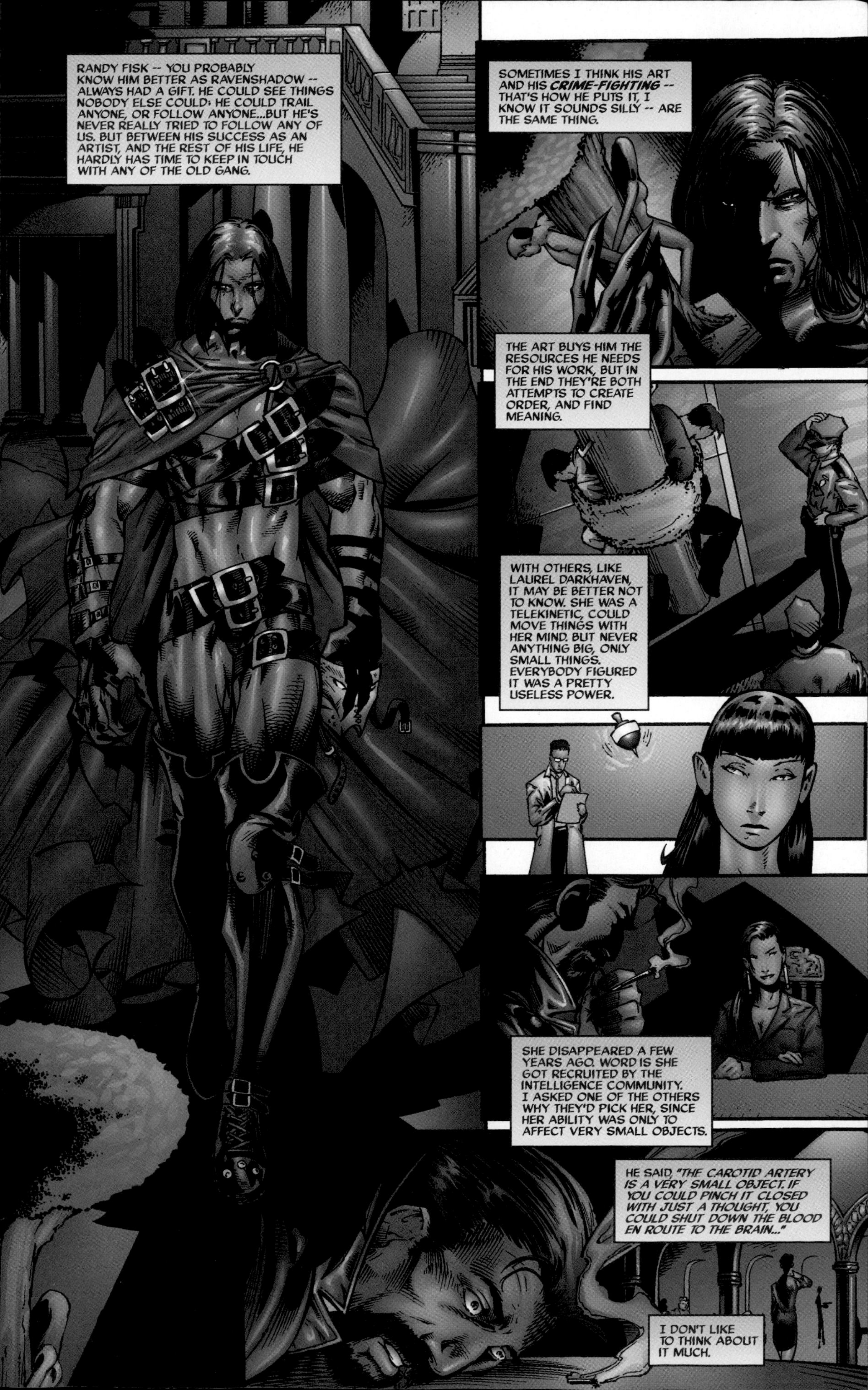
RANDY FISK -- YOU PROBABLY KNOW HIM BETTER AS RAVENSHADOW -- ALWAYS HAD A GIFT. HE COULD SEE THINGS NOBODY ELSE COULD; HE COULD TRAIL ANYONE, OR FOLLOW ANYONE...BUT HE'S NEVER REALLY TRIED TO FOLLOW ANY OF US. BUT BETWEEN HIS SUCCESS AS AN ARTIST, AND THE REST OF HIS LIFE, HE HARDLY HAS TIME TO KEEP IN TOUCH WITH ANY OF THE OLD GANG.
SOMETIMES I THINK HIS ART AND HIS CRIME-FIGHTING -- THAT'S HOW HE PUTS IT, I KNOW IT SOUNDS SILLY -- ARE THE SAME THING.
THE ART BUYS HIM THE RESOURCES HE NEEDS FOR HIS WORK, BUT IN THE END THEY'RE BOTH ATTEMPTS TO CREATE ORDER, AND FIND MEANING.
WITH OTHERS, LIKE LAUREL DARKHAVEN, IT MAY BE BETTER NOT TO KNOW. SHE WAS A TELEKINETIC, COULD MOVE THINGS WITH HER MIND. BUT NEVER ANYTHING BIG, ONLY SMALL THINGS. EVERYBODY FIGURED IT WAS A PRETTY USELESS POWER.
SHE DISAPPEARED A FEW YEARS AGO. WORD IS SHE GOT RECRUITED BY THE INTELLIGENCE COMMUNITY. I ASKED ONE OF THE OTHERS WHY THEY'D PICK HER, SINCE HER ABILITY WAS ONLY TO AFFECT VERY SMALL OBJECTS.
HE SAID, "THE CAROTID ARTERY IS A VERY SMALL OBJECT. IF YOU COULD PINCH IT CLOSED WITH JUST A THOUGHT, YOU COULD SHUT DOWN THE BLOOD EN ROUTE TO THE BRAIN..."
I DON'T LIKE TO THINK ABOUT IT MUCH.

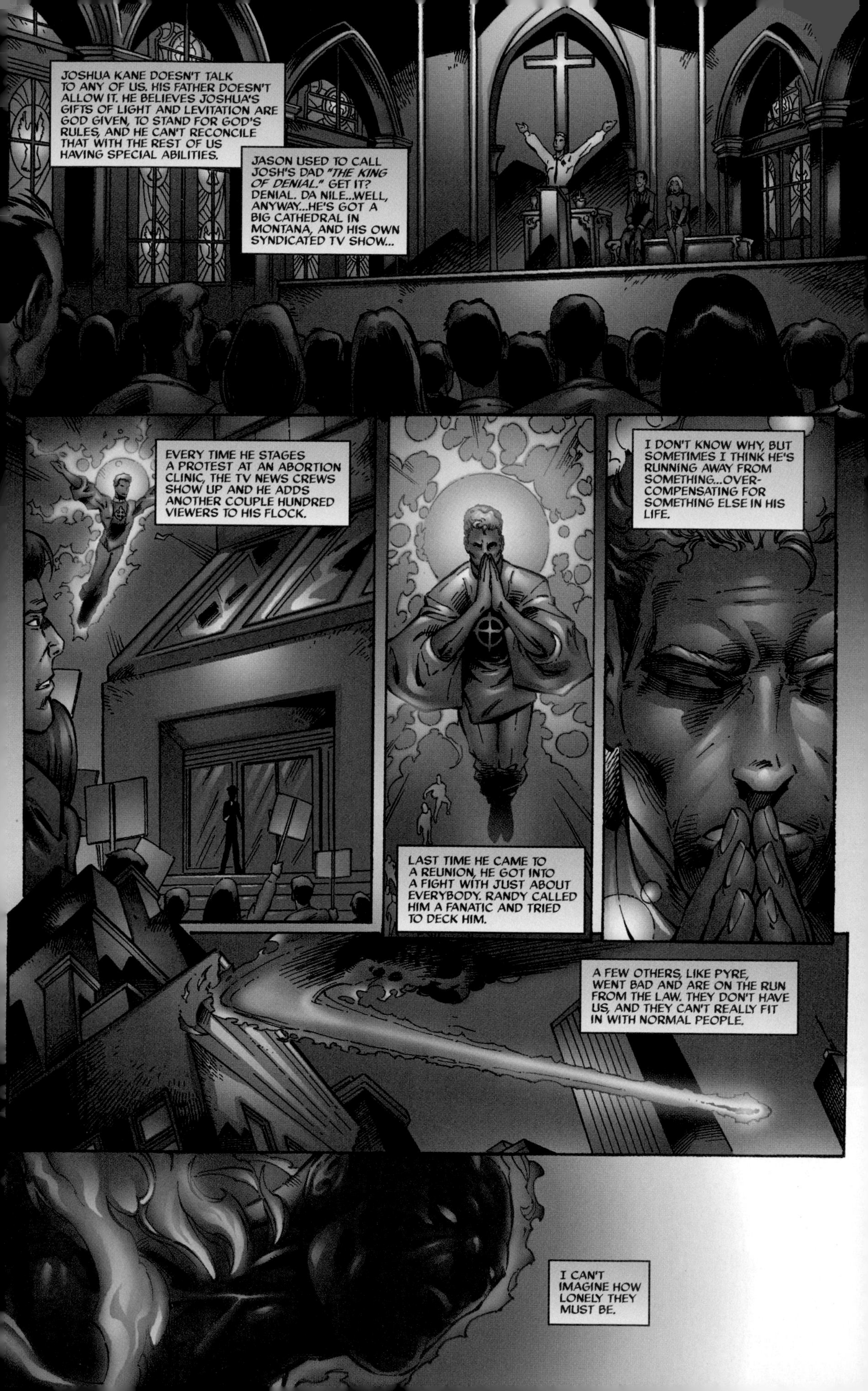
JOSHUA KANE DOESN'T TALK TO ANY OF US. HIS FATHER DOESN'T ALLOW IT. HE BELIEVES JOSHUA'S GIFTS OF LIGHT AND LEVITATION ARE GOD GIVEN, TO STAND FOR GOD'S RULES, AND HE CAN'T RECONCILE THAT WITH THE REST OF US HAVING SPECIAL ABILITIES.
JASON USED TO CALL JOSH'S DAD "THE KING OF DENIAL." GET IT? DENIAL. DA NILE...WELL, ANYWAY...HE'S GOT A BIG CATHEDRAL IN MONTANA, AND HIS OWN SYNDICATED TV SHOW...
EVERY TIME HE STAGES A PROTEST AT AN ABORTION CLINIC, THE TV NEWS CREWS SHOW UP AND HE ADDS ANOTHER COUPLE HUNDRED VIEWERS TO HIS FLOCK.
LAST TIME HE CAME TO A REUNION, HE GOT INTO A FIGHT WITH JUST ABOUT EVERYBODY. RANDY CALLED HIM A FANATIC AND TRIED TO DECK HIM.
I DON'T KNOW WHY, BUT SOMETIMES I THINK HE'S RUNNING AWAY FROM SOMETHING...OVER-COMPENSATING FOR SOMETHING ELSE IN HIS LIFE.
A FEW OTHERS, LIKE PYRE, WENT BAD AND ARE ON THE RUN FROM THE LAW. THEY DON'T HAVE US, AND THEY CAN'T REALLY FIT IN WITH NORMAL PEOPLE.
I CAN'T IMAGINE HOW LONELY THEY MUST BE.

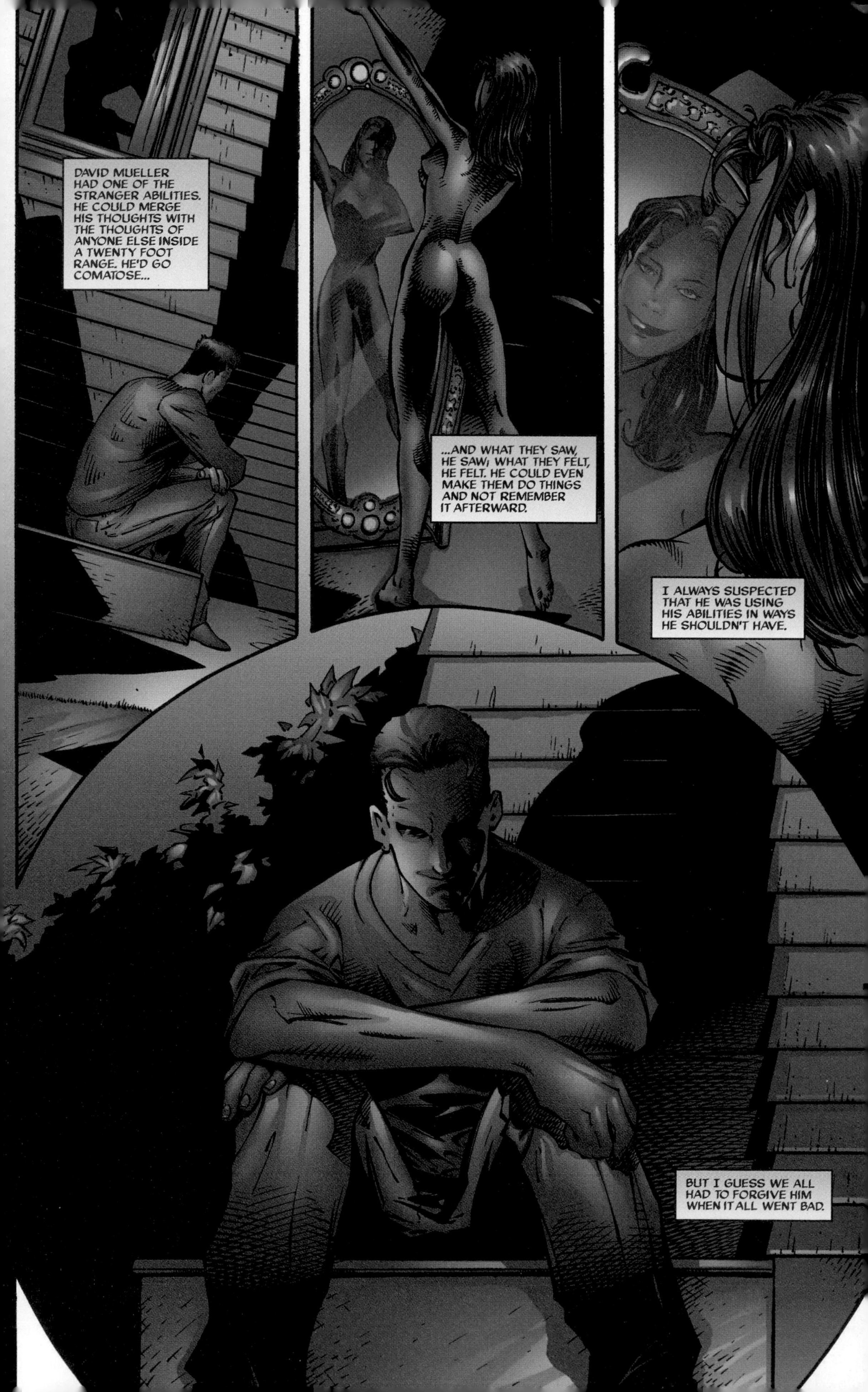
DAVID MUELLER HAD ONE OF THE STRANGER ABILITIES. HE COULD MERGE HIS THOUGHTS WITH THE THOUGHTS OF ANYONE ELSE INSIDE A TWENTY FOOT RANGE. HE'D GO COMATOSE...
...AND WHAT THEY SAW, HE SAW; WHAT THEY FELT, HE FELT. HE COULD EVEN MAKE THEM DO THINGS AND NOT REMEMBER IT AFTERWARD.
I ALWAYS SUSPECTED THAT HE WAS USING HIS ABILITIES IN WAYS HE SHOULDN'T HAVE.
BUT I GUESS WE ALL HAD TO FORGIVE HIM WHEN IT ALL WENT BAD.

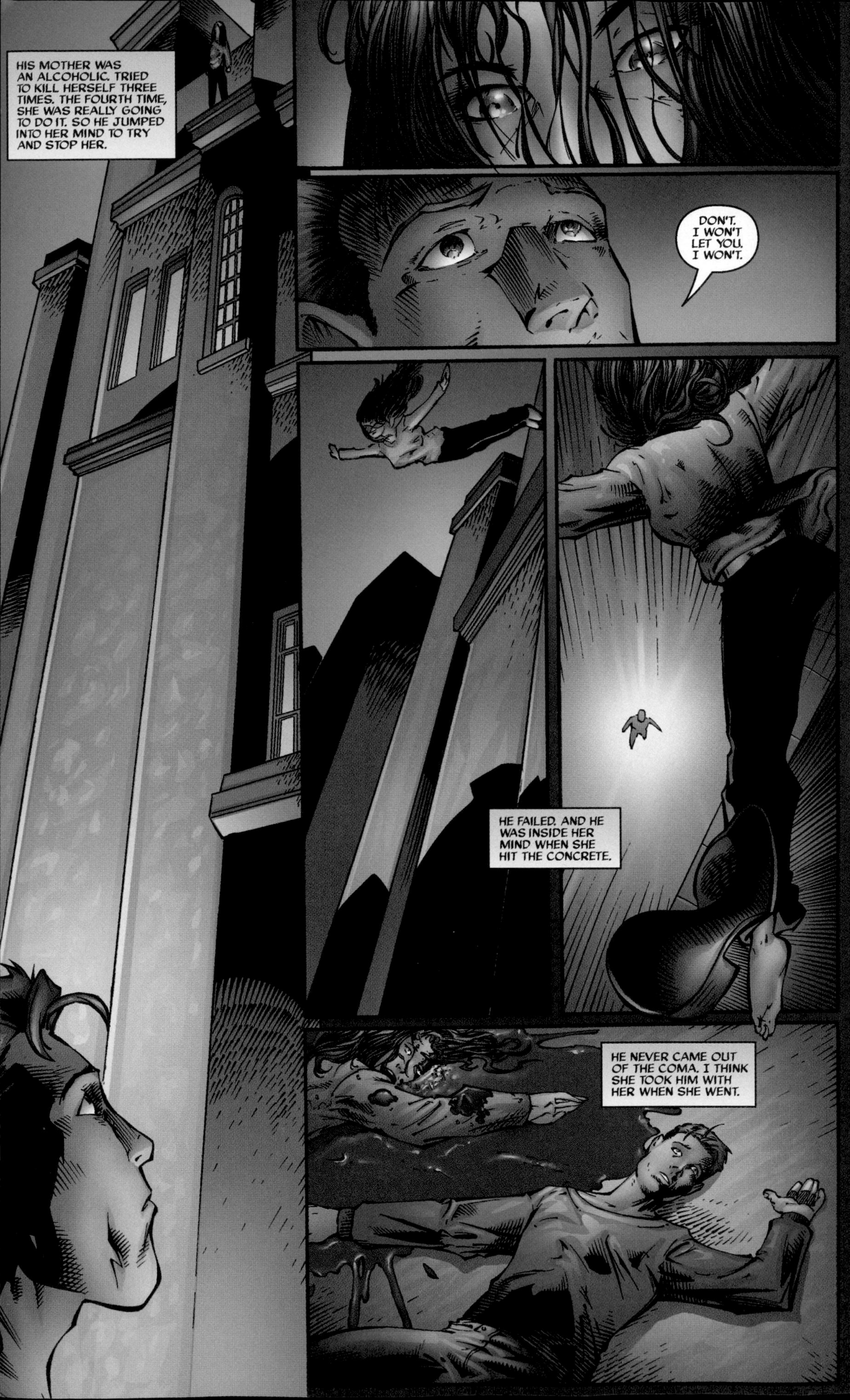
HIS MOTHER WAS AN ALCOHOLIC. TRIED TO KILL HERSELF THREE TIMES. THE FOURTH TIME, SHE WAS REALLY GOING TO DO IT. SO HE JUMPED INTO HER MIND TO TRY AND STOP HER.
DON'T. I WON'T LET YOU. I WON'T.
HE FAILED. AND HE WAS INSIDE HER MIND WHEN SHE HIT THE CONCRETE.
HE NEVER CAME OUT OF THE COMA. I THINK SHE TOOK HIM WITH HER WHEN SHE WENT.

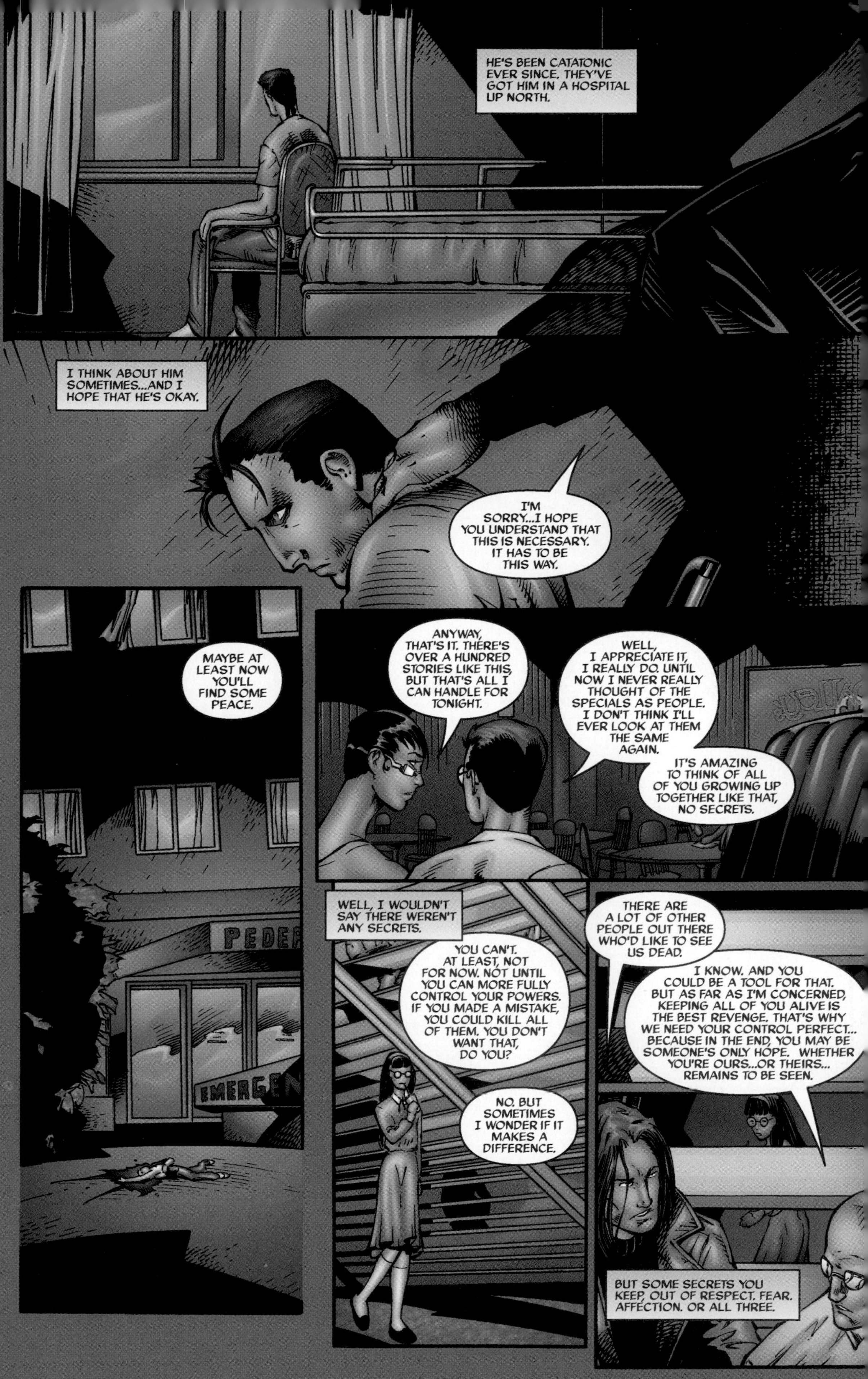
HE'S BEEN CATATONIC EVER SINCE. THEY'VE GOT HIM IN A HOSPITAL UP NORTH.
I THINK ABOUT HIM SOMETIMES...AND I HOPE THAT HE'S OKAY.
I'M SORRY...I HOPE YOU UNDERSTAND THAT THIS IS NECESSARY. IT HAS TO BE THIS WAY.
MAYBE AT LEAST NOW YOU'LL FIND SOME PEACE.
PEDER
EMERGEN
ANYWAY, THAT'S IT. THERE'S OVER A HUNDRED STORIES LIKE THIS, BUT THAT'S ALL I CAN HANDLE FOR TONIGHT.
WELL, I APPRECIATE IT, I REALLY DO. UNTIL NOW I NEVER REALLY THOUGHT OF THE SPECIALS AS PEOPLE. I DON'T THINK I'LL EVER LOOK AT THEM THE SAME AGAIN.
IT'S AMAZING TO THINK OF ALL OF YOU GROWING UP TOGETHER LIKE THAT, NO SECRETS.
WELL, I WOULDN'T SAY THERE WEREN'T ANY SECRETS.
YOU CAN'T. AT LEAST, NOT FOR NOW. NOT UNTIL YOU CAN MORE FULLY CONTROL YOUR POWERS. IF YOU MADE A MISTAKE, YOU COULD KILL ALL OF THEM. YOU DON'T WANT THAT, DO YOU?
NO. BUT SOMETIMES I WONDER IF IT MAKES A DIFFERENCE.
THERE ARE A LOT OF OTHER PEOPLE OUT THERE WHO'D LIKE TO SEE US DEAD.
I KNOW. AND YOU COULD BE A TOOL FOR THAT. BUT AS FAR AS I'M CONCERNED, KEEPING ALL OF YOU ALIVE IS THE BEST REVENGE. THAT'S WHY WE NEED YOUR CONTROL PERFECT... BECAUSE IN THE END, YOU MAY BE SOMEONE'S ONLY HOPE. WHETHER YOU'RE OURS...OR THEIRS... REMAINS TO BE SEEN.
BUT SOME SECRETS YOU KEEP, OUT OF RESPECT. FEAR. AFFECTION. OR ALL THREE.

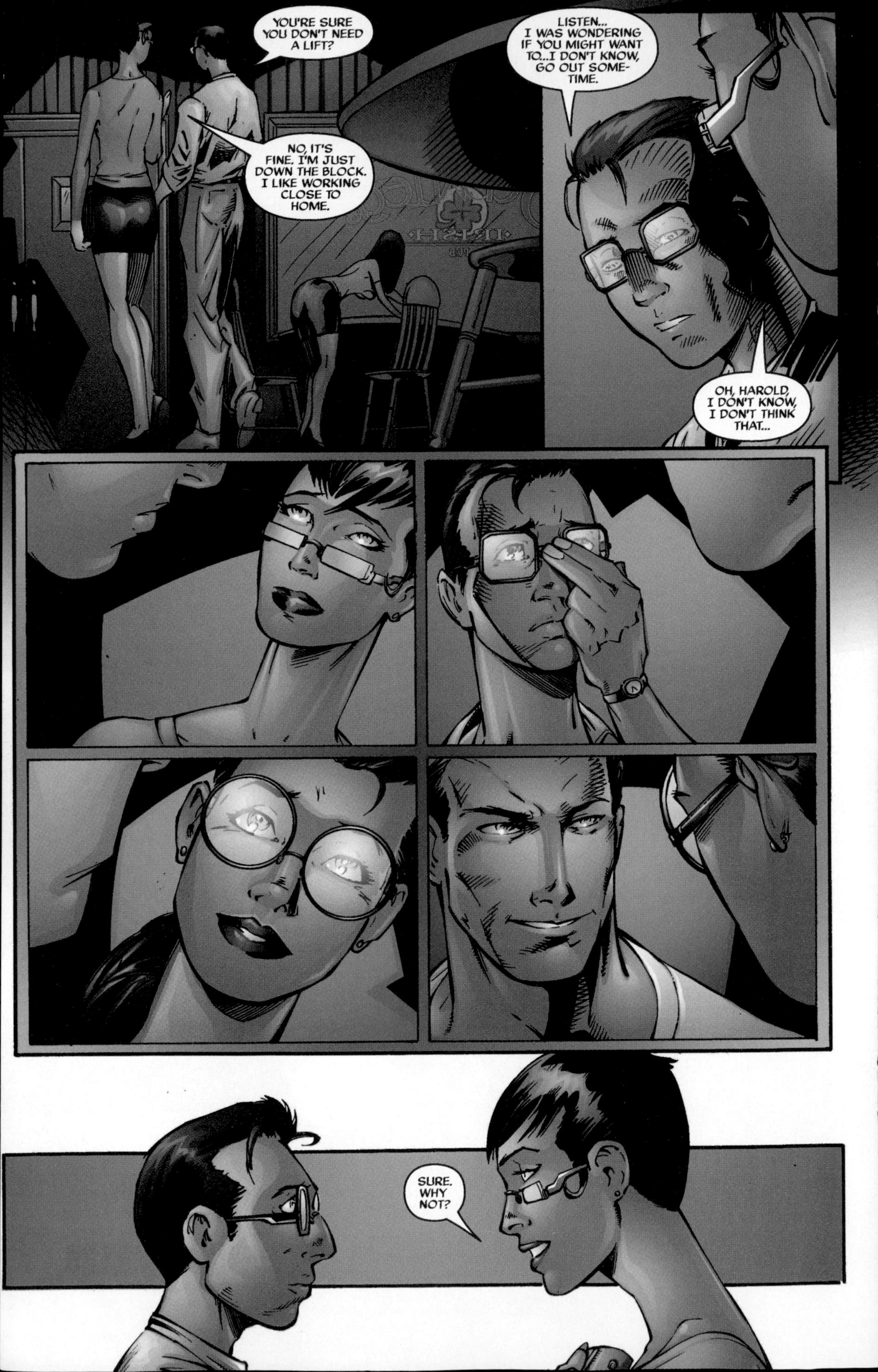
YOU'RE SURE YOU DON'T NEED A LIFT?
NO, IT'S FINE. I'M JUST DOWN THE BLOCK. I LIKE WORKING CLOSE TO HOME.
LISTEN... I WAS WONDERING IF YOU MIGHT WANT TO...I DON'T KNOW, GO OUT SOME-TIME.
OH, HAROLD, I DON'T KNOW, I DON'T THINK THAT...
SURE. WHY NOT?

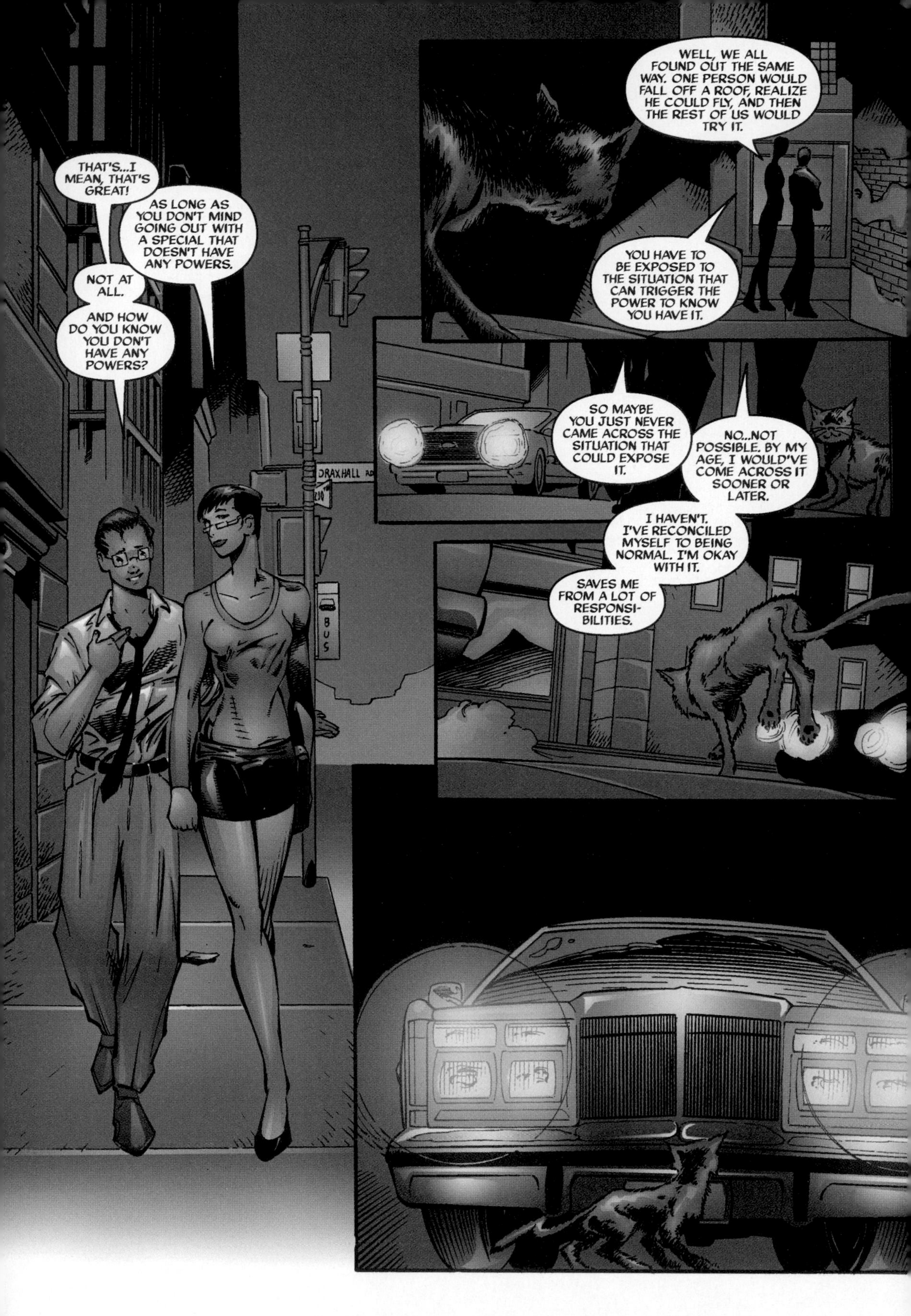
THAT'S...I MEAN, THAT'S GREAT!
AS LONG AS YOU DON'T MIND GOING OUT WITH A SPECIAL THAT DOESN'T HAVE ANY POWERS.
NOT AT ALL.
AND HOW DO YOU KNOW YOU DON'T HAVE ANY POWERS?
DRAXHALL RD
BUS
WELL, WE ALL FOUND OUT THE SAME WAY. ONE PERSON WOULD FALL OFF A ROOF, REALIZE HE COULD FLY, AND THEN THE REST OF US WOULD TRY IT.
YOU HAVE TO BE EXPOSED TO THE SITUATION THAT CAN TRIGGER THE POWER TO KNOW YOU HAVE IT.
SO MAYBE YOU JUST NEVER CAME ACROSS THE SITUATION THAT COULD EXPOSE IT.
NO...NOT POSSIBLE. BY MY AGE, I WOULD'VE COME ACROSS IT SOONER OR LATER.
I HAVEN'T. I'VE RECONCILED MYSELF TO BEING NORMAL. I'M OKAY WITH IT.
SAVES ME FROM A LOT OF RESPONSI-BILITIES.

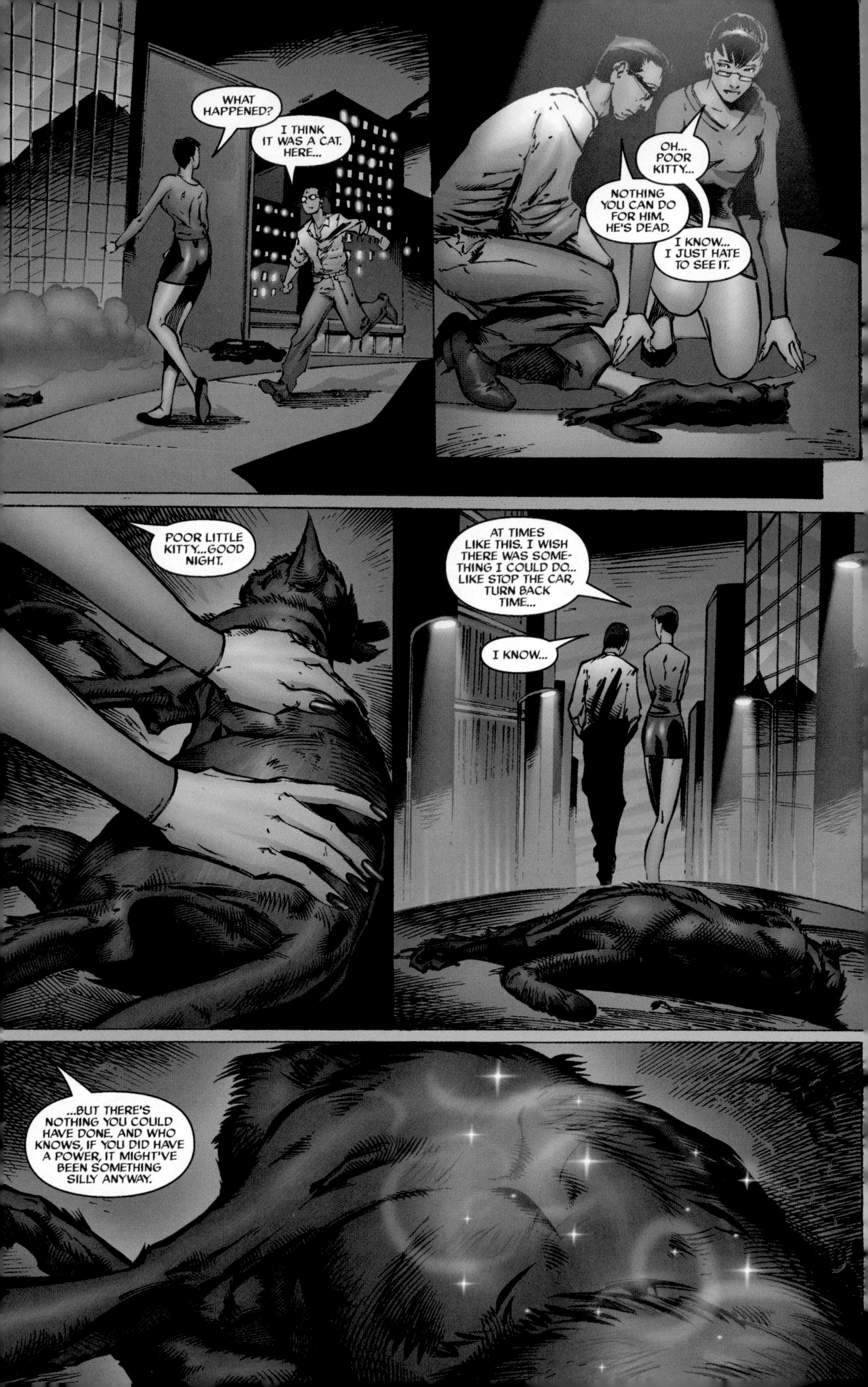
WHAT HAPPENED?
I THINK IT WAS A CAT. HERE...
OH... POOR KITTY...
NOTHING YOU CAN DO FOR HIM. HE'S DEAD.
I KNOW... I JUST HATE TO SEE IT.
POOR LITTLE KITTY...GOOD NIGHT.
AT TIMES LIKE THIS, I WISH THERE WAS SOMETHING I COULD DO... LIKE STOP THE CAR, TURN BACK TIME...
I KNOW...
...BUT THERE'S NOTHING YOU COULD HAVE DONE. AND WHO KNOWS, IF YOU DID HAVE A POWER, IT MIGHT'VE BEEN SOMETHING SILLY ANYWAY.

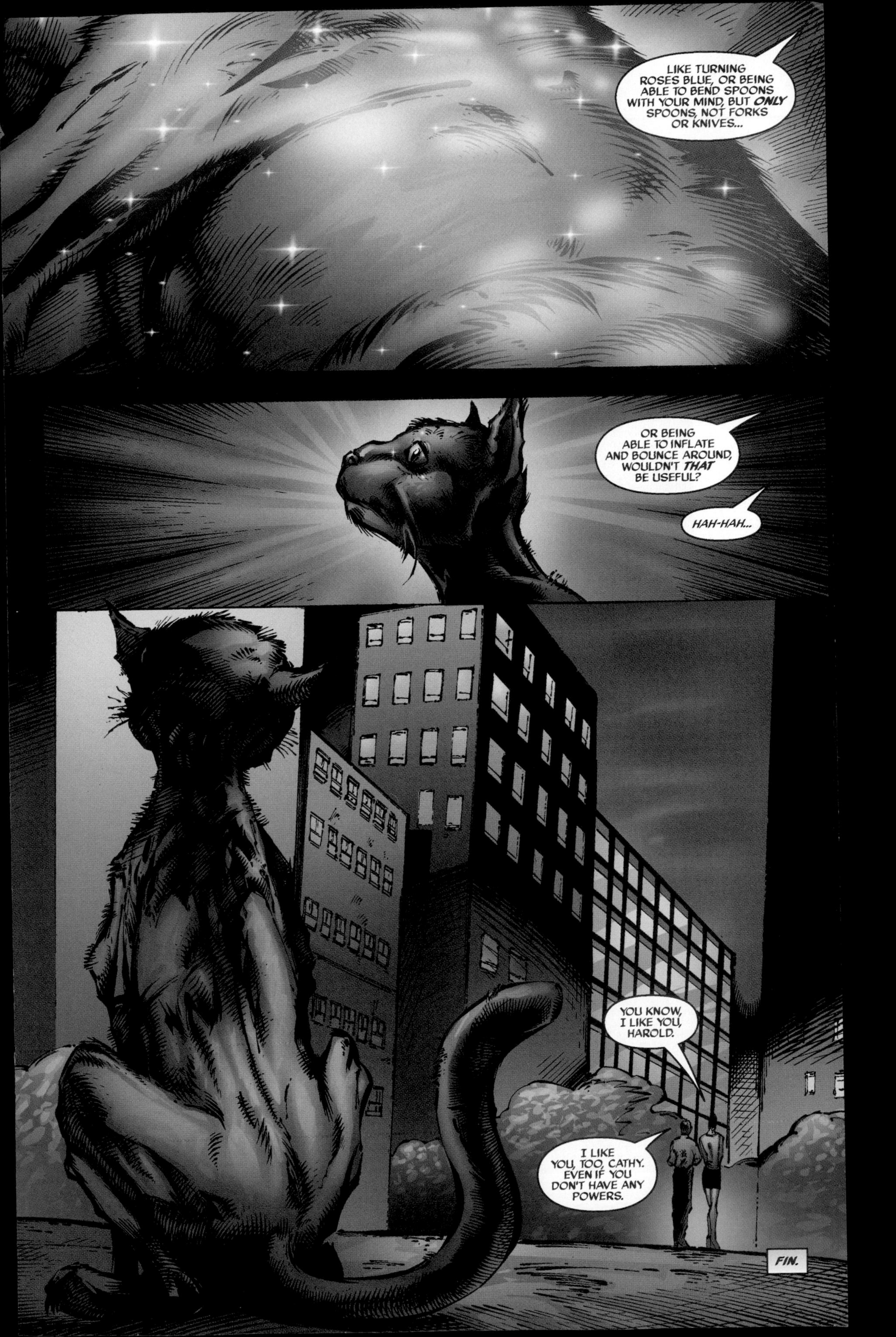
LIKE TURNING ROSES BLUE, OR BEING ABLE TO BEND SPOONS WITH YOUR MIND, BUT ONLY SPOONS, NOT FORKS OR KNIVES...
OR BEING ABLE TO INFLATE AND BOUNCE AROUND, WOULDN'T THAT BE USEFUL?
HAH-HAH...
YOU KNOW, I LIKE YOU, HAROLD.
I LIKE YOU, TOO, CATHY. EVEN IF YOU DON'T HAVE ANY POWERS.
FIN.

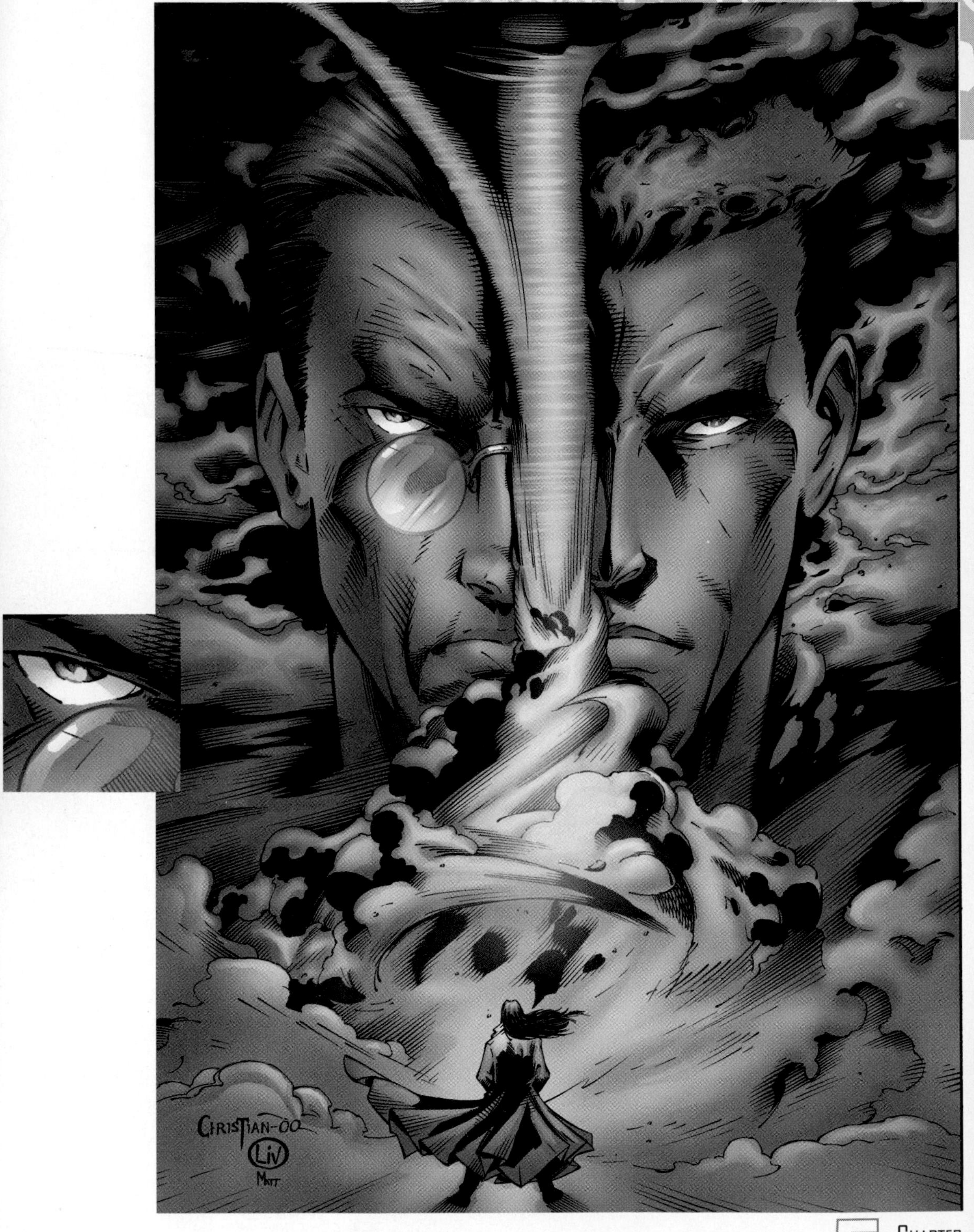
CRISTIAN-00
LIV
MATT

Chapter 5
The World Between

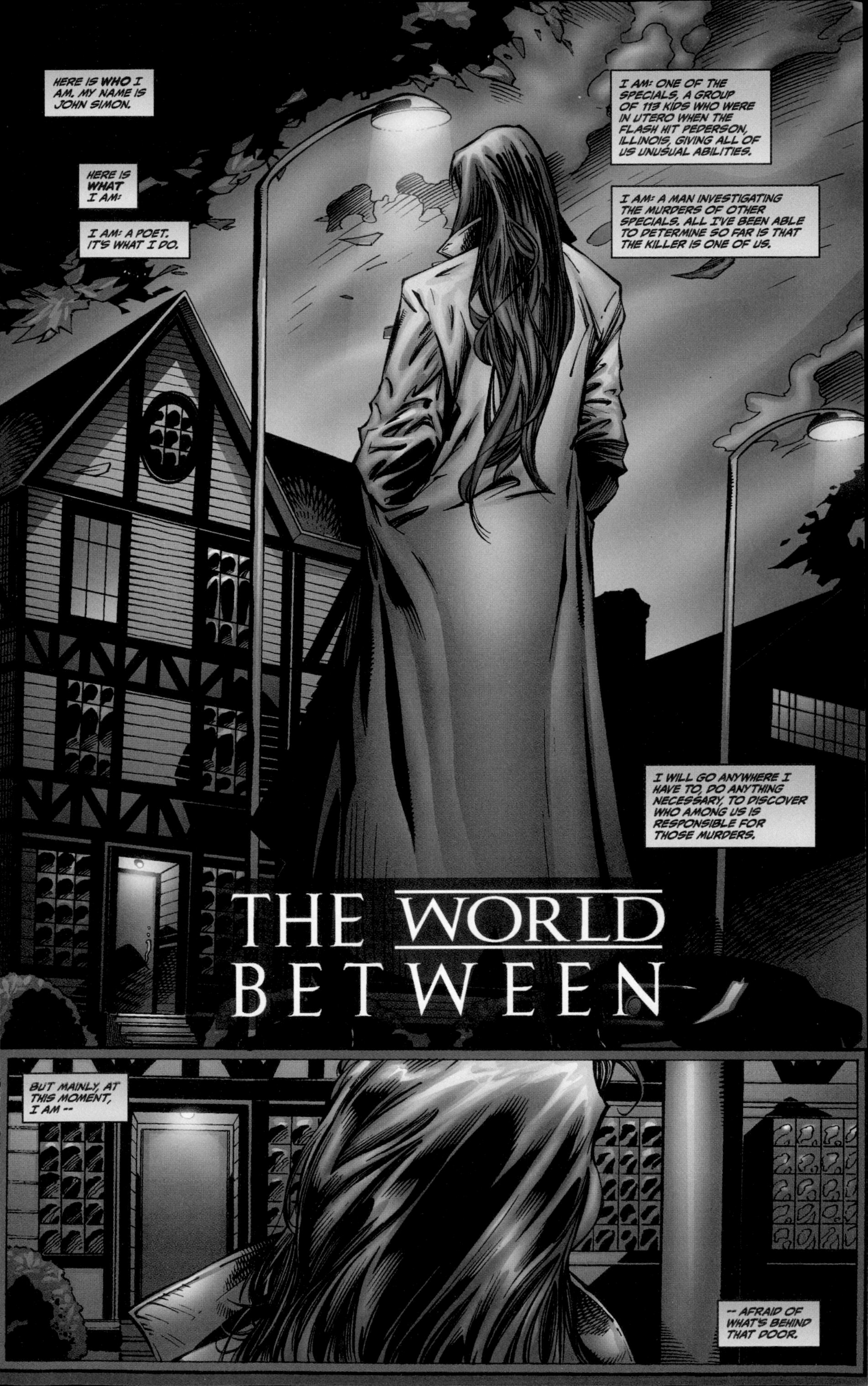
HERE IS WHO I AM. MY NAME IS JOHN SIMON.
HERE IS WHAT I AM:
I AM: A POET. IT'S WHAT I DO.
I AM: ONE OF THE SPECIALS, A GROUP OF 113 KIDS WHO WERE IN UTERO WHEN THE FLASH HIT PEDERSON, ILLINOIS, GIVING ALL OF US UNUSUAL ABILITIES.
I AM: A MAN INVESTIGATING THE MURDERS OF OTHER SPECIALS. ALL I'VE BEEN ABLE TO DETERMINE SO FAR IS THAT THE KILLER IS ONE OF US.
I WILL GO ANYWHERE I HAVE TO, DO ANYTHING NECESSARY, TO DISCOVER WHO AMONG US IS RESPONSIBLE FOR THOSE MURDERS.
THE WORLD BETWEEN
BUT MAINLY, AT THIS MOMENT, I AM --
-- AFRAID OF WHAT'S BEHIND THAT DOOR.

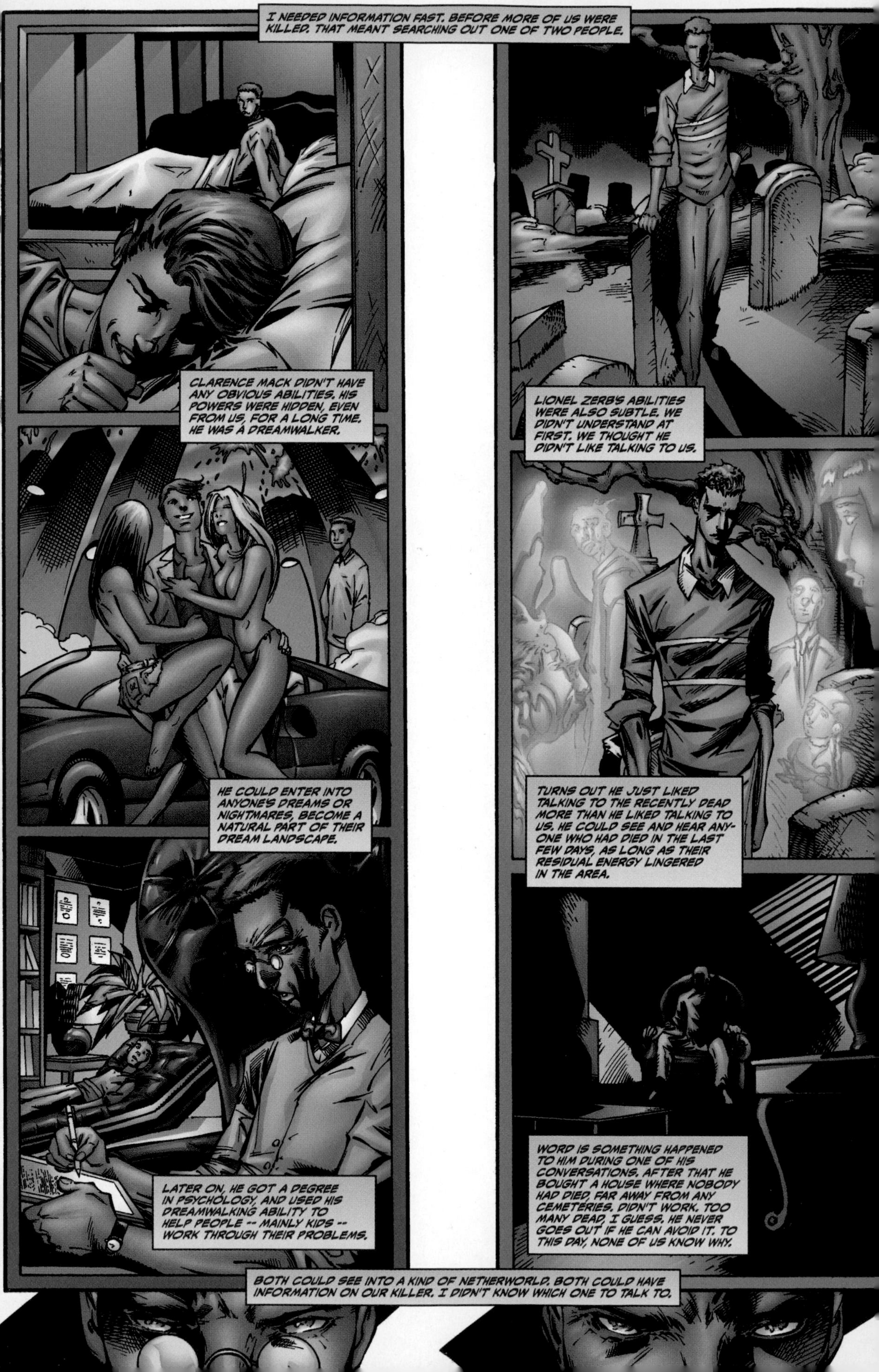
I NEEDED INFORMATION FAST. BEFORE MORE OF US WERE KILLED. THAT MEANT SEARCHING OUT ONE OF TWO PEOPLE.
CLARENCE MACK DIDN'T HAVE ANY OBVIOUS ABILITIES. HIS POWERS WERE HIDDEN, EVEN FROM US, FOR A LONG TIME. HE WAS A DREAMWALKER.
HE COULD ENTER INTO ANYONE'S DREAMS OR NIGHTMARES, BECOME A NATURAL PART OF THEIR DREAM LANDSCAPE.
LATER ON, HE GOT A DEGREE IN PSYCHOLOGY, AND USED HIS DREAMWALKING ABILITY TO HELP PEOPLE -- MAINLY KIDS -- WORK THROUGH THEIR PROBLEMS.
LIONEL ZERB'S ABILITIES WERE ALSO SUBTLE. WE DIDN'T UNDERSTAND AT FIRST. WE THOUGHT HE DIDN'T LIKE TALKING TO US.
TURNS OUT HE JUST LIKED TALKING TO THE RECENTLY DEAD MORE THAN HE LIKED TALKING TO US. HE COULD SEE AND HEAR ANY-ONE WHO HAD DIED IN THE LAST FEW DAYS, AS LONG AS THEIR RESIDUAL ENERGY LINGERED IN THE AREA.
WORD IS SOMETHING HAPPENED TO HIM DURING ONE OF HIS CONVERSATIONS. AFTER THAT HE BOUGHT A HOUSE WHERE NOBODY HAD DIED, FAR AWAY FROM ANY CEMETERIES. DIDN'T WORK. TOO MANY DEAD, I GUESS. HE NEVER GOES OUT IF HE CAN AVOID IT. TO THIS DAY, NONE OF US KNOW WHY.
BOTH COULD SEE INTO A KIND OF NETHERWORLD. BOTH COULD HAVE INFORMATION ON OUR KILLER. I DIDN'T KNOW WHICH ONE TO TALK TO.

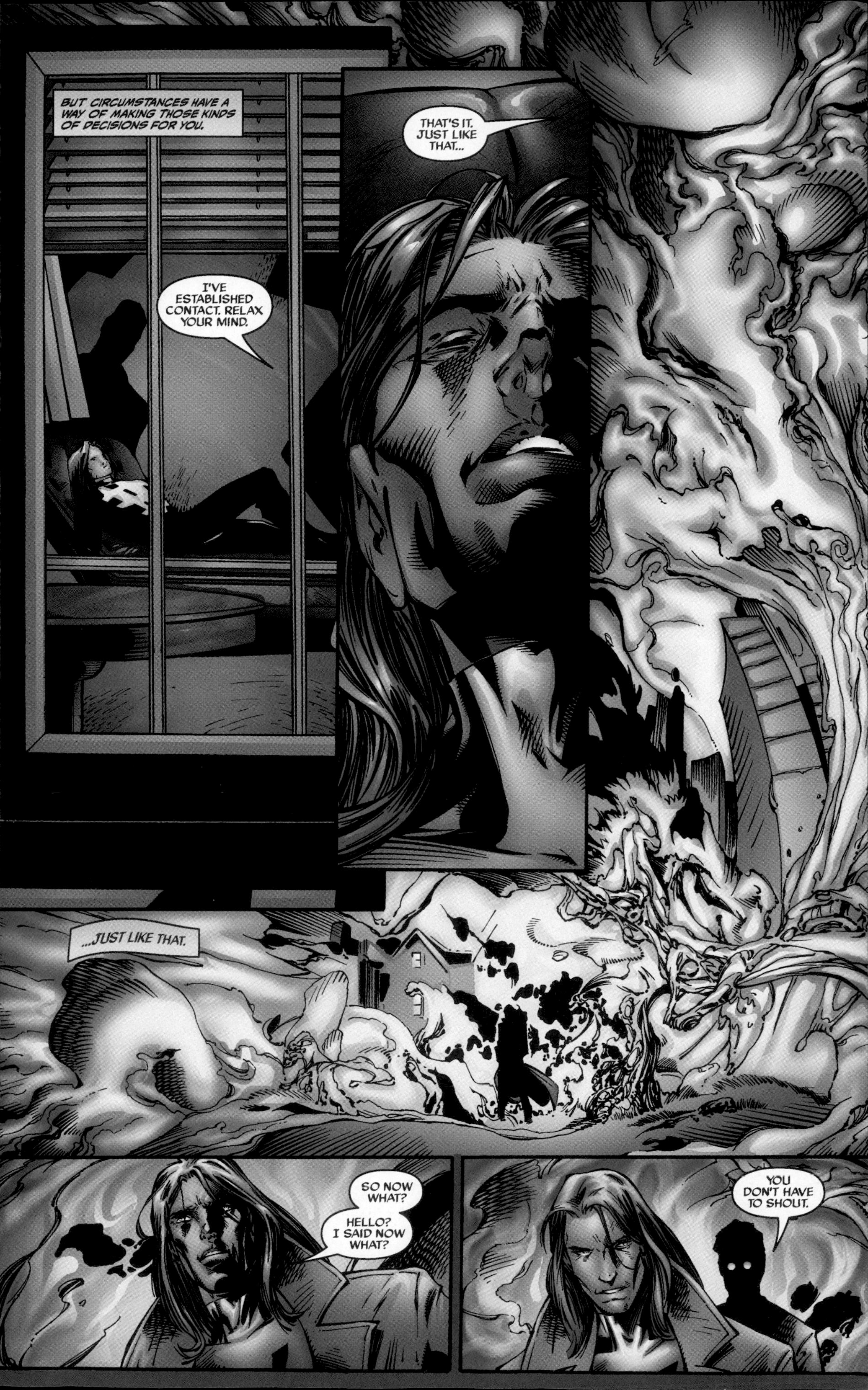
BUT CIRCUMSTANCES HAVE A WAY OF MAKING THOSE KINDS OF DECISIONS FOR YOU.
I'VE ESTABLISHED CONTACT. RELAX YOUR MIND.
THAT'S IT. JUST LIKE THAT...
...JUST LIKE THAT.
SO NOW WHAT?
HELLO? I SAID NOW WHAT?
YOU DON'T HAVE TO SHOUT.

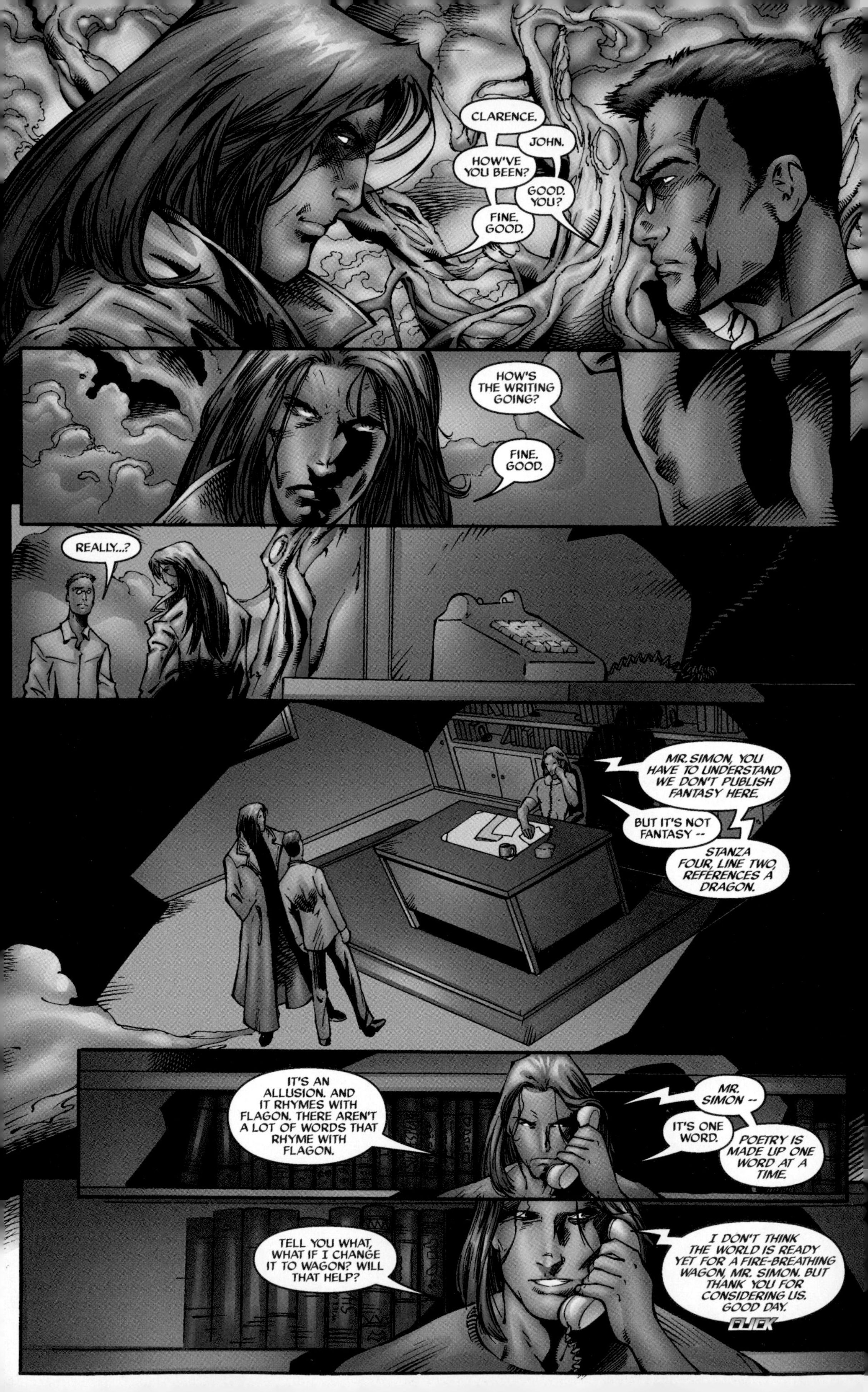
CLARENCE.
JOHN.
HOW'VE YOU BEEN?
GOOD. YOU?
FINE. GOOD.
HOW'S THE WRITING GOING?
FINE. GOOD.
REALLY...?
MR. SIMON, YOU HAVE TO UNDERSTAND WE DON'T PUBLISH FANTASY HERE.
BUT IT'S NOT FANTASY --
STANZA FOUR, LINE TWO, REFERENCES A DRAGON.
IT'S AN ALLUSION. AND IT RHYMES WITH FLAGON. THERE AREN'T A LOT OF WORDS THAT RHYME WITH FLAGON.
MR. SIMON --
IT'S ONE WORD.
POETRY IS MADE UP ONE WORD AT A TIME.
TELL YOU WHAT, WHAT IF I CHANGE IT TO WAGON? WILL THAT HELP?
I DON'T THINK THE WORLD IS READY YET FOR A FIRE-BREATHING WAGON, MR. SIMON. BUT THANK YOU FOR CONSIDERING US. GOOD DAY.
CLICK

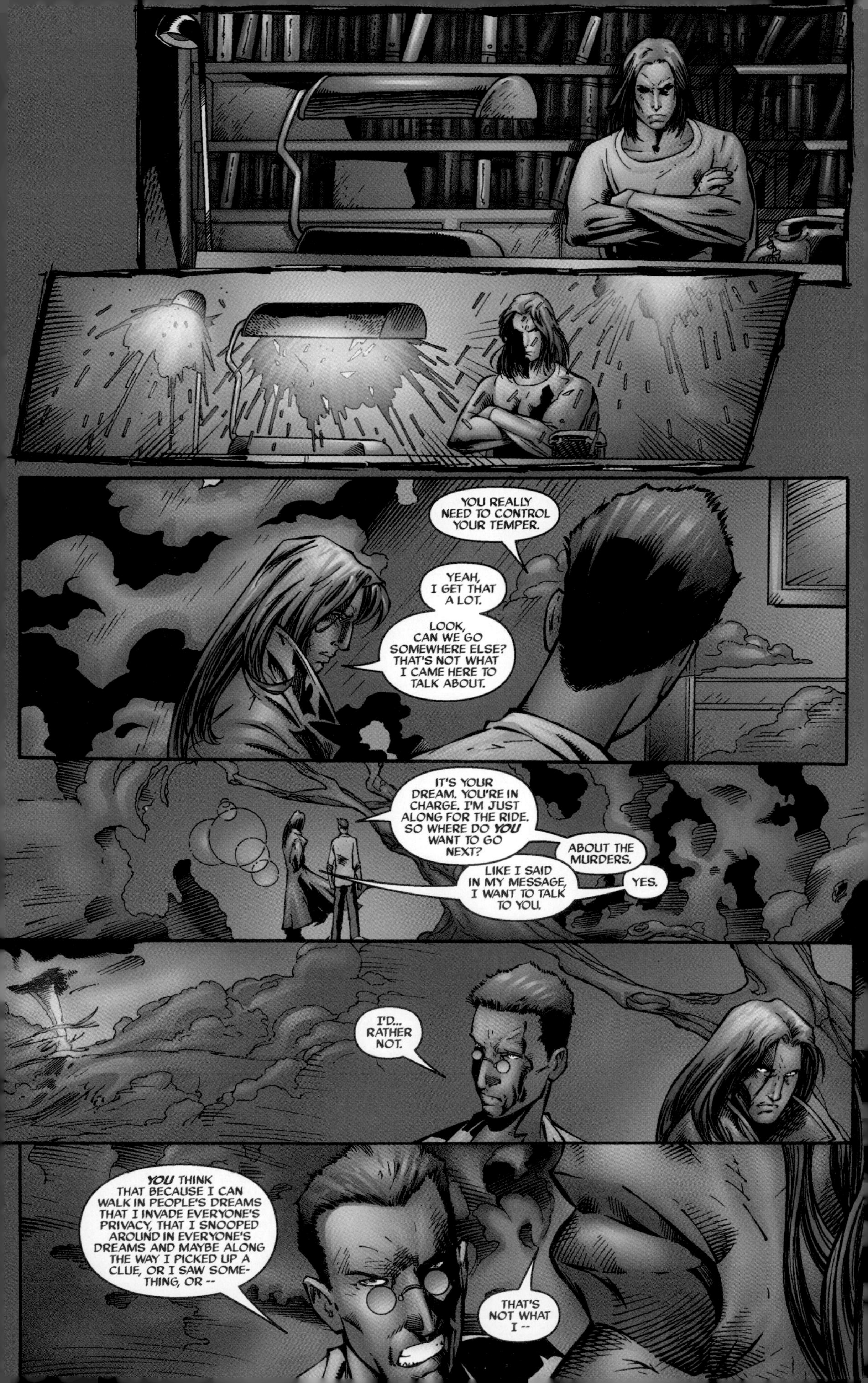

YOU REALLY NEED TO CONTROL YOUR TEMPER.
YEAH, I GET THAT A LOT.
LOOK, CAN WE GO SOMEWHERE ELSE? THAT'S NOT WHAT I CAME HERE TO TALK ABOUT.
IT'S YOUR DREAM. YOU'RE IN CHARGE. I'M JUST ALONG FOR THE RIDE. SO WHERE DO *YOU* WANT TO GO NEXT?
LIKE I SAID IN MY MESSAGE, I WANT TO TALK TO YOU.
YES.
ABOUT THE MURDERS.
I'D... RATHER NOT.
YOU THINK THAT BECAUSE I CAN WALK IN PEOPLE'S DREAMS THAT I INVADE EVERYONE'S PRIVACY, THAT I SNOOPED AROUND IN EVERYONE'S DREAMS AND MAYBE ALONG THE WAY I PICKED UP A CLUE, OR I SAW SOME-THING, OR --
THAT'S NOT WHAT I --

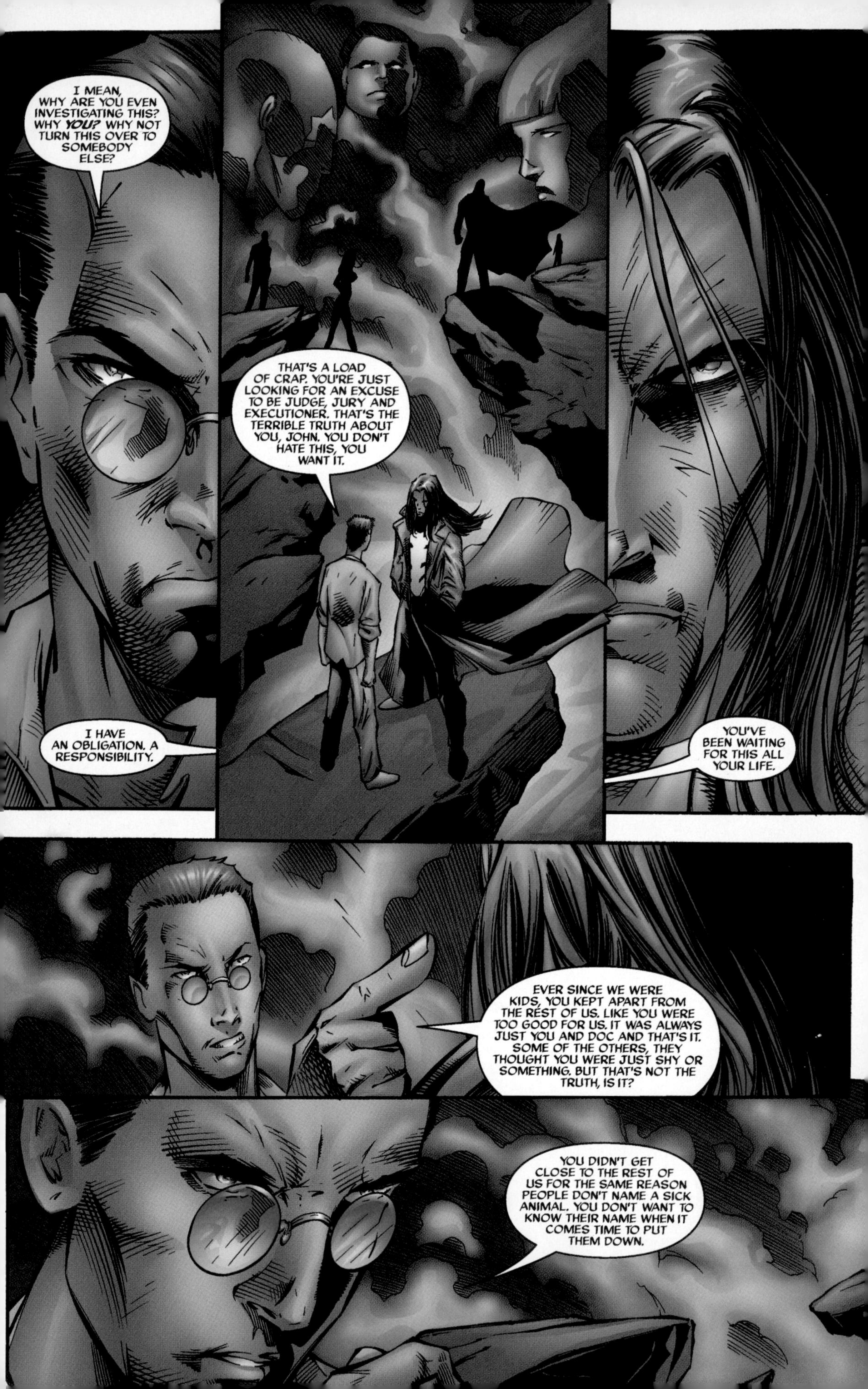
I MEAN, WHY ARE YOU EVEN INVESTIGATING THIS? WHY *YOU?* WHY NOT TURN THIS OVER TO SOMEBODY ELSE?
I HAVE AN OBLIGATION. A RESPONSIBILITY.
THAT'S A LOAD OF CRAP. YOU'RE JUST LOOKING FOR AN EXCUSE TO BE JUDGE, JURY AND EXECUTIONER. THAT'S THE TERRIBLE TRUTH ABOUT YOU, JOHN. YOU DON'T HATE THIS, YOU WANT IT.
YOU'VE BEEN WAITING FOR THIS ALL YOUR LIFE.
EVER SINCE WE WERE KIDS, YOU KEPT APART FROM THE REST OF US. LIKE YOU WERE TOO GOOD FOR US. IT WAS ALWAYS JUST YOU AND DOC AND THAT'S IT. SOME OF THE OTHERS, THEY THOUGHT YOU WERE JUST SHY OR SOMETHING. BUT THAT'S NOT THE TRUTH, IS IT?
YOU DIDN'T GET CLOSE TO THE REST OF US FOR THE SAME REASON PEOPLE DON'T NAME A SICK ANIMAL. YOU DON'T WANT TO KNOW THEIR NAME WHEN IT COMES TIME TO PUT THEM DOWN.

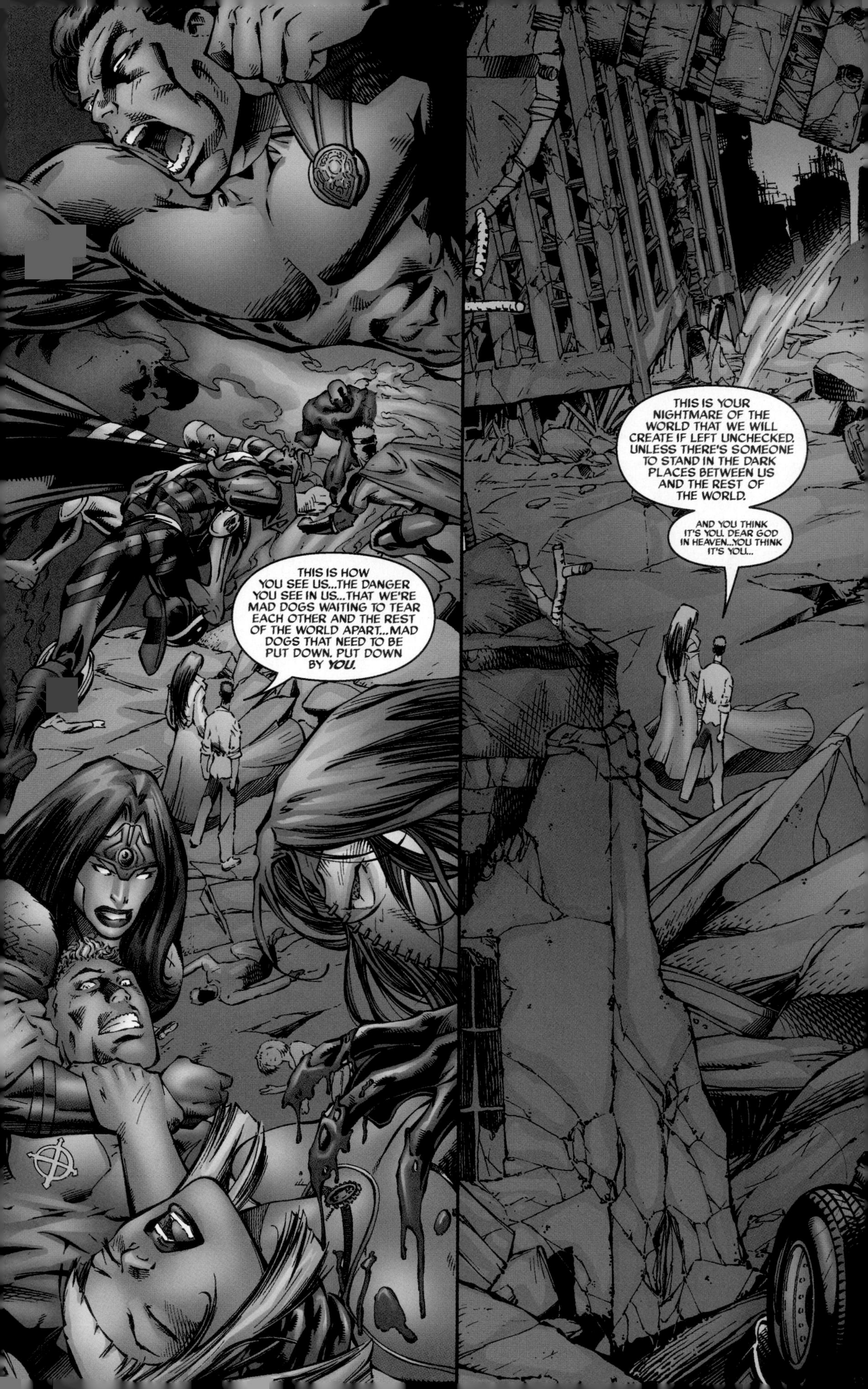
THIS IS HOW YOU SEE US...THE DANGER YOU SEE IN US...THAT WE'RE MAD DOGS WAITING TO TEAR EACH OTHER AND THE REST OF THE WORLD APART...MAD DOGS THAT NEED TO BE PUT DOWN. PUT DOWN BY *YOU.*
THIS IS YOUR NIGHTMARE OF THE WORLD THAT WE WILL CREATE IF LEFT UNCHECKED. UNLESS THERE'S SOMEONE TO STAND IN THE DARK PLACES BETWEEN US AND THE REST OF THE WORLD.
AND YOU THINK IT'S YOU. DEAR GOD IN HEAVEN...YOU THINK IT'S YOU...

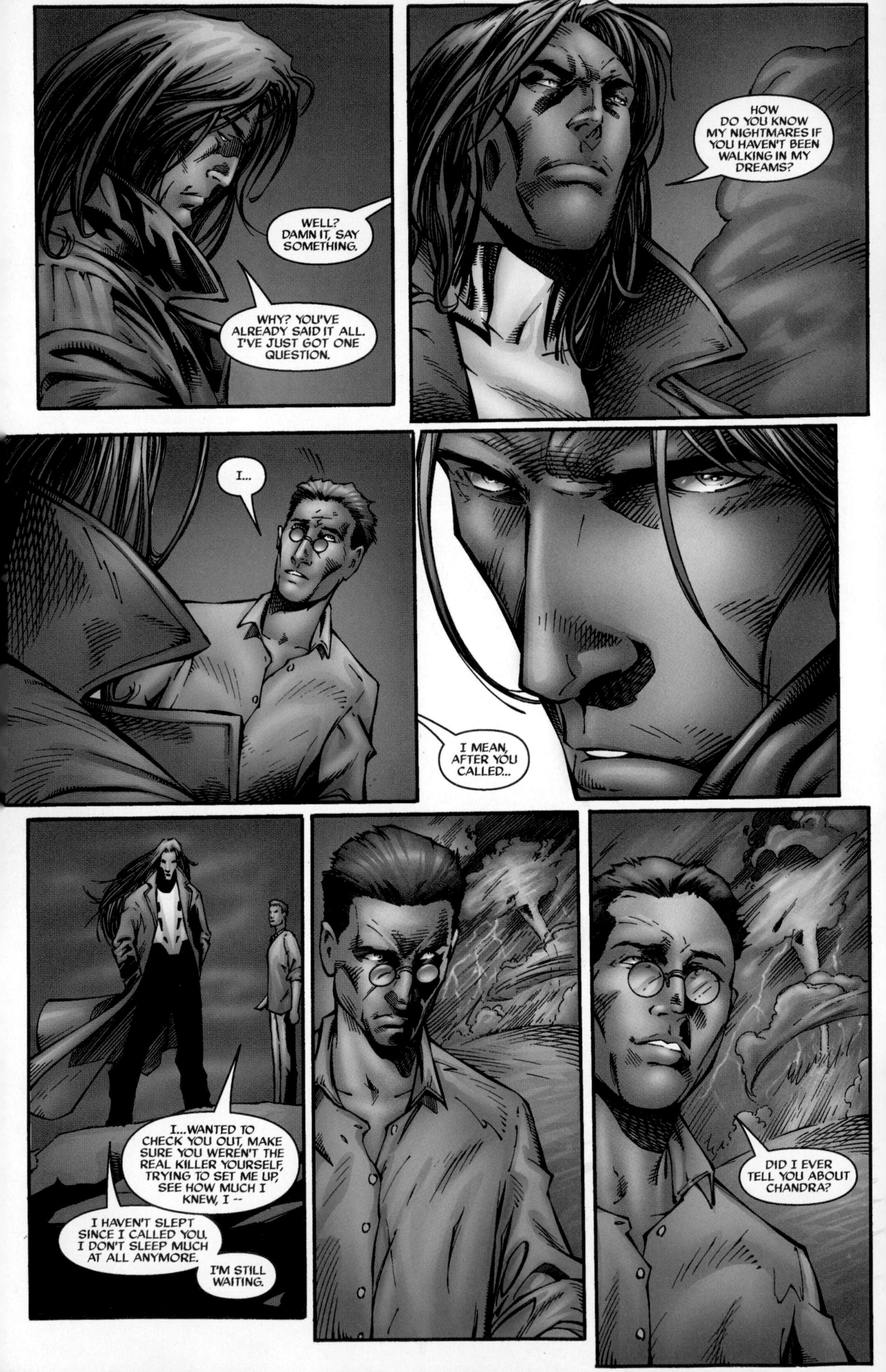
WELL? DAMN IT, SAY SOMETHING.
WHY? YOU'VE ALREADY SAID IT ALL. I'VE JUST GOT ONE QUESTION.
HOW DO YOU KNOW MY NIGHTMARES IF YOU HAVEN'T BEEN WALKING IN MY DREAMS?
I...
I MEAN, AFTER YOU CALLED...
I...WANTED TO CHECK YOU OUT, MAKE SURE YOU WEREN'T THE REAL KILLER YOURSELF, TRYING TO SET ME UP, SEE HOW MUCH I KNEW, I --
I HAVEN'T SLEPT SINCE I CALLED YOU. I DON'T SLEEP MUCH AT ALL ANYMORE.
I'M STILL WAITING.
DID I EVER TELL YOU ABOUT CHANDRA?

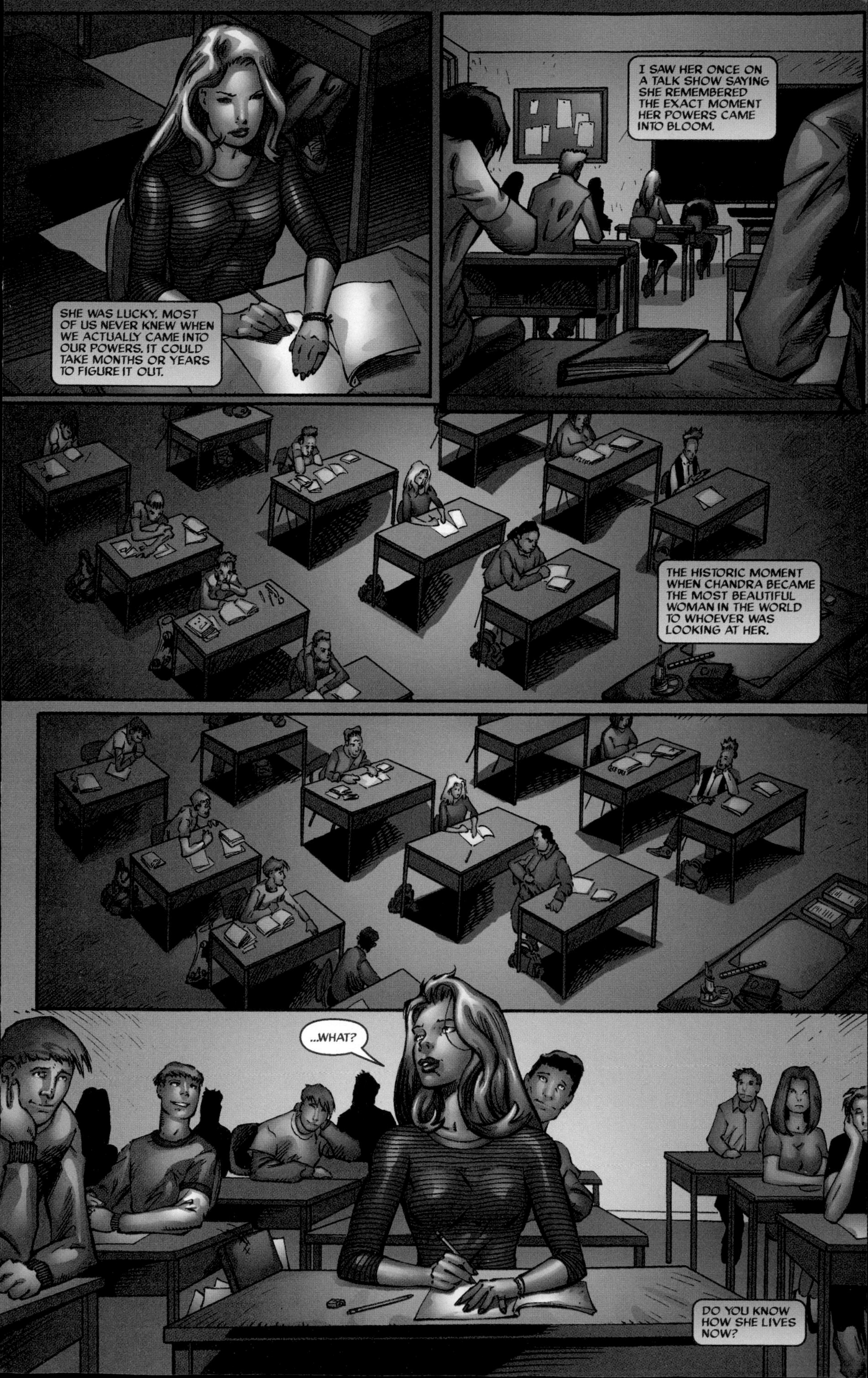
SHE WAS LUCKY. MOST OF US NEVER KNEW WHEN WE ACTUALLY CAME INTO OUR POWERS. IT COULD TAKE MONTHS OR YEARS TO FIGURE IT OUT.
I SAW HER ONCE ON A TALK SHOW SAYING SHE REMEMBERED THE EXACT MOMENT HER POWERS CAME INTO BLOOM.
THE HISTORIC MOMENT WHEN CHANDRA BECAME THE MOST BEAUTIFUL WOMAN IN THE WORLD TO WHOEVER WAS LOOKING AT HER.
...WHAT?
DO YOU KNOW HOW SHE LIVES NOW?

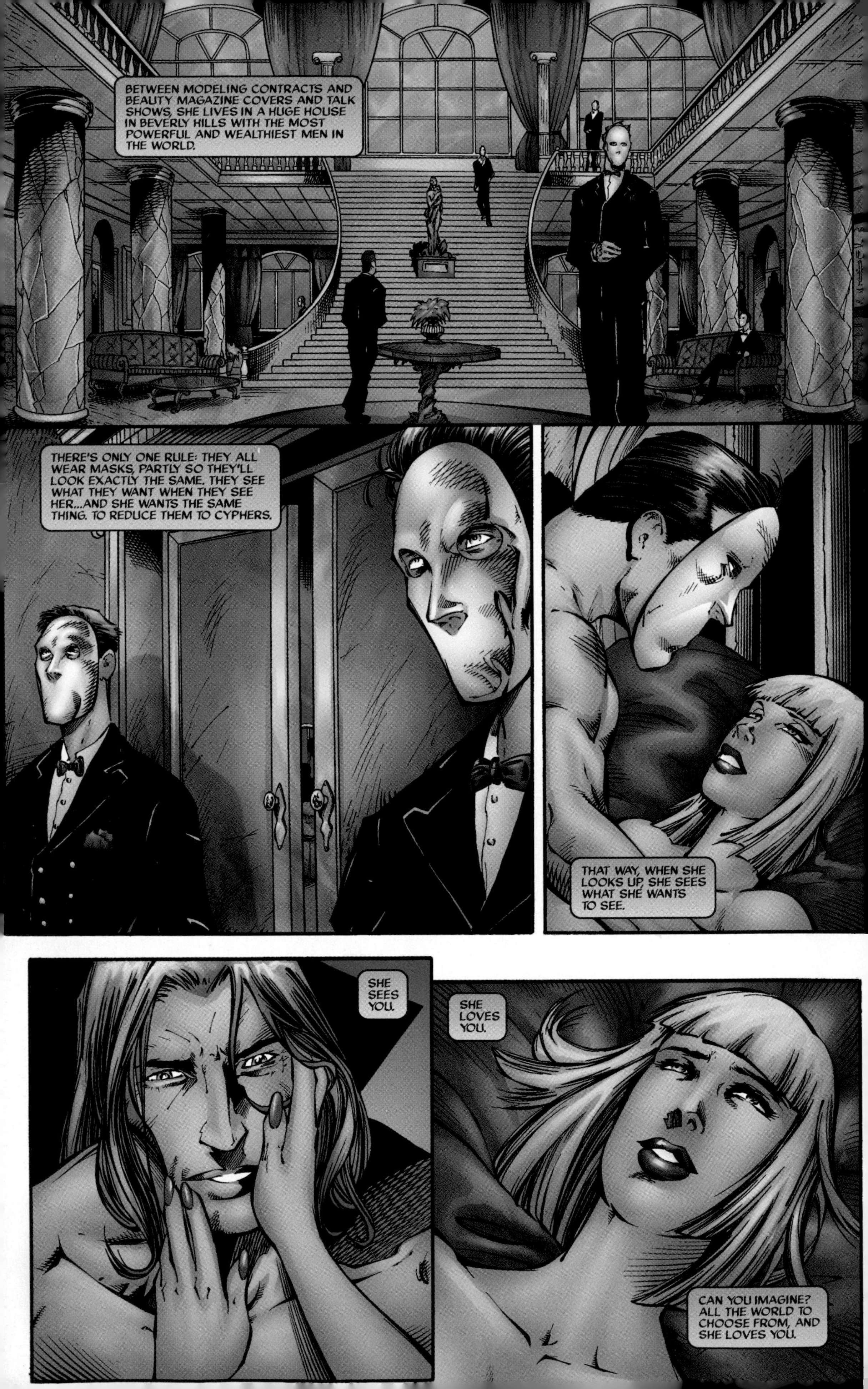
BETWEEN MODELING CONTRACTS AND BEAUTY MAGAZINE COVERS AND TALK SHOWS, SHE LIVES IN A HUGE HOUSE IN BEVERLY HILLS WITH THE MOST POWERFUL AND WEALTHIEST MEN IN THE WORLD.
THERE'S ONLY ONE RULE: THEY ALL WEAR MASKS, PARTLY SO THEY'LL LOOK EXACTLY THE SAME. THEY SEE WHAT THEY WANT WHEN THEY SEE HER...AND SHE WANTS THE SAME THING. TO REDUCE THEM TO CYPHERS.
THAT WAY, WHEN SHE LOOKS UP, SHE SEES WHAT SHE WANTS TO SEE.
SHE SEES YOU.
SHE LOVES YOU.
CAN YOU IMAGINE? ALL THE WORLD TO CHOOSE FROM, AND SHE LOVES YOU.

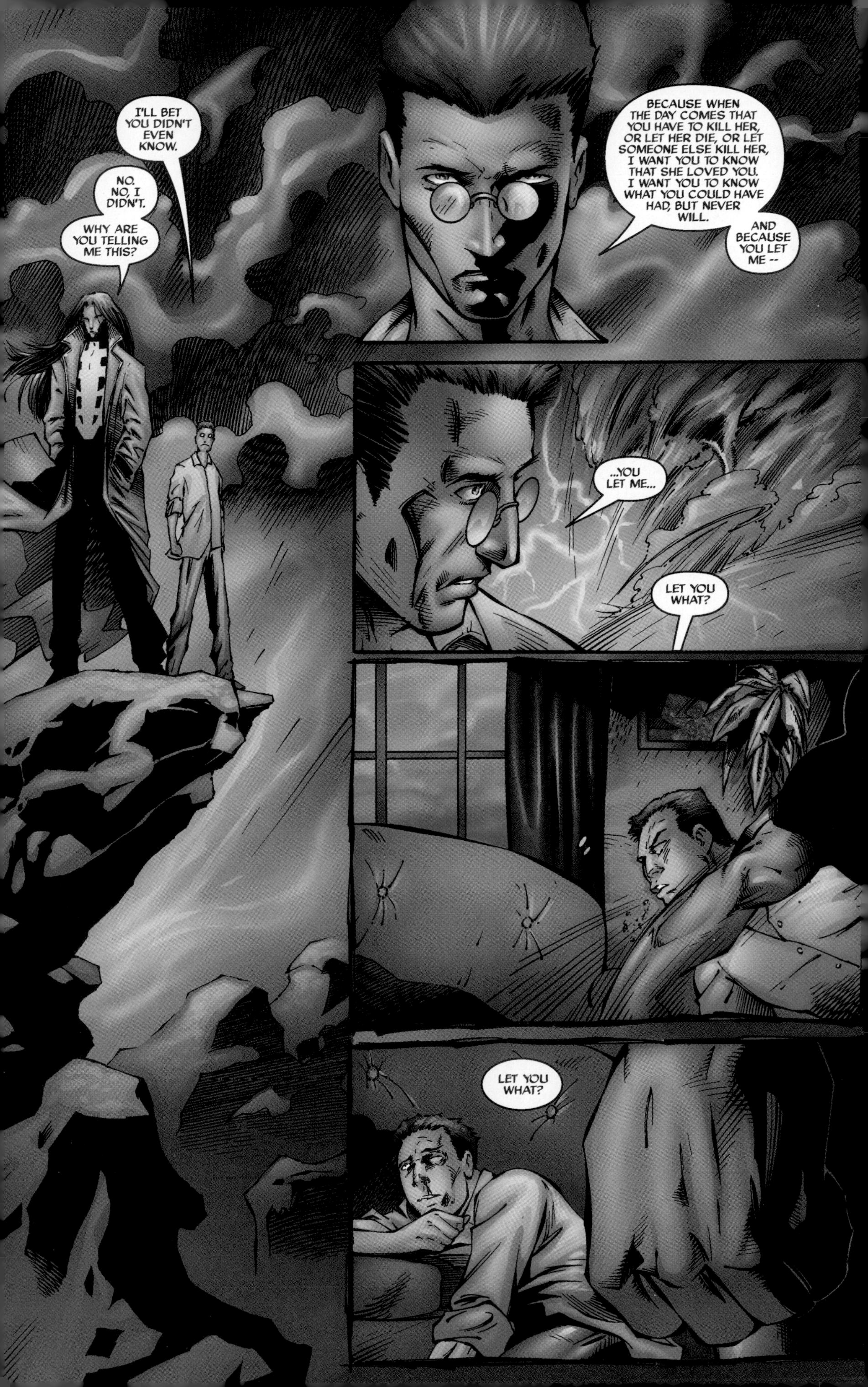
I'LL BET YOU DIDN'T EVEN KNOW.
NO. NO, I DIDN'T.
WHY ARE YOU TELLING ME THIS?
BECAUSE WHEN THE DAY COMES THAT YOU HAVE TO KILL HER, OR LET HER DIE, OR LET SOMEONE ELSE KILL HER, I WANT YOU TO KNOW THAT SHE LOVED YOU. I WANT YOU TO KNOW WHAT YOU COULD HAVE HAD, BUT NEVER WILL.
AND BECAUSE YOU LET ME --
...YOU LET ME...
LET YOU WHAT?
LET YOU WHAT?

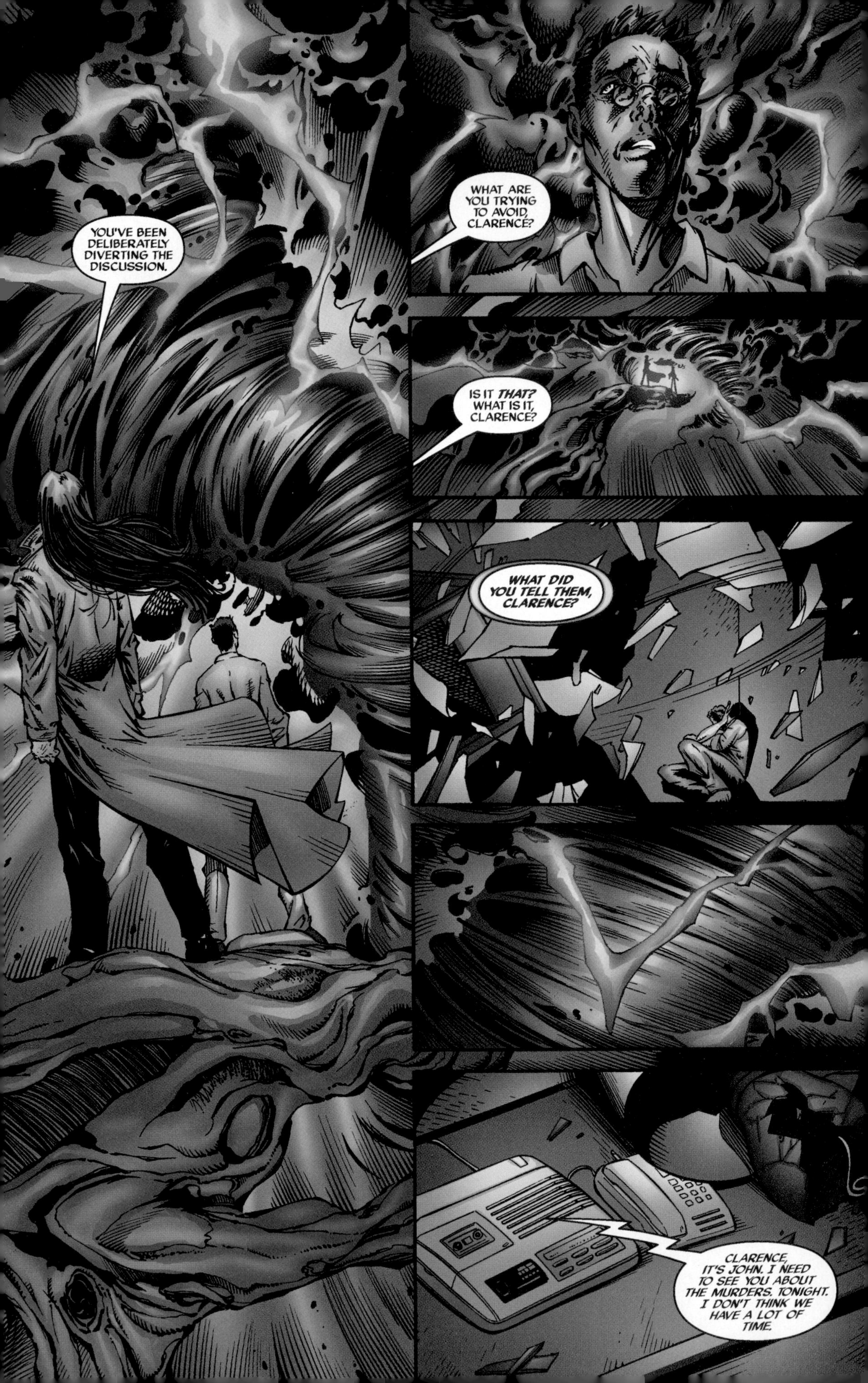
YOU'VE BEEN DELIBERATELY DIVERTING THE DISCUSSION.
WHAT ARE YOU TRYING TO AVOID, CLARENCE?
IS IT *THAT?* WHAT IS IT, CLARENCE?
WHAT DID YOU TELL THEM, CLARENCE?
CLARENCE, IT'S JOHN. I NEED TO SEE YOU ABOUT THE MURDERS. TONIGHT. I DON'T THINK WE HAVE A LOT OF TIME.

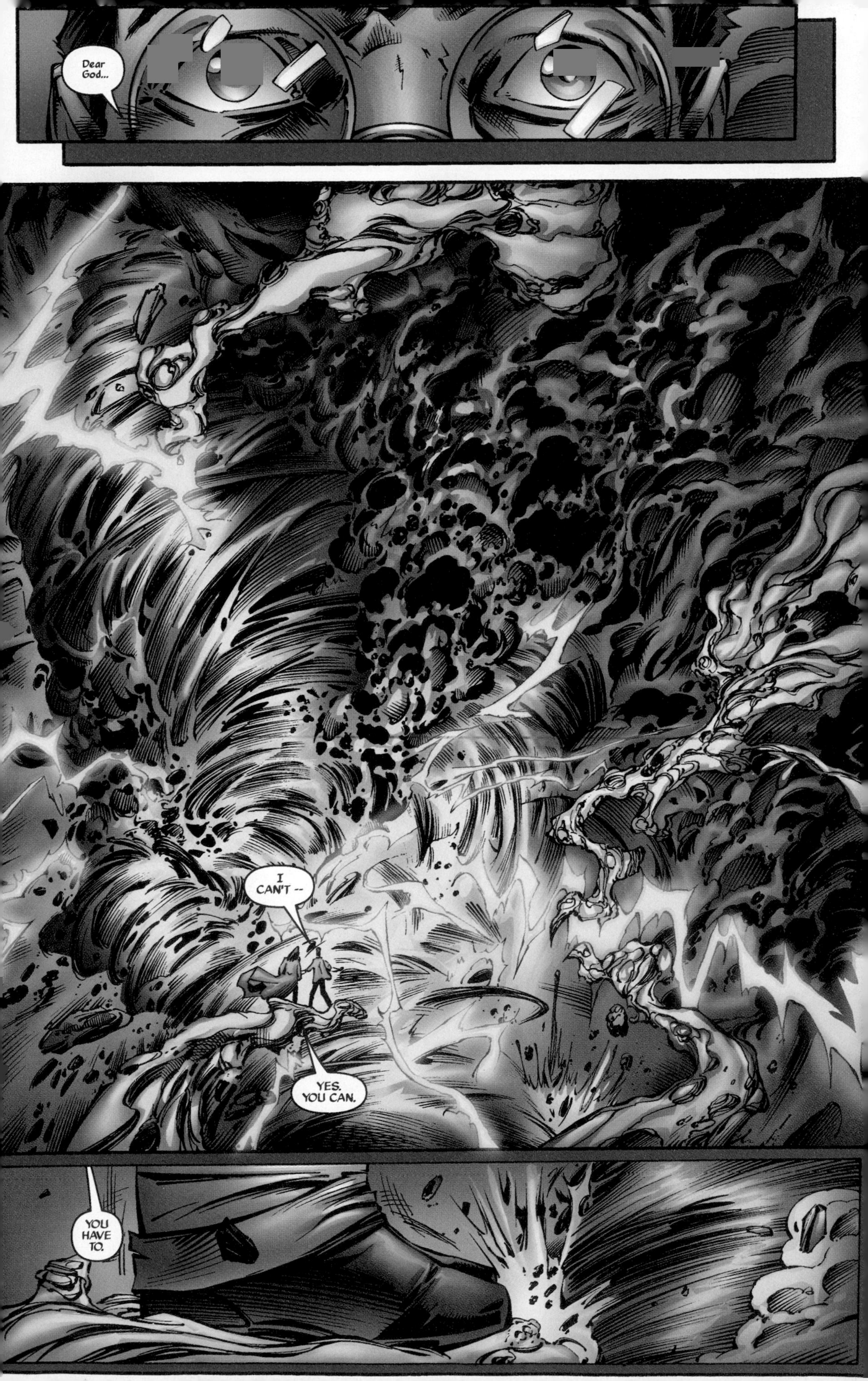
Dear God...
I CAN'T --
YES. YOU CAN.
YOU HAVE TO.

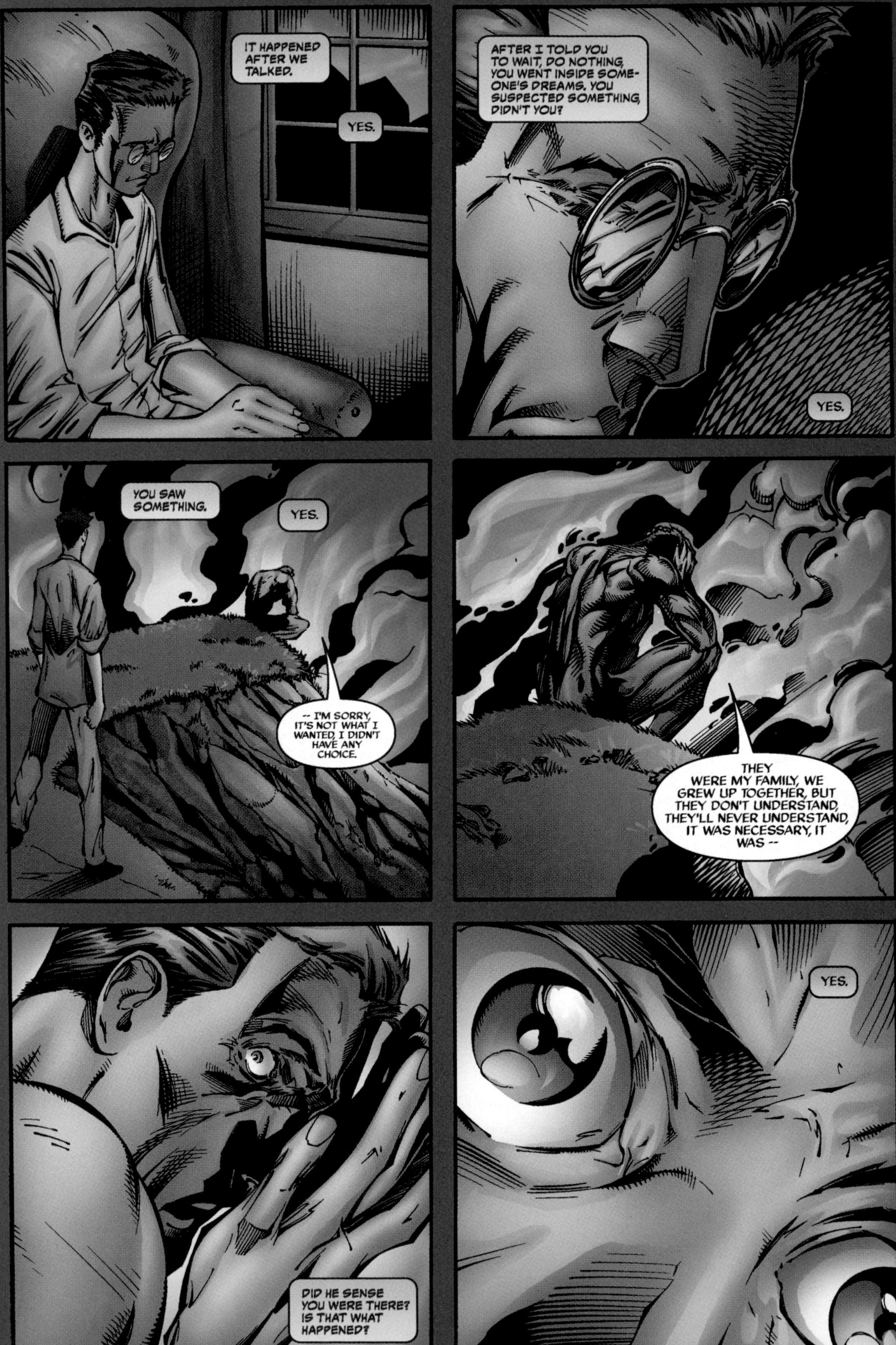
IT HAPPENED AFTER WE TALKED.
YES.
AFTER I TOLD YOU TO WAIT, DO NOTHING, YOU WENT INSIDE SOMEONE'S DREAMS. YOU SUSPECTED SOMETHING, DIDN'T YOU?
YES.
YOU SAW SOMETHING.
YES.
-- I'M SORRY, IT'S NOT WHAT I WANTED, I DIDN'T HAVE ANY CHOICE.
THEY WERE MY FAMILY, WE GREW UP TOGETHER, BUT THEY DON'T UNDERSTAND, THEY'LL NEVER UNDERSTAND, IT WAS NECESSARY, IT WAS --
DID HE SENSE YOU WERE THERE? IS THAT WHAT HAPPENED?
YES.

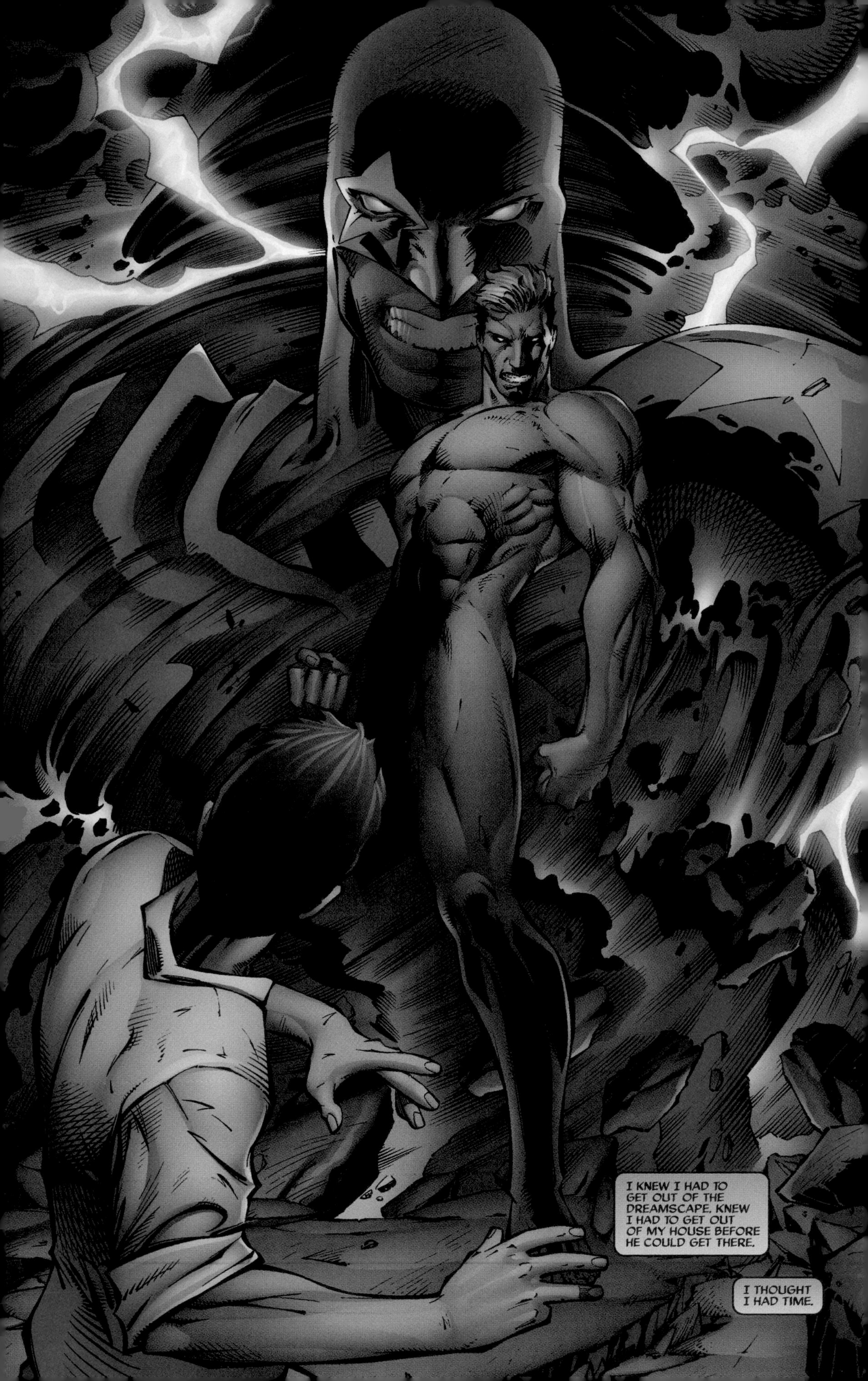
I KNEW I HAD TO GET OUT OF THE DREAMSCAPE. KNEW I HAD TO GET OUT OF MY HOUSE BEFORE HE COULD GET THERE.
I THOUGHT I HAD TIME.

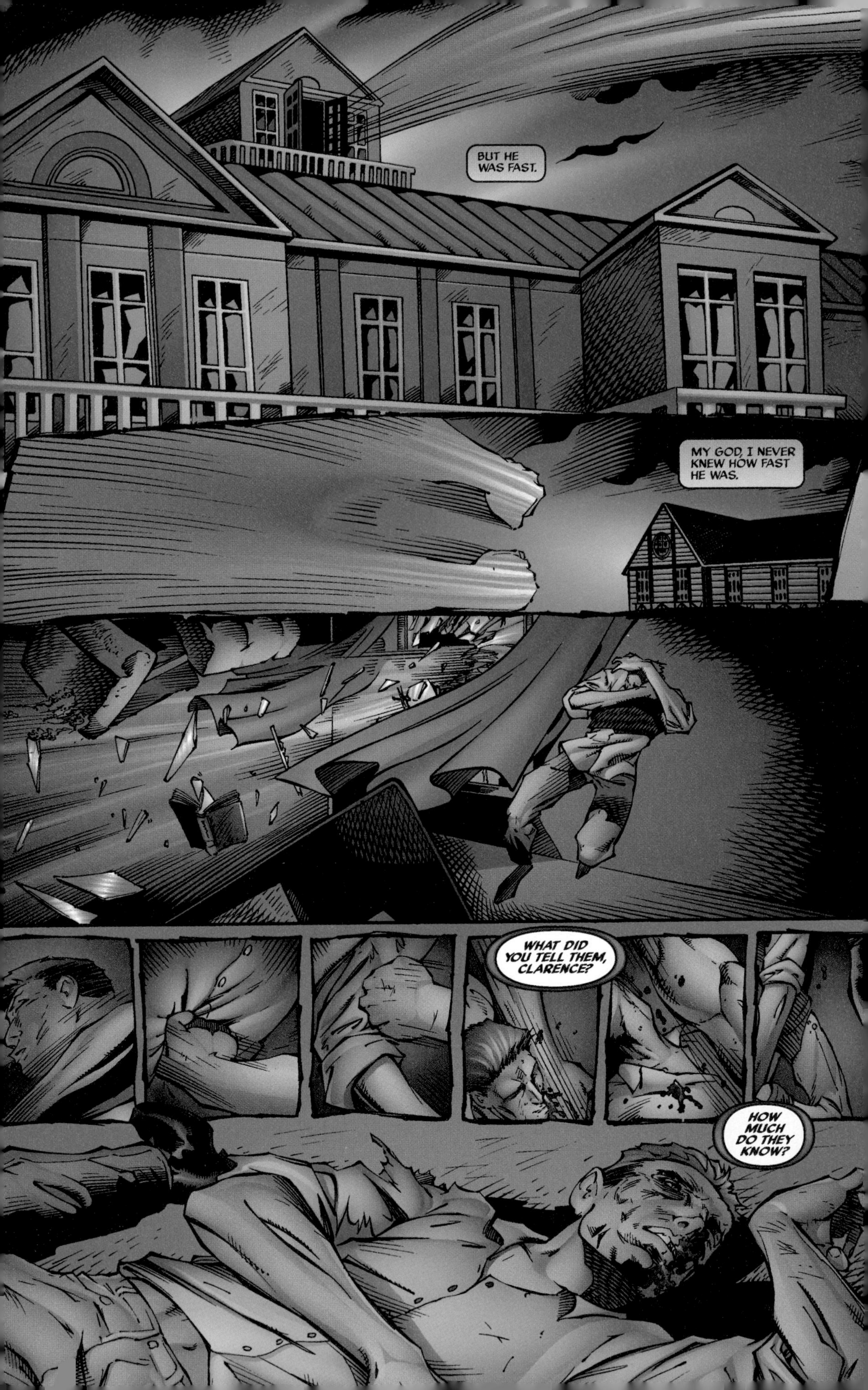
BUT HE WAS FAST.
MY GOD, I NEVER KNEW HOW FAST HE WAS.
WHAT DID YOU TELL THEM, CLARENCE?
HOW MUCH DO THEY KNOW?

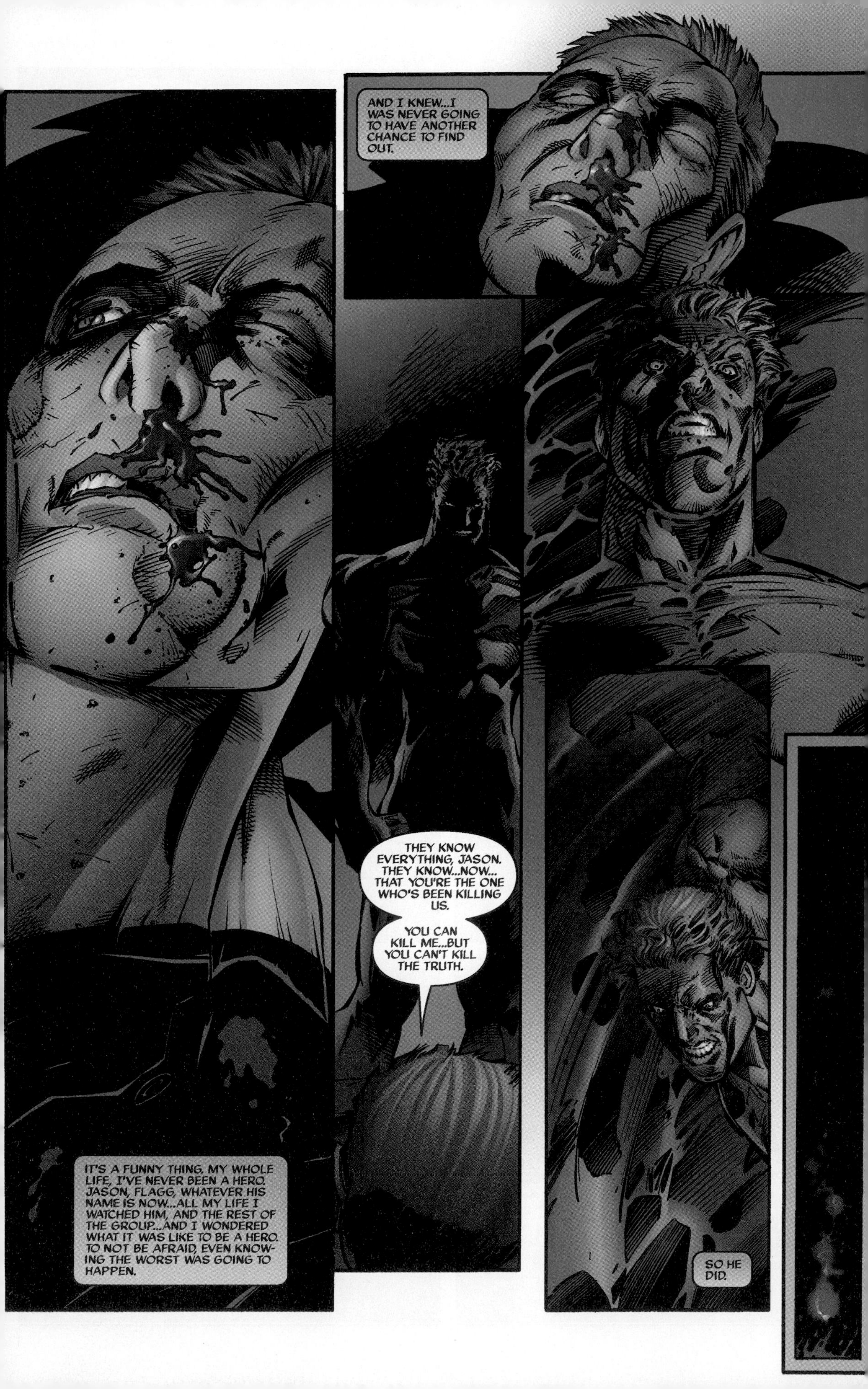
AND I KNEW...I WAS NEVER GOING TO HAVE ANOTHER CHANCE TO FIND OUT.
IT'S A FUNNY THING. MY WHOLE LIFE, I'VE NEVER BEEN A HERO. JASON, FLAGG, WHATEVER HIS NAME IS NOW...ALL MY LIFE I WATCHED HIM, AND THE REST OF THE GROUP...AND I WONDERED WHAT IT WAS LIKE TO BE A HERO. TO NOT BE AFRAID, EVEN KNOWING THE WORST WAS GOING TO HAPPEN.
THEY KNOW EVERYTHING, JASON. THEY KNOW...NOW... THAT YOU'RE THE ONE WHO'S BEEN KILLING US.
YOU CAN KILL ME...BUT YOU CAN'T KILL THE TRUTH.
SO HE DID.

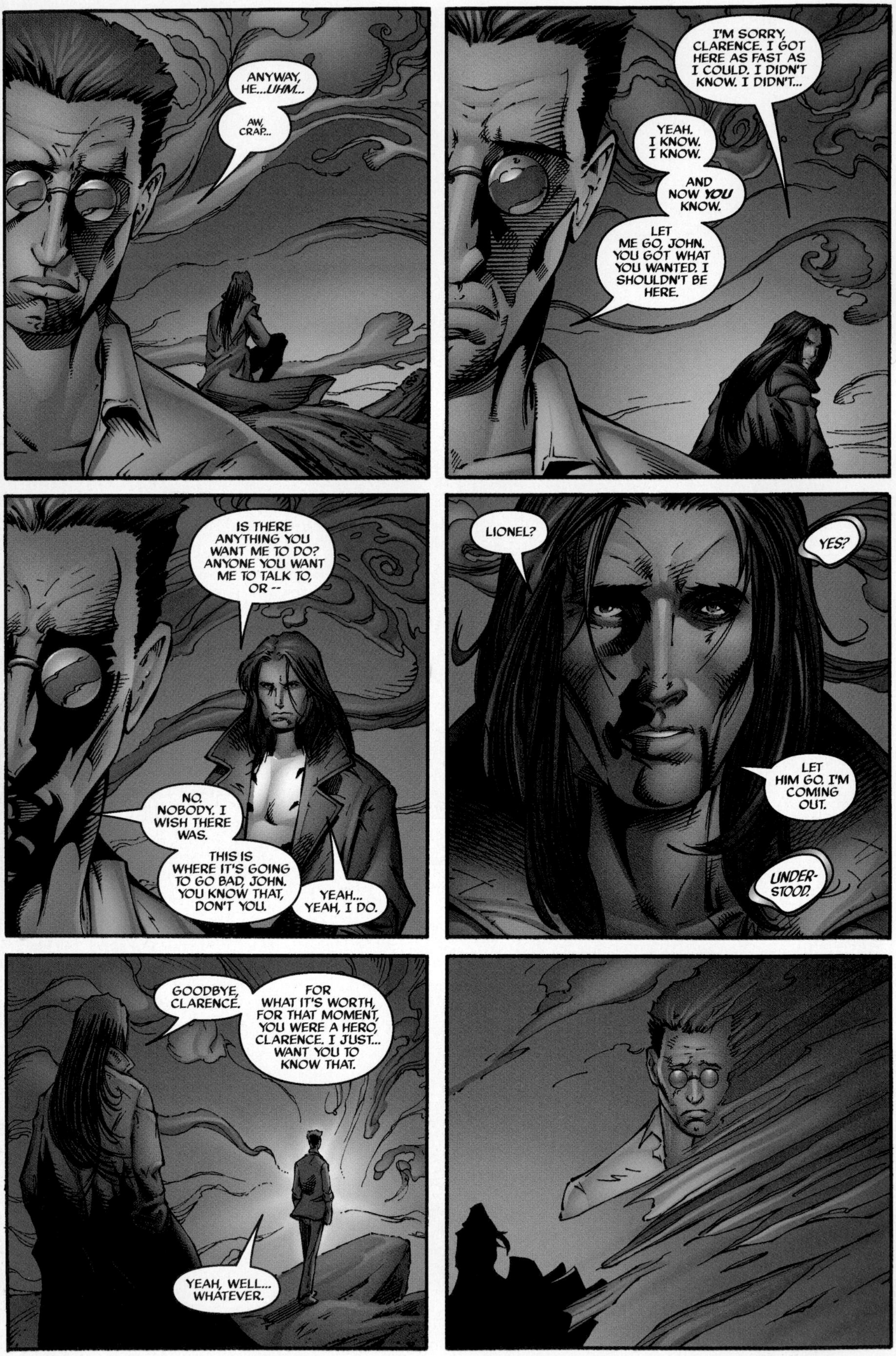
ANYWAY, HE...UHM...
AW, CRAP...
I'M SORRY, CLARENCE. I GOT HERE AS FAST AS I COULD. I DIDN'T KNOW. I DIDN'T...
YEAH. I KNOW. I KNOW.
AND NOW YOU KNOW.
LET ME GO, JOHN. YOU GOT WHAT YOU WANTED. I SHOULDN'T BE HERE.
IS THERE ANYTHING YOU WANT ME TO DO? ANYONE YOU WANT ME TO TALK TO, OR --
NO. NOBODY. I WISH THERE WAS.
THIS IS WHERE IT'S GOING TO GO BAD, JOHN. YOU KNOW THAT, DON'T YOU.
YEAH... YEAH, I DO.
LIONEL?
YES?
LET HIM GO. I'M COMING OUT.
UNDER-STOOD.
GOODBYE, CLARENCE.
FOR WHAT IT'S WORTH, FOR THAT MOMENT, YOU WERE A HERO, CLARENCE. I JUST... WANT YOU TO KNOW THAT.
YEAH, WELL... WHATEVER.

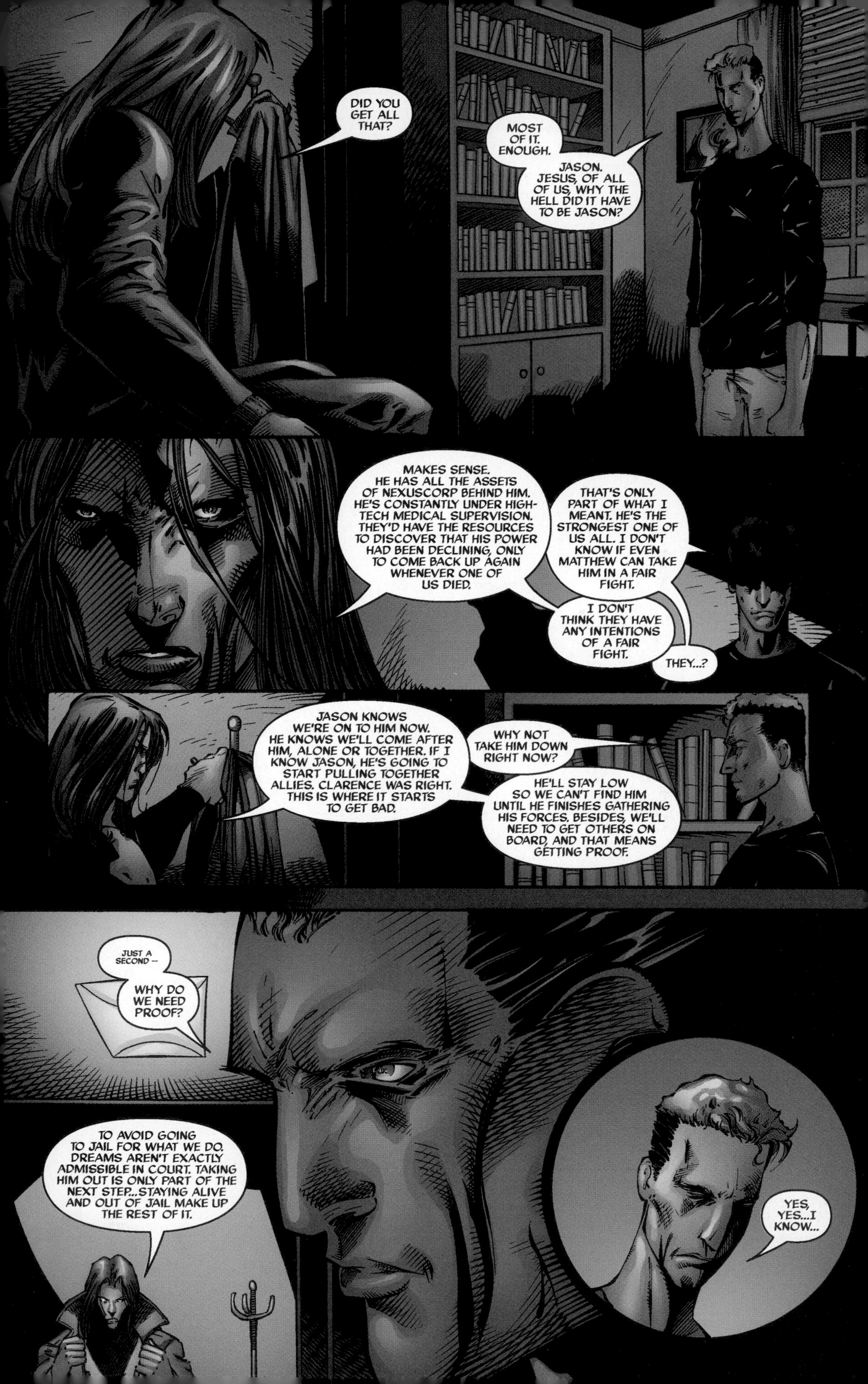
DID YOU GET ALL THAT?
MOST OF IT. ENOUGH.
JASON. JESUS, OF ALL OF US, WHY THE HELL DID IT HAVE TO BE JASON?
MAKES SENSE. HE HAS ALL THE ASSETS OF NEXUSCORP BEHIND HIM. HE'S CONSTANTLY UNDER HIGH-TECH MEDICAL SUPERVISION. THEY'D HAVE THE RESOURCES TO DISCOVER THAT HIS POWER HAD BEEN DECLINING, ONLY TO COME BACK UP AGAIN WHENEVER ONE OF US DIED.
THAT'S ONLY PART OF WHAT I MEANT. HE'S THE STRONGEST ONE OF US ALL. I DON'T KNOW IF EVEN MATTHEW CAN TAKE HIM IN A FAIR FIGHT.
I DON'T THINK THEY HAVE ANY INTENTIONS OF A FAIR FIGHT.
THEY...?
JASON KNOWS WE'RE ON TO HIM NOW. HE KNOWS WE'LL COME AFTER HIM, ALONE OR TOGETHER. IF I KNOW JASON, HE'S GOING TO START PULLING TOGETHER ALLIES. CLARENCE WAS RIGHT. THIS IS WHERE IT STARTS TO GET BAD.
WHY NOT TAKE HIM DOWN RIGHT NOW?
HE'LL STAY LOW SO WE CAN'T FIND HIM UNTIL HE FINISHES GATHERING HIS FORCES. BESIDES, WE'LL NEED TO GET OTHERS ON BOARD, AND THAT MEANS GETTING PROOF.
JUST A SECOND --
WHY DO WE NEED PROOF?
TO AVOID GOING TO JAIL FOR WHAT WE DO. DREAMS AREN'T EXACTLY ADMISSIBLE IN COURT. TAKING HIM OUT IS ONLY PART OF THE NEXT STEP...STAYING ALIVE AND OUT OF JAIL MAKE UP THE REST OF IT.
YES, YES...I KNOW...

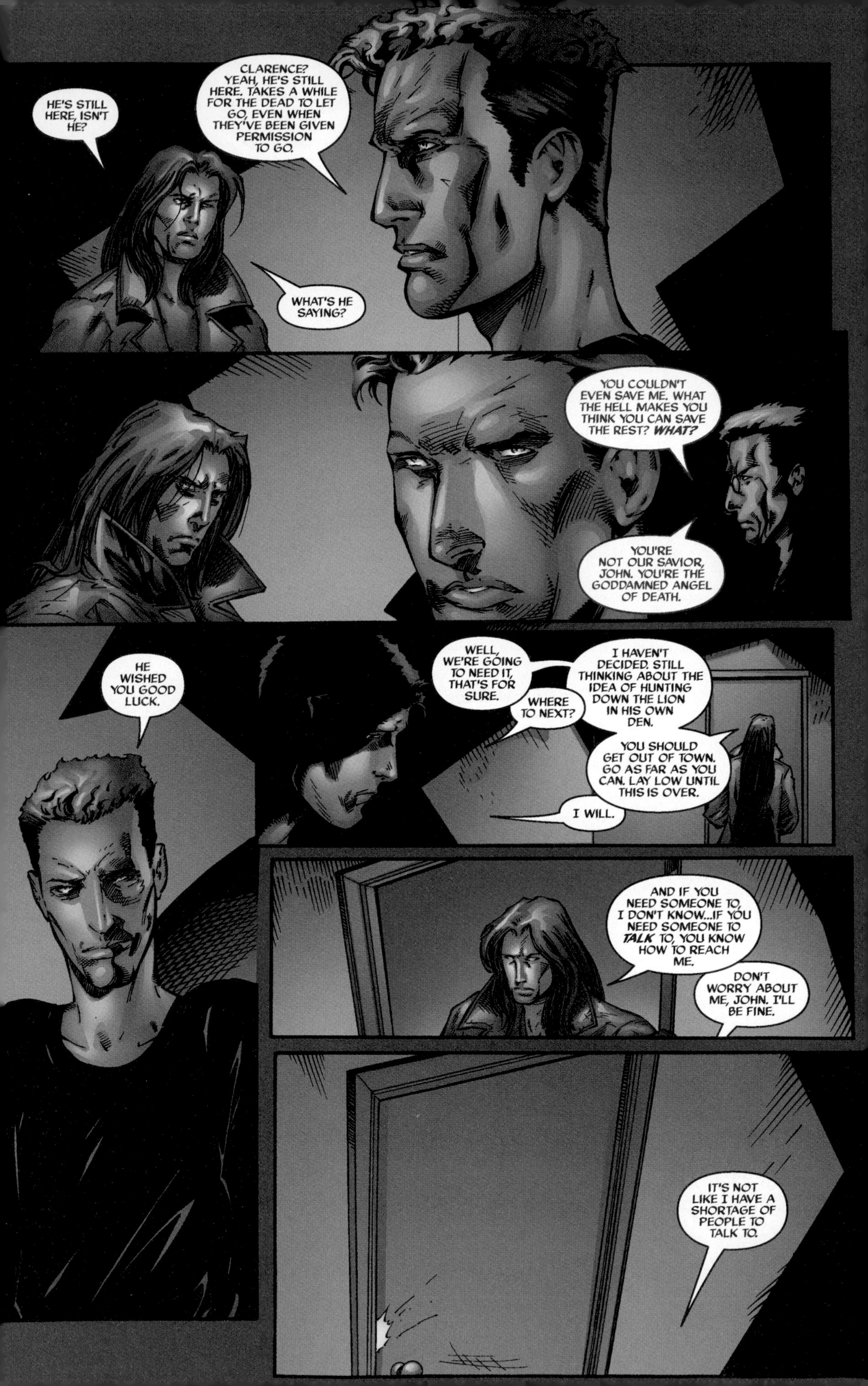
HE'S STILL HERE, ISN'T HE?
CLARENCE? YEAH, HE'S STILL HERE. TAKES A WHILE FOR THE DEAD TO LET GO, EVEN WHEN THEY'VE BEEN GIVEN PERMISSION TO GO.
WHAT'S HE SAYING?
YOU COULDN'T EVEN SAVE ME. WHAT THE HELL MAKES YOU THINK YOU CAN SAVE THE REST? WHAT?
YOU'RE NOT OUR SAVIOR, JOHN. YOU'RE THE GODDAMNED ANGEL OF DEATH.
HE WISHED YOU GOOD LUCK.
WELL, WE'RE GOING TO NEED IT, THAT'S FOR SURE.
WHERE TO NEXT?
I HAVEN'T DECIDED. STILL THINKING ABOUT THE IDEA OF HUNTING DOWN THE LION IN HIS OWN DEN.
YOU SHOULD GET OUT OF TOWN. GO AS FAR AS YOU CAN. LAY LOW UNTIL THIS IS OVER.
I WILL.
AND IF YOU NEED SOMEONE TO, I DON'T KNOW...IF YOU NEED SOMEONE TO TALK TO, YOU KNOW HOW TO REACH ME.
DON'T WORRY ABOUT ME, JOHN. I'LL BE FINE.
IT'S NOT LIKE I HAVE A SHORTAGE OF PEOPLE TO TALK TO.

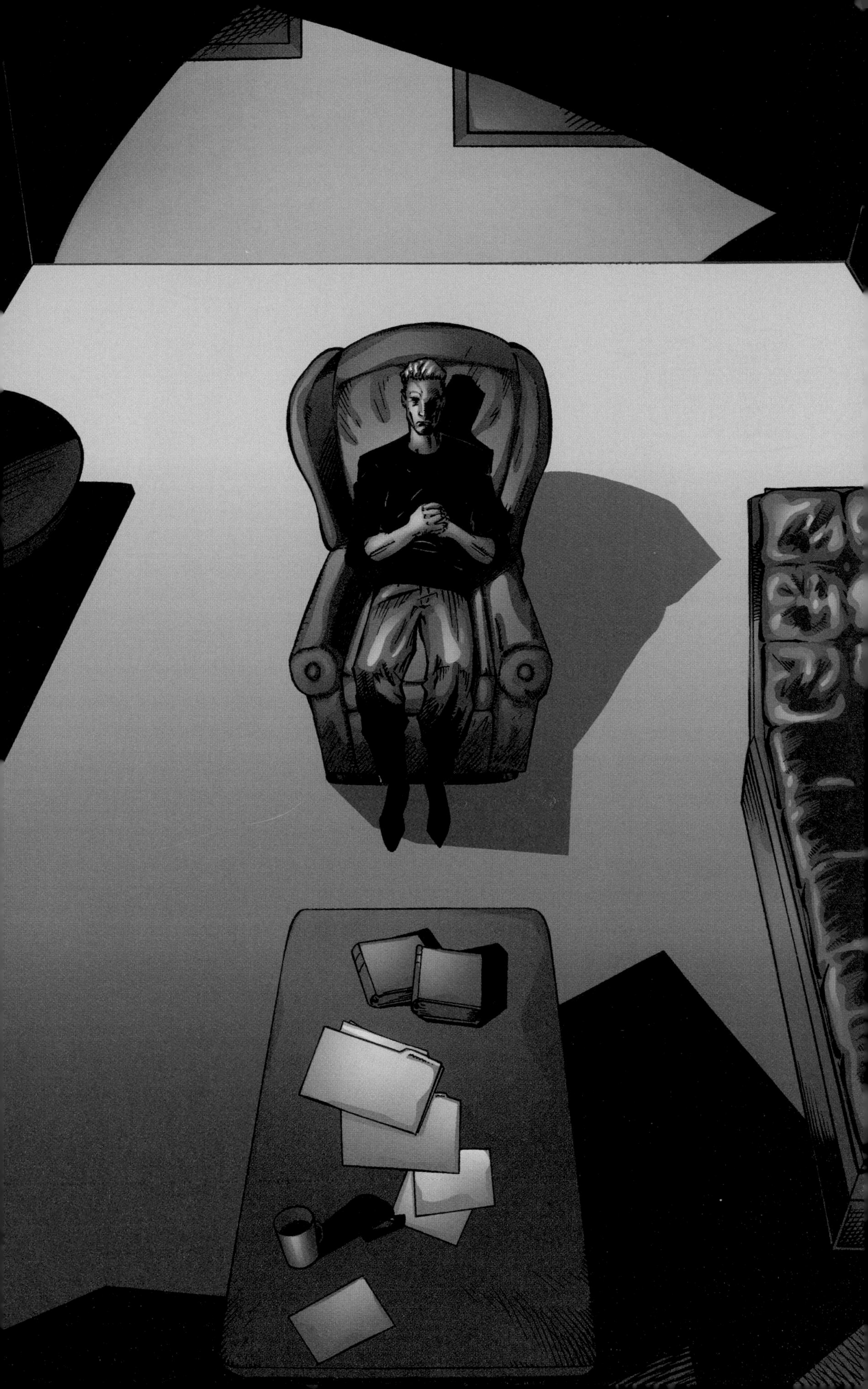

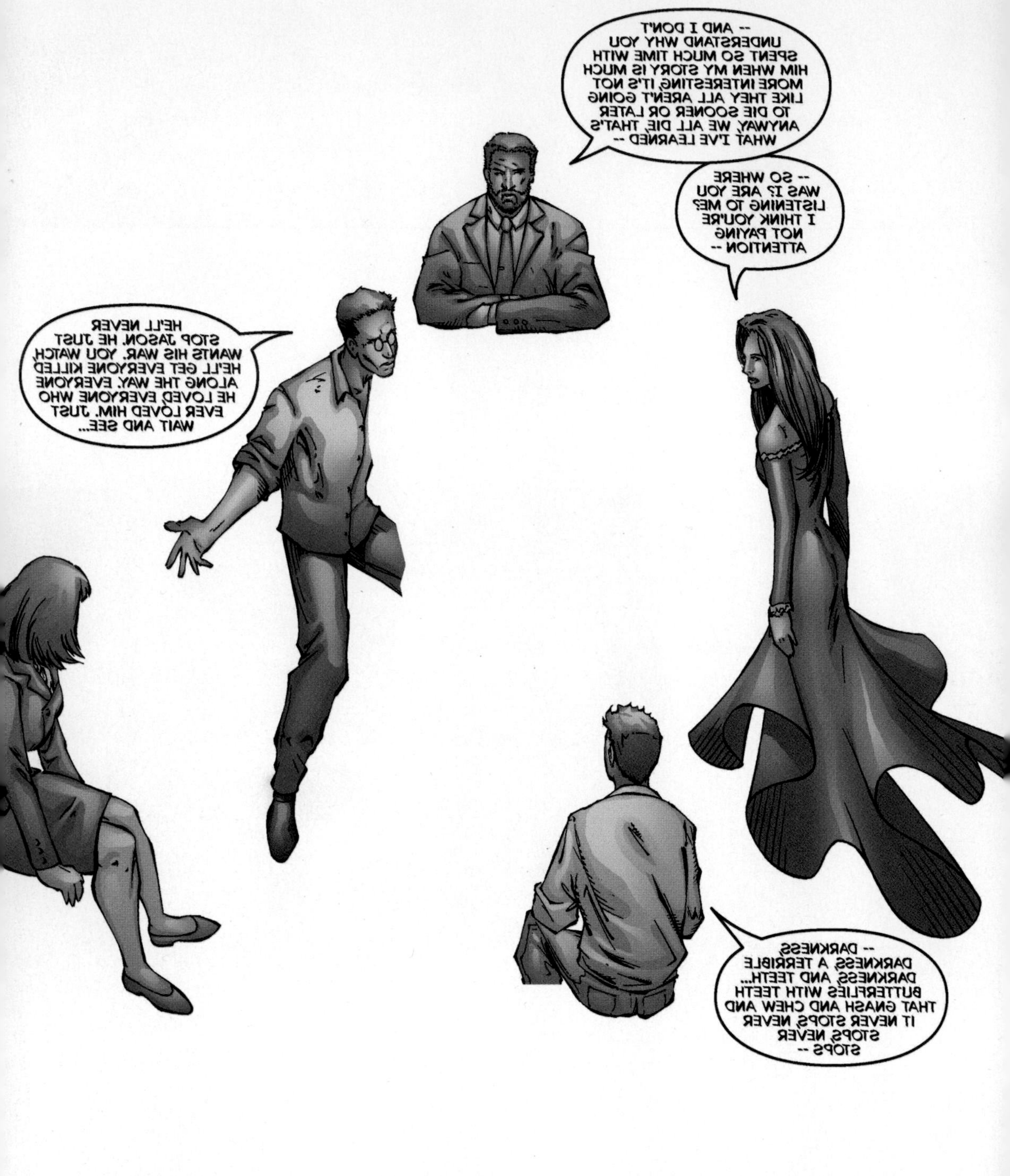
-- AND I DON'T UNDERSTAND WHY YOU SPENT SO MUCH TIME WITH HIM WHEN MY STORY IS MUCH MORE INTERESTING, IT'S NOT LIKE THEY ALL AREN'T GOING TO DIE SOONER OR LATER ANYWAY, WE ALL DIE, THAT'S WHAT I'VE LEARNED --
-- SO WHERE WAS I? ARE YOU LISTENING TO ME? I THINK YOU'RE NOT PAYING ATTENTION --
HE'LL NEVER STOP JASON. HE JUST WANTS HIS WAR. YOU WATCH, HE'LL GET EVERYONE KILLED ALONG THE WAY. EVERYONE HE LOVED, EVERYONE WHO EVER LOVED HIM. JUST WAIT AND SEE...
-- DARKNESS, DARKNESS, A TERRIBLE DARKNESS, AND TEETH... BUTTERFLIES WITH TEETH THAT GNASH AND CHEW AND IT NEVER STOPS, NEVER STOPS, NEVER STOPS --

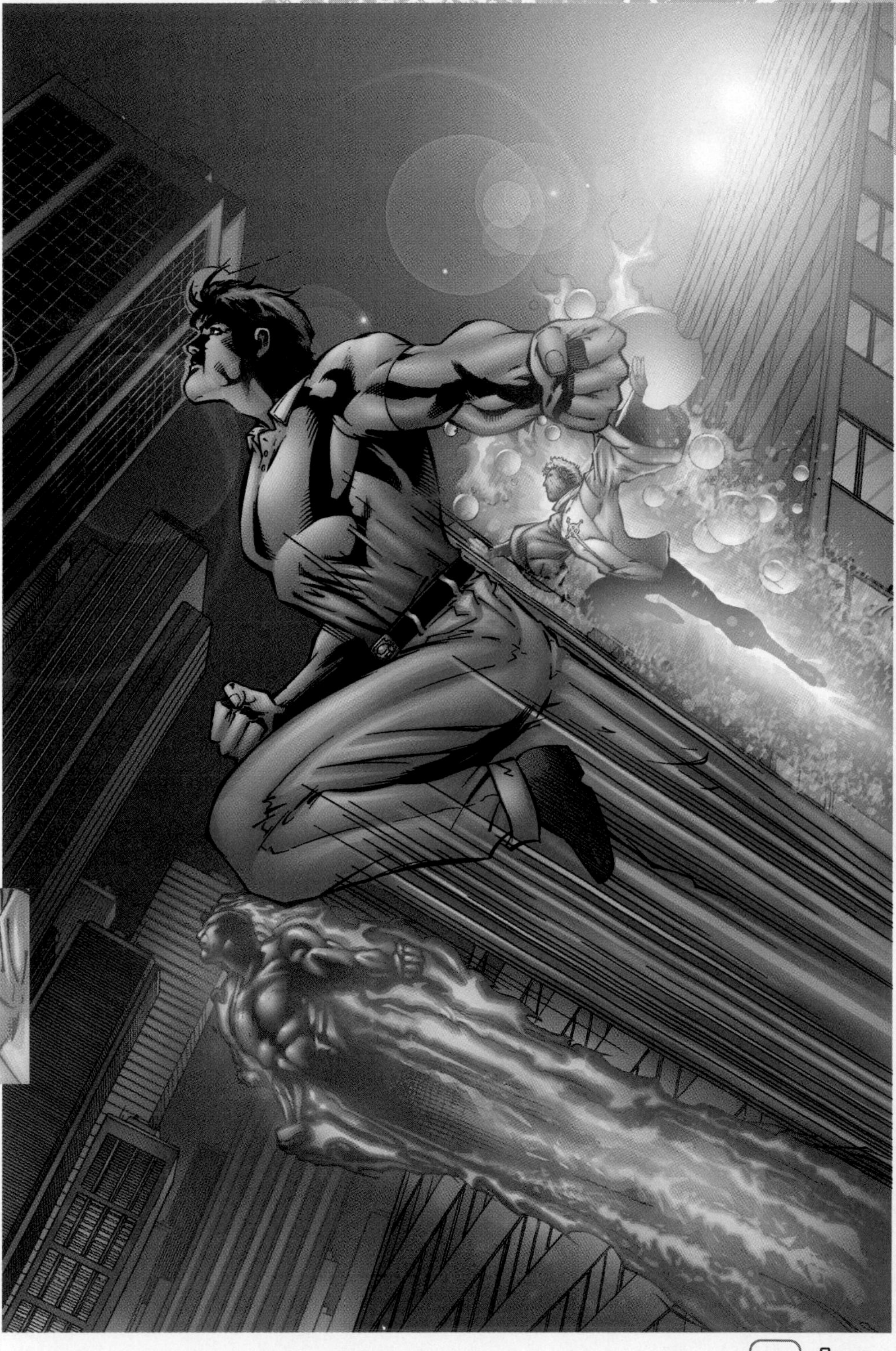

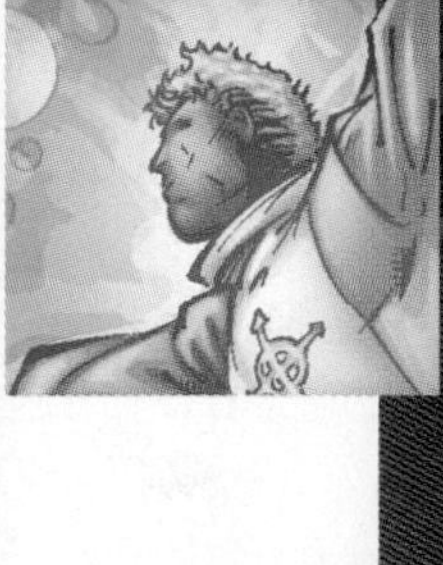

Chapter 6
Things Fall Apart—one

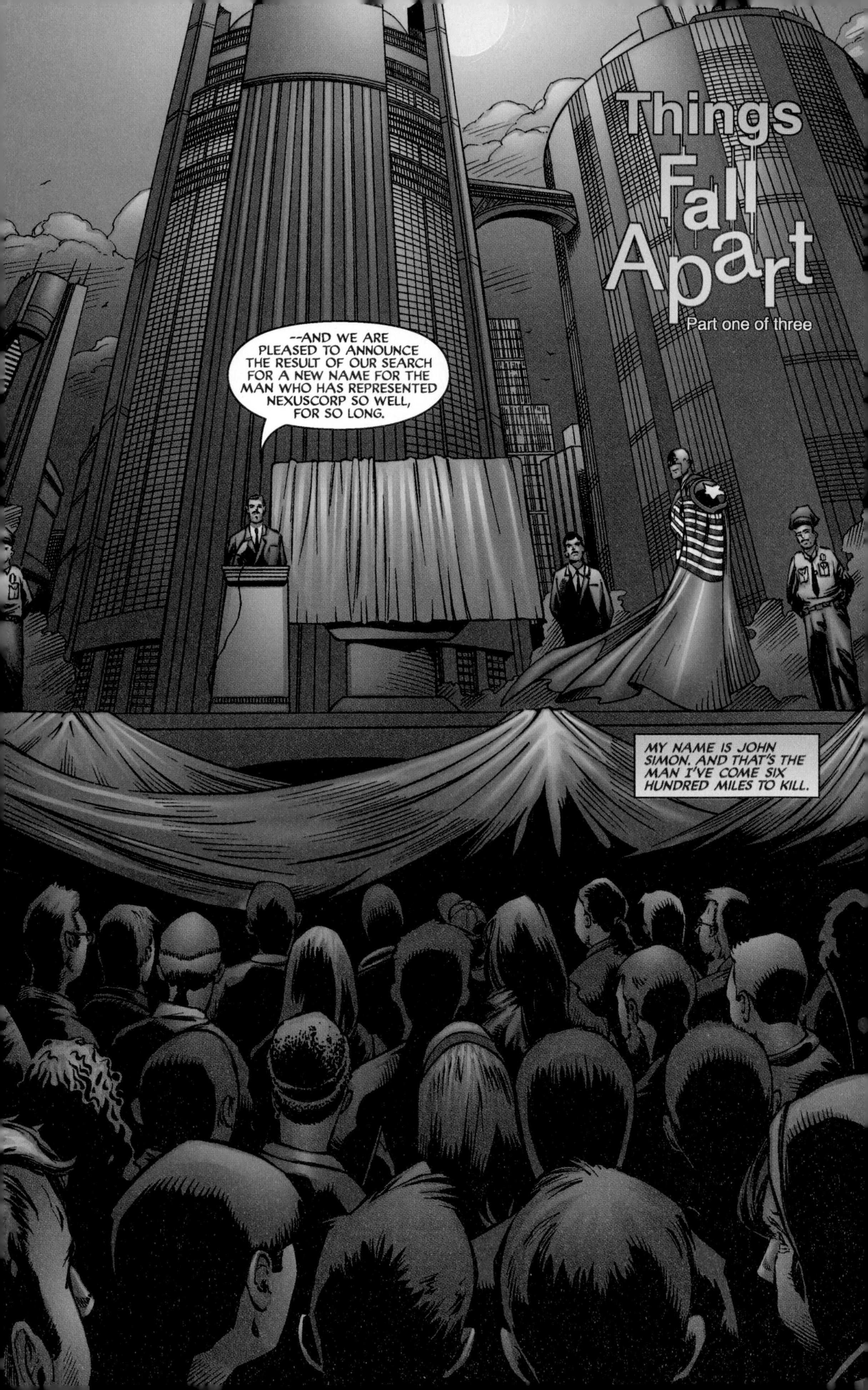
Things Fall Apart
Part one of three
--AND WE ARE PLEASED TO ANNOUNCE THE RESULT OF OUR SEARCH FOR A NEW NAME FOR THE MAN WHO HAS REPRESENTED NEXUSCORP SO WELL, FOR SO LONG.
MY NAME IS JOHN SIMON. AND THAT'S THE MAN I'VE COME SIX HUNDRED MILES TO KILL.

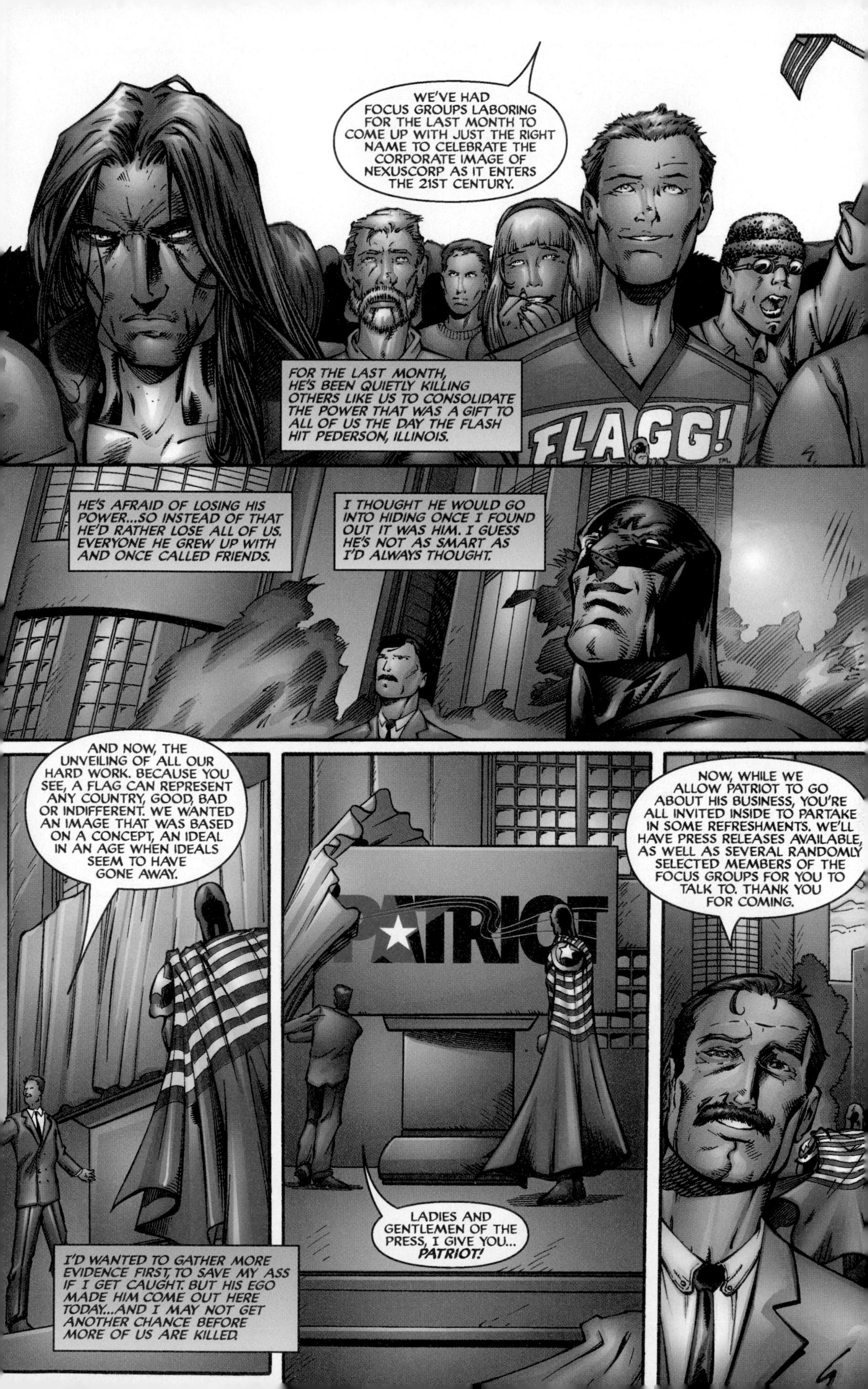
WE'VE HAD FOCUS GROUPS LABORING FOR THE LAST MONTH TO COME UP WITH JUST THE RIGHT NAME TO CELEBRATE THE CORPORATE IMAGE OF NEXUSCORP AS IT ENTERS THE 21ST CENTURY.
FOR THE LAST MONTH, HE'S BEEN QUIETLY KILLING OTHERS LIKE US TO CONSOLIDATE THE POWER THAT WAS A GIFT TO ALL OF US THE DAY THE FLASH HIT PEDERSON, ILLINOIS.
FLAGG!
HE'S AFRAID OF LOSING HIS POWER...SO INSTEAD OF THAT HE'D RATHER LOSE ALL OF US. EVERYONE HE GREW UP WITH AND ONCE CALLED FRIENDS.
I THOUGHT HE WOULD GO INTO HIDING ONCE I FOUND OUT IT WAS HIM. I GUESS HE'S NOT AS SMART AS I'D ALWAYS THOUGHT.
AND NOW, THE UNVEILING OF ALL OUR HARD WORK. BECAUSE YOU SEE, A FLAG CAN REPRESENT ANY COUNTRY, GOOD, BAD OR INDIFFERENT. WE WANTED AN IMAGE THAT WAS BASED ON A CONCEPT, AN IDEAL IN AN AGE WHEN IDEALS SEEM TO HAVE GONE AWAY.
I'D WANTED TO GATHER MORE EVIDENCE FIRST, TO SAVE MY ASS IF I GET CAUGHT. BUT HIS EGO MADE HIM COME OUT HERE TODAY...AND I MAY NOT GET ANOTHER CHANCE BEFORE MORE OF US ARE KILLED.
PATRIOT
LADIES AND GENTLEMEN OF THE PRESS, I GIVE YOU... *PATRIOT!*
NOW, WHILE WE ALLOW PATRIOT TO GO ABOUT HIS BUSINESS, YOU'RE ALL INVITED INSIDE TO PARTAKE IN SOME REFRESHMENTS. WE'LL HAVE PRESS RELEASES AVAILABLE, AS WELL AS SEVERAL RANDOMLY SELECTED MEMBERS OF THE FOCUS GROUPS FOR YOU TO TALK TO. THANK YOU FOR COMING.

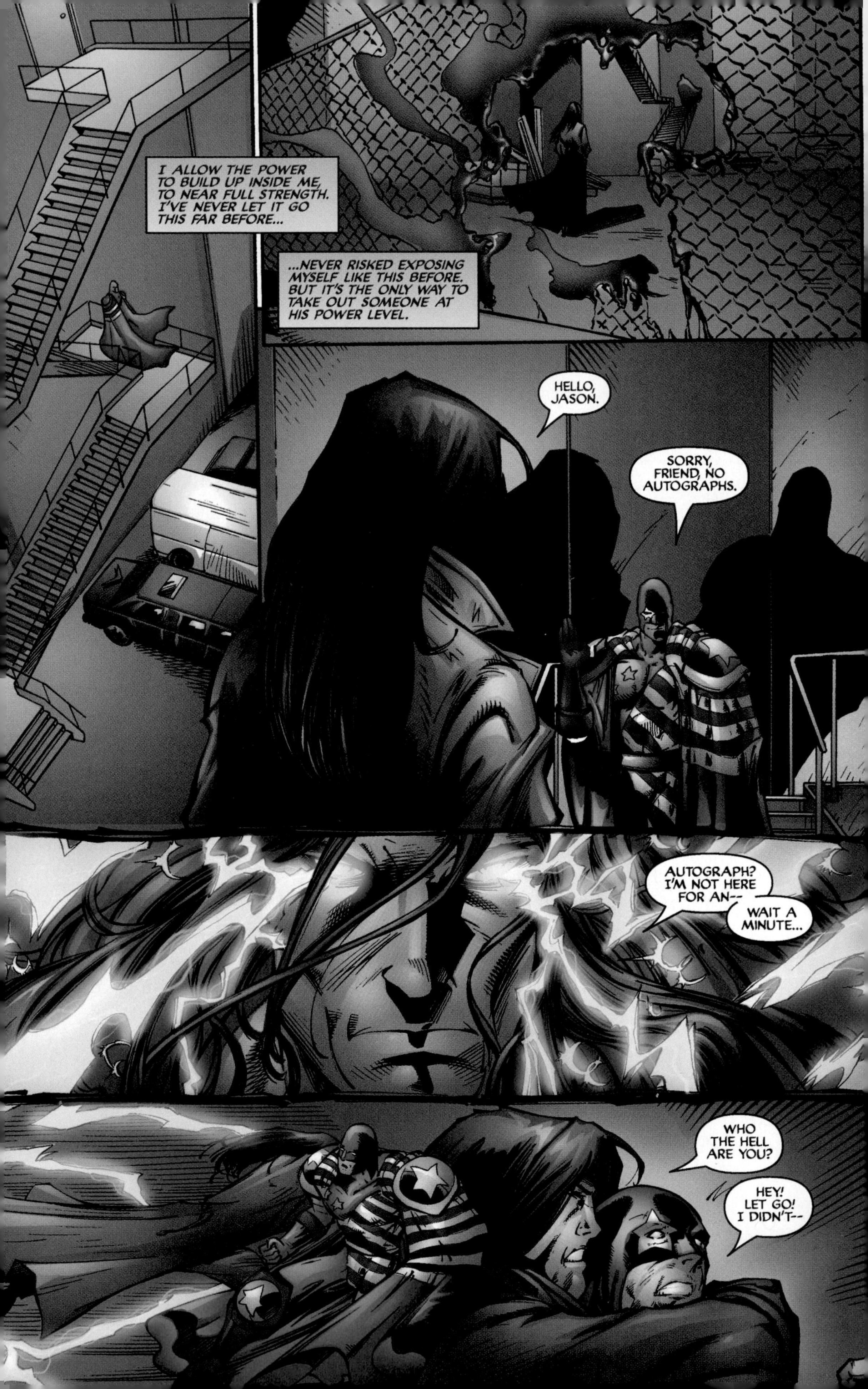

I ALLOW THE POWER TO BUILD UP INSIDE ME, TO NEAR FULL STRENGTH. I'VE NEVER LET IT GO THIS FAR BEFORE...
...NEVER RISKED EXPOSING MYSELF LIKE THIS BEFORE. BUT IT'S THE ONLY WAY TO TAKE OUT SOMEONE AT HIS POWER LEVEL.
HELLO, JASON.
SORRY, FRIEND, NO AUTOGRAPHS.
AUTOGRAPH? I'M NOT HERE FOR AN--
WAIT A MINUTE...
WHO THE HELL ARE YOU?
HEY! LET GO! I DIDN'T--

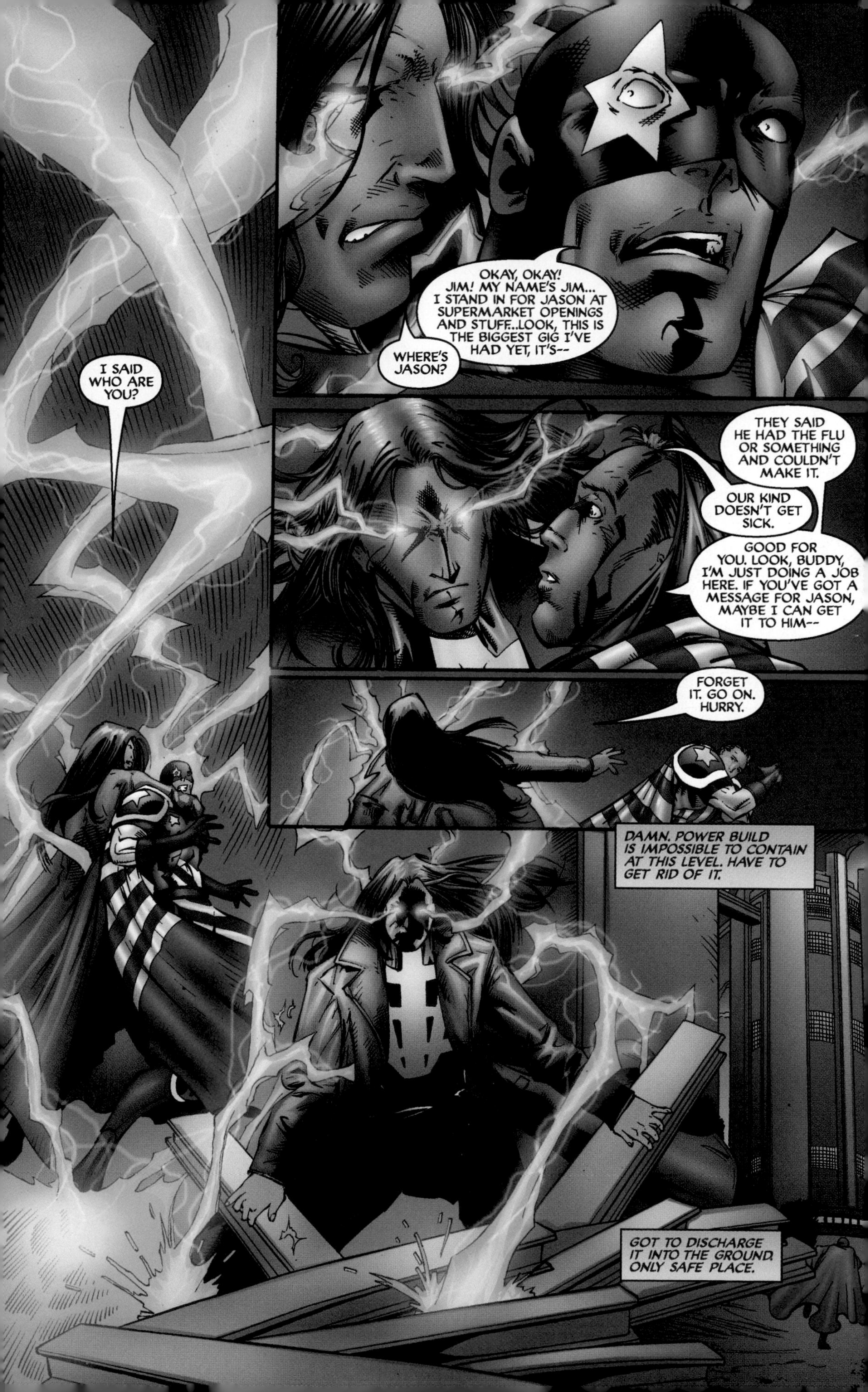
I SAID WHO ARE YOU?
WHERE'S JASON?
OKAY, OKAY! JIM! MY NAME'S JIM... I STAND IN FOR JASON AT SUPERMARKET OPENINGS AND STUFF...LOOK, THIS IS THE BIGGEST GIG I'VE HAD YET, IT'S--
THEY SAID HE HAD THE FLU OR SOMETHING AND COULDN'T MAKE IT.
OUR KIND DOESN'T GET SICK.
GOOD FOR YOU. LOOK, BUDDY, I'M JUST DOING A JOB HERE. IF YOU'VE GOT A MESSAGE FOR JASON, MAYBE I CAN GET IT TO HIM--
FORGET IT. GO ON. HURRY.
DAMN. POWER BUILD IS IMPOSSIBLE TO CONTAIN AT THIS LEVEL. HAVE TO GET RID OF IT.
GOT TO DISCHARGE IT INTO THE GROUND. ONLY SAFE PLACE.

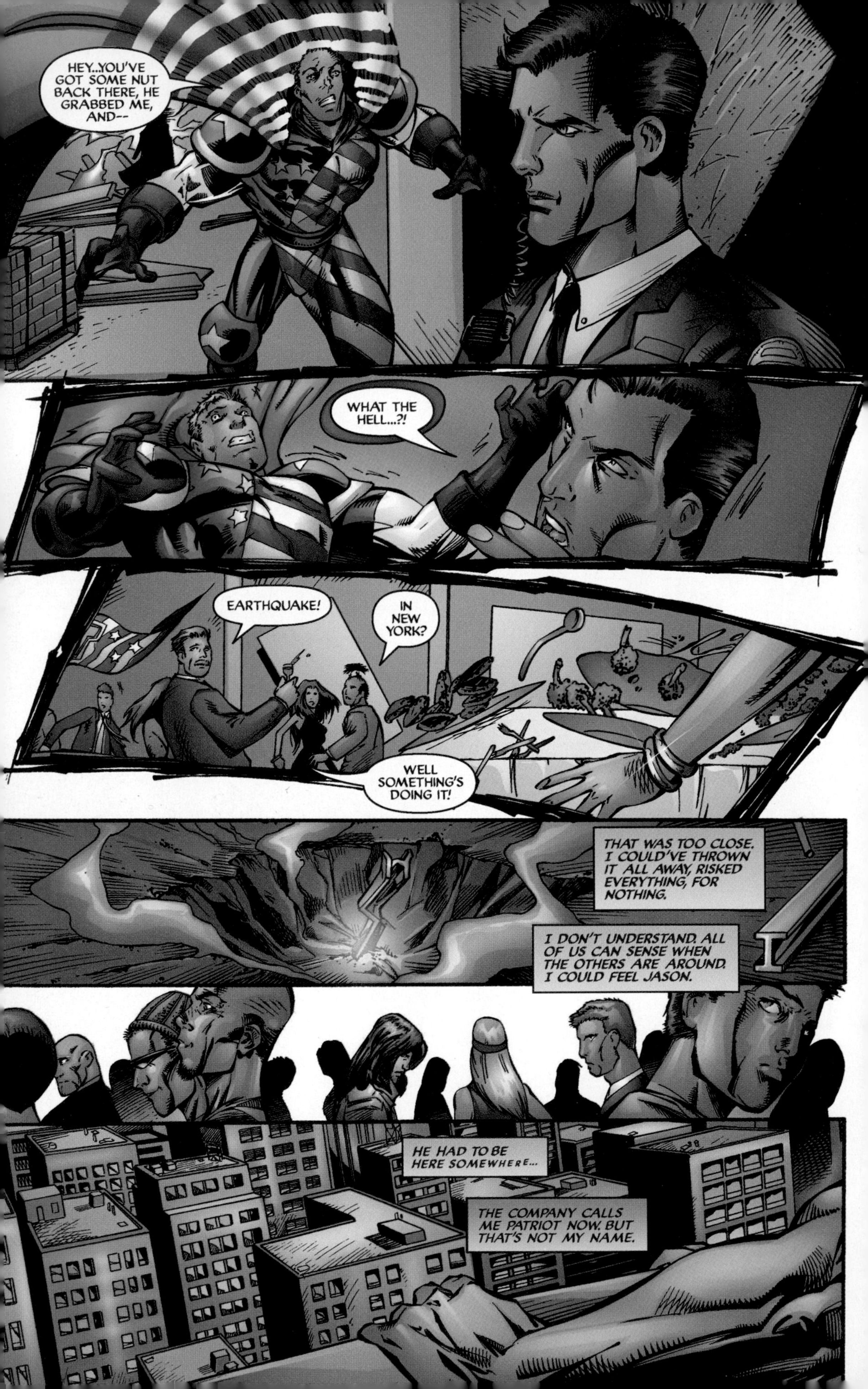
HEY...YOU'VE GOT SOME NUT BACK THERE, HE GRABBED ME, AND--
WHAT THE HELL...?!
EARTHQUAKE!
IN NEW YORK?
WELL SOMETHING'S DOING IT!
THAT WAS TOO CLOSE. I COULD'VE THROWN IT ALL AWAY, RISKED EVERYTHING, FOR NOTHING.
I DON'T UNDERSTAND. ALL OF US CAN SENSE WHEN THE OTHERS ARE AROUND. I COULD FEEL JASON.
HE HAD TO BE HERE SOMEWHERE...
THE COMPANY CALLS ME PATRIOT NOW. BUT THAT'S NOT MY NAME.

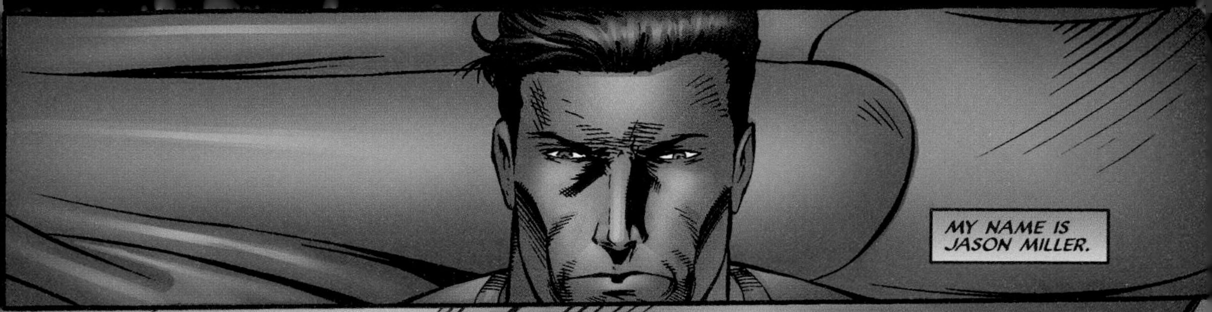
MY NAME IS
JASON MILLER.

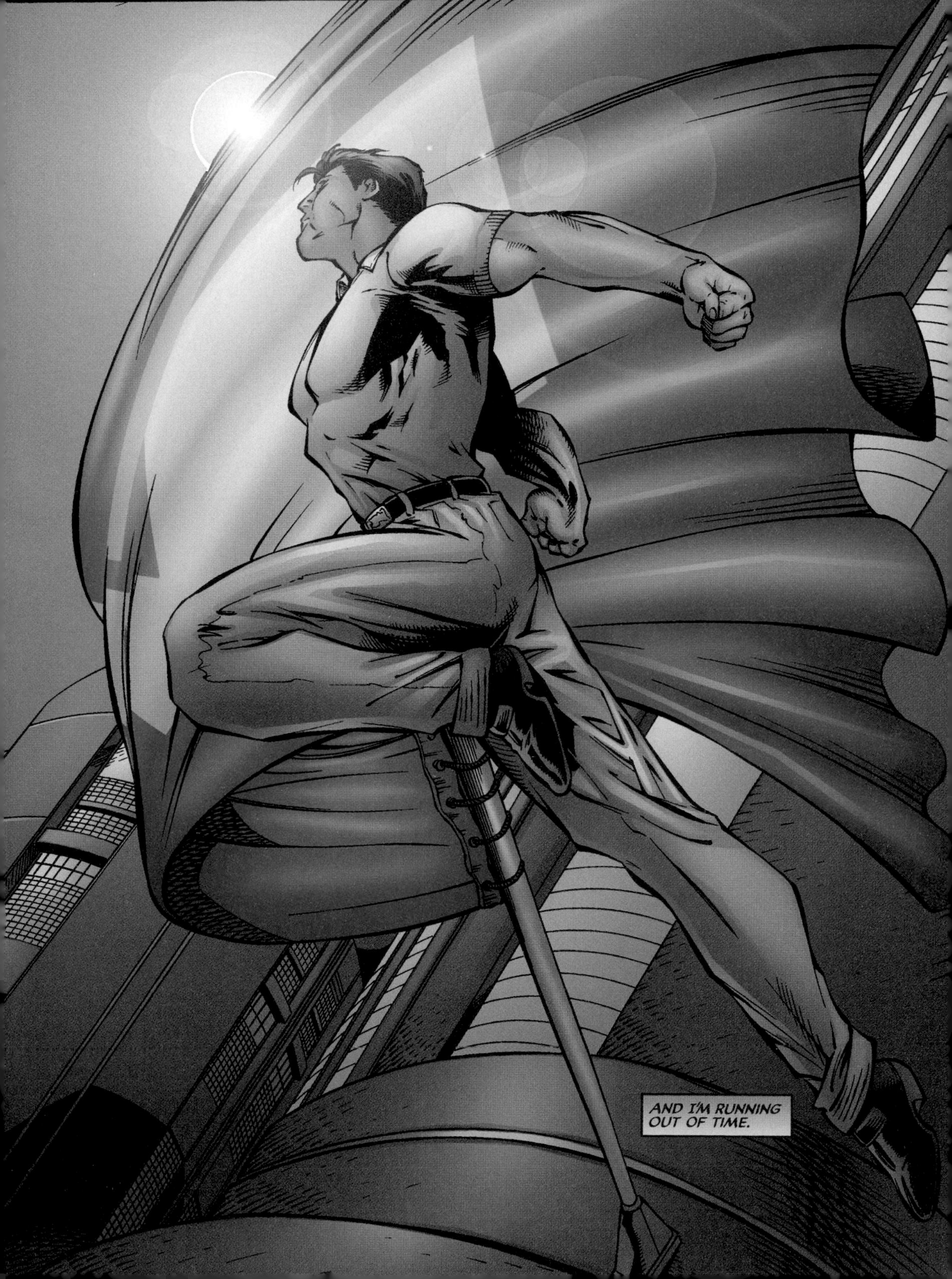
AND I'M RUNNING
OUT OF TIME.

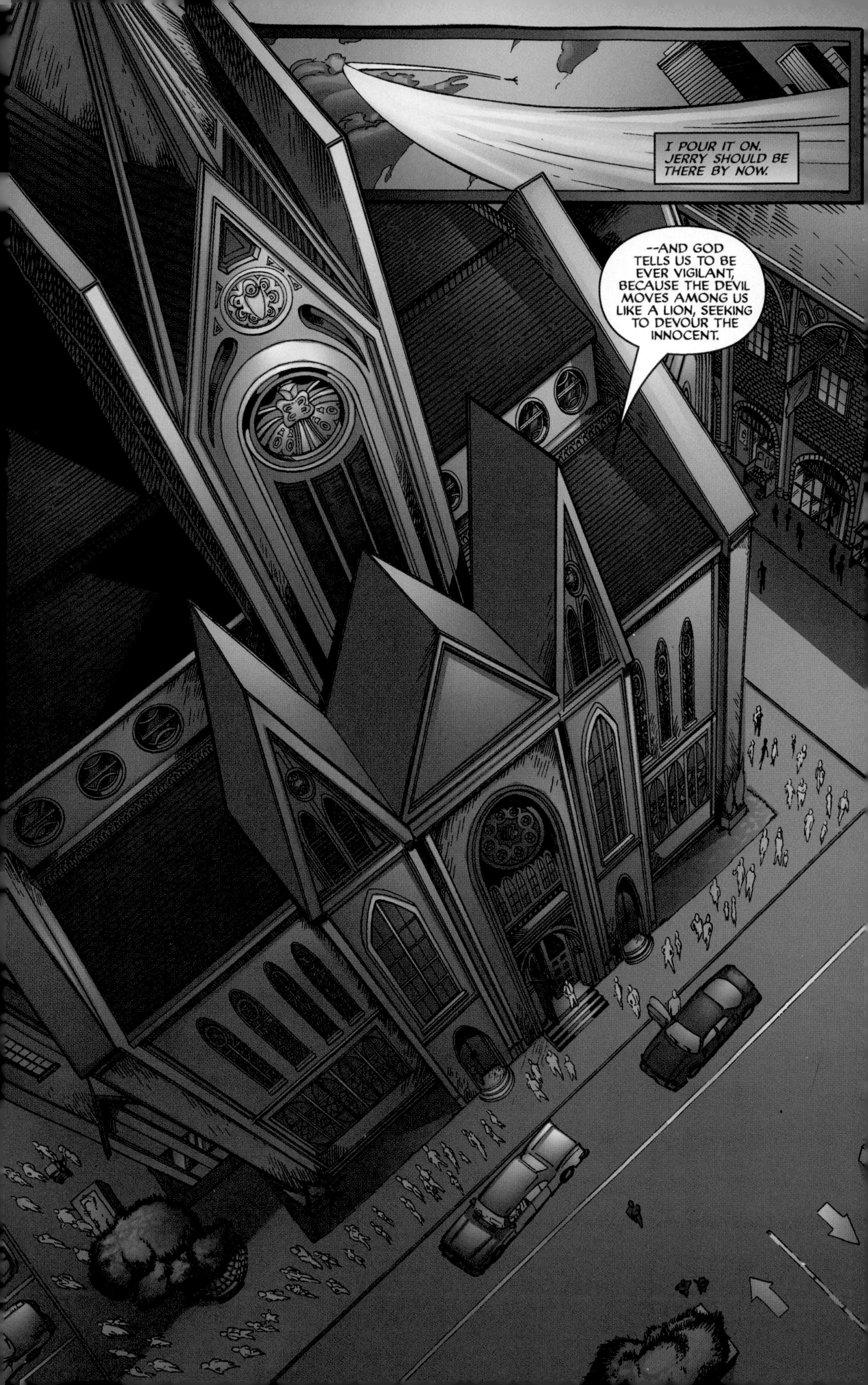
I POUR IT ON. JERRY SHOULD BE THERE BY NOW.
--AND GOD TELLS US TO BE EVER VIGILANT, BECAUSE THE DEVIL MOVES AMONG US LIKE A LION, SEEKING TO DEVOUR THE INNOCENT.

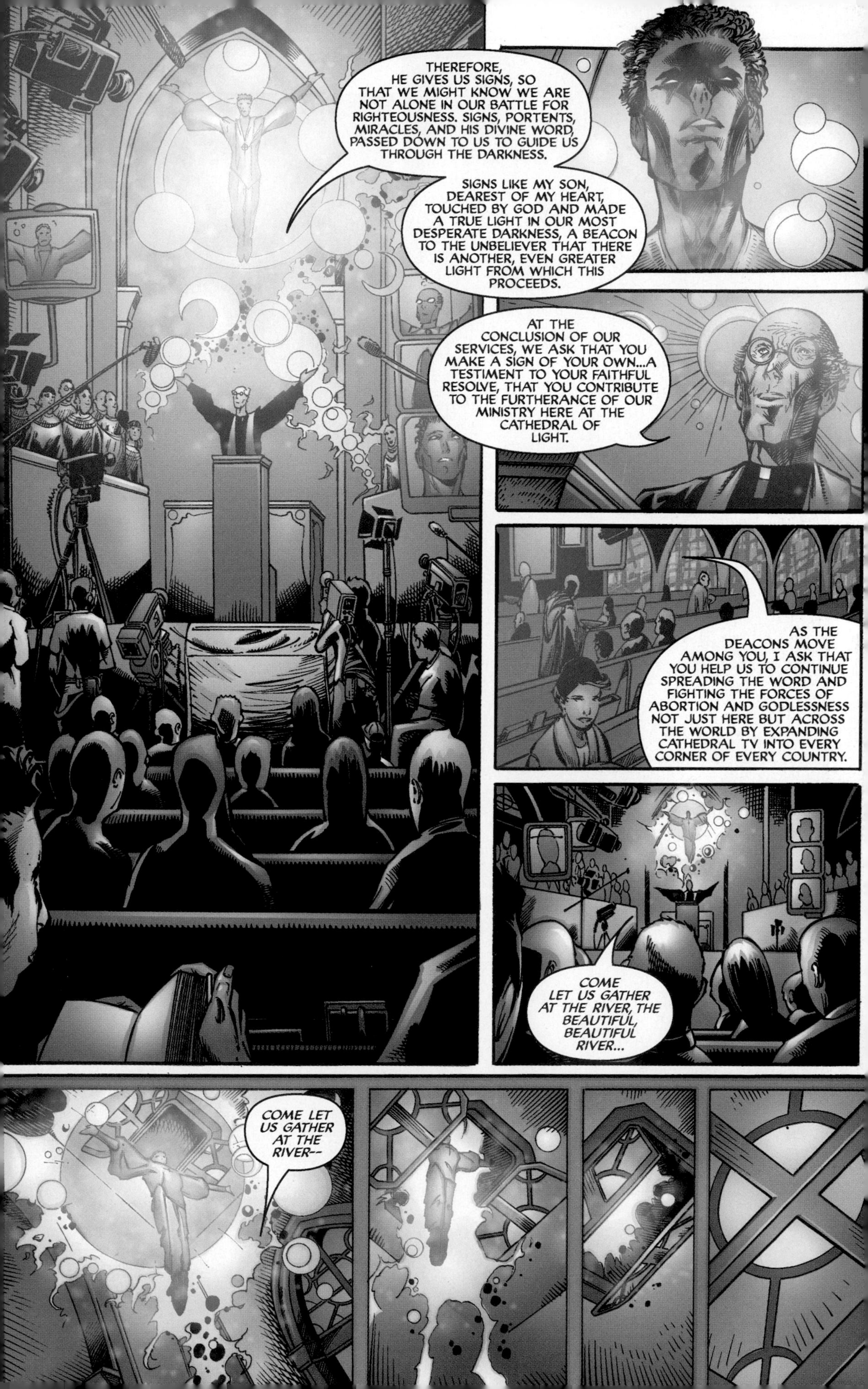
THEREFORE, HE GIVES US SIGNS, SO THAT WE MIGHT KNOW WE ARE NOT ALONE IN OUR BATTLE FOR RIGHTEOUSNESS. SIGNS, PORTENTS, MIRACLES, AND HIS DIVINE WORD, PASSED DOWN TO US TO GUIDE US THROUGH THE DARKNESS.
SIGNS LIKE MY SON, DEAREST OF MY HEART, TOUCHED BY GOD AND MADE A TRUE LIGHT IN OUR MOST DESPERATE DARKNESS, A BEACON TO THE UNBELIEVER THAT THERE IS ANOTHER, EVEN GREATER LIGHT FROM WHICH THIS PROCEEDS.
AT THE CONCLUSION OF OUR SERVICES, WE ASK THAT YOU MAKE A SIGN OF YOUR OWN...A TESTIMENT TO YOUR FAITHFUL RESOLVE, THAT YOU CONTRIBUTE TO THE FURTHERANCE OF OUR MINISTRY HERE AT THE CATHEDRAL OF LIGHT.
AS THE DEACONS MOVE AMONG YOU, I ASK THAT YOU HELP US TO CONTINUE SPREADING THE WORD AND FIGHTING THE FORCES OF ABORTION AND GODLESSNESS NOT JUST HERE BUT ACROSS THE WORLD BY EXPANDING CATHEDRAL TV INTO EVERY CORNER OF EVERY COUNTRY.
COME LET US GATHER AT THE RIVER, THE BEAUTIFUL, BEAUTIFUL RIVER...
COME LET US GATHER AT THE RIVER--

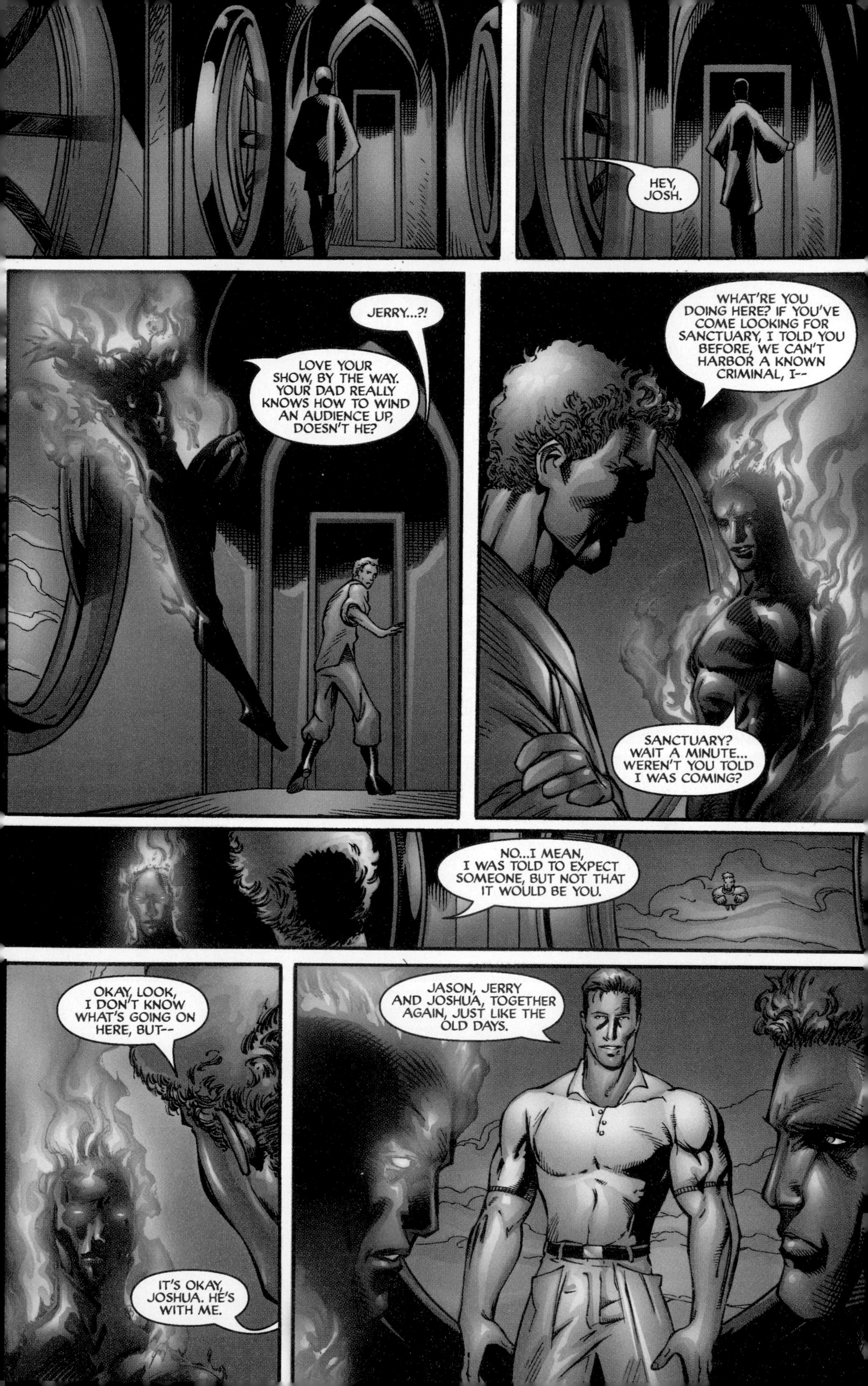
HEY, JOSH.
JERRY...?!
LOVE YOUR SHOW, BY THE WAY. YOUR DAD REALLY KNOWS HOW TO WIND AN AUDIENCE UP, DOESN'T HE?
WHAT'RE YOU DOING HERE? IF YOU'VE COME LOOKING FOR SANCTUARY, I TOLD YOU BEFORE, WE CAN'T HARBOR A KNOWN CRIMINAL, I--
SANCTUARY? WAIT A MINUTE... WEREN'T YOU TOLD I WAS COMING?
NO...I MEAN, I WAS TOLD TO EXPECT SOMEONE, BUT NOT THAT IT WOULD BE YOU.
OKAY, LOOK, I DON'T KNOW WHAT'S GOING ON HERE, BUT--
IT'S OKAY, JOSHUA. HE'S WITH ME.
JASON, JERRY AND JOSHUA, TOGETHER AGAIN, JUST LIKE THE OLD DAYS.

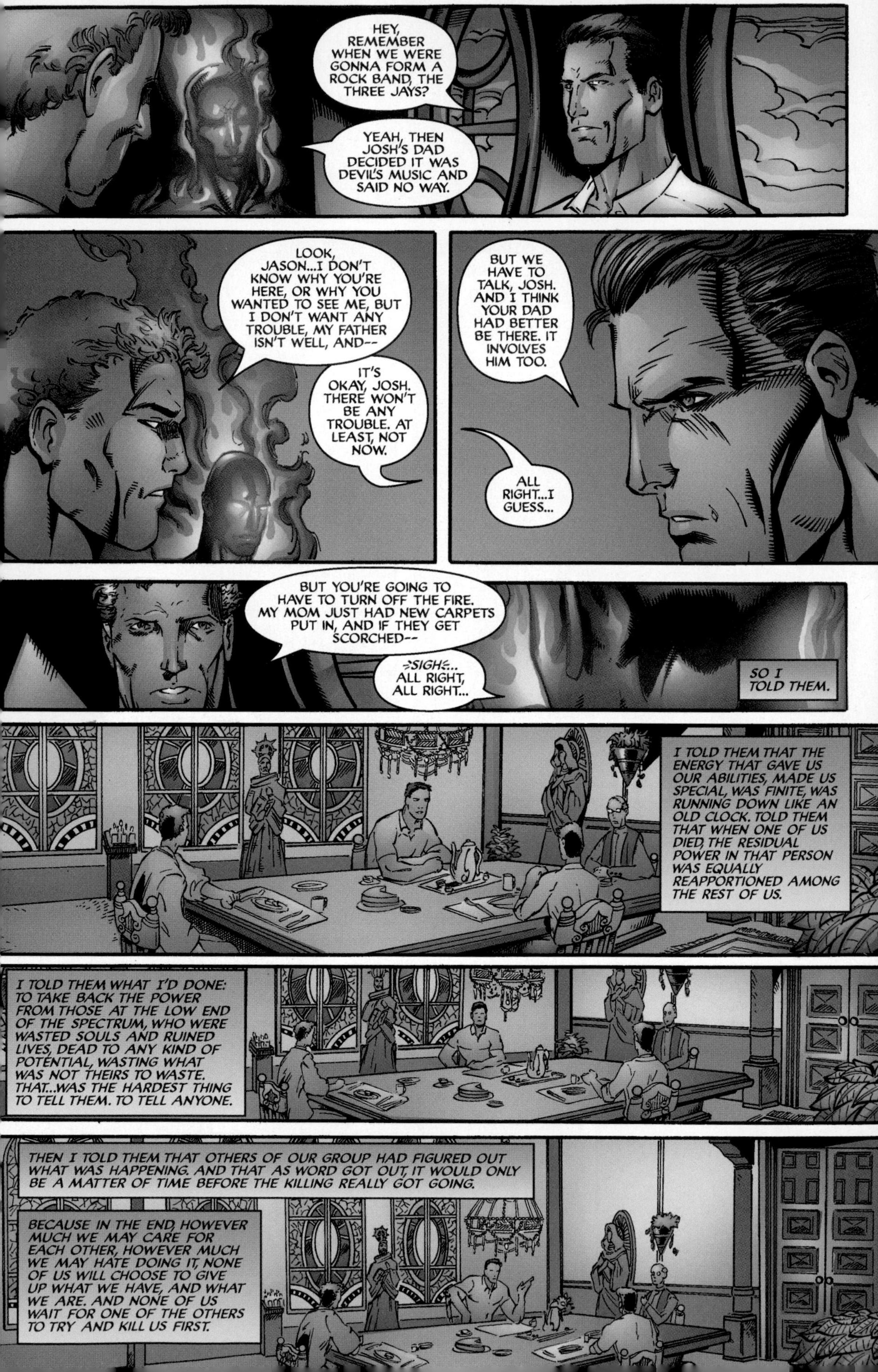
HEY, REMEMBER WHEN WE WERE GONNA FORM A ROCK BAND, THE THREE JAYS?
YEAH, THEN JOSH'S DAD DECIDED IT WAS DEVIL'S MUSIC AND SAID NO WAY.
LOOK, JASON...I DON'T KNOW WHY YOU'RE HERE, OR WHY YOU WANTED TO SEE ME, BUT I DON'T WANT ANY TROUBLE, MY FATHER ISN'T WELL, AND--
IT'S OKAY, JOSH. THERE WON'T BE ANY TROUBLE. AT LEAST, NOT NOW.
BUT WE HAVE TO TALK, JOSH. AND I THINK YOUR DAD HAD BETTER BE THERE. IT INVOLVES HIM TOO.
ALL RIGHT...I GUESS...
BUT YOU'RE GOING TO HAVE TO TURN OFF THE FIRE. MY MOM JUST HAD NEW CARPETS PUT IN, AND IF THEY GET SCORCHED--
SIGH... ALL RIGHT, ALL RIGHT...
SO I TOLD THEM.
I TOLD THEM THAT THE ENERGY THAT GAVE US OUR ABILITIES, MADE US SPECIAL, WAS FINITE, WAS RUNNING DOWN LIKE AN OLD CLOCK. TOLD THEM THAT WHEN ONE OF US DIED, THE RESIDUAL POWER IN THAT PERSON WAS EQUALLY REAPPORTIONED AMONG THE REST OF US.
I TOLD THEM WHAT I'D DONE: TO TAKE BACK THE POWER FROM THOSE AT THE LOW END OF THE SPECTRUM, WHO WERE WASTED SOULS AND RUINED LIVES, DEAD TO ANY KIND OF POTENTIAL, WASTING WHAT WAS NOT THEIRS TO WASTE. THAT...WAS THE HARDEST THING TO TELL THEM. TO TELL ANYONE.
THEN I TOLD THEM THAT OTHERS OF OUR GROUP HAD FIGURED OUT WHAT WAS HAPPENING. AND THAT AS WORD GOT OUT, IT WOULD ONLY BE A MATTER OF TIME BEFORE THE KILLING REALLY GOT GOING.
BECAUSE IN THE END, HOWEVER MUCH WE MAY CARE FOR EACH OTHER, HOWEVER MUCH WE MAY HATE DOING IT, NONE OF US WILL CHOOSE TO GIVE UP WHAT WE HAVE, AND WHAT WE ARE. AND NONE OF US WAIT FOR ONE OF THE OTHERS TO TRY AND KILL US FIRST.

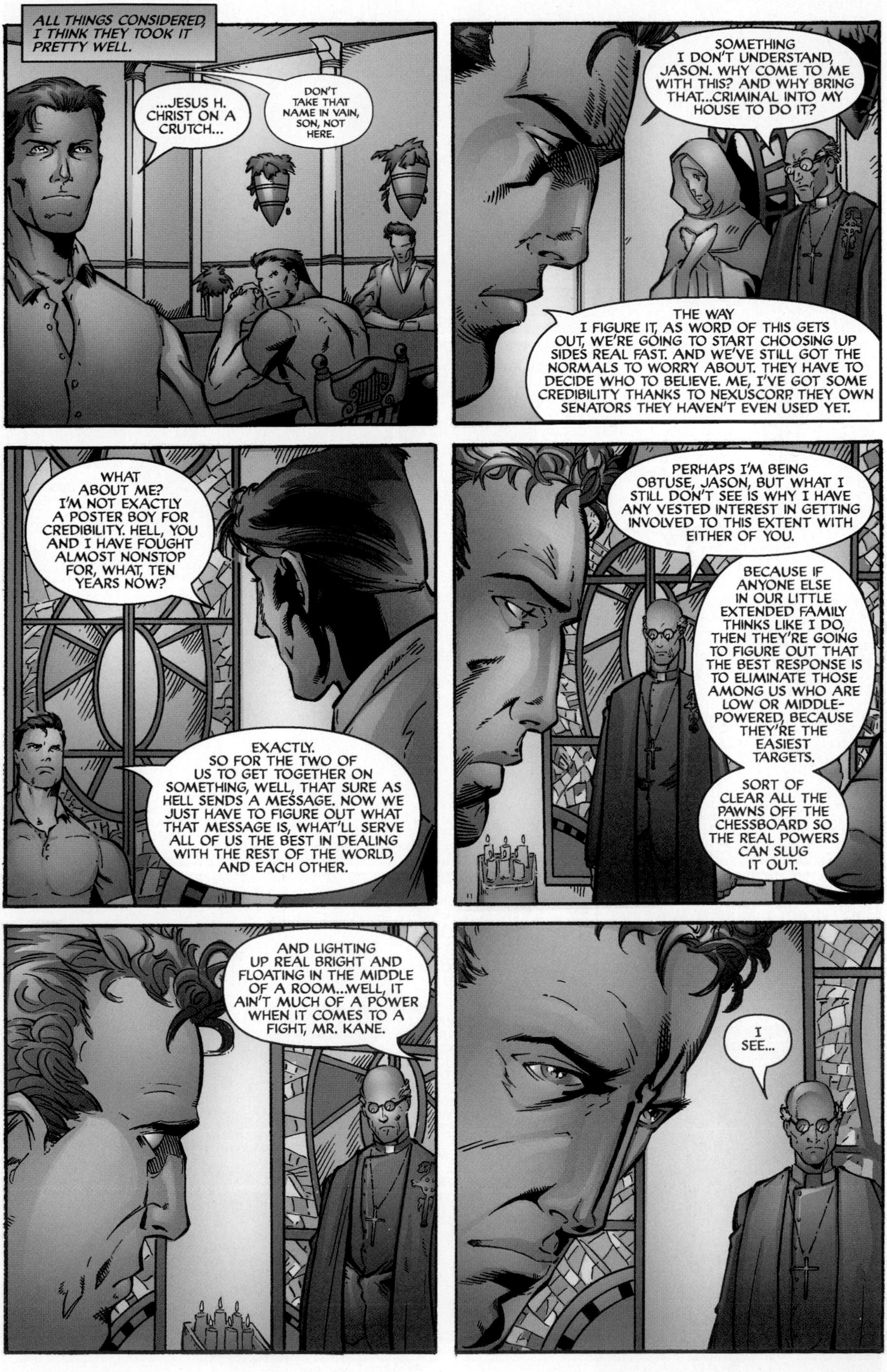

ALL THINGS CONSIDERED, I THINK THEY TOOK IT PRETTY WELL.
...JESUS H. CHRIST ON A CRUTCH...
DON'T TAKE THAT NAME IN VAIN, SON, NOT HERE.
SOMETHING I DON'T UNDERSTAND, JASON. WHY COME TO ME WITH THIS? AND WHY BRING THAT...CRIMINAL INTO MY HOUSE TO DO IT?
THE WAY I FIGURE IT, AS WORD OF THIS GETS OUT, WE'RE GOING TO START CHOOSING UP SIDES REAL FAST. AND WE'VE STILL GOT THE NORMALS TO WORRY ABOUT. THEY HAVE TO DECIDE WHO TO BELIEVE. ME, I'VE GOT SOME CREDIBILITY THANKS TO NEXUSCORP. THEY OWN SENATORS THEY HAVEN'T EVEN USED YET.
WHAT ABOUT ME? I'M NOT EXACTLY A POSTER BOY FOR CREDIBILITY. HELL, YOU AND I HAVE FOUGHT ALMOST NONSTOP FOR, WHAT, TEN YEARS NOW?
EXACTLY. SO FOR THE TWO OF US TO GET TOGETHER ON SOMETHING, WELL, THAT SURE AS HELL SENDS A MESSAGE. NOW WE JUST HAVE TO FIGURE OUT WHAT THAT MESSAGE IS, WHAT'LL SERVE ALL OF US THE BEST IN DEALING WITH THE REST OF THE WORLD, AND EACH OTHER.
PERHAPS I'M BEING OBTUSE, JASON, BUT WHAT I STILL DON'T SEE IS WHY I HAVE ANY VESTED INTEREST IN GETTING INVOLVED TO THIS EXTENT WITH EITHER OF YOU.
BECAUSE IF ANYONE ELSE IN OUR LITTLE EXTENDED FAMILY THINKS LIKE I DO, THEN THEY'RE GOING TO FIGURE OUT THAT THE BEST RESPONSE IS TO ELIMINATE THOSE AMONG US WHO ARE LOW OR MIDDLE-POWERED, BECAUSE THEY'RE THE EASIEST TARGETS.
SORT OF CLEAR ALL THE PAWNS OFF THE CHESSBOARD SO THE REAL POWERS CAN SLUG IT OUT.
AND LIGHTING UP REAL BRIGHT AND FLOATING IN THE MIDDLE OF A ROOM...WELL, IT AIN'T MUCH OF A POWER WHEN IT COMES TO A FIGHT, MR. KANE.
I SEE...

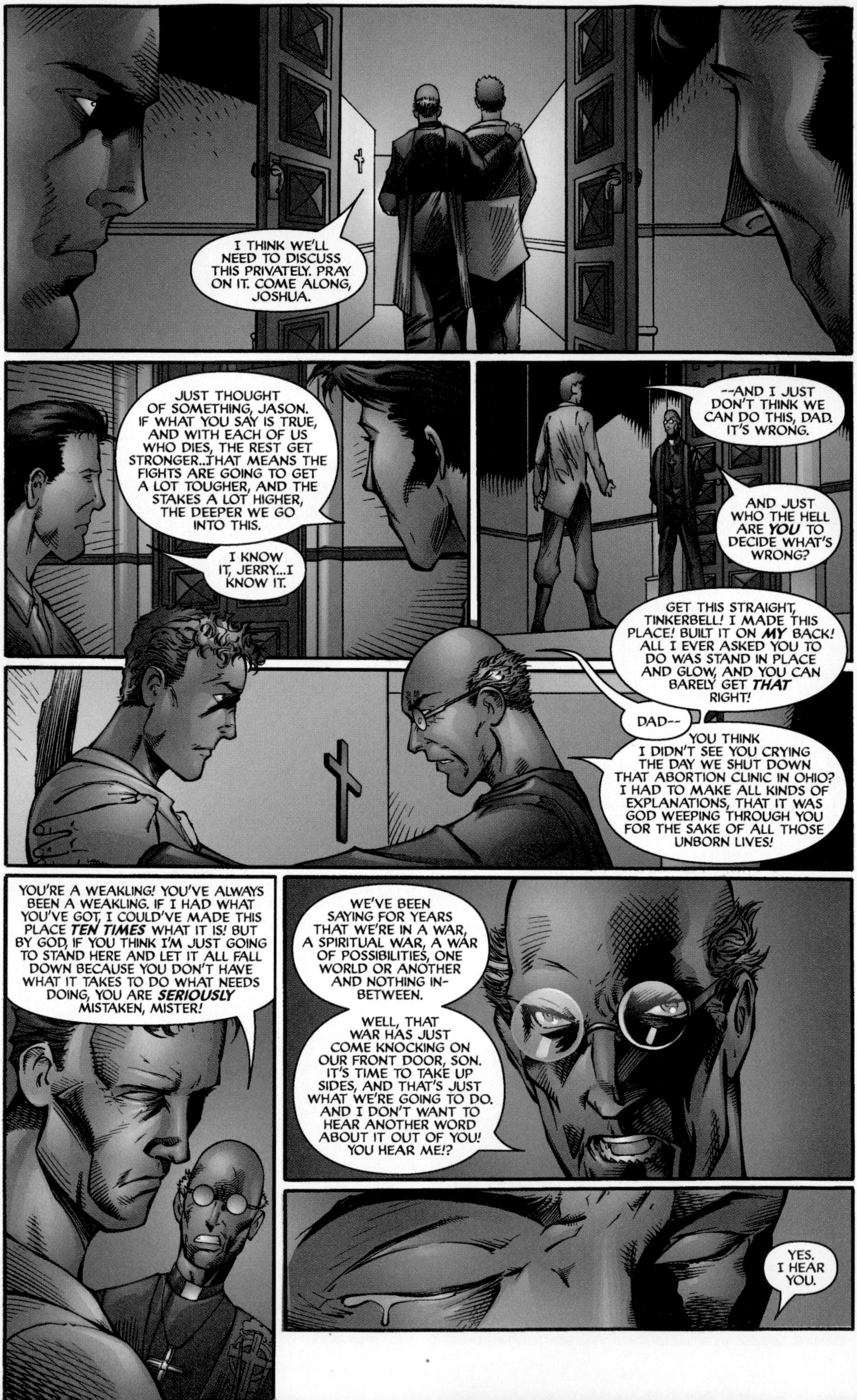
I THINK WE'LL NEED TO DISCUSS THIS PRIVATELY. PRAY ON IT. COME ALONG, JOSHUA.
JUST THOUGHT OF SOMETHING, JASON. IF WHAT YOU SAY IS TRUE, AND WITH EACH OF US WHO DIES, THE REST GET STRONGER...THAT MEANS THE FIGHTS ARE GOING TO GET A LOT TOUGHER, AND THE STAKES A LOT HIGHER, THE DEEPER WE GO INTO THIS.
I KNOW IT, JERRY...I KNOW IT.
--AND I JUST DON'T THINK WE CAN DO THIS, DAD. IT'S WRONG.
AND JUST WHO THE HELL ARE YOU TO DECIDE WHAT'S WRONG?
GET THIS STRAIGHT, TINKERBELL! I MADE THIS PLACE! BUILT IT ON MY BACK! ALL I EVER ASKED YOU TO DO WAS STAND IN PLACE AND GLOW, AND YOU CAN BARELY GET THAT RIGHT!
DAD--
YOU THINK I DIDN'T SEE YOU CRYING THE DAY WE SHUT DOWN THAT ABORTION CLINIC IN OHIO? I HAD TO MAKE ALL KINDS OF EXPLANATIONS, THAT IT WAS GOD WEEPING THROUGH YOU FOR THE SAKE OF ALL THOSE UNBORN LIVES!
YOU'RE A WEAKLING! YOU'VE ALWAYS BEEN A WEAKLING. IF I HAD WHAT YOU'VE GOT, I COULD'VE MADE THIS PLACE TEN TIMES WHAT IT IS! BUT BY GOD, IF YOU THINK I'M JUST GOING TO STAND HERE AND LET IT ALL FALL DOWN BECAUSE YOU DON'T HAVE WHAT IT TAKES TO DO WHAT NEEDS DOING, YOU ARE SERIOUSLY MISTAKEN, MISTER!
WE'VE BEEN SAYING FOR YEARS THAT WE'RE IN A WAR, A SPIRITUAL WAR, A WAR OF POSSIBILITIES, ONE WORLD OR ANOTHER AND NOTHING IN-BETWEEN.
WELL, THAT WAR HAS JUST COME KNOCKING ON OUR FRONT DOOR, SON. IT'S TIME TO TAKE UP SIDES, AND THAT'S JUST WHAT WE'RE GOING TO DO. AND I DON'T WANT TO HEAR ANOTHER WORD ABOUT IT OUT OF YOU! YOU HEAR ME!?
YES. I HEAR YOU.

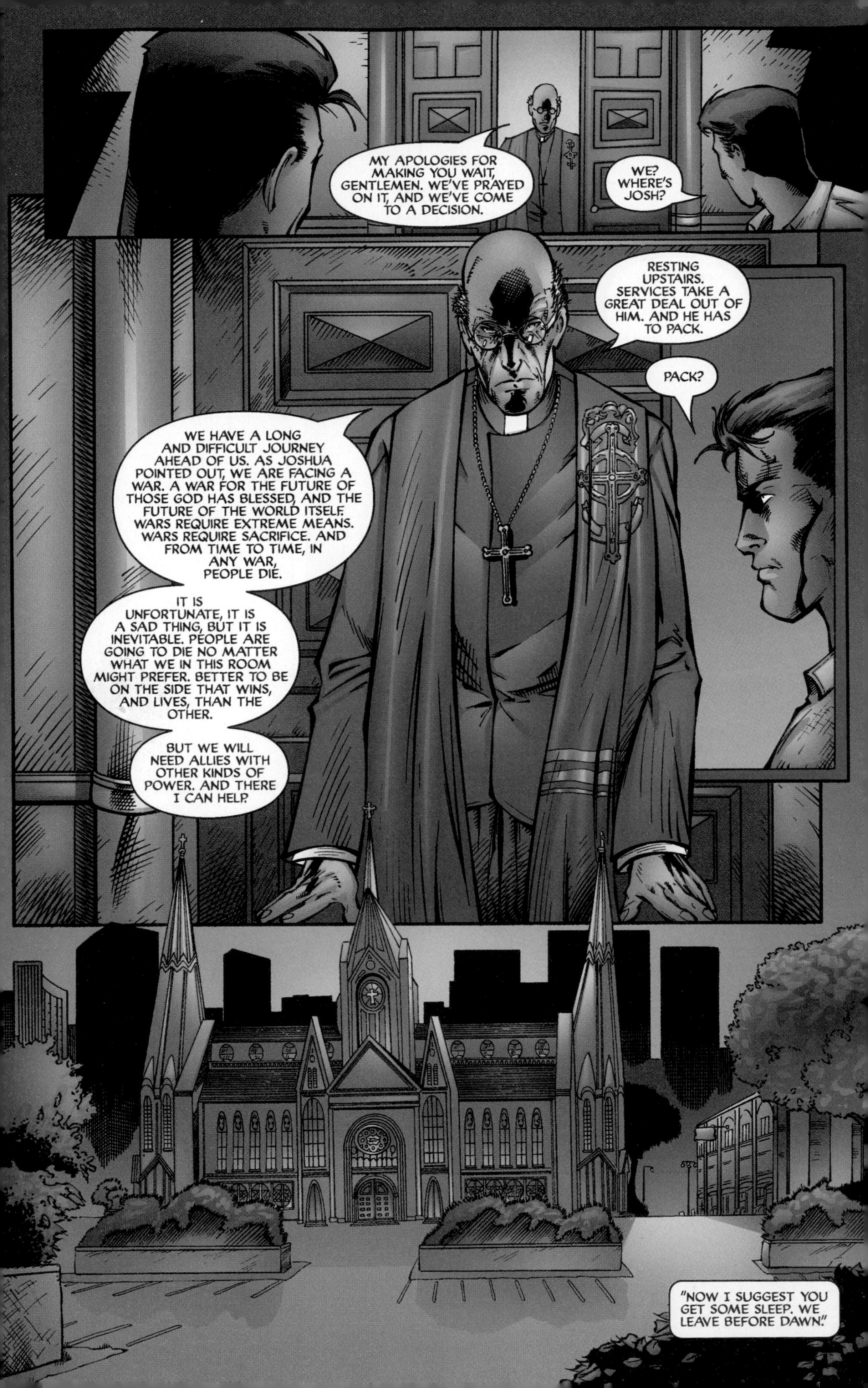
MY APOLOGIES FOR MAKING YOU WAIT, GENTLEMEN. WE'VE PRAYED ON IT, AND WE'VE COME TO A DECISION.
WE? WHERE'S JOSH?
RESTING UPSTAIRS. SERVICES TAKE A GREAT DEAL OUT OF HIM. AND HE HAS TO PACK.
PACK?
WE HAVE A LONG AND DIFFICULT JOURNEY AHEAD OF US. AS JOSHUA POINTED OUT, WE ARE FACING A WAR. A WAR FOR THE FUTURE OF THOSE GOD HAS BLESSED, AND THE FUTURE OF THE WORLD ITSELF. WARS REQUIRE EXTREME MEANS. WARS REQUIRE SACRIFICE. AND FROM TIME TO TIME, IN ANY WAR, PEOPLE DIE.
IT IS UNFORTUNATE, IT IS A SAD THING, BUT IT IS INEVITABLE. PEOPLE ARE GOING TO DIE NO MATTER WHAT WE IN THIS ROOM MIGHT PREFER. BETTER TO BE ON THE SIDE THAT WINS, AND LIVES, THAN THE OTHER.
BUT WE WILL NEED ALLIES WITH OTHER KINDS OF POWER. AND THERE I CAN HELP.
"NOW I SUGGEST YOU GET SOME SLEEP. WE LEAVE BEFORE DAWN."

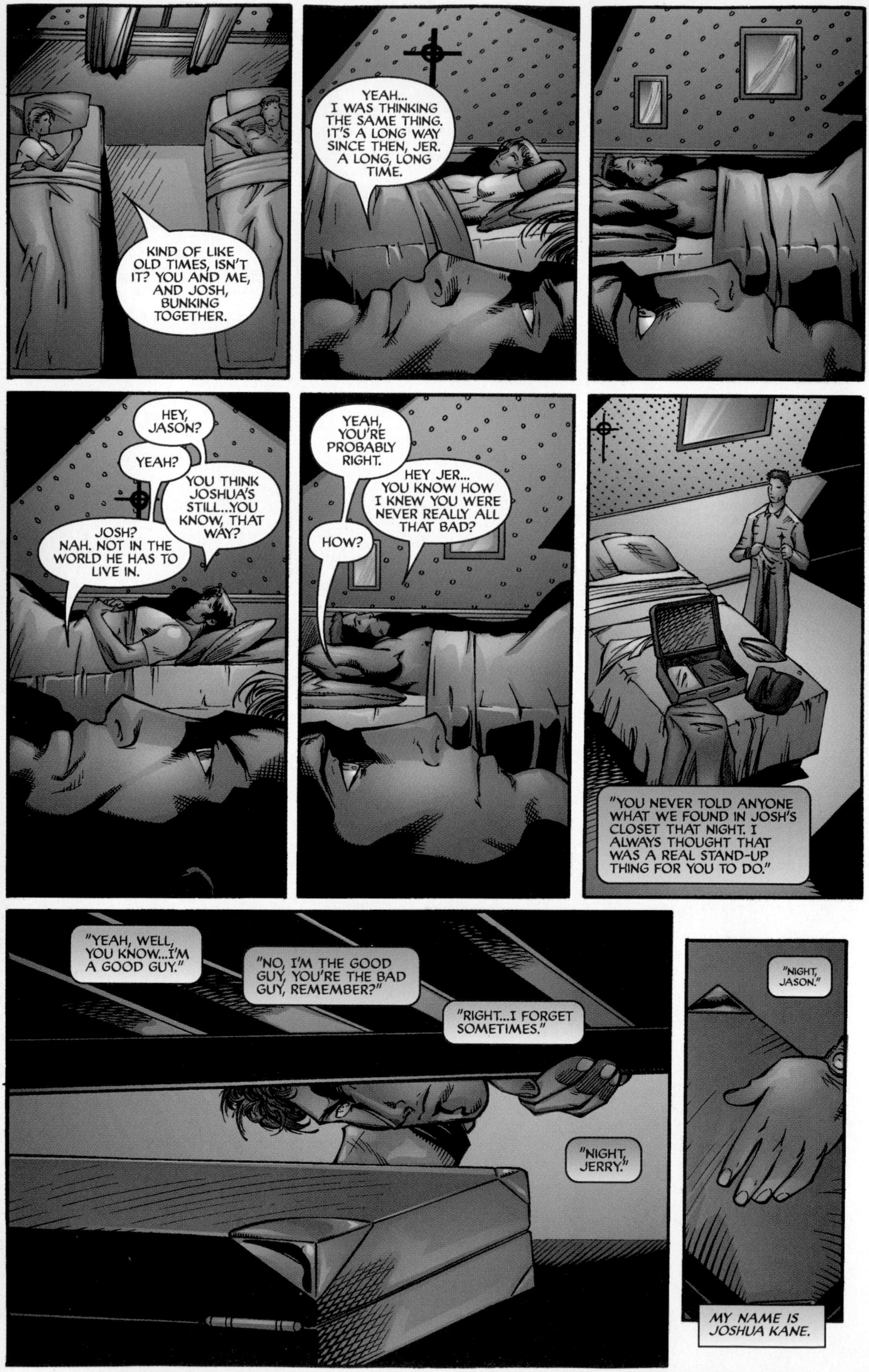
KIND OF LIKE OLD TIMES, ISN'T IT? YOU AND ME, AND JOSH, BUNKING TOGETHER.
YEAH... I WAS THINKING THE SAME THING. IT'S A LONG WAY SINCE THEN, JER. A LONG, LONG TIME.
HEY, JASON?
YEAH?
YOU THINK JOSHUA'S STILL...YOU KNOW, THAT WAY?
JOSH? NAH. NOT IN THE WORLD HE HAS TO LIVE IN.
YEAH, YOU'RE PROBABLY RIGHT.
HEY JER... YOU KNOW HOW I KNEW YOU WERE NEVER REALLY ALL THAT BAD?
HOW?
"YOU NEVER TOLD ANYONE WHAT WE FOUND IN JOSH'S CLOSET THAT NIGHT. I ALWAYS THOUGHT THAT WAS A REAL STAND-UP THING FOR YOU TO DO."
"YEAH, WELL, YOU KNOW...I'M A GOOD GUY."
"NO, I'M THE GOOD GUY, YOU'RE THE BAD GUY, REMEMBER?"
"RIGHT...I FORGET SOMETIMES."
"NIGHT, JERRY."
"NIGHT, JASON."
MY NAME IS JOSHUA KANE.

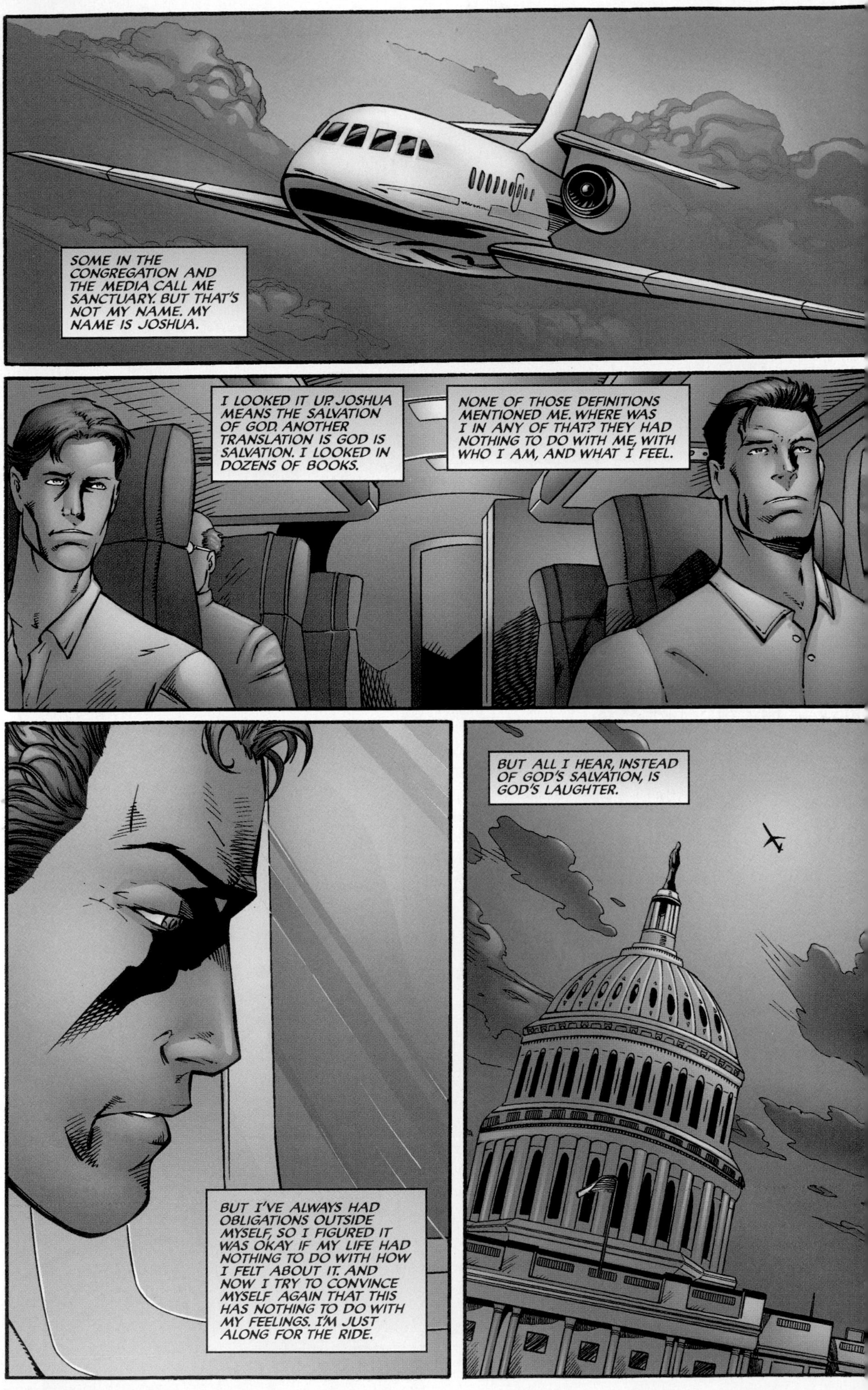
SOME IN THE CONGREGATION AND THE MEDIA CALL ME SANCTUARY. BUT THAT'S NOT MY NAME. MY NAME IS JOSHUA.
I LOOKED IT UP. JOSHUA MEANS THE SALVATION OF GOD. ANOTHER TRANSLATION IS GOD IS SALVATION. I LOOKED IN DOZENS OF BOOKS.
NONE OF THOSE DEFINITIONS MENTIONED ME. WHERE WAS I IN ANY OF THAT? THEY HAD NOTHING TO DO WITH ME, WITH WHO I AM, AND WHAT I FEEL.
BUT I'VE ALWAYS HAD OBLIGATIONS OUTSIDE MYSELF, SO I FIGURED IT WAS OKAY IF MY LIFE HAD NOTHING TO DO WITH HOW I FELT ABOUT IT. AND NOW I TRY TO CONVINCE MYSELF AGAIN THAT THIS HAS NOTHING TO DO WITH MY FEELINGS. I'M JUST ALONG FOR THE RIDE.
BUT ALL I HEAR, INSTEAD OF GOD'S SALVATION, IS GOD'S LAUGHTER.

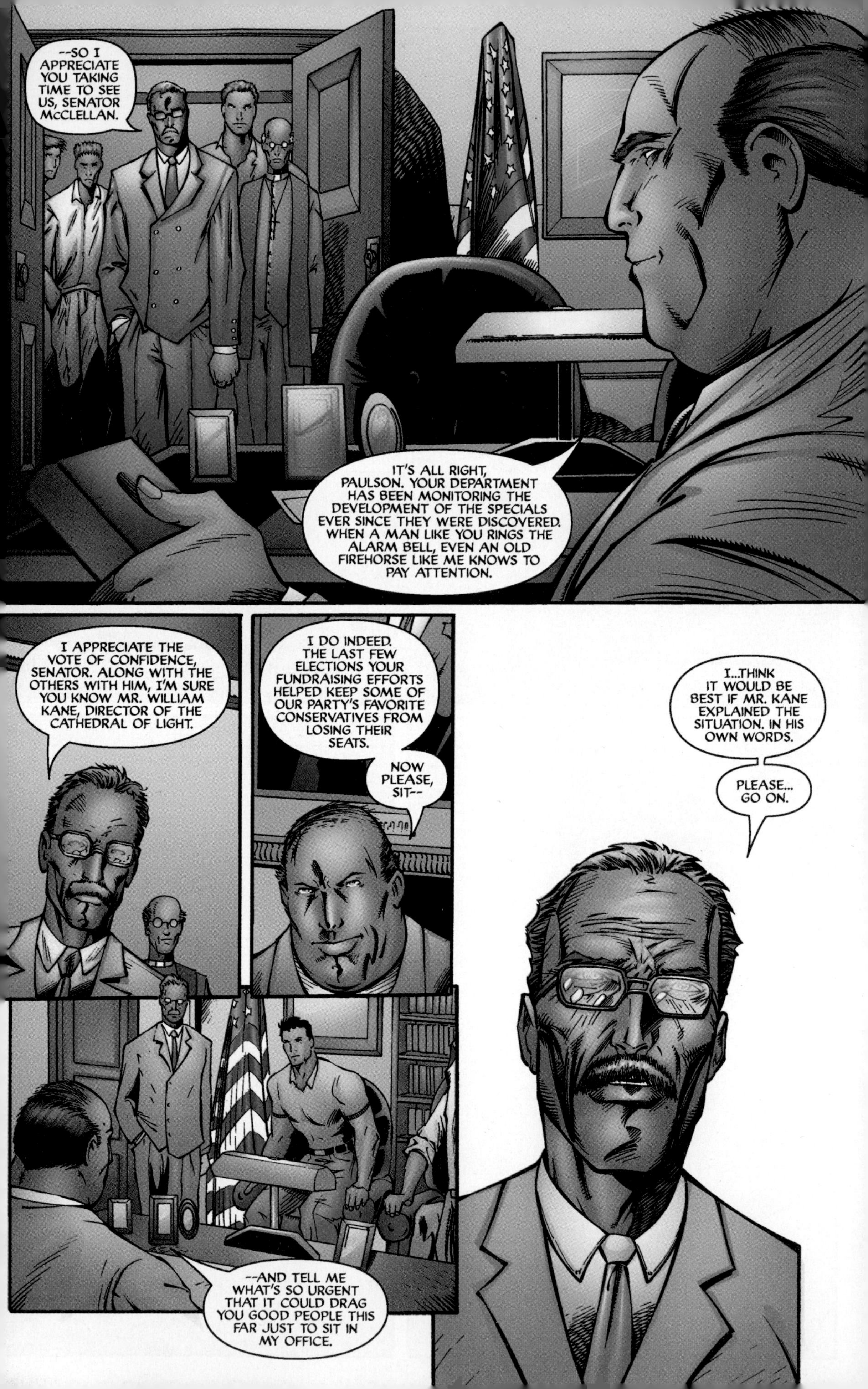
--SO I APPRECIATE YOU TAKING TIME TO SEE US, SENATOR McCLELLAN.
IT'S ALL RIGHT, PAULSON. YOUR DEPARTMENT HAS BEEN MONITORING THE DEVELOPMENT OF THE SPECIALS EVER SINCE THEY WERE DISCOVERED. WHEN A MAN LIKE YOU RINGS THE ALARM BELL, EVEN AN OLD FIREHORSE LIKE ME KNOWS TO PAY ATTENTION.
I APPRECIATE THE VOTE OF CONFIDENCE, SENATOR. ALONG WITH THE OTHERS WITH HIM, I'M SURE YOU KNOW MR. WILLIAM KANE, DIRECTOR OF THE CATHEDRAL OF LIGHT.
I DO INDEED. THE LAST FEW ELECTIONS YOUR FUNDRAISING EFFORTS HELPED KEEP SOME OF OUR PARTY'S FAVORITE CONSERVATIVES FROM LOSING THEIR SEATS.
NOW PLEASE, SIT--
--AND TELL ME WHAT'S SO URGENT THAT IT COULD DRAG YOU GOOD PEOPLE THIS FAR JUST TO SIT IN MY OFFICE.
I...THINK IT WOULD BE BEST IF MR. KANE EXPLAINED THE SITUATION. IN HIS OWN WORDS.
PLEASE... GO ON.

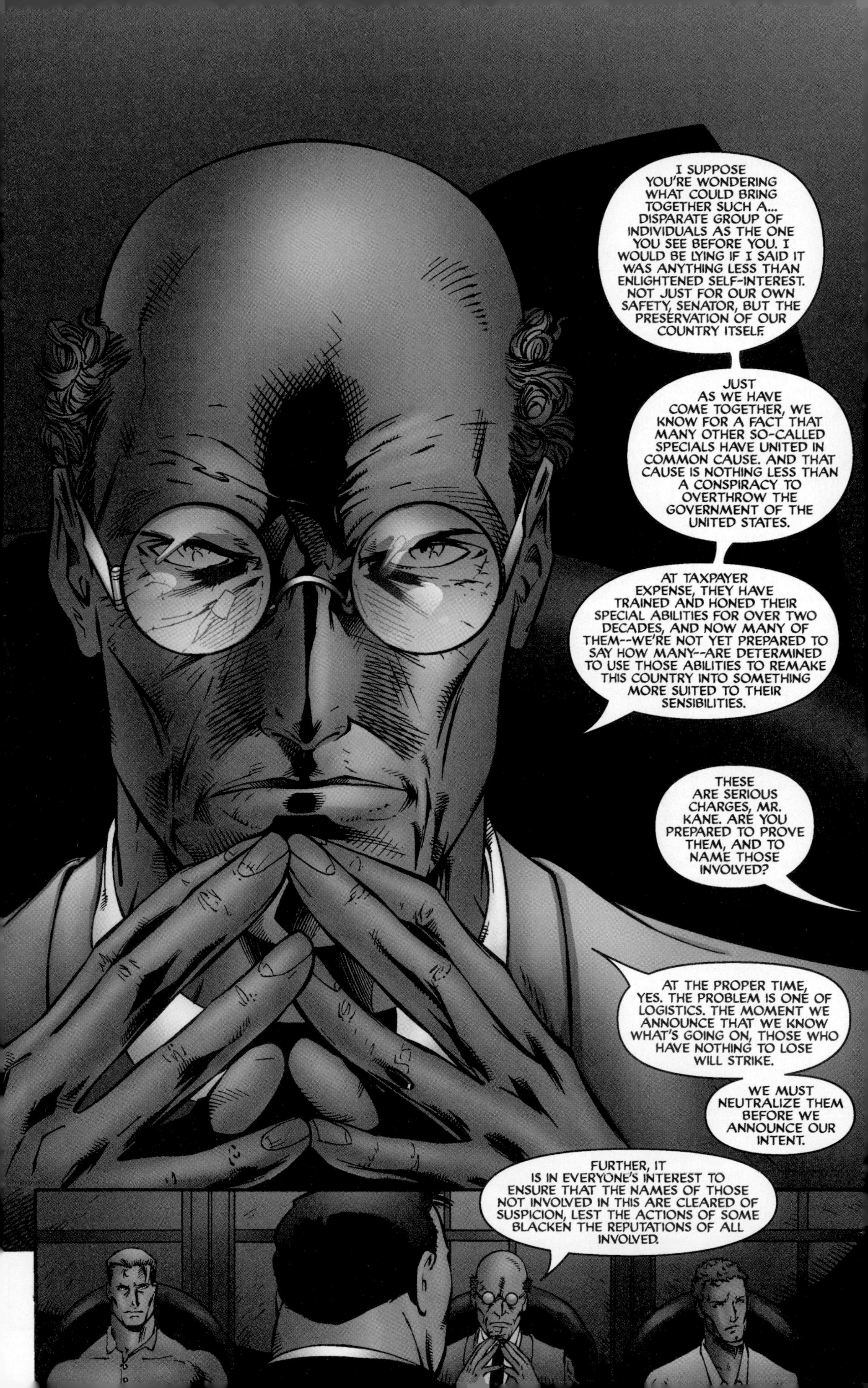
I SUPPOSE YOU'RE WONDERING WHAT COULD BRING TOGETHER SUCH A... DISPARATE GROUP OF INDIVIDUALS AS THE ONE YOU SEE BEFORE YOU. I WOULD BE LYING IF I SAID IT WAS ANYTHING LESS THAN ENLIGHTENED SELF-INTEREST. NOT JUST FOR OUR OWN SAFETY, SENATOR, BUT THE PRESERVATION OF OUR COUNTRY ITSELF.
JUST AS WE HAVE COME TOGETHER, WE KNOW FOR A FACT THAT MANY OTHER SO-CALLED SPECIALS HAVE UNITED IN COMMON CAUSE. AND THAT CAUSE IS NOTHING LESS THAN A CONSPIRACY TO OVERTHROW THE GOVERNMENT OF THE UNITED STATES.
AT TAXPAYER EXPENSE, THEY HAVE TRAINED AND HONED THEIR SPECIAL ABILITIES FOR OVER TWO DECADES, AND NOW MANY OF THEM--WE'RE NOT YET PREPARED TO SAY HOW MANY--ARE DETERMINED TO USE THOSE ABILITIES TO REMAKE THIS COUNTRY INTO SOMETHING MORE SUITED TO THEIR SENSIBILITIES.
THESE ARE SERIOUS CHARGES, MR. KANE. ARE YOU PREPARED TO PROVE THEM, AND TO NAME THOSE INVOLVED?
AT THE PROPER TIME, YES. THE PROBLEM IS ONE OF LOGISTICS. THE MOMENT WE ANNOUNCE THAT WE KNOW WHAT'S GOING ON, THOSE WHO HAVE NOTHING TO LOSE WILL STRIKE.
WE MUST NEUTRALIZE THEM BEFORE WE ANNOUNCE OUR INTENT.
FURTHER, IT IS IN EVERYONE'S INTEREST TO ENSURE THAT THE NAMES OF THOSE NOT INVOLVED IN THIS ARE CLEARED OF SUSPICION, LEST THE ACTIONS OF SOME BLACKEN THE REPUTATIONS OF ALL INVOLVED.

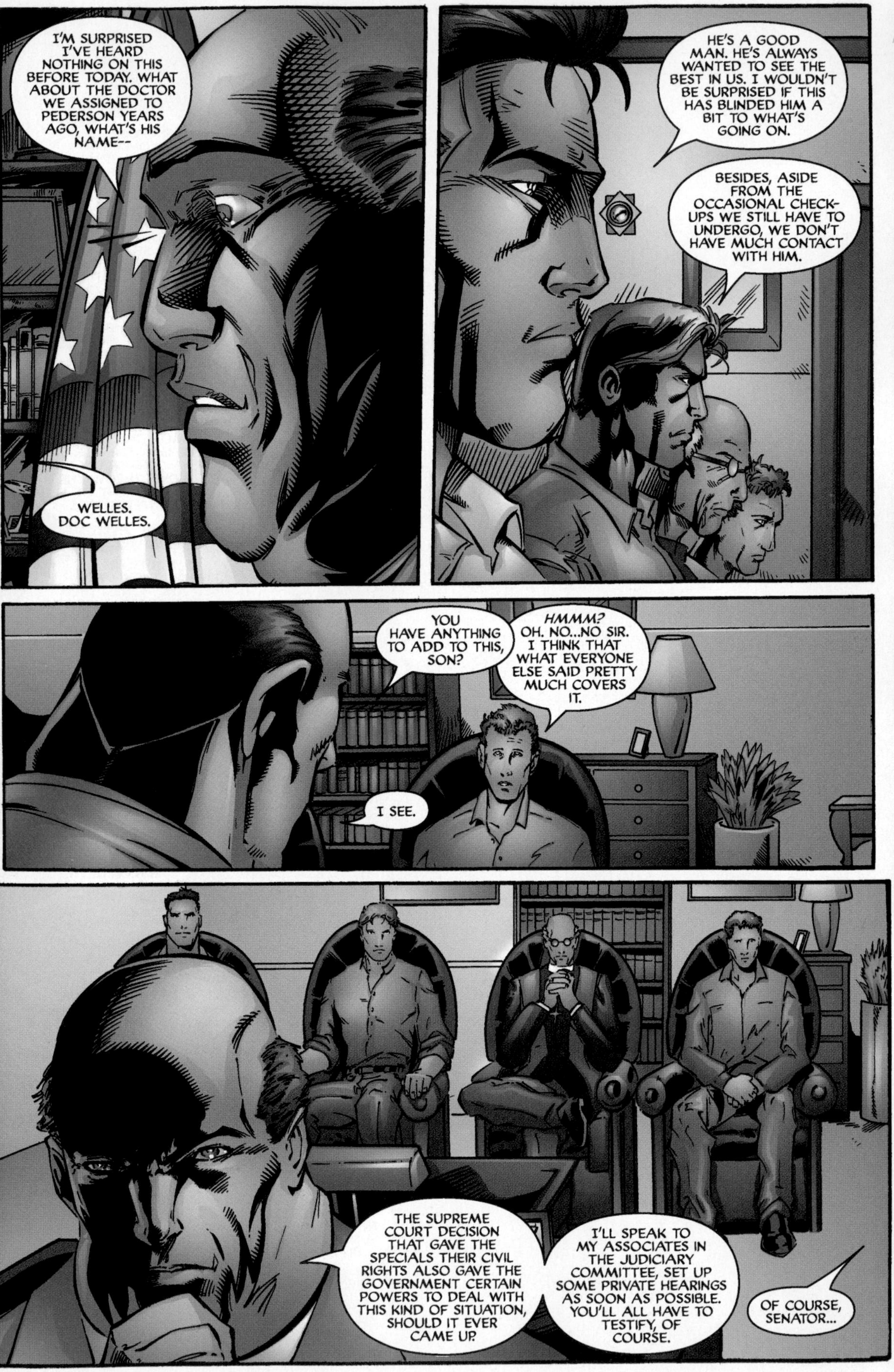
I'M SURPRISED I'VE HEARD NOTHING ON THIS BEFORE TODAY. WHAT ABOUT THE DOCTOR WE ASSIGNED TO PEDERSON YEARS AGO, WHAT'S HIS NAME--
WELLES. DOC WELLES.
HE'S A GOOD MAN. HE'S ALWAYS WANTED TO SEE THE BEST IN US. I WOULDN'T BE SURPRISED IF THIS HAS BLINDED HIM A BIT TO WHAT'S GOING ON.
BESIDES, ASIDE FROM THE OCCASIONAL CHECK-UPS WE STILL HAVE TO UNDERGO, WE DON'T HAVE MUCH CONTACT WITH HIM.
YOU HAVE ANYTHING TO ADD TO THIS, SON?
HMMM? OH. NO...NO SIR. I THINK THAT WHAT EVERYONE ELSE SAID PRETTY MUCH COVERS IT.
I SEE.
THE SUPREME COURT DECISION THAT GAVE THE SPECIALS THEIR CIVIL RIGHTS ALSO GAVE THE GOVERNMENT CERTAIN POWERS TO DEAL WITH THIS KIND OF SITUATION, SHOULD IT EVER CAME UP?
I'LL SPEAK TO MY ASSOCIATES IN THE JUDICIARY COMMITTEE, SET UP SOME PRIVATE HEARINGS AS SOON AS POSSIBLE. YOU'LL ALL HAVE TO TESTIFY, OF COURSE.
OF COURSE, SENATOR...

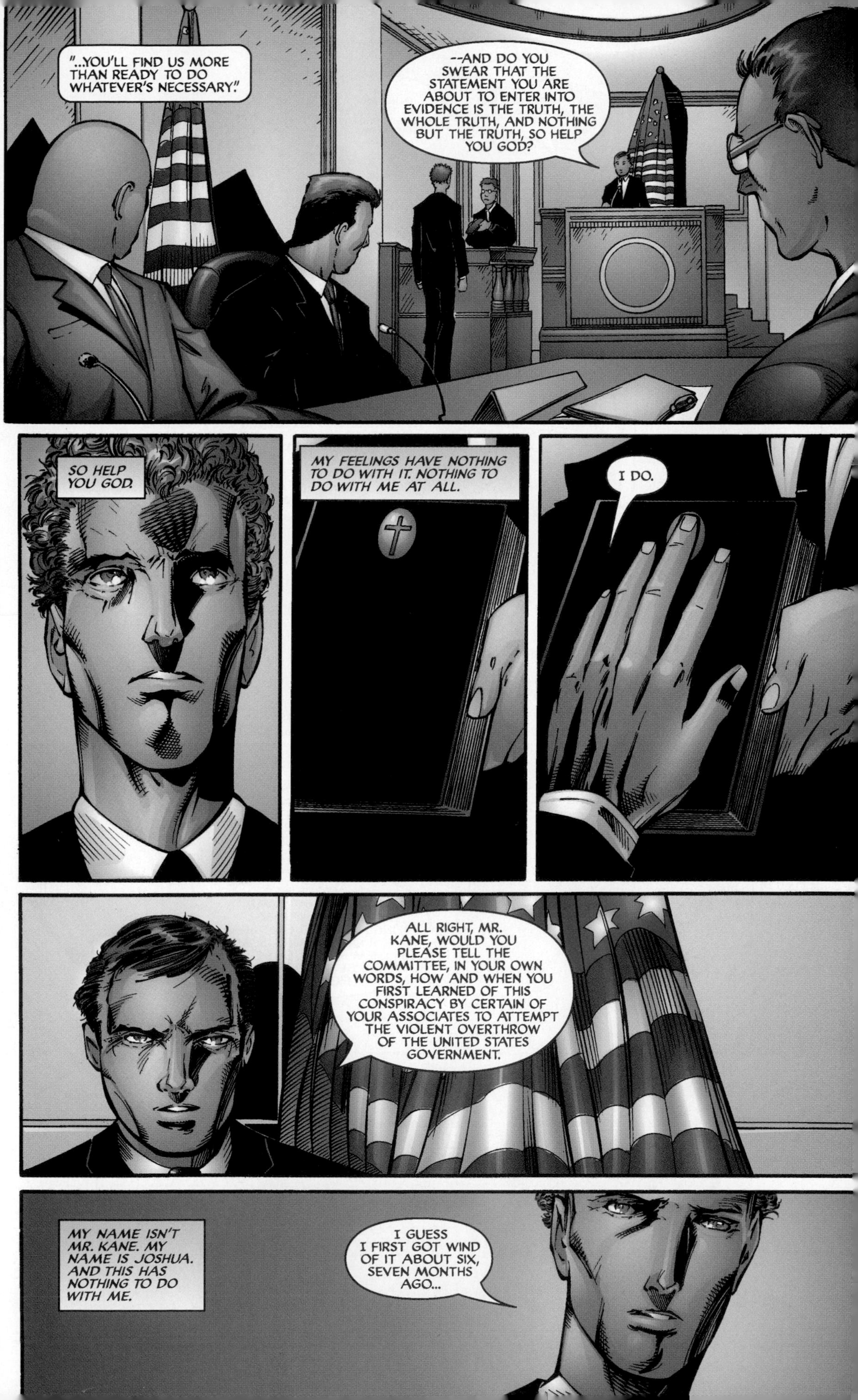
"...YOU'LL FIND US MORE THAN READY TO DO WHATEVER'S NECESSARY."
--AND DO YOU SWEAR THAT THE STATEMENT YOU ARE ABOUT TO ENTER INTO EVIDENCE IS THE TRUTH, THE WHOLE TRUTH, AND NOTHING BUT THE TRUTH, SO HELP YOU GOD?
SO HELP YOU GOD.
MY FEELINGS HAVE NOTHING TO DO WITH IT. NOTHING TO DO WITH ME AT ALL.
I DO.
ALL RIGHT, MR. KANE, WOULD YOU PLEASE TELL THE COMMITTEE, IN YOUR OWN WORDS, HOW AND WHEN YOU FIRST LEARNED OF THIS CONSPIRACY BY CERTAIN OF YOUR ASSOCIATES TO ATTEMPT THE VIOLENT OVERTHROW OF THE UNITED STATES GOVERNMENT.
MY NAME ISN'T MR. KANE. MY NAME IS JOSHUA. AND THIS HAS NOTHING TO DO WITH ME.
I GUESS I FIRST GOT WIND OF IT ABOUT SIX, SEVEN MONTHS AGO...

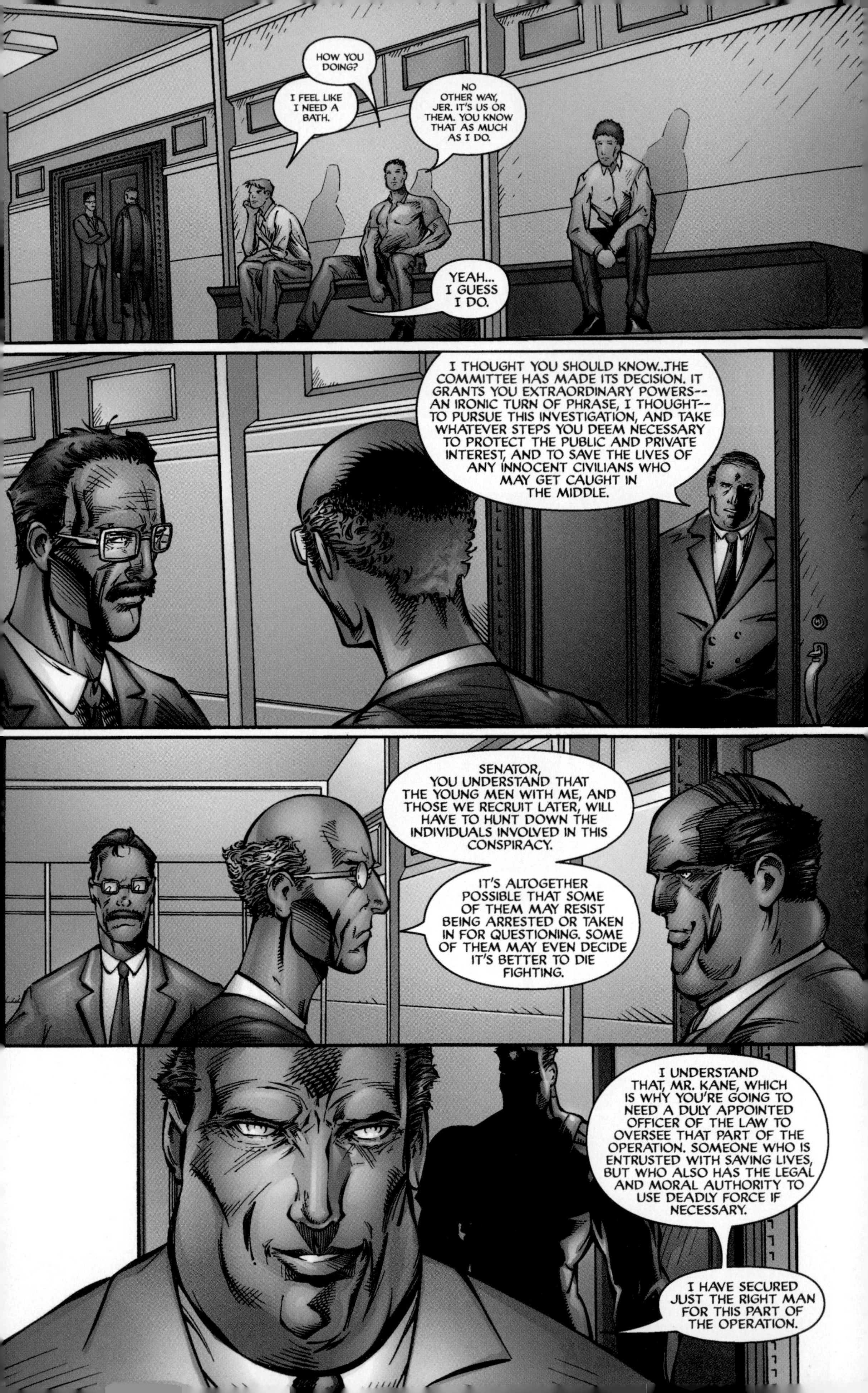
HOW YOU DOING?
I FEEL LIKE I NEED A BATH.
NO OTHER WAY, JER. IT'S US OR THEM. YOU KNOW THAT AS MUCH AS I DO.
YEAH... I GUESS I DO.
I THOUGHT YOU SHOULD KNOW..THE COMMITTEE HAS MADE ITS DECISION. IT GRANTS YOU EXTRAORDINARY POWERS-- AN IRONIC TURN OF PHRASE, I THOUGHT-- TO PURSUE THIS INVESTIGATION, AND TAKE WHATEVER STEPS YOU DEEM NECESSARY TO PROTECT THE PUBLIC AND PRIVATE INTEREST, AND TO SAVE THE LIVES OF ANY INNOCENT CIVILIANS WHO MAY GET CAUGHT IN THE MIDDLE.
SENATOR, YOU UNDERSTAND THAT THE YOUNG MEN WITH ME, AND THOSE WE RECRUIT LATER, WILL HAVE TO HUNT DOWN THE INDIVIDUALS INVOLVED IN THIS CONSPIRACY.
IT'S ALTOGETHER POSSIBLE THAT SOME OF THEM MAY RESIST BEING ARRESTED OR TAKEN IN FOR QUESTIONING. SOME OF THEM MAY EVEN DECIDE IT'S BETTER TO DIE FIGHTING.
I UNDERSTAND THAT, MR. KANE, WHICH IS WHY YOU'RE GOING TO NEED A DULY APPOINTED OFFICER OF THE LAW TO OVERSEE THAT PART OF THE OPERATION. SOMEONE WHO IS ENTRUSTED WITH SAVING LIVES, BUT WHO ALSO HAS THE LEGAL AND MORAL AUTHORITY TO USE DEADLY FORCE IF NECESSARY.
I HAVE SECURED JUST THE RIGHT MAN FOR THIS PART OF THE OPERATION.

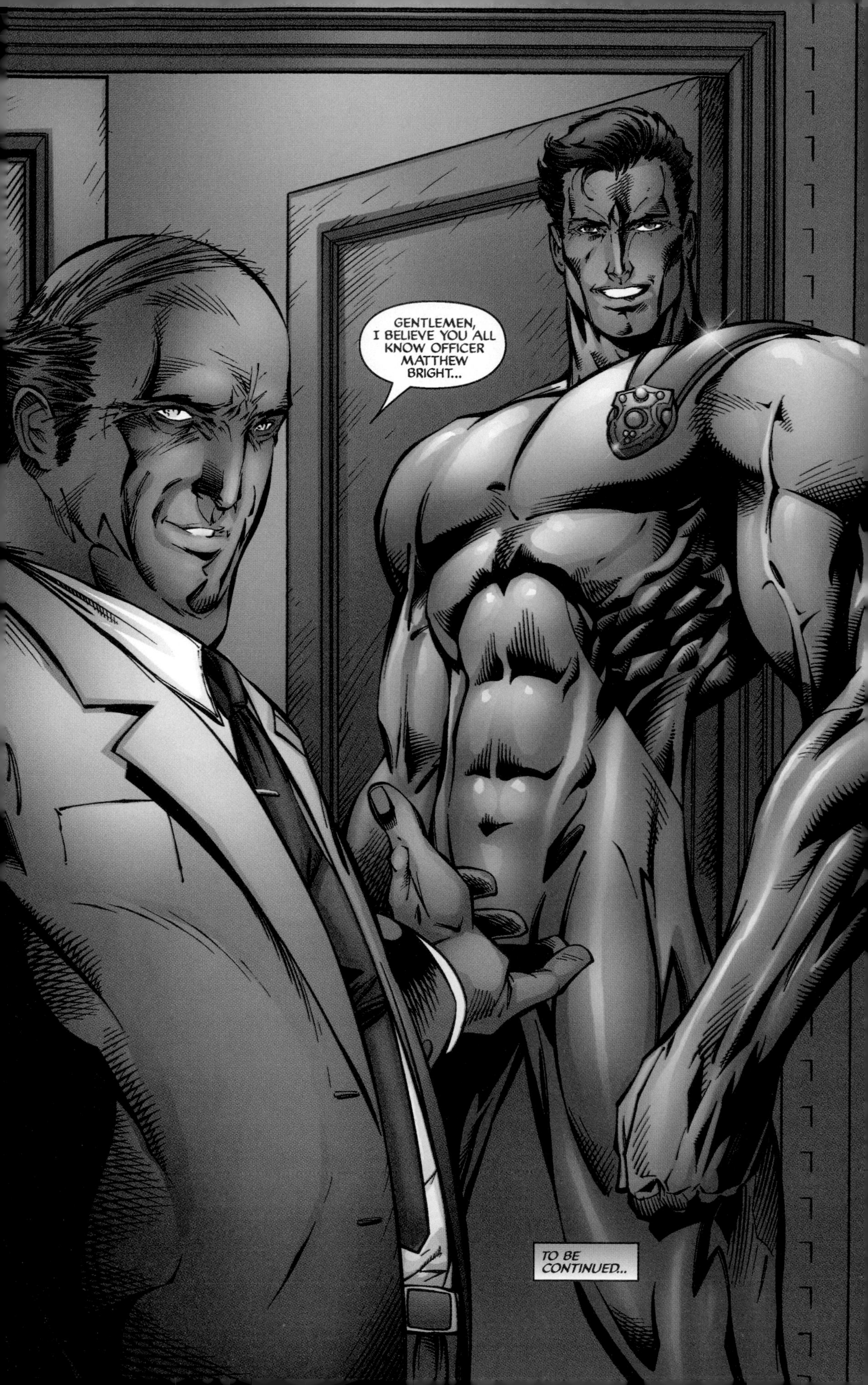
GENTLEMEN, I BELIEVE YOU ALL KNOW OFFICER MATTHEW BRIGHT...
TO BE CONTINUED...

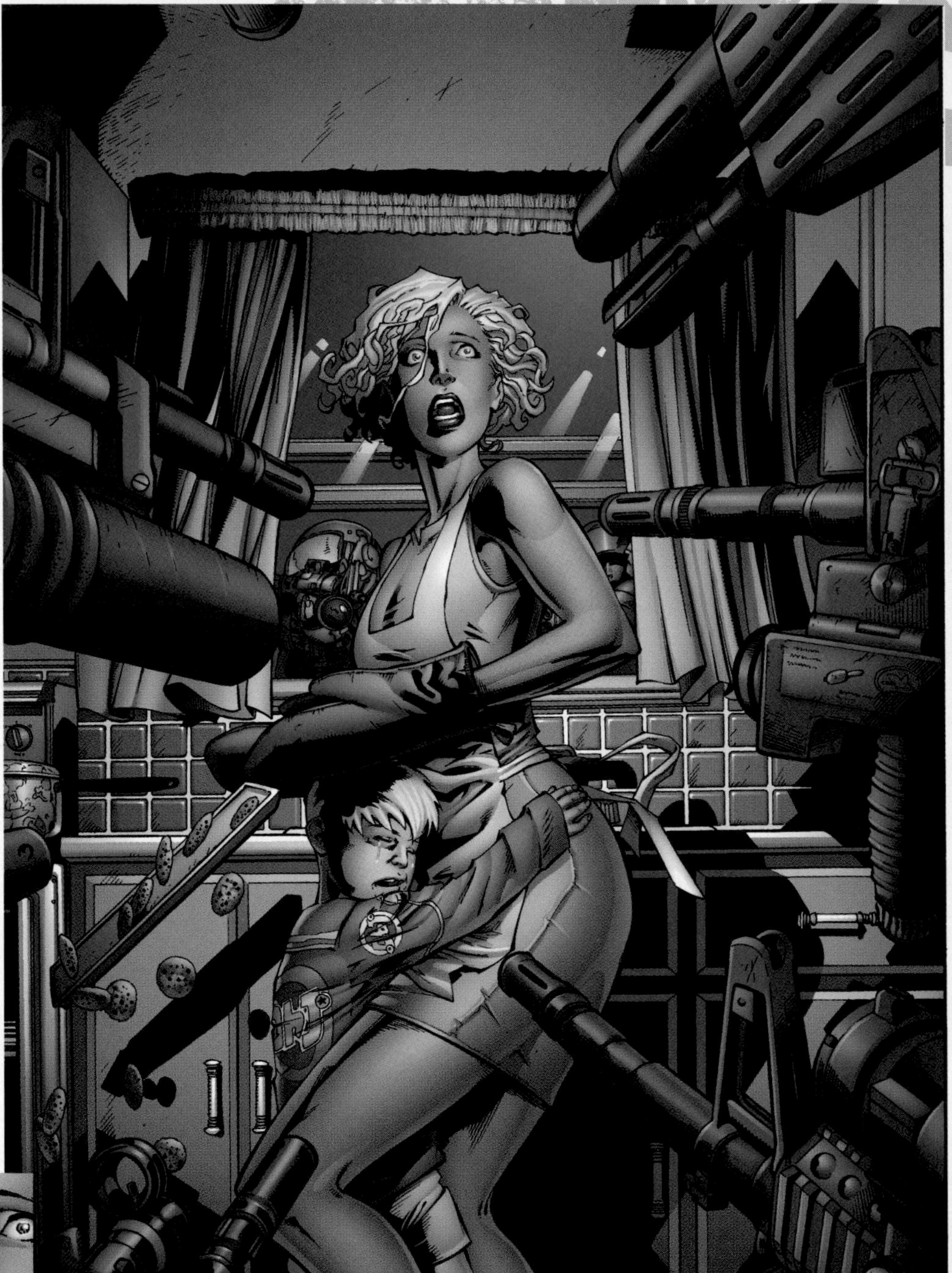

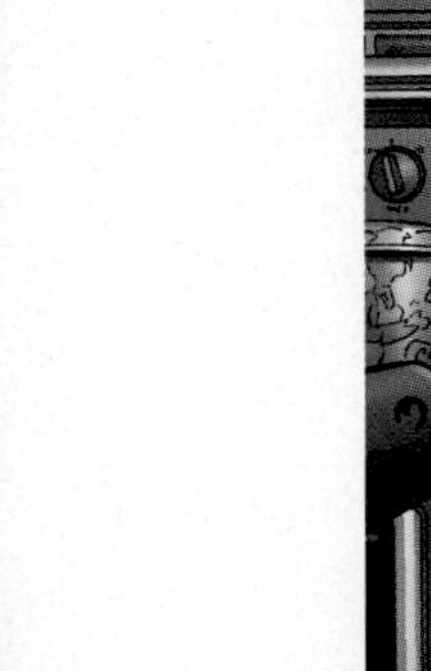

CHAPTER 7
THINGS FALL APART—TWO

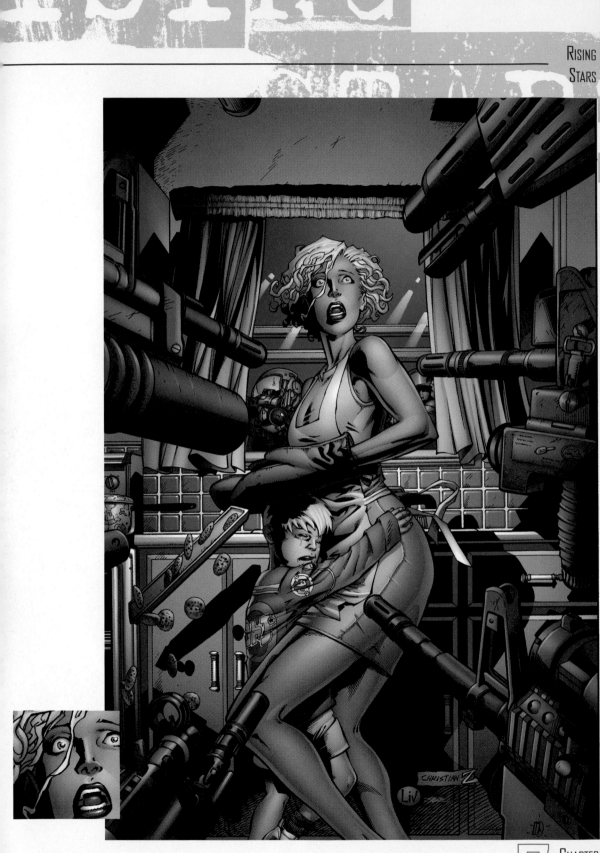

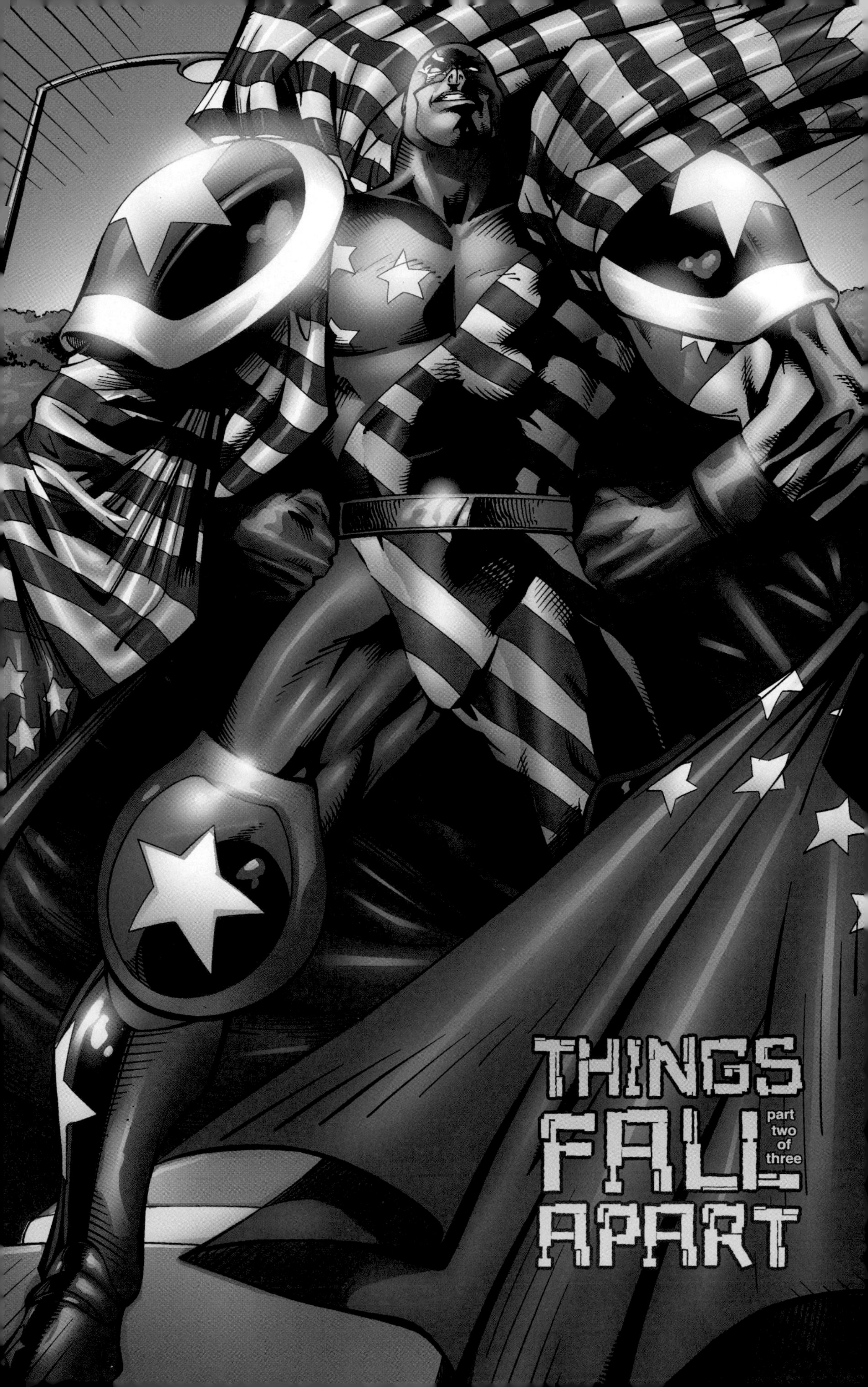
THINGS FALL APART
part two of three

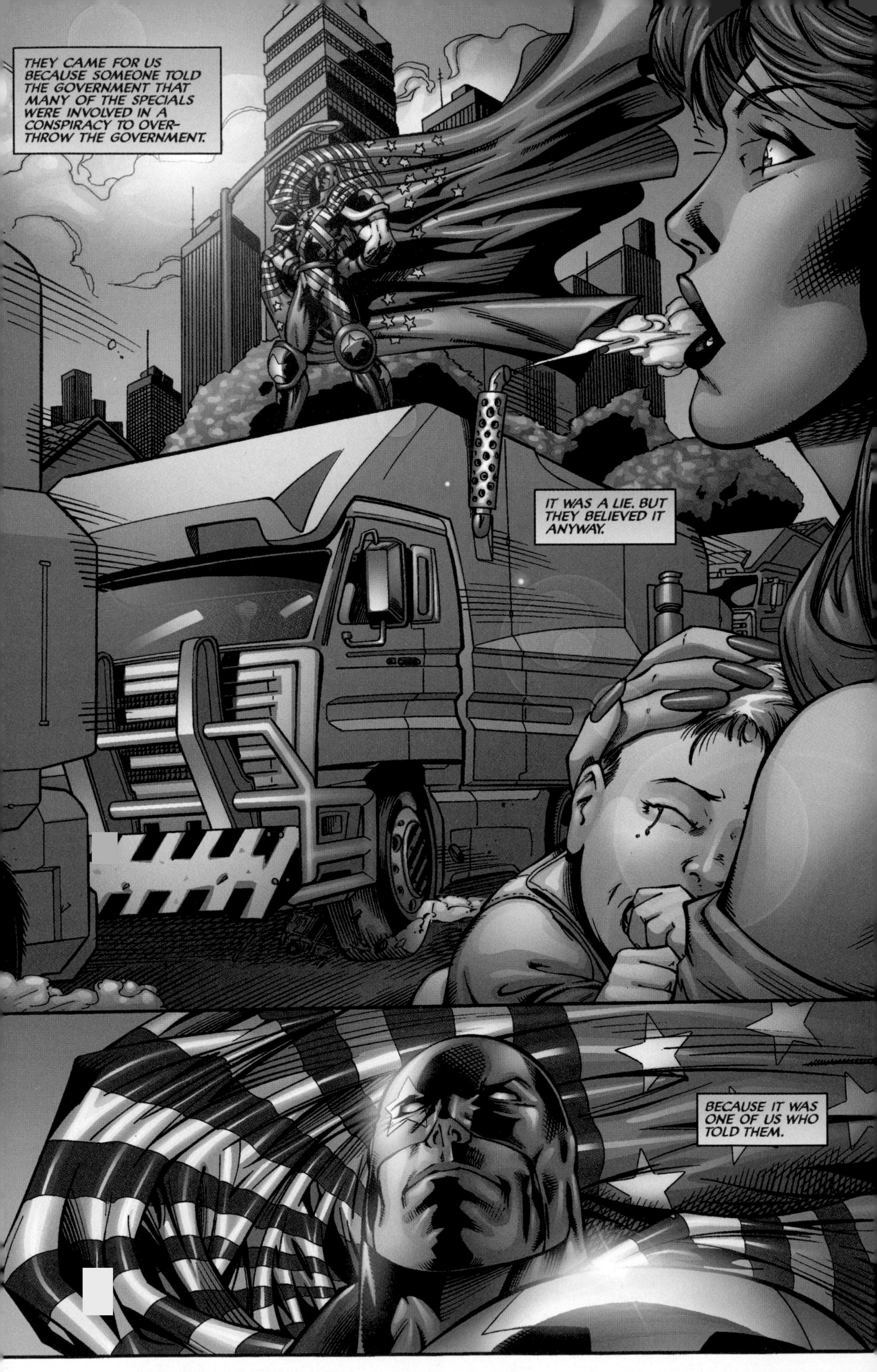
THEY CAME FOR US BECAUSE SOMEONE TOLD THE GOVERNMENT THAT MANY OF THE SPECIALS WERE INVOLVED IN A CONSPIRACY TO OVER-THROW THE GOVERNMENT.
IT WAS A LIE. BUT THEY BELIEVED IT ANYWAY.
BECAUSE IT WAS ONE OF US WHO TOLD THEM.

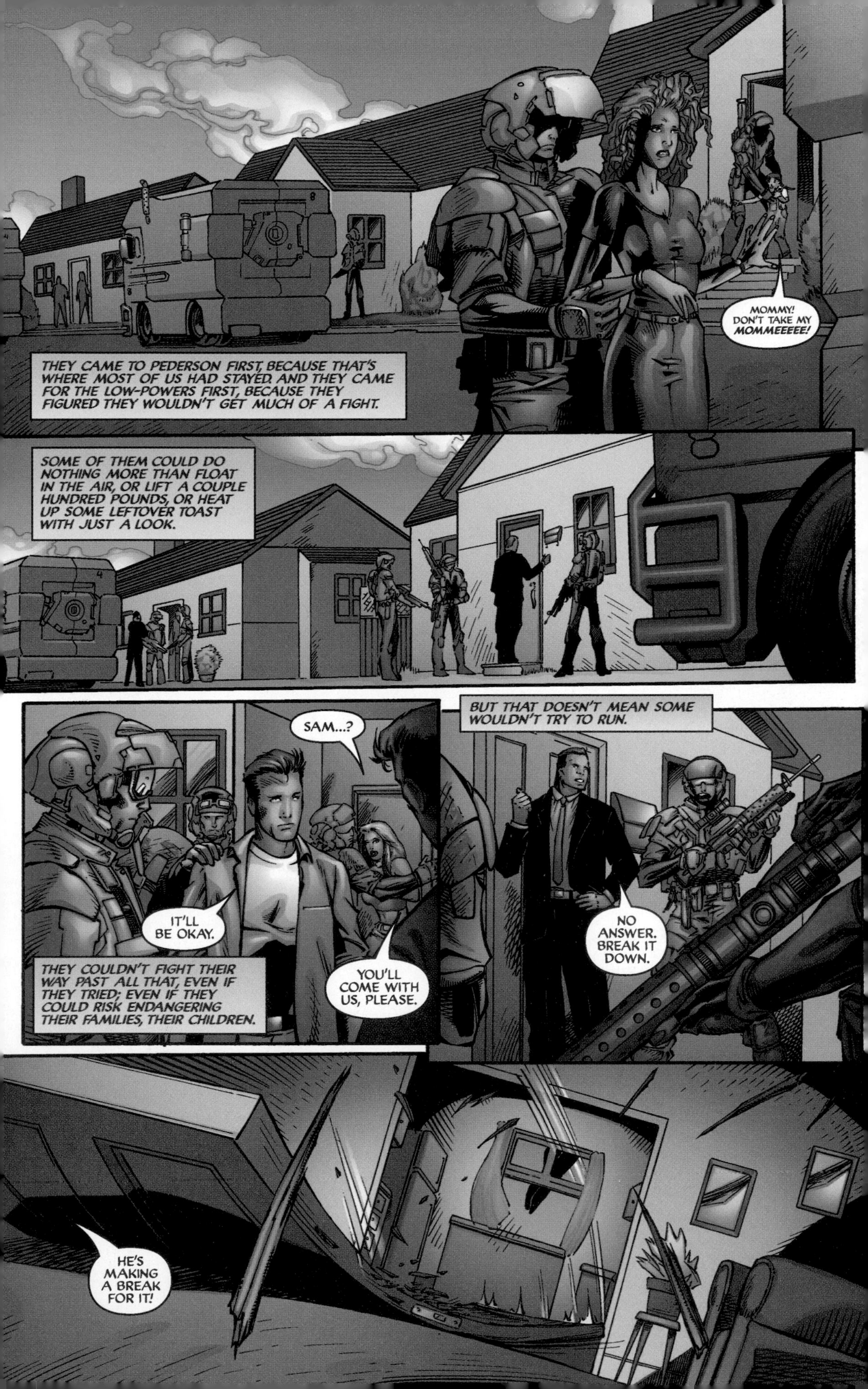
THEY CAME TO PEDERSON FIRST, BECAUSE THAT'S WHERE MOST OF US HAD STAYED. AND THEY CAME FOR THE LOW-POWERS FIRST, BECAUSE THEY FIGURED THEY WOULDN'T GET MUCH OF A FIGHT.
MOMMY! DON'T TAKE MY MOMMEEEEE!
SOME OF THEM COULD DO NOTHING MORE THAN FLOAT IN THE AIR, OR LIFT A COUPLE HUNDRED POUNDS, OR HEAT UP SOME LEFTOVER TOAST WITH JUST A LOOK.
SAM...?
IT'LL BE OKAY.
THEY COULDN'T FIGHT THEIR WAY PAST ALL THAT, EVEN IF THEY TRIED; EVEN IF THEY COULD RISK ENDANGERING THEIR FAMILIES, THEIR CHILDREN.
YOU'LL COME WITH US, PLEASE.
BUT THAT DOESN'T MEAN SOME WOULDN'T TRY TO RUN.
NO ANSWER. BREAK IT DOWN.
HE'S MAKING A BREAK FOR IT!

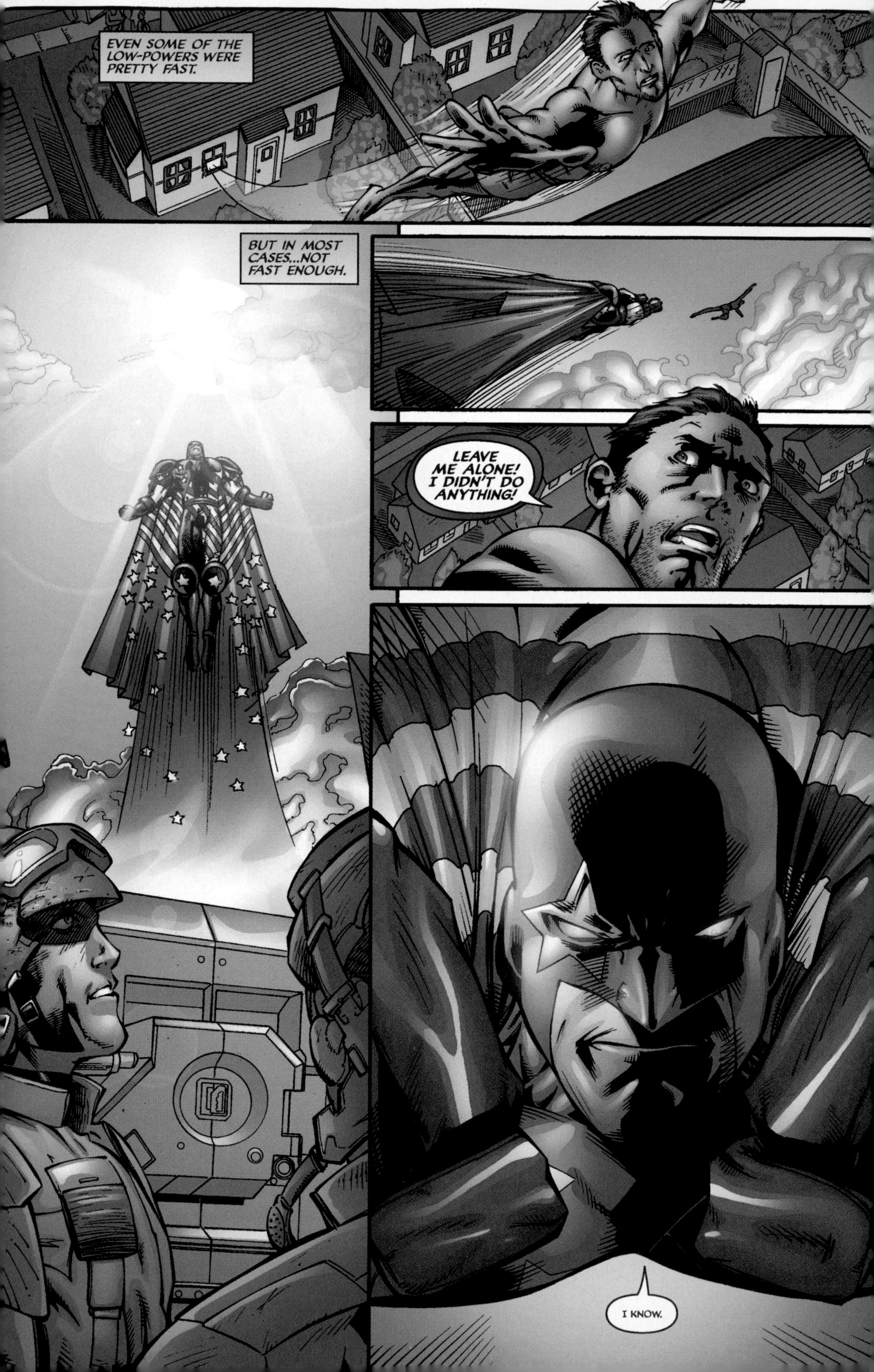
EVEN SOME OF THE LOW-POWERS WERE PRETTY FAST.
BUT IN MOST CASES...NOT FAST ENOUGH.
LEAVE ME ALONE! I DIDN'T DO ANYTHING!
I KNOW.

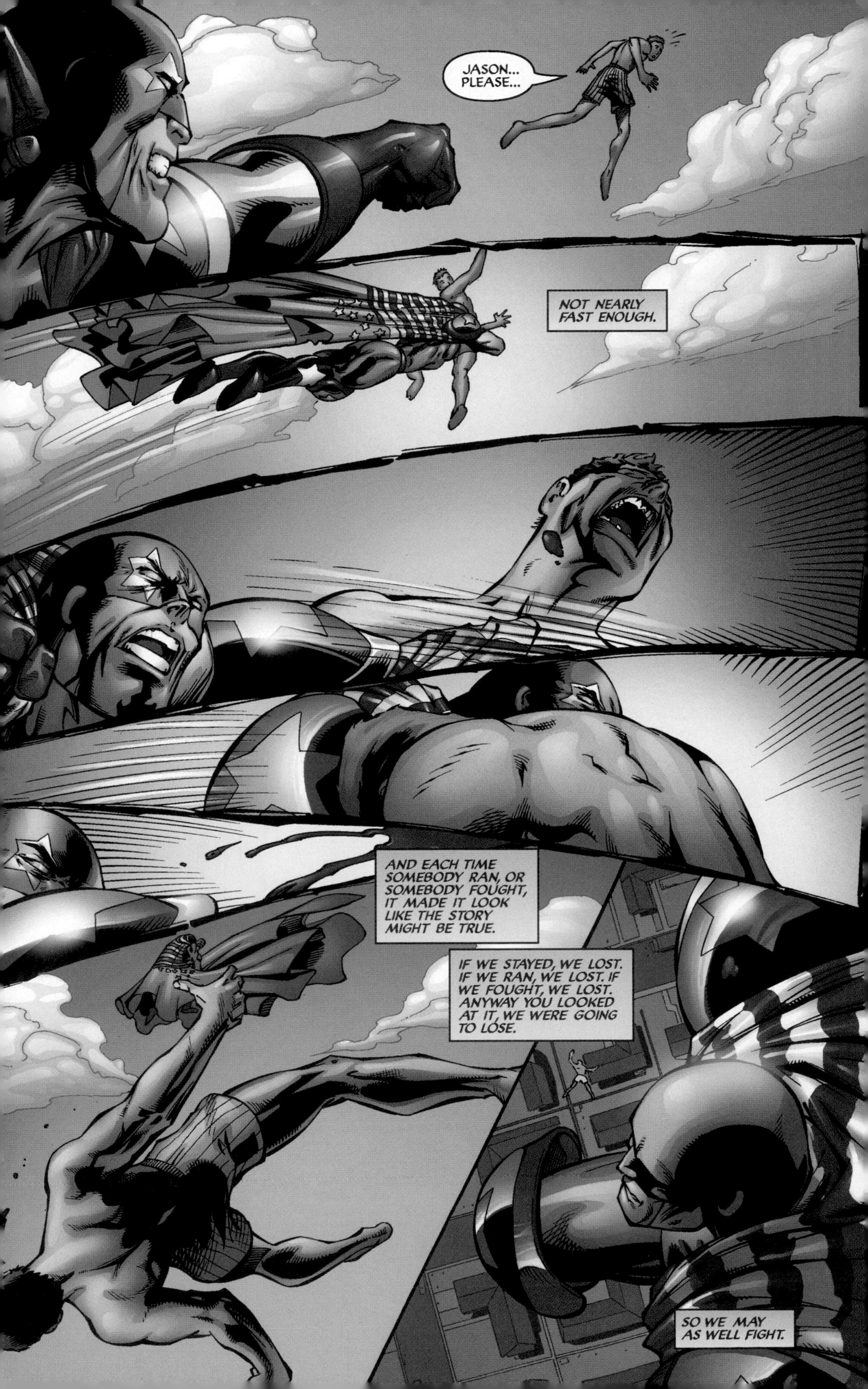
JASON... PLEASE...
NOT NEARLY FAST ENOUGH.
AND EACH TIME SOMEBODY RAN, OR SOMEBODY FOUGHT, IT MADE IT LOOK LIKE THE STORY MIGHT BE TRUE.
IF WE STAYED, WE LOST. IF WE RAN, WE LOST. IF WE FOUGHT, WE LOST. ANYWAY YOU LOOKED AT IT, WE WERE GOING TO LOSE.
SO WE MAY AS WELL FIGHT.

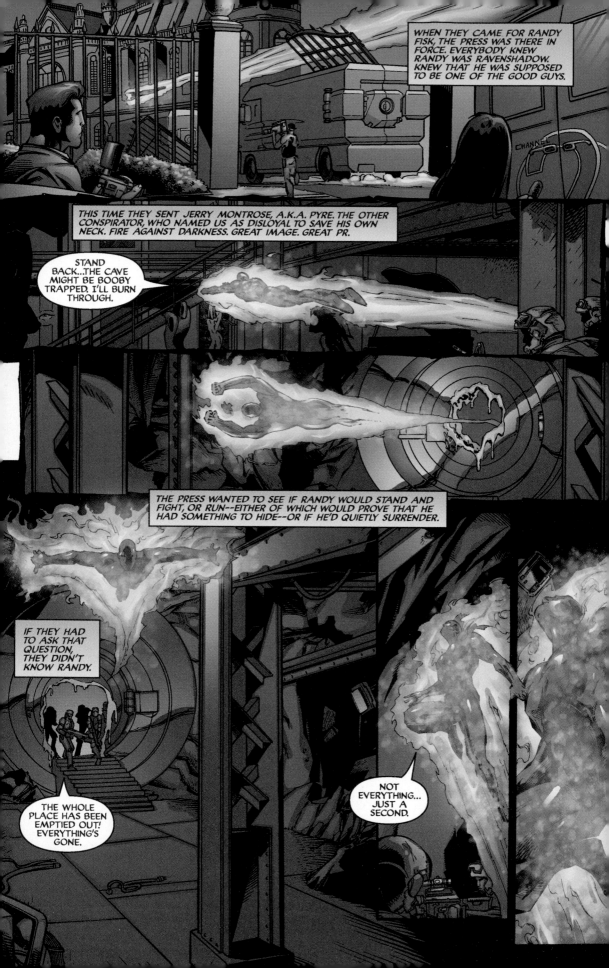

WHEN THEY CAME FOR RANDY FISK, THE PRESS WAS THERE IN FORCE. EVERYBODY KNEW RANDY WAS RAVENSHADOW. KNEW THAT HE WAS SUPPOSED TO BE ONE OF THE GOOD GUYS.

THIS TIME THEY SENT JERRY MONTROSE, A.K.A. PYRE. THE OTHER CONSPIRATOR, WHO NAMED US AS DISLOYAL TO SAVE HIS OWN NECK. FIRE AGAINST DARKNESS. GREAT IMAGE. GREAT PR.

STAND BACK...THE CAVE MIGHT BE BOOBY TRAPPED. I'LL BURN THROUGH.

THE PRESS WANTED TO SEE IF RANDY WOULD STAND AND FIGHT, OR RUN--EITHER OF WHICH WOULD PROVE THAT HE HAD SOMETHING TO HIDE--OR IF HE'D QUIETLY SURRENDER.

IF THEY HAD TO ASK THAT QUESTION, THEY DIDN'T KNOW RANDY.

THE WHOLE PLACE HAS BEEN EMPTIED OUT! EVERYTHING'S GONE.

NOT EVERYTHING... JUST A SECOND.

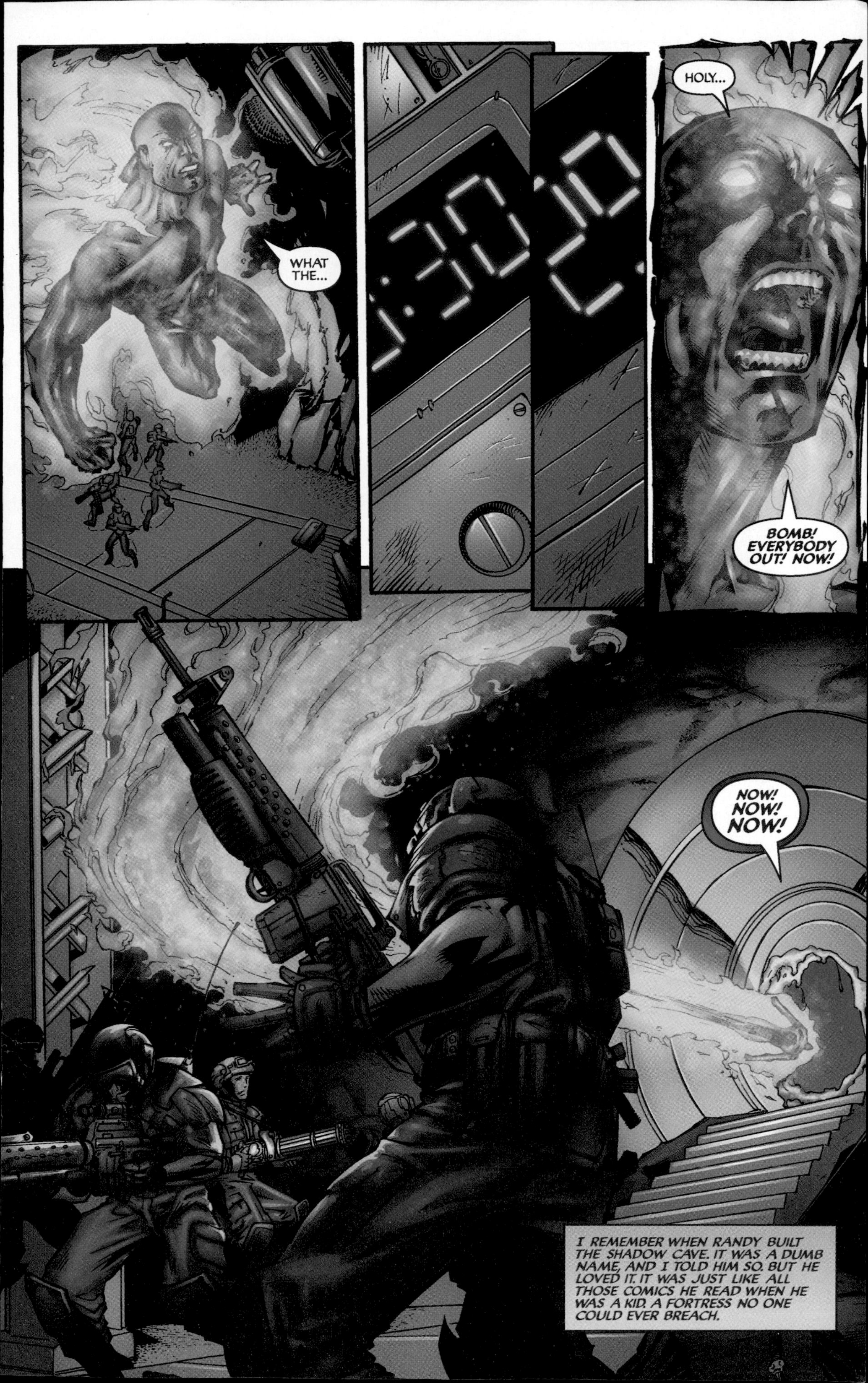
WHAT THE...
HOLY...
BOMB! EVERYBODY OUT! NOW!
NOW! NOW! NOW!
I REMEMBER WHEN RANDY BUILT THE SHADOW CAVE. IT WAS A DUMB NAME, AND I TOLD HIM SO. BUT HE LOVED IT. IT WAS JUST LIKE ALL THOSE COMICS HE READ WHEN HE WAS A KID. A FORTRESS NO ONE COULD EVER BREACH.

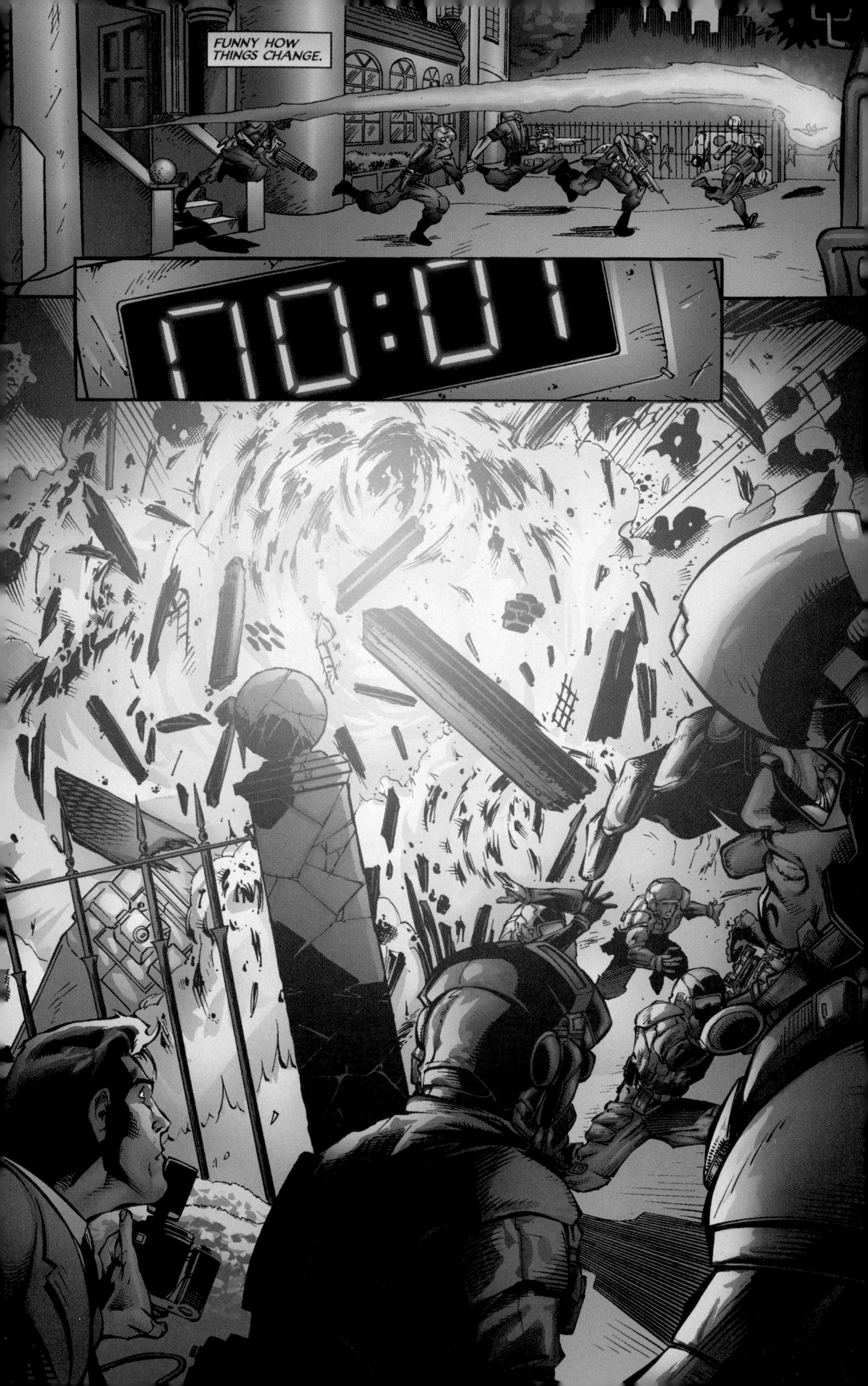
FUNNY HOW THINGS CHANGE.

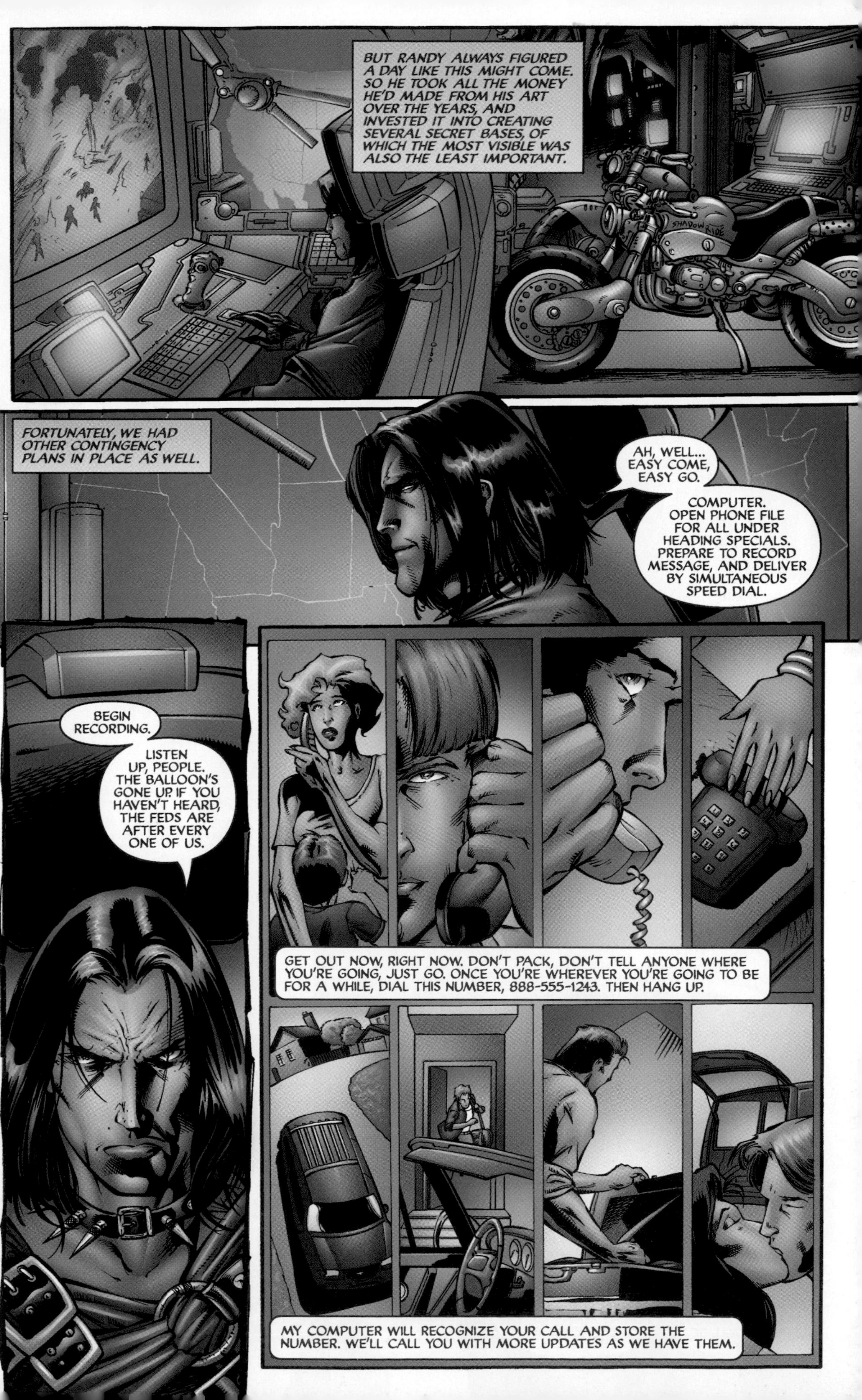
BUT RANDY ALWAYS FIGURED A DAY LIKE THIS MIGHT COME. SO HE TOOK ALL THE MONEY HE'D MADE FROM HIS ART OVER THE YEARS, AND INVESTED IT INTO CREATING SEVERAL SECRET BASES, OF WHICH THE MOST VISIBLE WAS ALSO THE LEAST IMPORTANT.
SHADOW RIDE
FORTUNATELY, WE HAD OTHER CONTINGENCY PLANS IN PLACE AS WELL.
AH, WELL... EASY COME, EASY GO.
COMPUTER. OPEN PHONE FILE FOR ALL UNDER HEADING SPECIALS. PREPARE TO RECORD MESSAGE, AND DELIVER BY SIMULTANEOUS SPEED DIAL.
BEGIN RECORDING.
LISTEN UP, PEOPLE. THE BALLOON'S GONE UP. IF YOU HAVEN'T HEARD, THE FEDS ARE AFTER EVERY ONE OF US.
GET OUT NOW, RIGHT NOW. DON'T PACK, DON'T TELL ANYONE WHERE YOU'RE GOING, JUST GO. ONCE YOU'RE WHEREVER YOU'RE GOING TO BE FOR A WHILE, DIAL THIS NUMBER, 888-555-1243. THEN HANG UP.
MY COMPUTER WILL RECOGNIZE YOUR CALL AND STORE THE NUMBER. WE'LL CALL YOU WITH MORE UPDATES AS WE HAVE THEM.

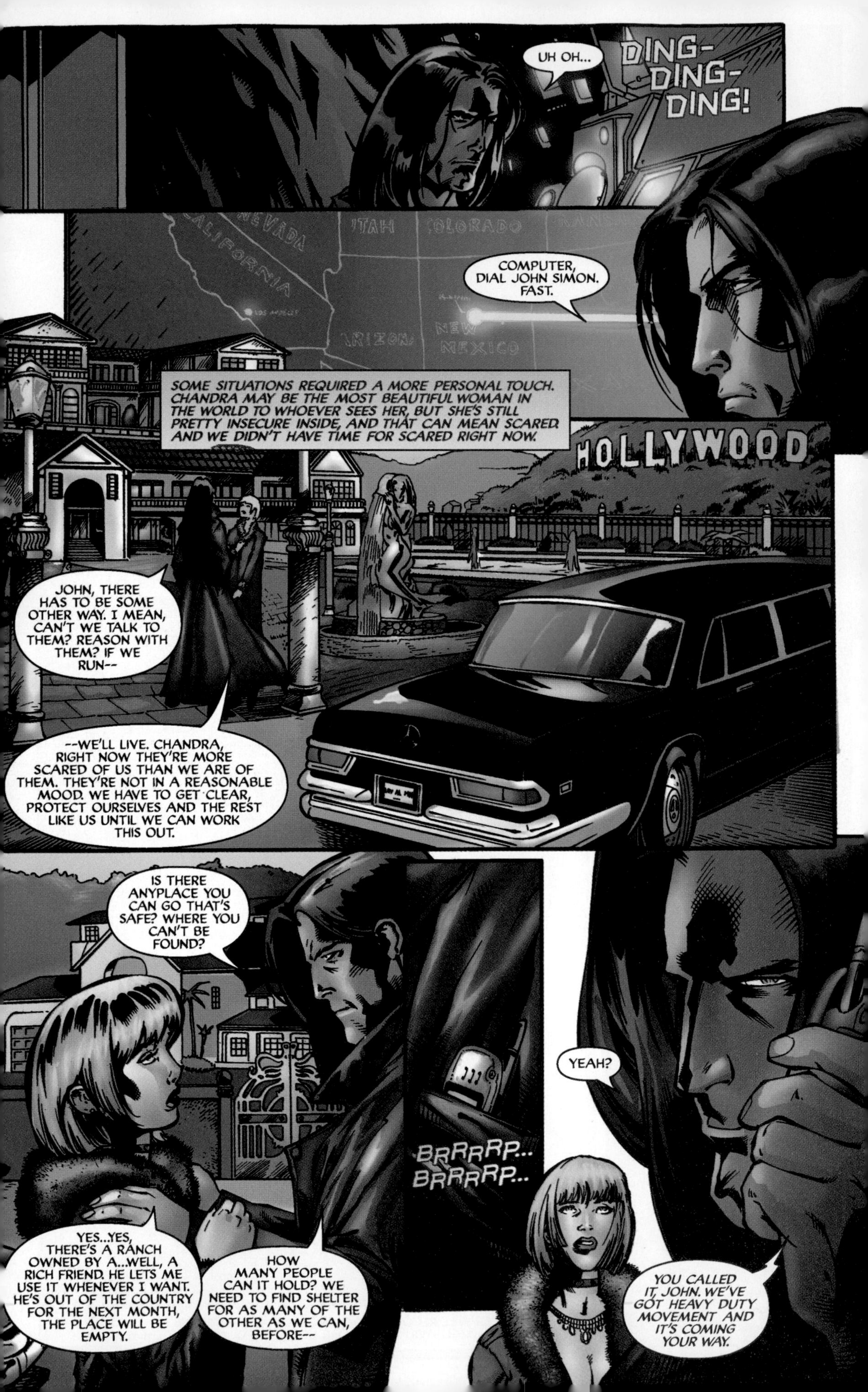
UH OH...
DING-DING-DING!
COMPUTER, DIAL JOHN SIMON. FAST.
NEVADA
CALIFORNIA
UTAH
COLORADO
ARIZONA
NEW MEXICO
SOME SITUATIONS REQUIRED A MORE PERSONAL TOUCH. CHANDRA MAY BE THE MOST BEAUTIFUL WOMAN IN THE WORLD TO WHOEVER SEES HER, BUT SHE'S STILL PRETTY INSECURE INSIDE, AND THAT CAN MEAN SCARED. AND WE DIDN'T HAVE TIME FOR SCARED RIGHT NOW.
HOLLYWOOD
JOHN, THERE HAS TO BE SOME OTHER WAY. I MEAN, CAN'T WE TALK TO THEM? REASON WITH THEM? IF WE RUN--
--WE'LL LIVE. CHANDRA, RIGHT NOW THEY'RE MORE SCARED OF US THAN WE ARE OF THEM. THEY'RE NOT IN A REASONABLE MOOD. WE HAVE TO GET CLEAR, PROTECT OURSELVES AND THE REST LIKE US UNTIL WE CAN WORK THIS OUT.
IS THERE ANYPLACE YOU CAN GO THAT'S SAFE? WHERE YOU CAN'T BE FOUND?
YES...YES, THERE'S A RANCH OWNED BY A...WELL, A RICH FRIEND. HE LETS ME USE IT WHENEVER I WANT. HE'S OUT OF THE COUNTRY FOR THE NEXT MONTH, THE PLACE WILL BE EMPTY.
HOW MANY PEOPLE CAN IT HOLD? WE NEED TO FIND SHELTER FOR AS MANY OF THE OTHER AS WE CAN, BEFORE--
BRRRRP... BRRRRP...
YEAH?
YOU CALLED IT, JOHN. WE'VE GOT HEAVY DUTY MOVEMENT AND IT'S COMING YOUR WAY.

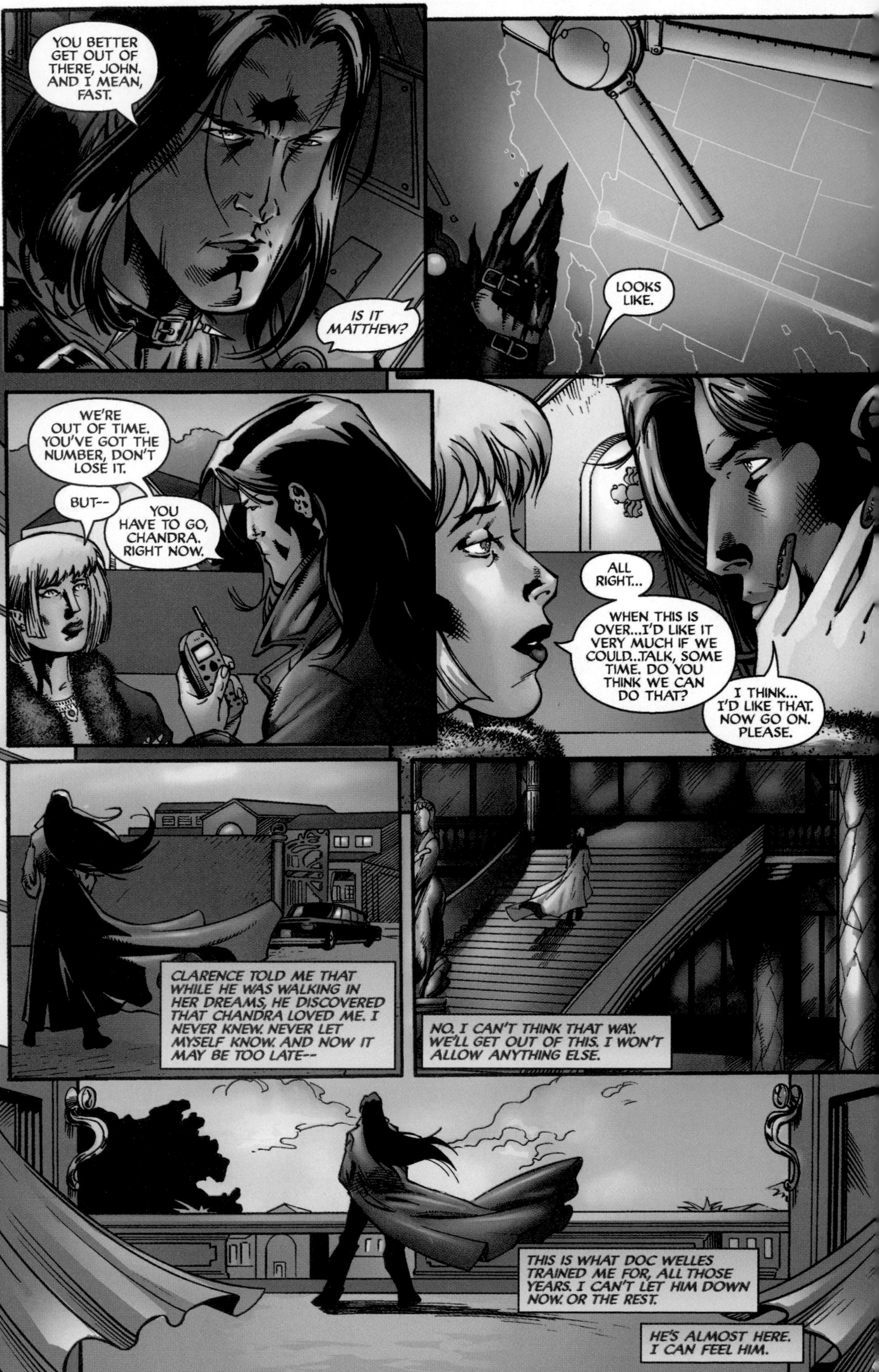

YOU BETTER GET OUT OF THERE, JOHN. AND I MEAN, FAST.
IS IT MATTHEW?
LOOKS LIKE.
WE'RE OUT OF TIME. YOU'VE GOT THE NUMBER, DON'T LOSE IT.
BUT--
YOU HAVE TO GO, CHANDRA. RIGHT NOW.
ALL RIGHT...
WHEN THIS IS OVER...I'D LIKE IT VERY MUCH IF WE COULD...TALK, SOME TIME. DO YOU THINK WE CAN DO THAT?
I THINK... I'D LIKE THAT. NOW GO ON. PLEASE.
CLARENCE TOLD ME THAT WHILE HE WAS WALKING IN HER DREAMS, HE DISCOVERED THAT CHANDRA LOVED ME. I NEVER KNEW. NEVER LET MYSELF KNOW. AND NOW IT MAY BE TOO LATE--
NO. I CAN'T THINK THAT WAY. WE'LL GET OUT OF THIS. I WON'T ALLOW ANYTHING ELSE.
THIS IS WHAT DOC WELLES TRAINED ME FOR, ALL THOSE YEARS. I CAN'T LET HIM DOWN NOW. OR THE REST.
HE'S ALMOST HERE. I CAN FEEL HIM.

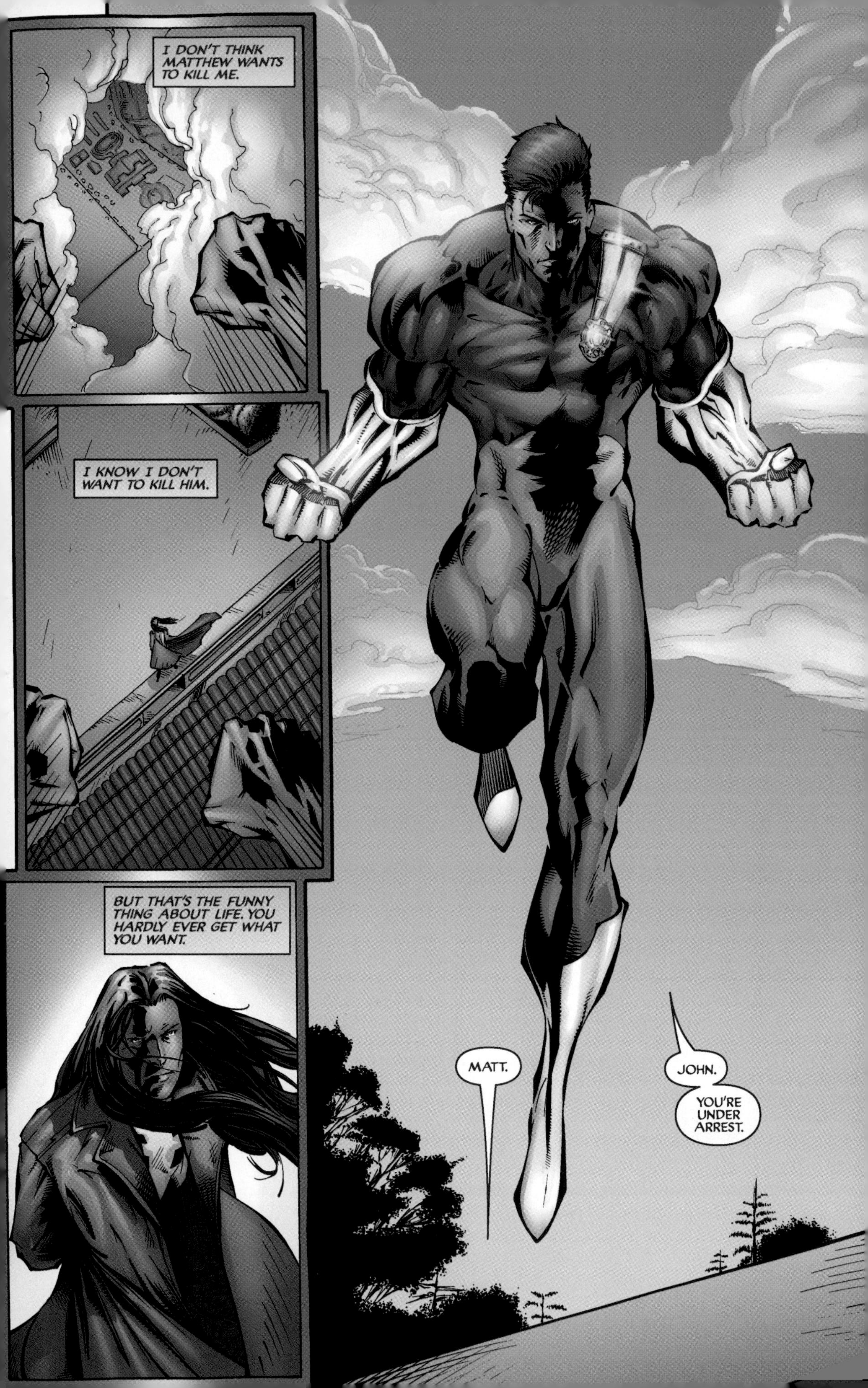
I DON'T THINK MATTHEW WANTS TO KILL ME.
I KNOW I DON'T WANT TO KILL HIM.
BUT THAT'S THE FUNNY THING ABOUT LIFE. YOU HARDLY EVER GET WHAT YOU WANT.
MATT.
JOHN.
YOU'RE UNDER ARREST.

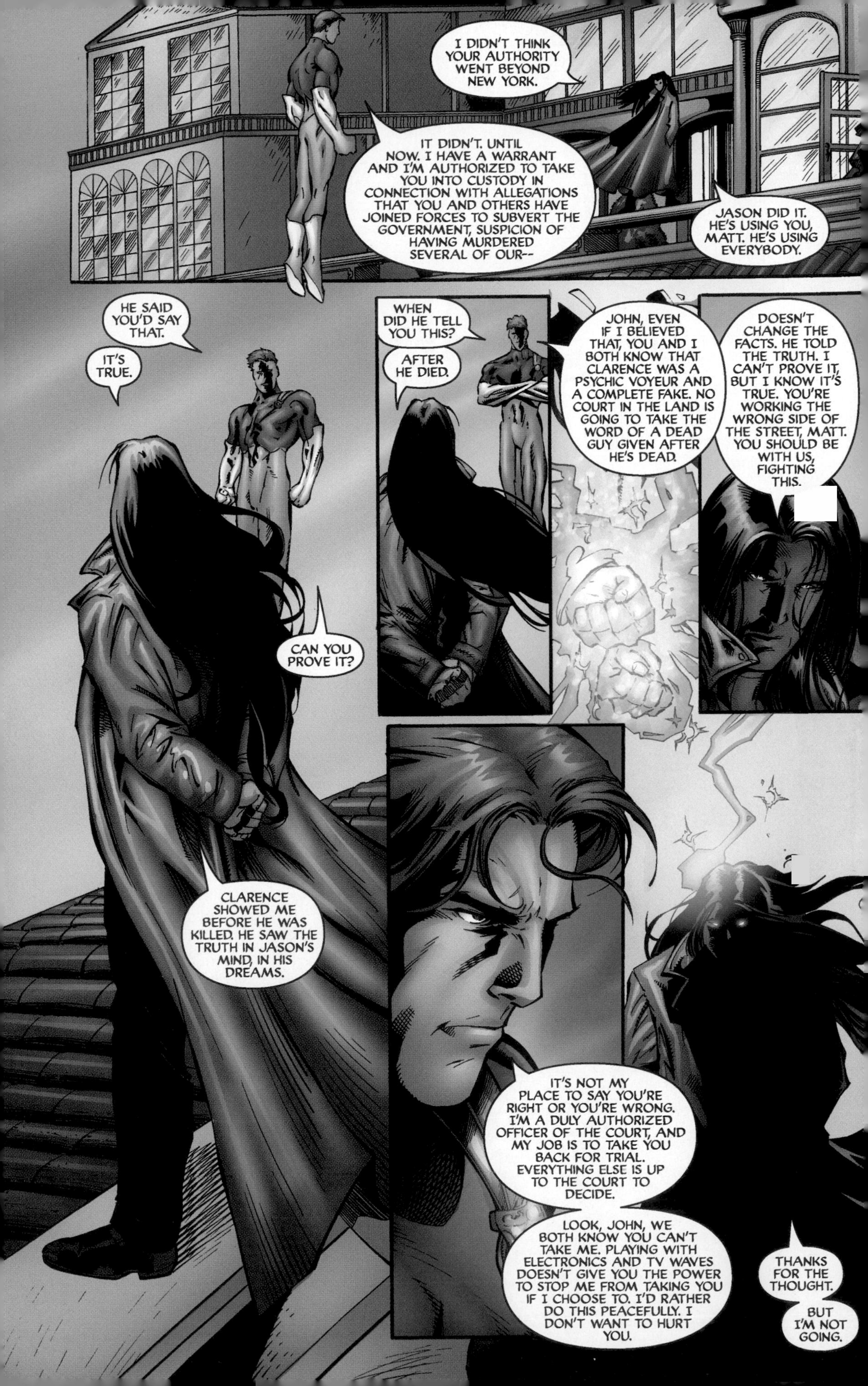
I DIDN'T THINK YOUR AUTHORITY WENT BEYOND NEW YORK.
IT DIDN'T. UNTIL NOW. I HAVE A WARRANT AND I'M AUTHORIZED TO TAKE YOU INTO CUSTODY IN CONNECTION WITH ALLEGATIONS THAT YOU AND OTHERS HAVE JOINED FORCES TO SUBVERT THE GOVERNMENT, SUSPICION OF HAVING MURDERED SEVERAL OF OUR--
JASON DID IT. HE'S USING YOU, MATT. HE'S USING EVERYBODY.
HE SAID YOU'D SAY THAT.
IT'S TRUE.
CAN YOU PROVE IT?
CLARENCE SHOWED ME BEFORE HE WAS KILLED. HE SAW THE TRUTH IN JASON'S MIND, IN HIS DREAMS.
WHEN DID HE TELL YOU THIS?
AFTER HE DIED.
JOHN, EVEN IF I BELIEVED THAT, YOU AND I BOTH KNOW THAT CLARENCE WAS A PSYCHIC VOYEUR AND A COMPLETE FAKE. NO COURT IN THE LAND IS GOING TO TAKE THE WORD OF A DEAD GUY GIVEN AFTER HE'S DEAD.
DOESN'T CHANGE THE FACTS. HE TOLD THE TRUTH. I CAN'T PROVE IT, BUT I KNOW IT'S TRUE. YOU'RE WORKING THE WRONG SIDE OF THE STREET, MATT. YOU SHOULD BE WITH US, FIGHTING THIS.
IT'S NOT MY PLACE TO SAY YOU'RE RIGHT OR YOU'RE WRONG. I'M A DULY AUTHORIZED OFFICER OF THE COURT, AND MY JOB IS TO TAKE YOU BACK FOR TRIAL. EVERYTHING ELSE IS UP TO THE COURT TO DECIDE.
LOOK, JOHN, WE BOTH KNOW YOU CAN'T TAKE ME. PLAYING WITH ELECTRONICS AND TV WAVES DOESN'T GIVE YOU THE POWER TO STOP ME FROM TAKING YOU IF I CHOOSE TO. I'D RATHER DO THIS PEACEFULLY. I DON'T WANT TO HURT YOU.
THANKS FOR THE THOUGHT.
BUT I'M NOT GOING.

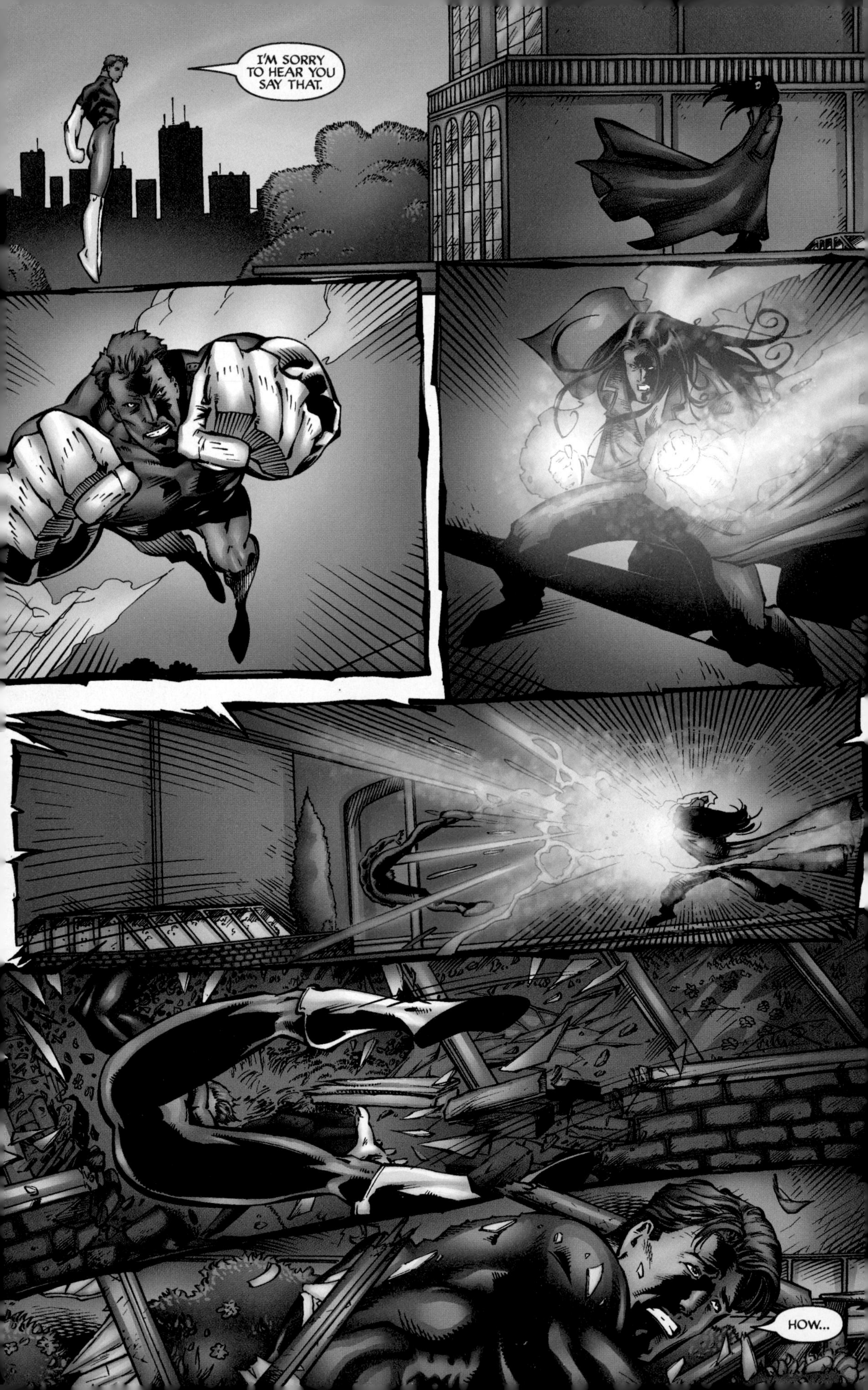
I'M SORRY TO HEAR YOU SAY THAT.
HOW...

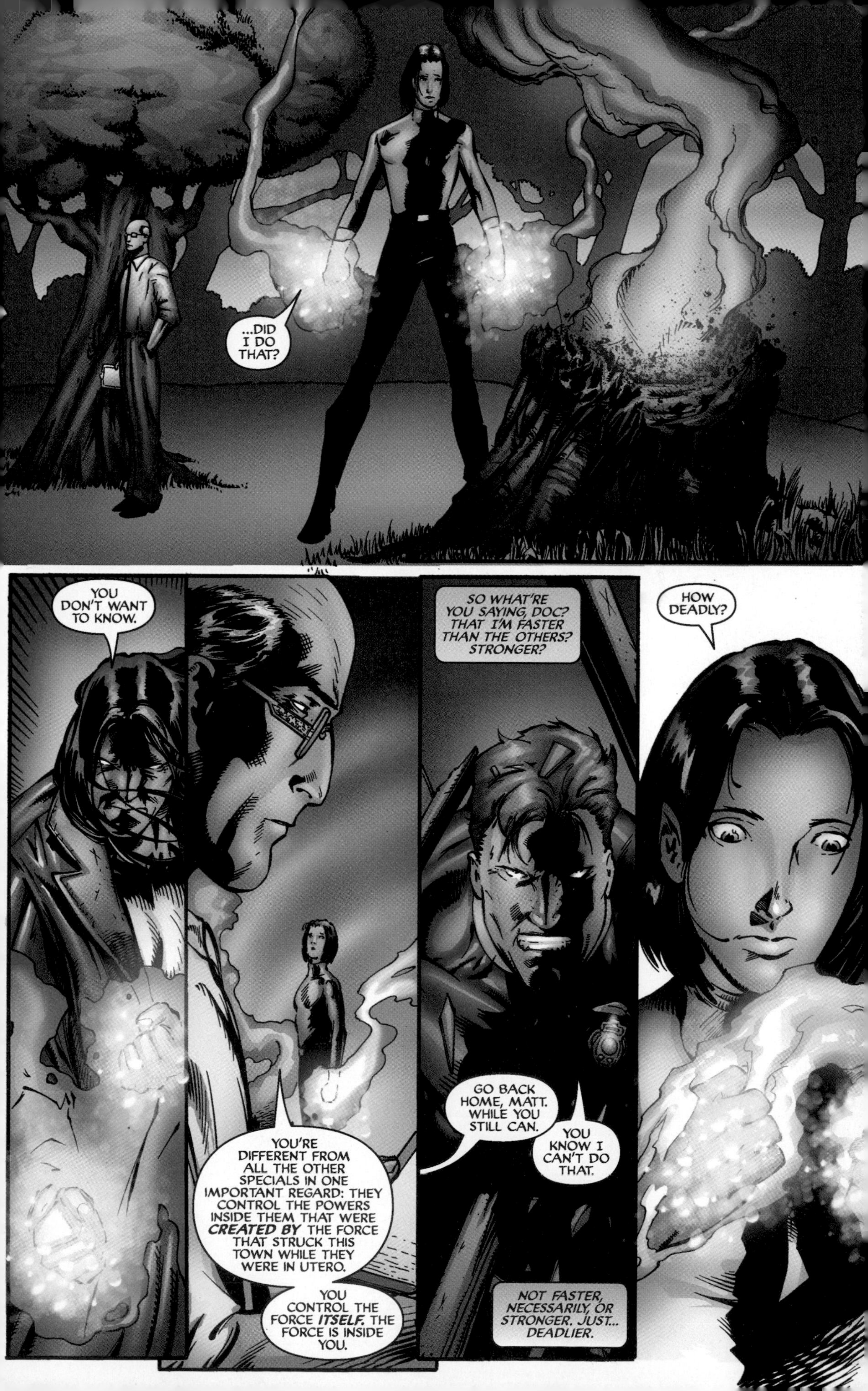
...DID I DO THAT?
YOU DON'T WANT TO KNOW.
YOU'RE DIFFERENT FROM ALL THE OTHER SPECIALS IN ONE IMPORTANT REGARD: THEY CONTROL THE POWERS INSIDE THEM THAT WERE CREATED BY THE FORCE THAT STRUCK THIS TOWN WHILE THEY WERE IN UTERO.
YOU CONTROL THE FORCE ITSELF. THE FORCE IS INSIDE YOU.
SO WHAT'RE YOU SAYING, DOC? THAT I'M FASTER THAN THE OTHERS? STRONGER?
GO BACK HOME, MATT. WHILE YOU STILL CAN.
YOU KNOW I CAN'T DO THAT.
NOT FASTER, NECESSARILY, OR STRONGER. JUST... DEADLIER.
HOW DEADLY?

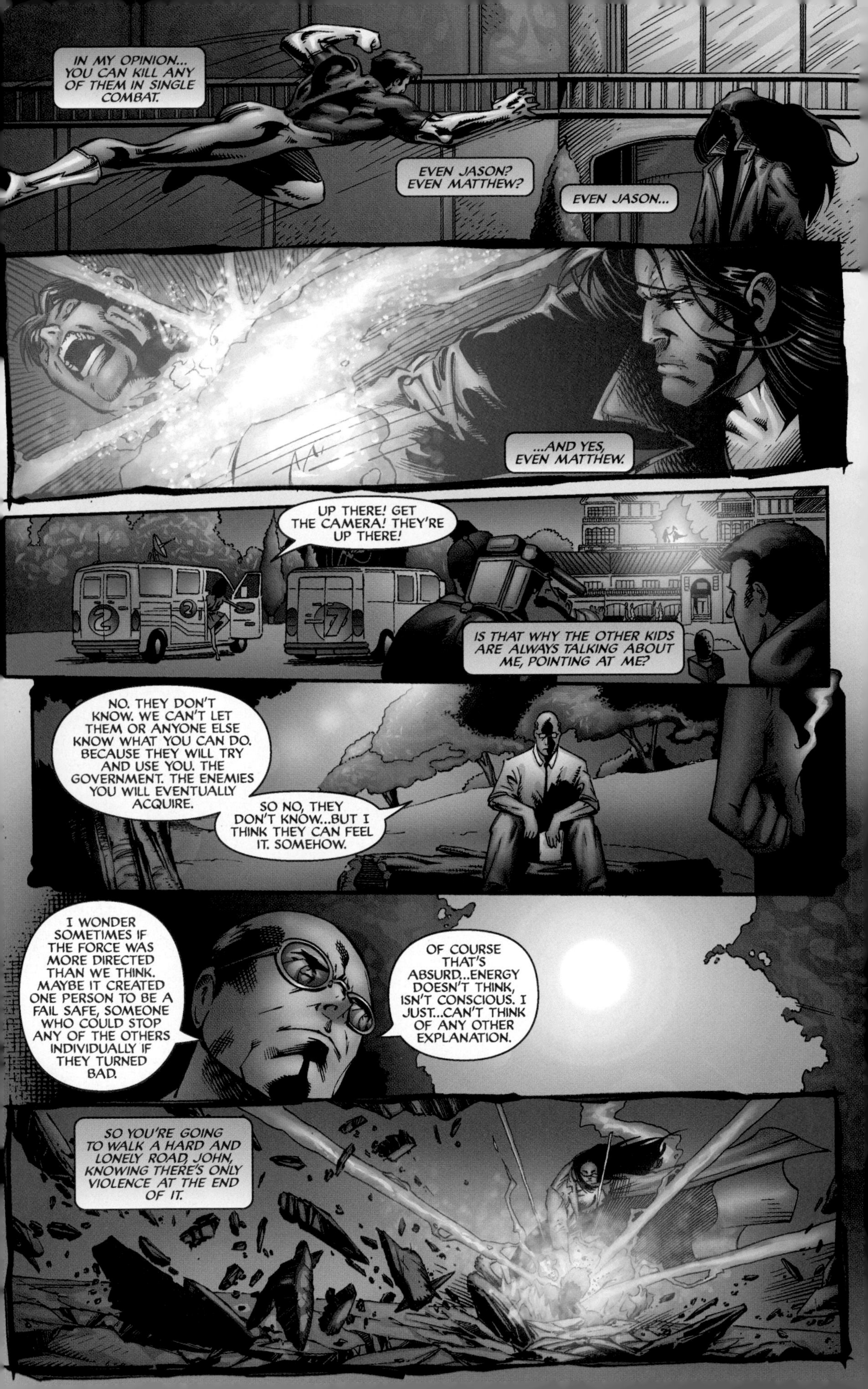
IN MY OPINION... YOU CAN KILL ANY OF THEM IN SINGLE COMBAT.
EVEN JASON? EVEN MATTHEW?
EVEN JASON...
...AND YES, EVEN MATTHEW.
UP THERE! GET THE CAMERA! THEY'RE UP THERE!
IS THAT WHY THE OTHER KIDS ARE ALWAYS TALKING ABOUT ME, POINTING AT ME?
NO. THEY DON'T KNOW. WE CAN'T LET THEM OR ANYONE ELSE KNOW WHAT YOU CAN DO. BECAUSE THEY WILL TRY AND USE YOU. THE GOVERNMENT. THE ENEMIES YOU WILL EVENTUALLY ACQUIRE.
SO NO, THEY DON'T KNOW...BUT I THINK THEY CAN FEEL IT. SOMEHOW.
I WONDER SOMETIMES IF THE FORCE WAS MORE DIRECTED THAN WE THINK. MAYBE IT CREATED ONE PERSON TO BE A FAIL SAFE, SOMEONE WHO COULD STOP ANY OF THE OTHERS INDIVIDUALLY IF THEY TURNED BAD.
OF COURSE THAT'S ABSURD...ENERGY DOESN'T THINK, ISN'T CONSCIOUS. I JUST...CAN'T THINK OF ANY OTHER EXPLANATION.
SO YOU'RE GOING TO WALK A HARD AND LONELY ROAD, JOHN, KNOWING THERE'S ONLY VIOLENCE AT THE END OF IT.

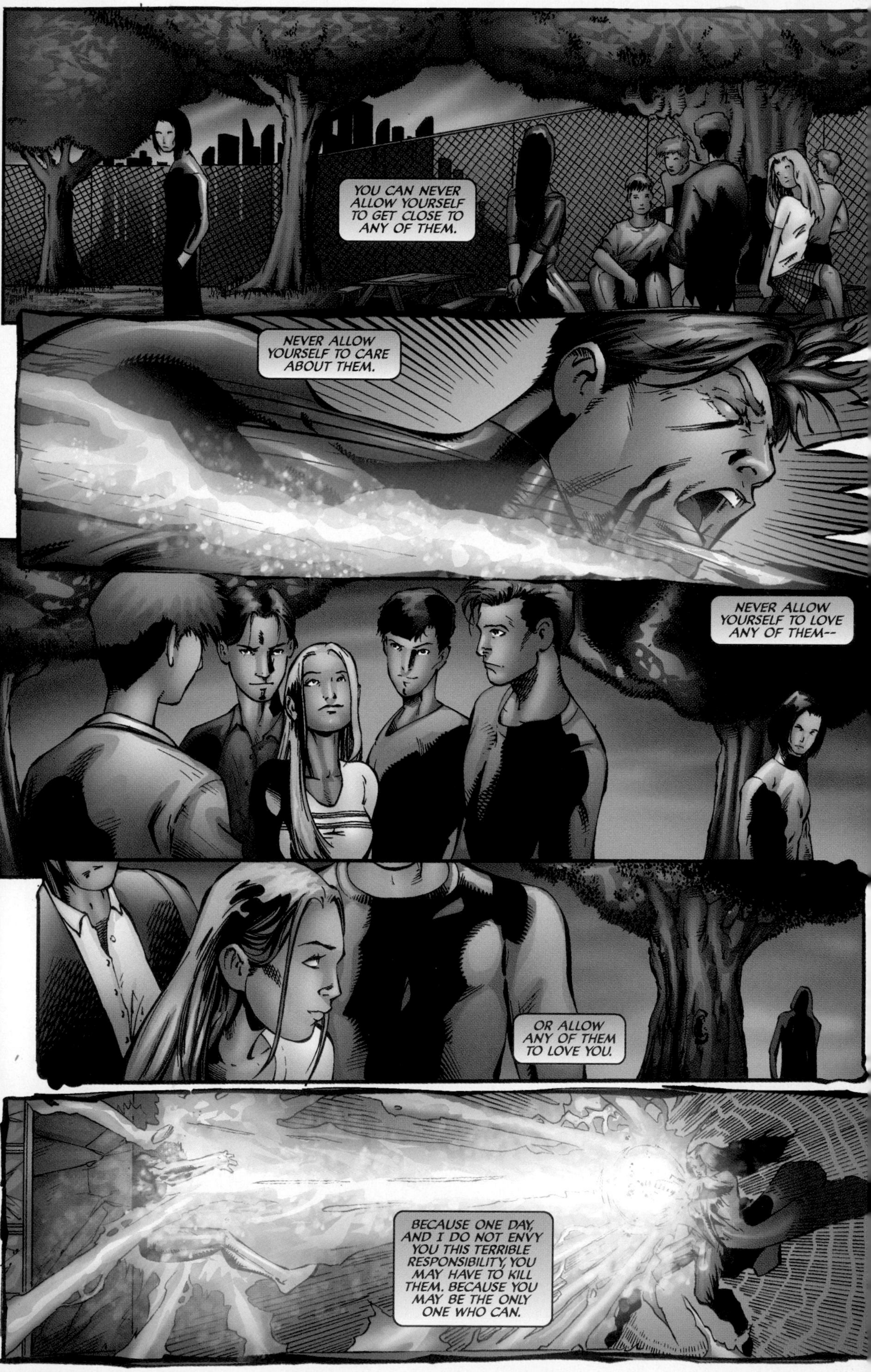
YOU CAN NEVER ALLOW YOURSELF TO GET CLOSE TO ANY OF THEM.
NEVER ALLOW YOURSELF TO CARE ABOUT THEM.
NEVER ALLOW YOURSELF TO LOVE ANY OF THEM--
OR ALLOW ANY OF THEM TO LOVE YOU.
BECAUSE ONE DAY, AND I DO NOT ENVY YOU THIS TERRIBLE RESPONSIBILITY, YOU MAY HAVE TO KILL THEM. BECAUSE YOU MAY BE THE ONLY ONE WHO CAN.

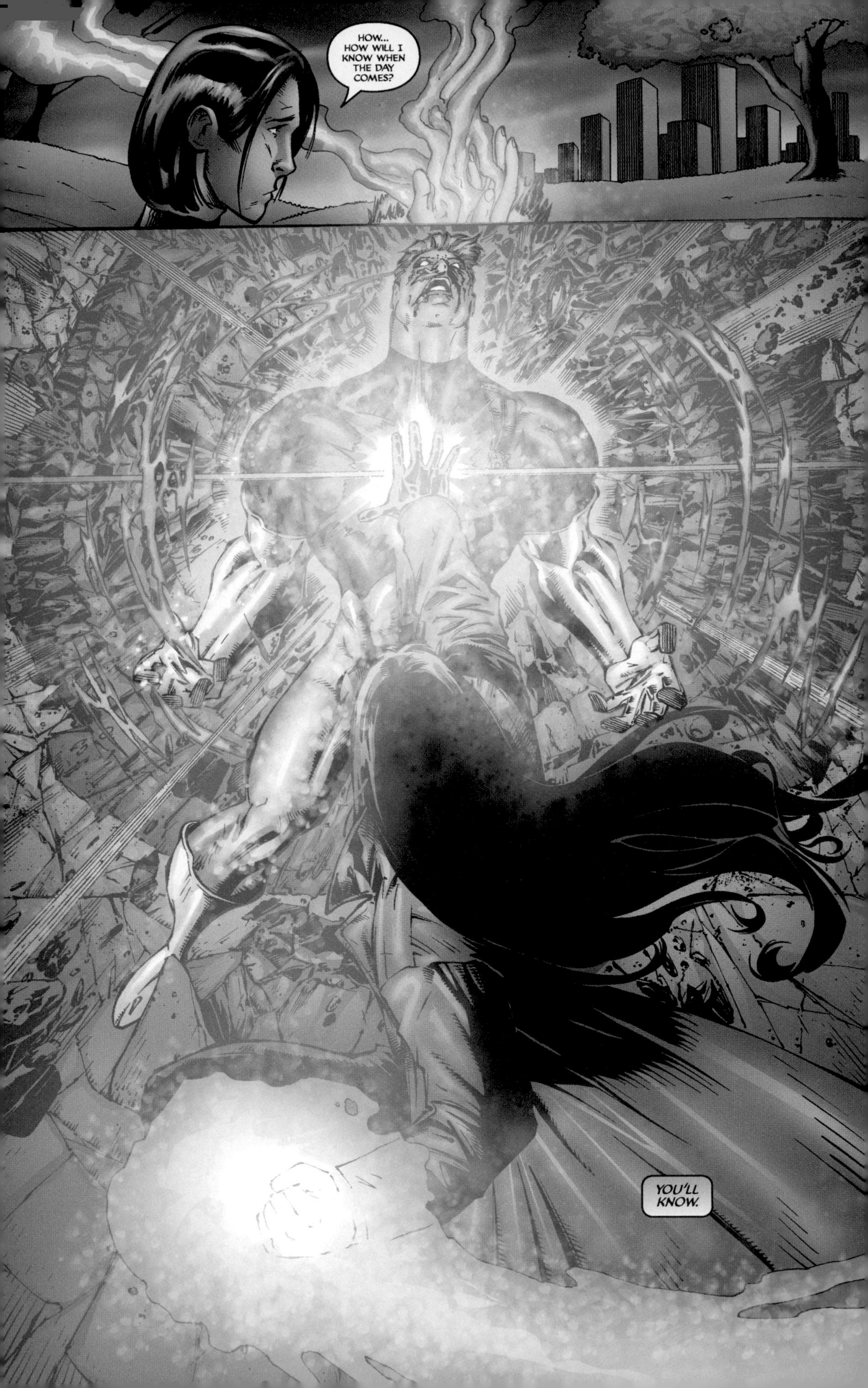
HOW... HOW WILL I KNOW WHEN THE DAY COMES?
YOU'LL KNOW.

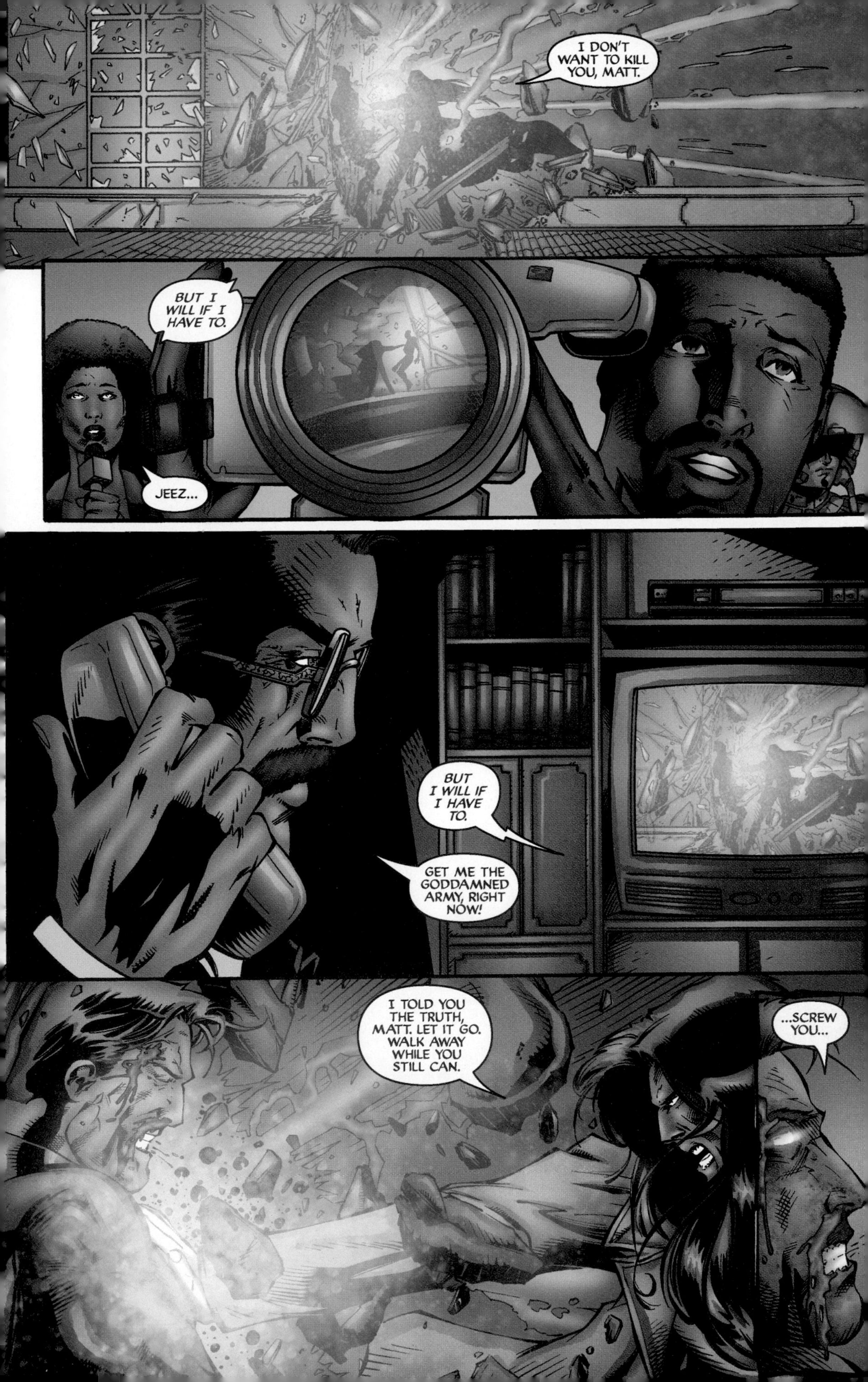
I DON'T WANT TO KILL YOU, MATT.
BUT I WILL IF I HAVE TO.
JEEZ...
BUT I WILL IF I HAVE TO.
GET ME THE GODDAMNED ARMY, RIGHT NOW!
I TOLD YOU THE TRUTH, MATT. LET IT GO. WALK AWAY WHILE YOU STILL CAN.
...SCREW YOU...

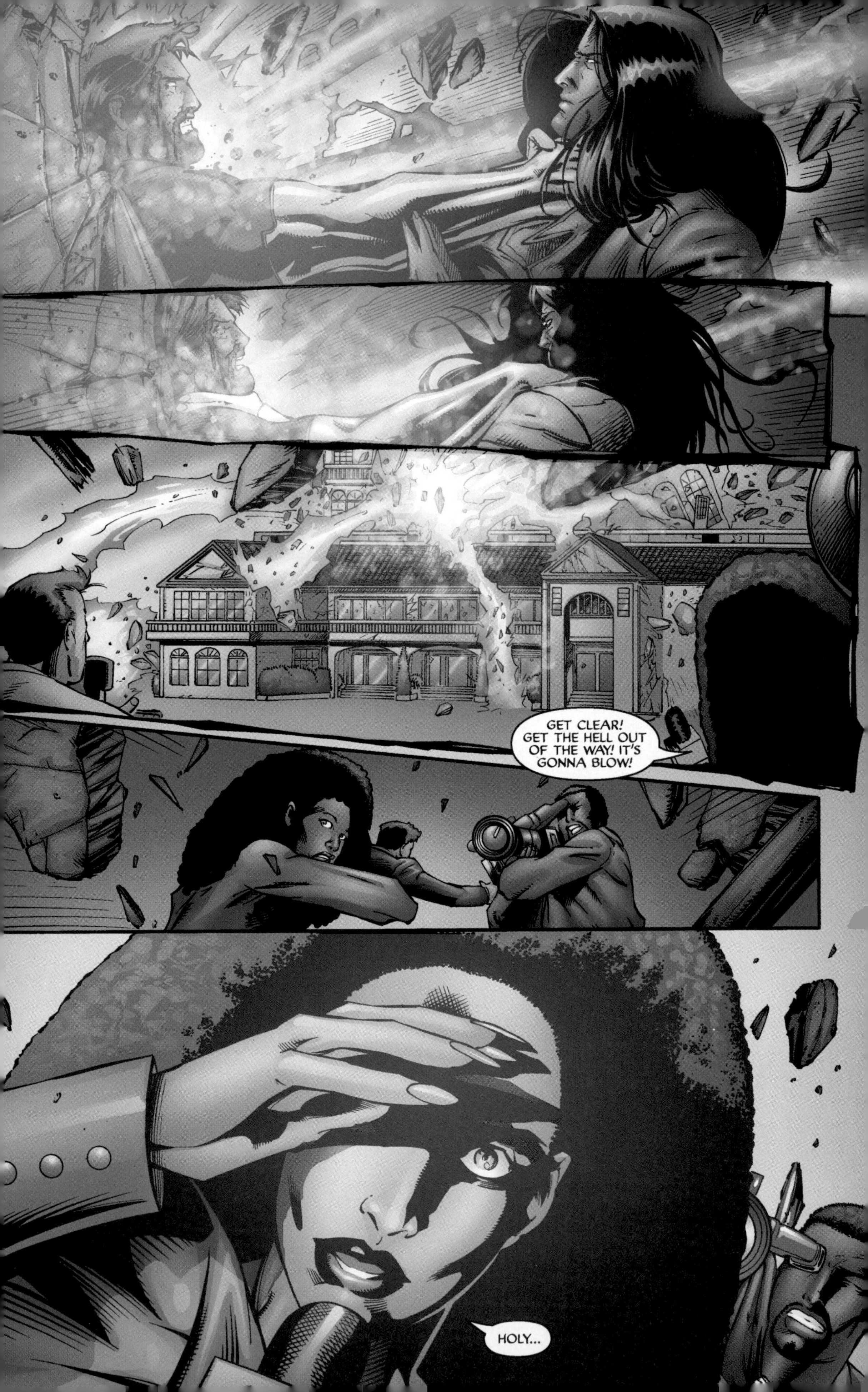
GET CLEAR! GET THE HELL OUT OF THE WAY! IT'S GONNA BLOW!
HOLY...

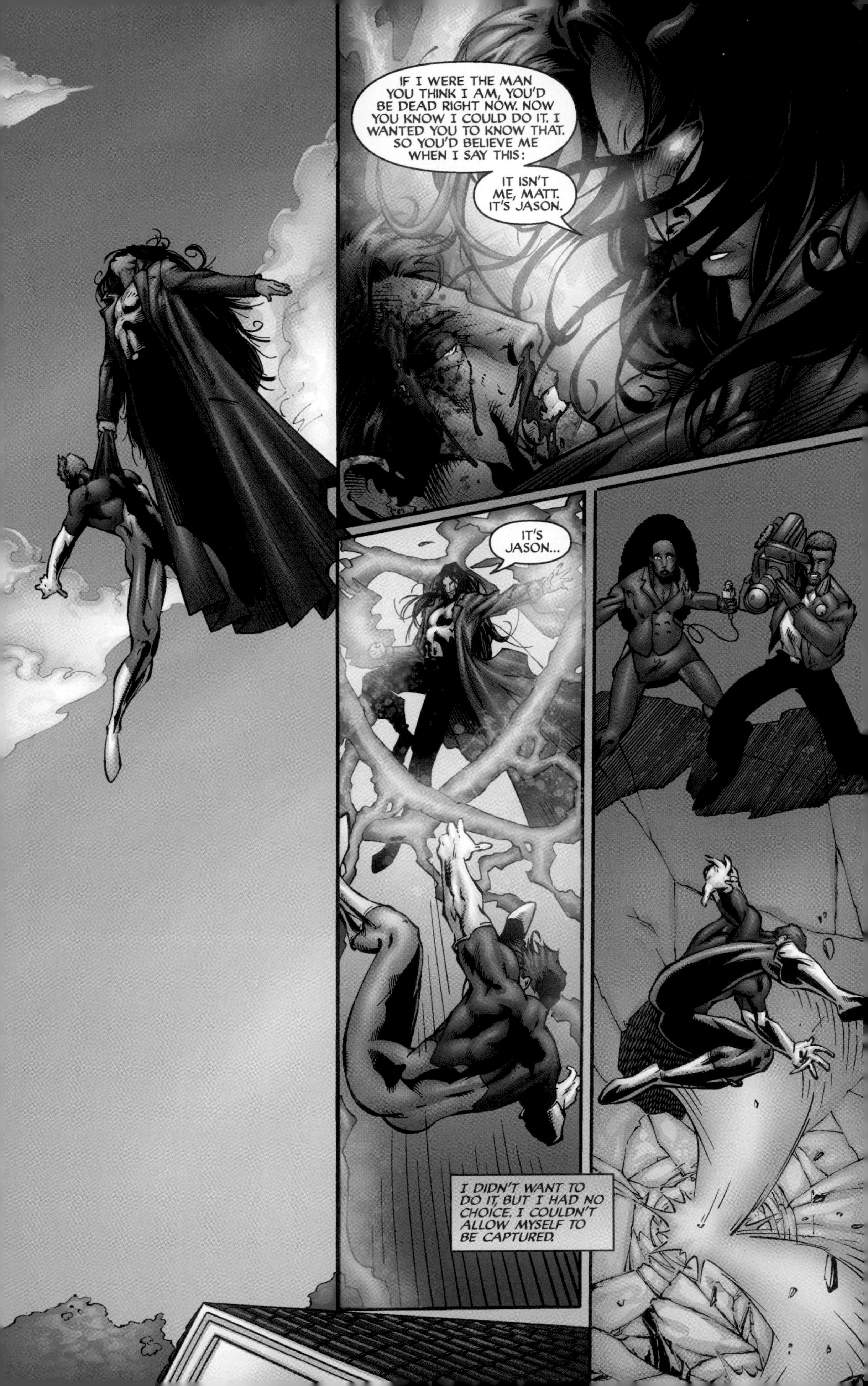
IF I WERE THE MAN YOU THINK I AM, YOU'D BE DEAD RIGHT NOW. NOW YOU KNOW I COULD DO IT. I WANTED YOU TO KNOW THAT. SO YOU'D BELIEVE ME WHEN I SAY THIS:
IT ISN'T ME, MATT. IT'S JASON.
IT'S JASON...
I DIDN'T WANT TO DO IT, BUT I HAD NO CHOICE. I COULDN'T ALLOW MYSELF TO BE CAPTURED.

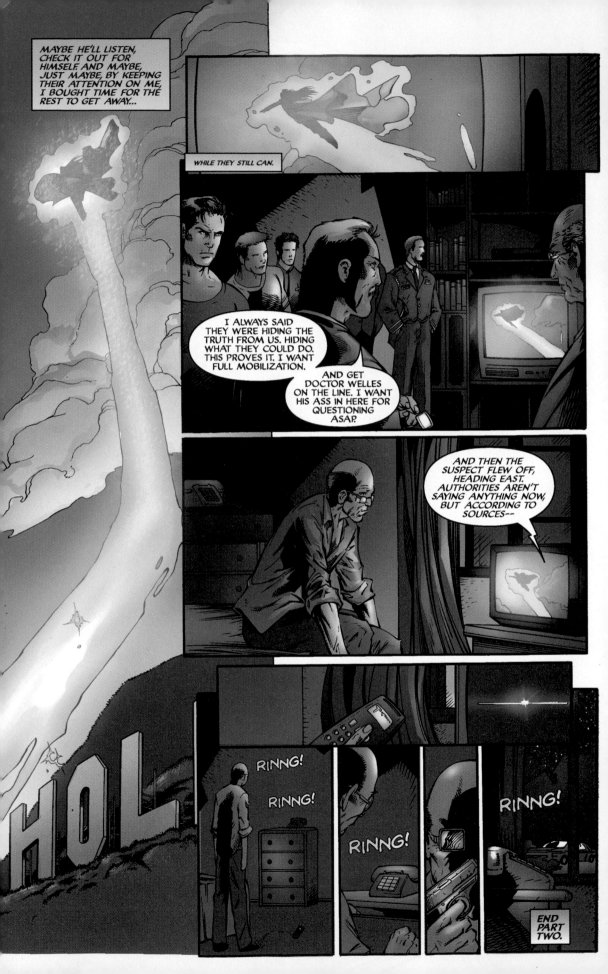

MAYBE HE'LL LISTEN, CHECK IT OUT FOR HIMSELF AND MAYBE, JUST MAYBE, BY KEEPING THEIR ATTENTION ON ME, I BOUGHT TIME FOR THE REST TO GET AWAY...

WHILE THEY STILL CAN.

I ALWAYS SAID THEY WERE HIDING THE TRUTH FROM US. HIDING WHAT THEY COULD DO. THIS PROVES IT. I WANT FULL MOBILIZATION.

AND GET DOCTOR WELLES ON THE LINE. I WANT HIS ASS IN HERE FOR QUESTIONING ASAP.

AND THEN THE SUSPECT FLEW OFF, HEADING EAST. AUTHORITIES AREN'T SAYING ANYTHING NOW, BUT ACCORDING TO SOURCES--

RINNG!

RINNG!

RINNG!

RINNG!

END PART TWO.

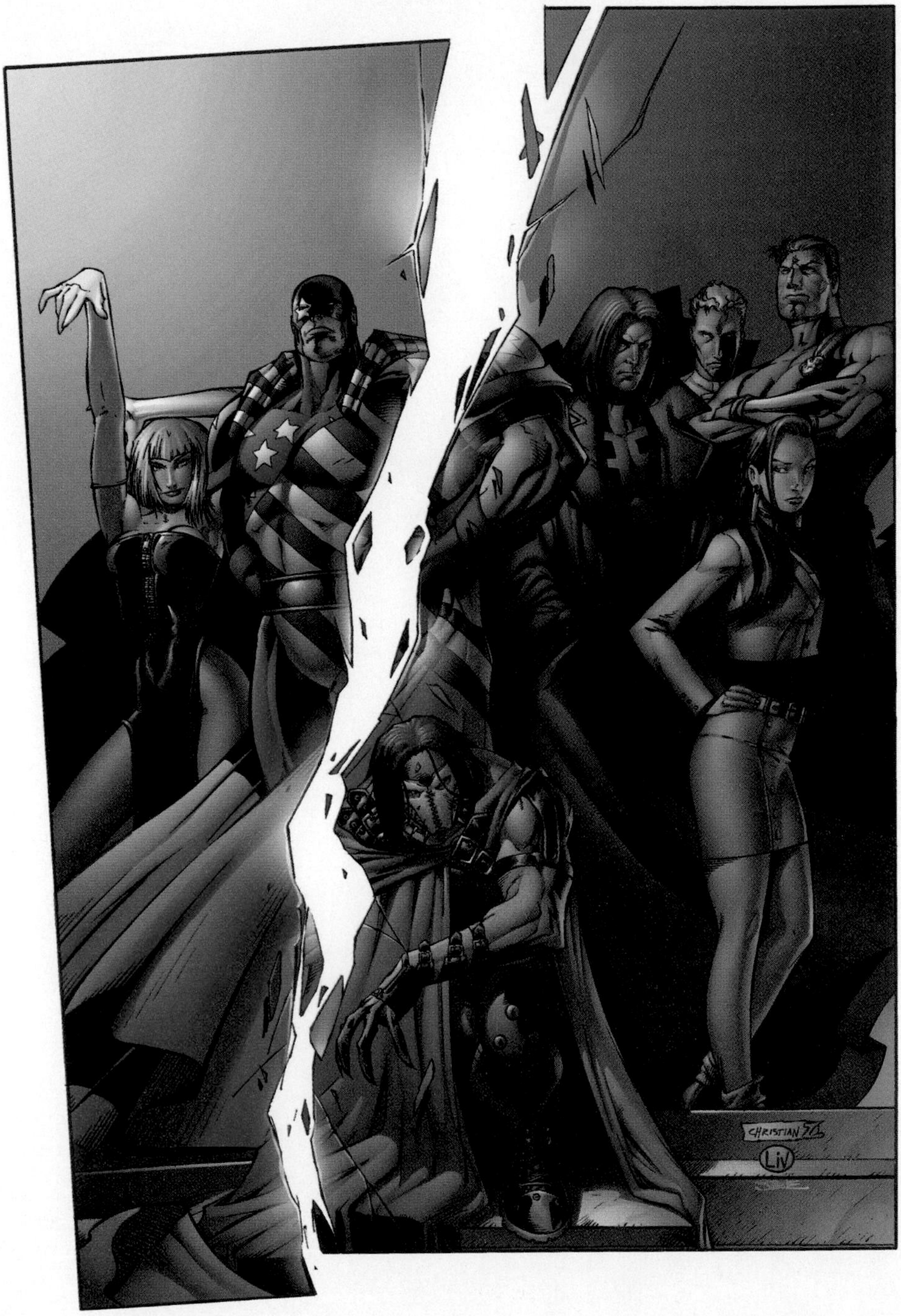

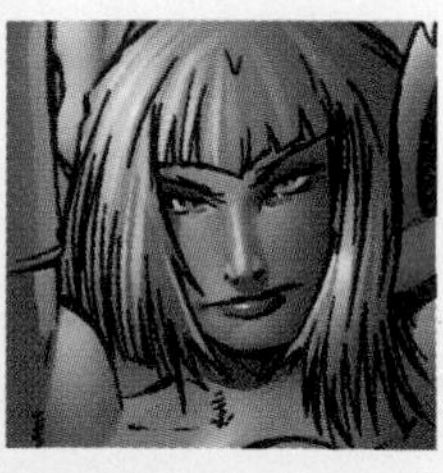

Chapter 8
Things Fall Apart—Three

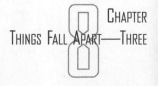

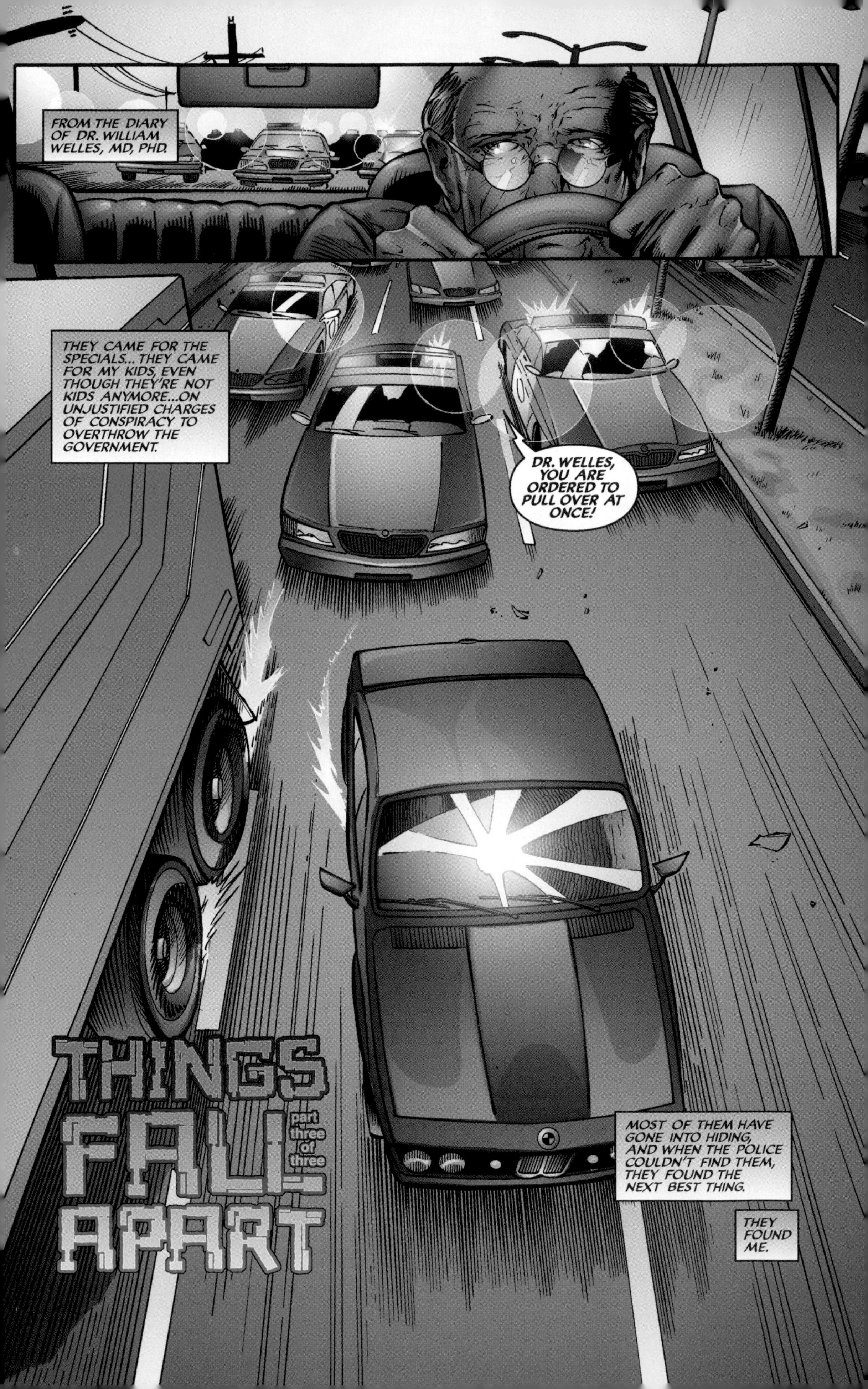
FROM THE DIARY OF DR. WILLIAM WELLES, MD, PHD.
THEY CAME FOR THE SPECIALS... THEY CAME FOR MY KIDS, EVEN THOUGH THEY'RE NOT KIDS ANYMORE...ON UNJUSTIFIED CHARGES OF CONSPIRACY TO OVERTHROW THE GOVERNMENT.
DR. WELLES, YOU ARE ORDERED TO PULL OVER AT ONCE!
THINGS FALL APART
part three of three
MOST OF THEM HAVE GONE INTO HIDING, AND WHEN THE POLICE COULDN'T FIND THEM, THEY FOUND THE NEXT BEST THING.
THEY FOUND ME.

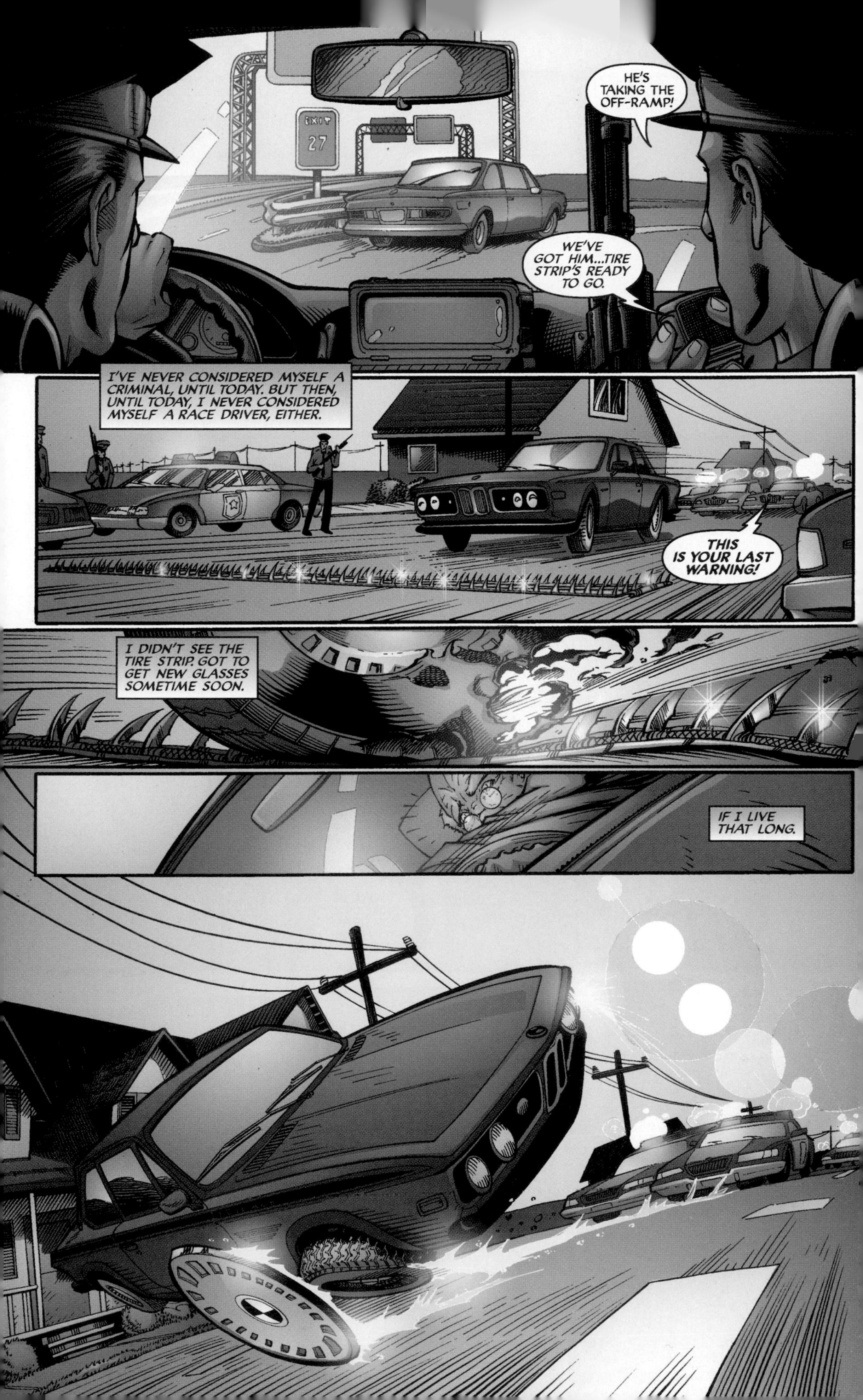
HE'S TAKING THE OFF-RAMP!
EXIT 27
WE'VE GOT HIM...TIRE STRIP'S READY TO GO.
I'VE NEVER CONSIDERED MYSELF A CRIMINAL, UNTIL TODAY. BUT THEN, UNTIL TODAY, I NEVER CONSIDERED MYSELF A RACE DRIVER, EITHER.
THIS IS YOUR LAST WARNING!
I DIDN'T SEE THE TIRE STRIP. GOT TO GET NEW GLASSES SOMETIME SOON.
IF I LIVE THAT LONG.

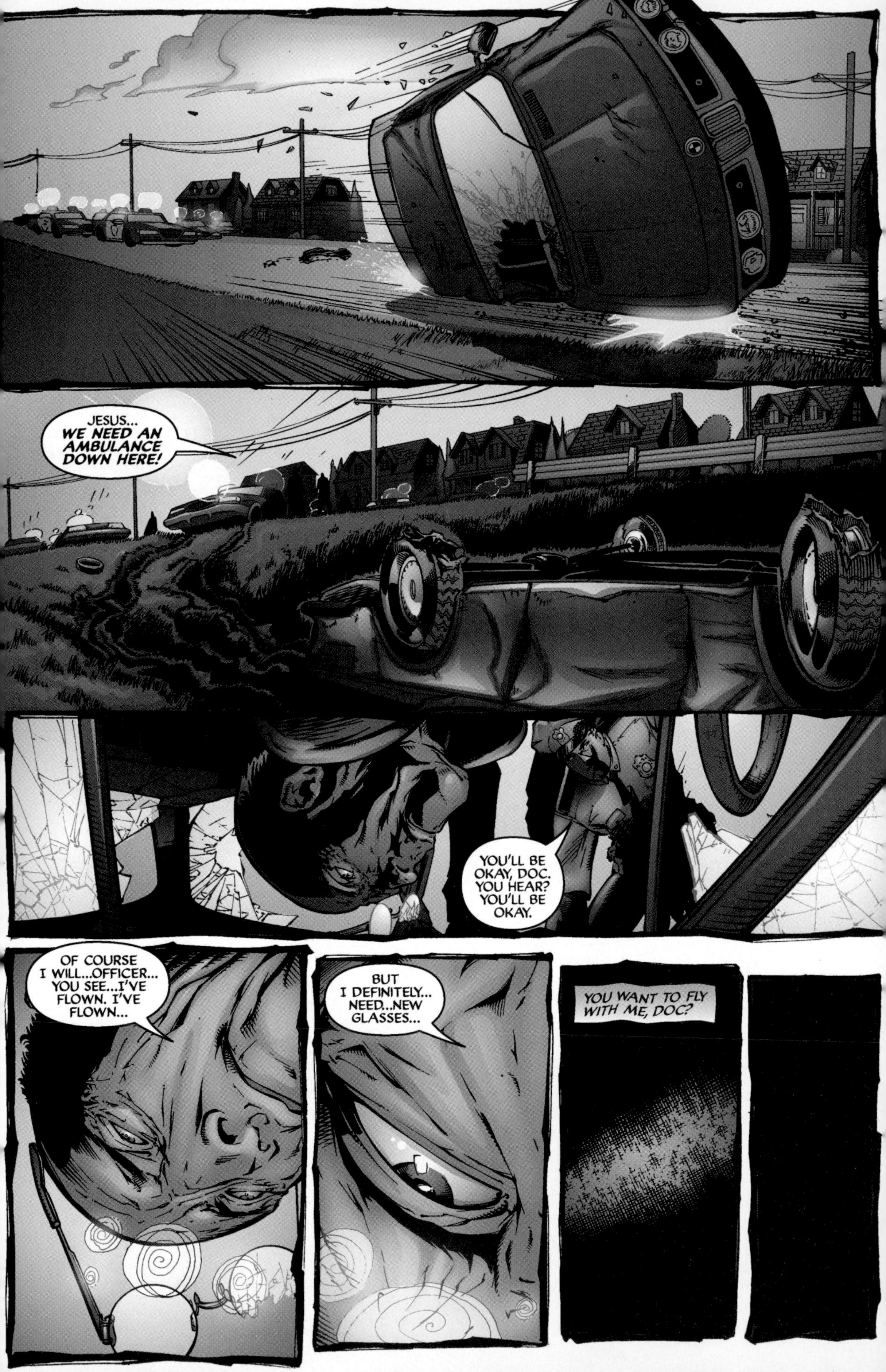
JESUS... WE NEED AN AMBULANCE DOWN HERE!
YOU'LL BE OKAY, DOC. YOU HEAR? YOU'LL BE OKAY.
OF COURSE I WILL...OFFICER... YOU SEE...I'VE FLOWN. I'VE FLOWN...
BUT I DEFINITELY... NEED...NEW GLASSES...
YOU WANT TO FLY WITH ME, DOC?

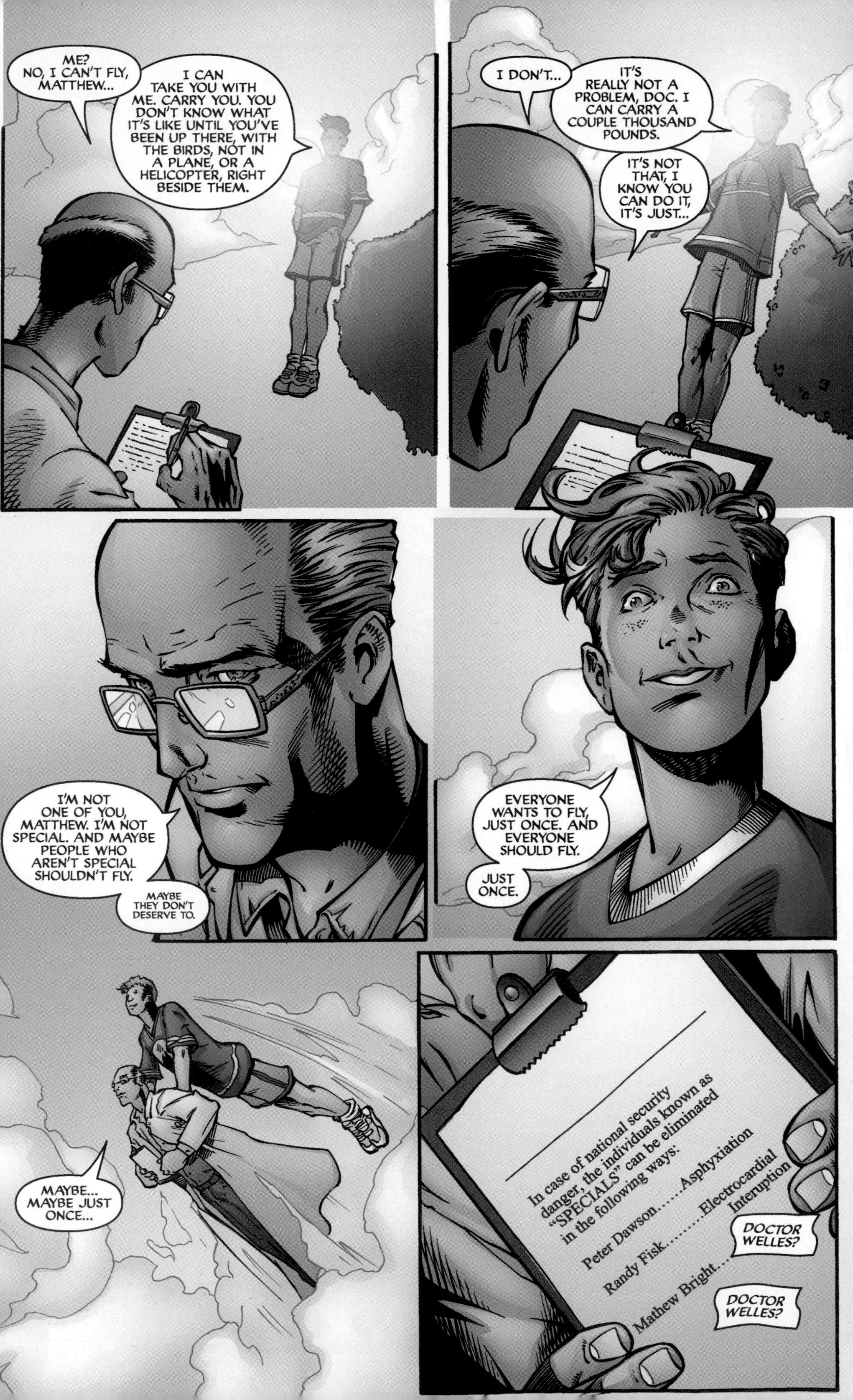

ME? NO, I CAN'T FLY, MATTHEW...
I CAN TAKE YOU WITH ME. CARRY YOU. YOU DON'T KNOW WHAT IT'S LIKE UNTIL YOU'VE BEEN UP THERE, WITH THE BIRDS, NOT IN A PLANE, OR A HELICOPTER, RIGHT BESIDE THEM.
I DON'T...
IT'S REALLY NOT A PROBLEM, DOC. I CAN CARRY A COUPLE THOUSAND POUNDS.
IT'S NOT THAT, I KNOW YOU CAN DO IT, IT'S JUST...
I'M NOT ONE OF YOU, MATTHEW. I'M NOT SPECIAL. AND MAYBE PEOPLE WHO AREN'T SPECIAL SHOULDN'T FLY.
MAYBE THEY DON'T DESERVE TO.
EVERYONE WANTS TO FLY, JUST ONCE. AND EVERYONE SHOULD FLY.
JUST ONCE.
MAYBE... MAYBE JUST ONCE...
In case of national security danger, the individuals known as "SPECIALS" can be eliminated in the following ways:
Peter Dawson.......Asphyxiation
Randy Fisk.........Electrocardial Interuption
Mathew Bright...
DOCTOR WELLES?
DOCTOR WELLES?

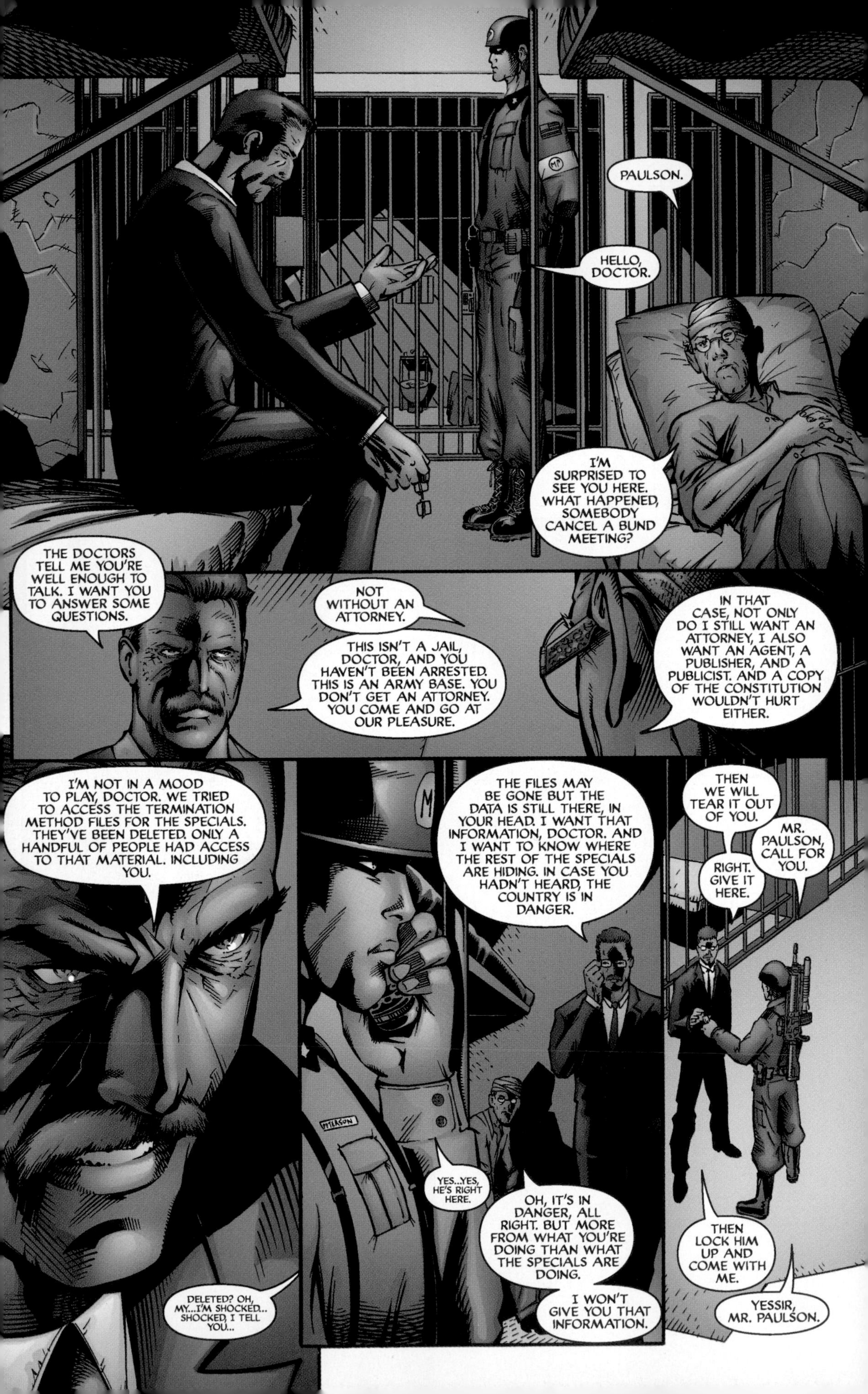
PAULSON.
HELLO, DOCTOR.
I'M SURPRISED TO SEE YOU HERE. WHAT HAPPENED, SOMEBODY CANCEL A BUND MEETING?
THE DOCTORS TELL ME YOU'RE WELL ENOUGH TO TALK. I WANT YOU TO ANSWER SOME QUESTIONS.
NOT WITHOUT AN ATTORNEY.
THIS ISN'T A JAIL, DOCTOR, AND YOU HAVEN'T BEEN ARRESTED. THIS IS AN ARMY BASE. YOU DON'T GET AN ATTORNEY. YOU COME AND GO AT OUR PLEASURE.
IN THAT CASE, NOT ONLY DO I STILL WANT AN ATTORNEY, I ALSO WANT AN AGENT, A PUBLISHER, AND A PUBLICIST. AND A COPY OF THE CONSTITUTION WOULDN'T HURT EITHER.
I'M NOT IN A MOOD TO PLAY, DOCTOR. WE TRIED TO ACCESS THE TERMINATION METHOD FILES FOR THE SPECIALS. THEY'VE BEEN DELETED. ONLY A HANDFUL OF PEOPLE HAD ACCESS TO THAT MATERIAL. INCLUDING YOU.
DELETED? OH, MY...I'M SHOCKED... SHOCKED, I TELL YOU...
THE FILES MAY BE GONE BUT THE DATA IS STILL THERE, IN YOUR HEAD. I WANT THAT INFORMATION, DOCTOR. AND I WANT TO KNOW WHERE THE REST OF THE SPECIALS ARE HIDING. IN CASE YOU HADN'T HEARD, THE COUNTRY IS IN DANGER.
YES...YES, HE'S RIGHT HERE.
OH, IT'S IN DANGER, ALL RIGHT. BUT MORE FROM WHAT YOU'RE DOING THAN WHAT THE SPECIALS ARE DOING.
I WON'T GIVE YOU THAT INFORMATION.
THEN WE WILL TEAR IT OUT OF YOU.
MR. PAULSON, CALL FOR YOU.
RIGHT. GIVE IT HERE.
THEN LOCK HIM UP AND COME WITH ME.
YESSIR, MR. PAULSON.

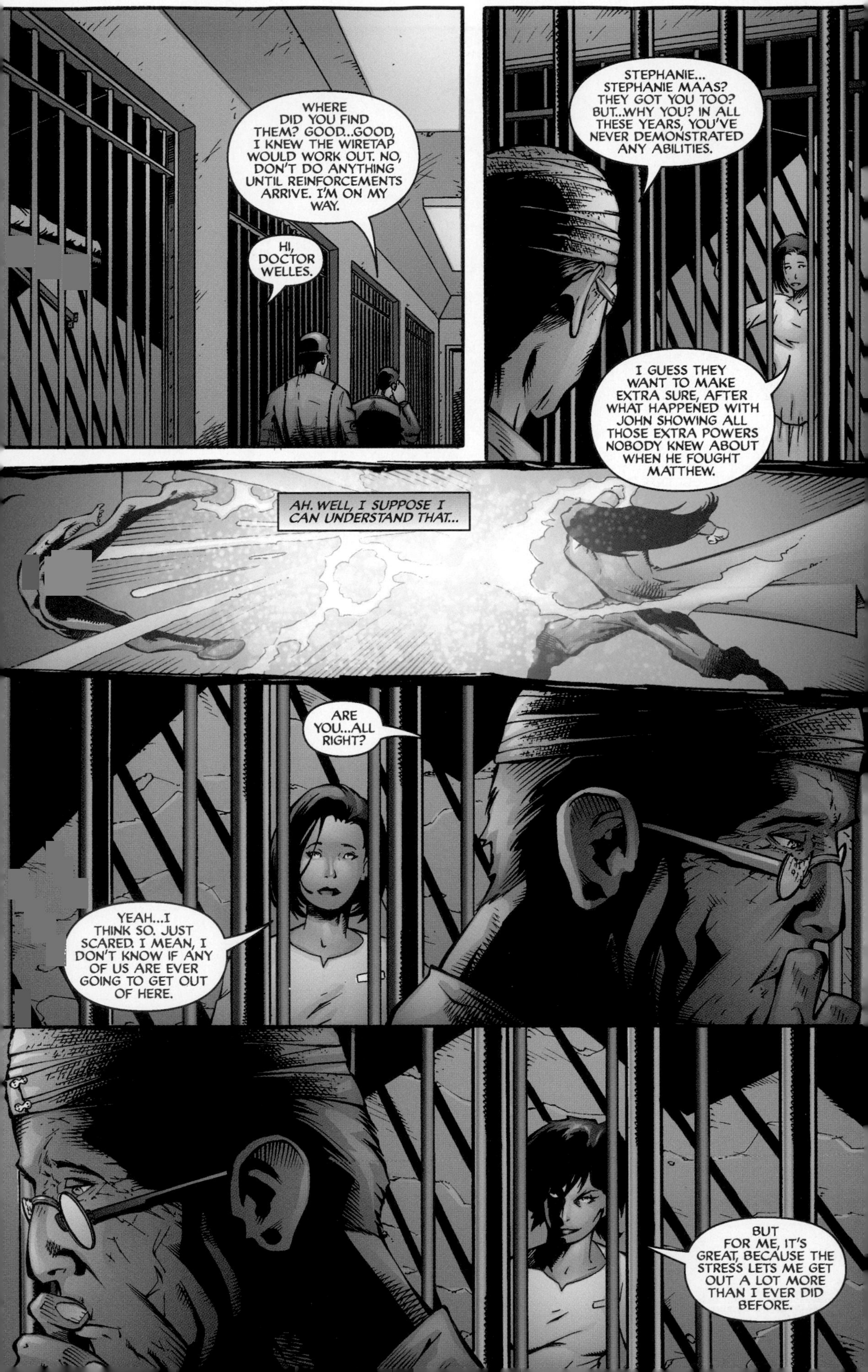
WHERE DID YOU FIND THEM? GOOD...GOOD, I KNEW THE WIRETAP WOULD WORK OUT. NO, DON'T DO ANYTHING UNTIL REINFORCEMENTS ARRIVE. I'M ON MY WAY.
HI, DOCTOR WELLES.
STEPHANIE... STEPHANIE MAAS? THEY GOT YOU TOO? BUT...WHY YOU? IN ALL THESE YEARS, YOU'VE NEVER DEMONSTRATED ANY ABILITIES.
I GUESS THEY WANT TO MAKE EXTRA SURE, AFTER WHAT HAPPENED WITH JOHN SHOWING ALL THOSE EXTRA POWERS NOBODY KNEW ABOUT WHEN HE FOUGHT MATTHEW.
AH. WELL, I SUPPOSE I CAN UNDERSTAND THAT...
ARE YOU...ALL RIGHT?
YEAH...I THINK SO. JUST SCARED. I MEAN, I DON'T KNOW IF ANY OF US ARE EVER GOING TO GET OUT OF HERE.
BUT FOR ME, IT'S GREAT, BECAUSE THE STRESS LETS ME GET OUT A LOT MORE THAN I EVER DID BEFORE.

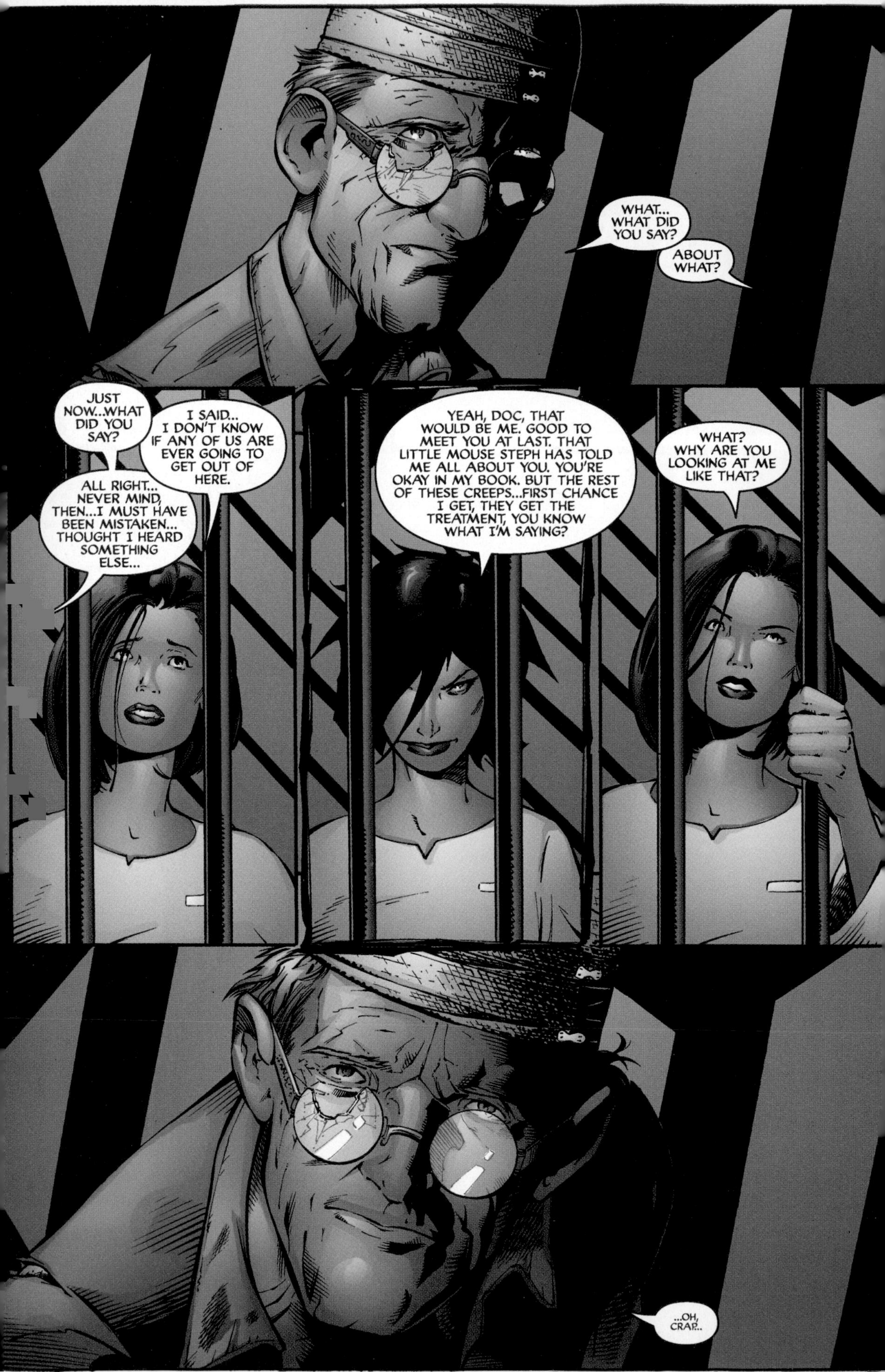
WHAT... WHAT DID YOU SAY?
ABOUT WHAT?
JUST NOW...WHAT DID YOU SAY?
I SAID... I DON'T KNOW IF ANY OF US ARE EVER GOING TO GET OUT OF HERE.
ALL RIGHT... NEVER MIND, THEN...I MUST HAVE BEEN MISTAKEN... THOUGHT I HEARD SOMETHING ELSE...
YEAH, DOC, THAT WOULD BE ME. GOOD TO MEET YOU AT LAST. THAT LITTLE MOUSE STEPH HAS TOLD ME ALL ABOUT YOU. YOU'RE OKAY IN MY BOOK. BUT THE REST OF THESE CREEPS...FIRST CHANCE I GET, THEY GET THE TREATMENT, YOU KNOW WHAT I'M SAYING?
WHAT? WHY ARE YOU LOOKING AT ME LIKE THAT?
...OH, CRAP...

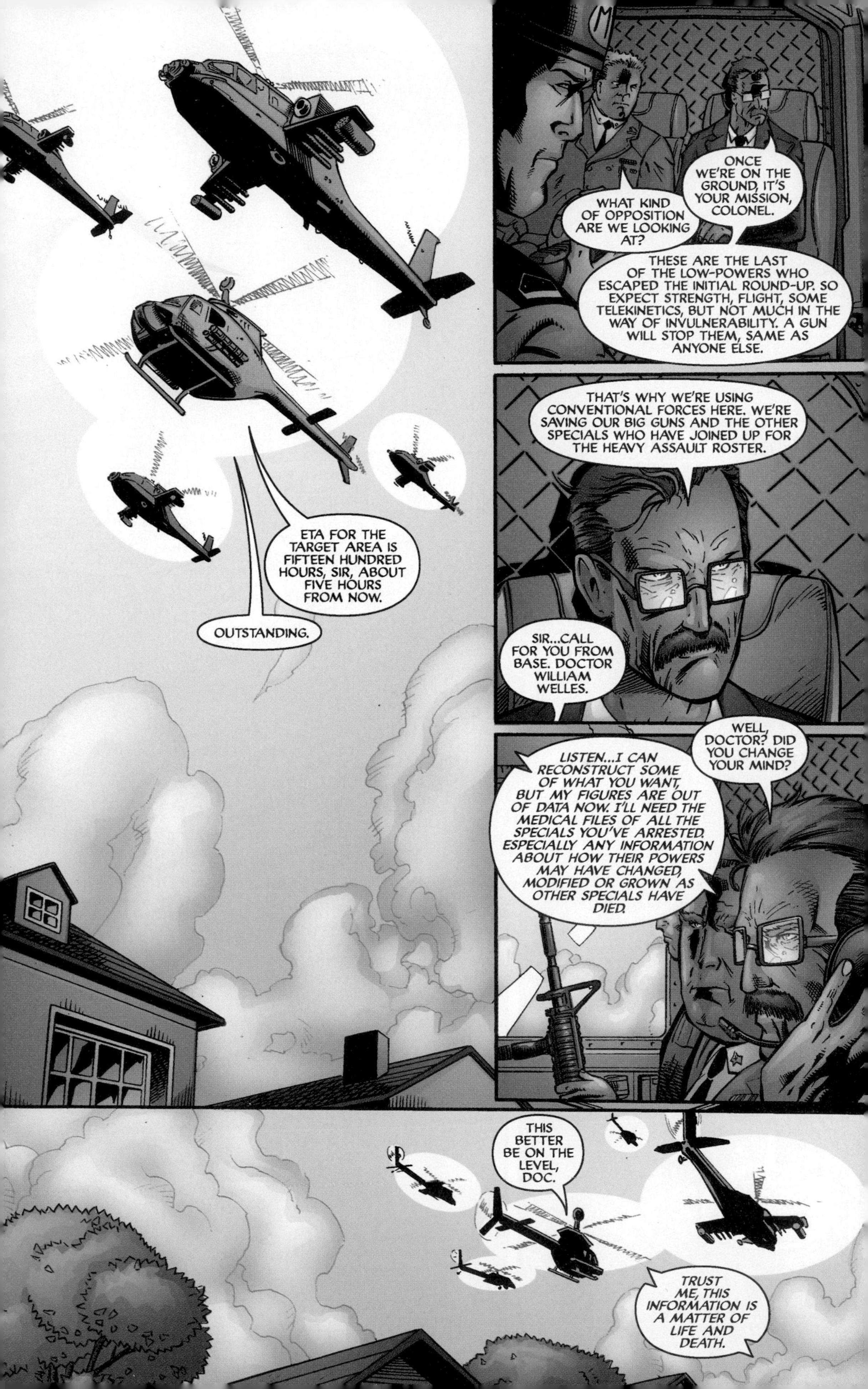
ETA FOR THE TARGET AREA IS FIFTEEN HUNDRED HOURS, SIR, ABOUT FIVE HOURS FROM NOW.
OUTSTANDING.
ONCE WE'RE ON THE GROUND, IT'S YOUR MISSION, COLONEL.
WHAT KIND OF OPPOSITION ARE WE LOOKING AT?
THESE ARE THE LAST OF THE LOW-POWERS WHO ESCAPED THE INITIAL ROUND-UP. SO EXPECT STRENGTH, FLIGHT, SOME TELEKINETICS, BUT NOT MUCH IN THE WAY OF INVULNERABILITY. A GUN WILL STOP THEM, SAME AS ANYONE ELSE.
THAT'S WHY WE'RE USING CONVENTIONAL FORCES HERE. WE'RE SAVING OUR BIG GUNS AND THE OTHER SPECIALS WHO HAVE JOINED UP FOR THE HEAVY ASSAULT ROSTER.
SIR...CALL FOR YOU FROM BASE. DOCTOR WILLIAM WELLES.
WELL, DOCTOR? DID YOU CHANGE YOUR MIND?
LISTEN...I CAN RECONSTRUCT SOME OF WHAT YOU WANT, BUT MY FIGURES ARE OUT OF DATA NOW. I'LL NEED THE MEDICAL FILES OF ALL THE SPECIALS YOU'VE ARRESTED. ESPECIALLY ANY INFORMATION ABOUT HOW THEIR POWERS MAY HAVE CHANGED, MODIFIED OR GROWN AS OTHER SPECIALS HAVE DIED.
THIS BETTER BE ON THE LEVEL, DOC.
TRUST ME, THIS INFORMATION IS A MATTER OF LIFE AND DEATH.

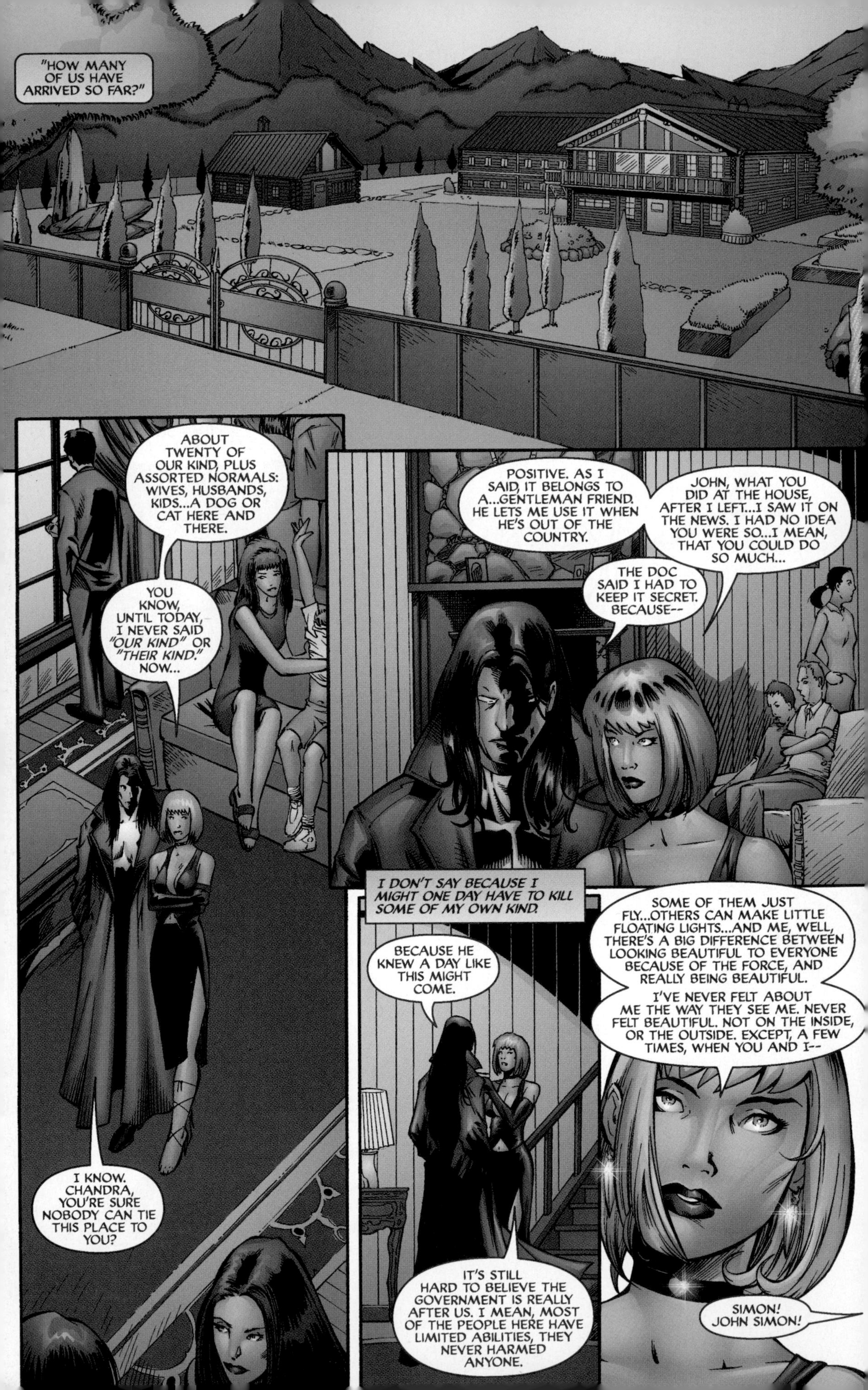
"HOW MANY OF US HAVE ARRIVED SO FAR?"
ABOUT TWENTY OF OUR KIND, PLUS ASSORTED NORMALS: WIVES, HUSBANDS, KIDS...A DOG OR CAT HERE AND THERE.
YOU KNOW, UNTIL TODAY, I NEVER SAID "OUR KIND" OR "THEIR KIND." NOW...
I KNOW. CHANDRA, YOU'RE SURE NOBODY CAN TIE THIS PLACE TO YOU?
POSITIVE. AS I SAID, IT BELONGS TO A...GENTLEMAN FRIEND. HE LETS ME USE IT WHEN HE'S OUT OF THE COUNTRY.
JOHN, WHAT YOU DID AT THE HOUSE, AFTER I LEFT...I SAW IT ON THE NEWS. I HAD NO IDEA YOU WERE SO...I MEAN, THAT YOU COULD DO SO MUCH...
THE DOC SAID I HAD TO KEEP IT SECRET. BECAUSE--
I DON'T SAY BECAUSE I MIGHT ONE DAY HAVE TO KILL SOME OF MY OWN KIND.
BECAUSE HE KNEW A DAY LIKE THIS MIGHT COME.
IT'S STILL HARD TO BELIEVE THE GOVERNMENT IS REALLY AFTER US. I MEAN, MOST OF THE PEOPLE HERE HAVE LIMITED ABILITIES, THEY NEVER HARMED ANYONE.
SOME OF THEM JUST FLY...OTHERS CAN MAKE LITTLE FLOATING LIGHTS...AND ME, WELL, THERE'S A BIG DIFFERENCE BETWEEN LOOKING BEAUTIFUL TO EVERYONE BECAUSE OF THE FORCE, AND REALLY BEING BEAUTIFUL.
I'VE NEVER FELT ABOUT ME THE WAY THEY SEE ME. NEVER FELT BEAUTIFUL. NOT ON THE INSIDE, OR THE OUTSIDE. EXCEPT, A FEW TIMES, WHEN YOU AND I--
SIMON! JOHN SIMON!

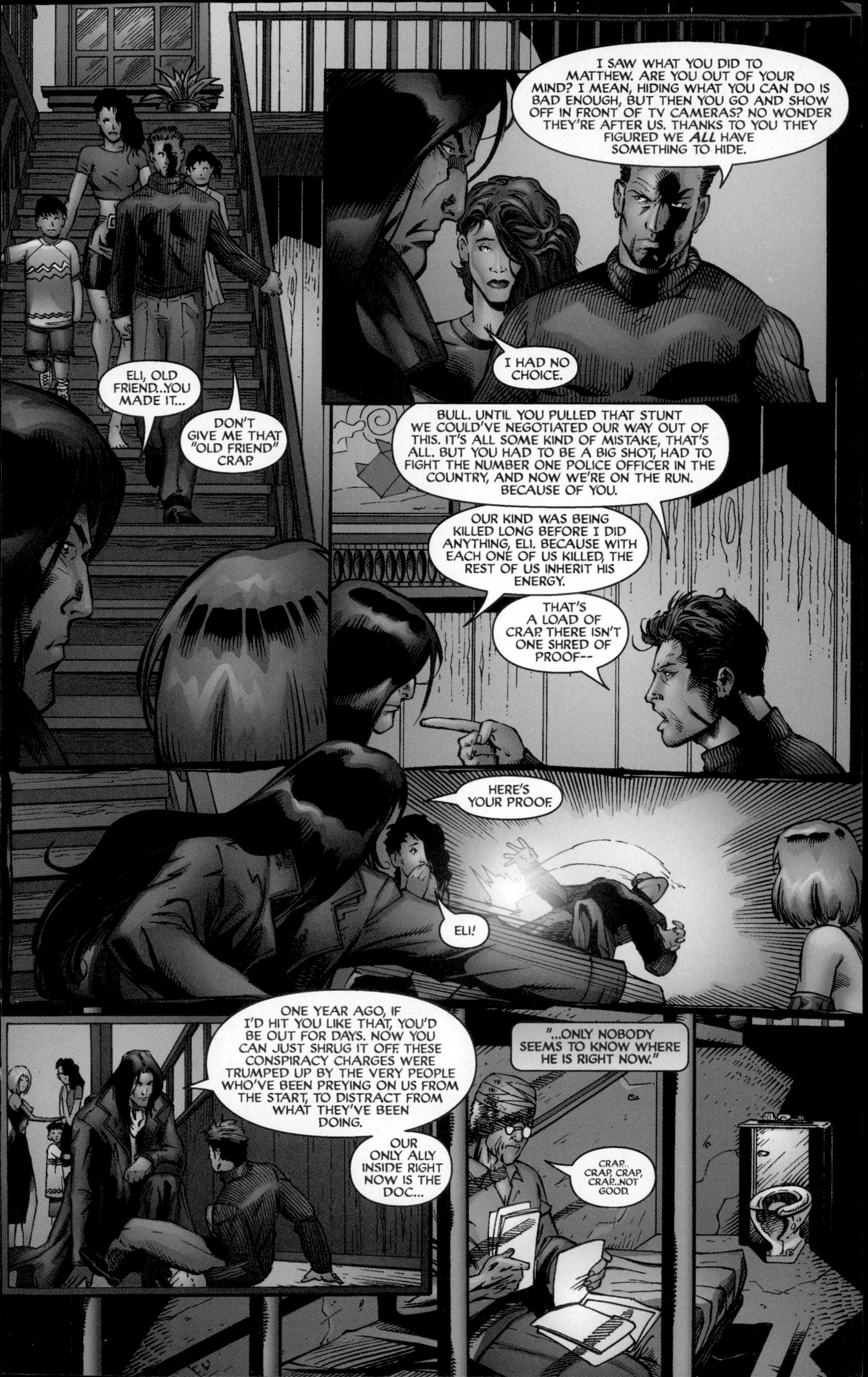
I SAW WHAT YOU DID TO MATTHEW. ARE YOU OUT OF YOUR MIND? I MEAN, HIDING WHAT YOU CAN DO IS BAD ENOUGH, BUT THEN YOU GO AND SHOW OFF IN FRONT OF TV CAMERAS? NO WONDER THEY'RE AFTER US. THANKS TO YOU THEY FIGURED WE ALL HAVE SOMETHING TO HIDE.
I HAD NO CHOICE.
ELI, OLD FRIEND...YOU MADE IT...
DON'T GIVE ME THAT "OLD FRIEND" CRAP.
BULL. UNTIL YOU PULLED THAT STUNT WE COULD'VE NEGOTIATED OUR WAY OUT OF THIS. IT'S ALL SOME KIND OF MISTAKE, THAT'S ALL. BUT YOU HAD TO BE A BIG SHOT, HAD TO FIGHT THE NUMBER ONE POLICE OFFICER IN THE COUNTRY, AND NOW WE'RE ON THE RUN. BECAUSE OF YOU.
OUR KIND WAS BEING KILLED LONG BEFORE I DID ANYTHING, ELI. BECAUSE WITH EACH ONE OF US KILLED, THE REST OF US INHERIT HIS ENERGY.
THAT'S A LOAD OF CRAP. THERE ISN'T ONE SHRED OF PROOF--
HERE'S YOUR PROOF.
ELI!
ONE YEAR AGO, IF I'D HIT YOU LIKE THAT, YOU'D BE OUT FOR DAYS. NOW YOU CAN JUST SHRUG IT OFF. THESE CONSPIRACY CHARGES WERE TRUMPED UP BY THE VERY PEOPLE WHO'VE BEEN PREYING ON US FROM THE START, TO DISTRACT FROM WHAT THEY'VE BEEN DOING.
OUR ONLY ALLY INSIDE RIGHT NOW IS THE DOC...
"...ONLY NOBODY SEEMS TO KNOW WHERE HE IS RIGHT NOW."
CRAP... CRAP, CRAP, CRAP...NOT GOOD.

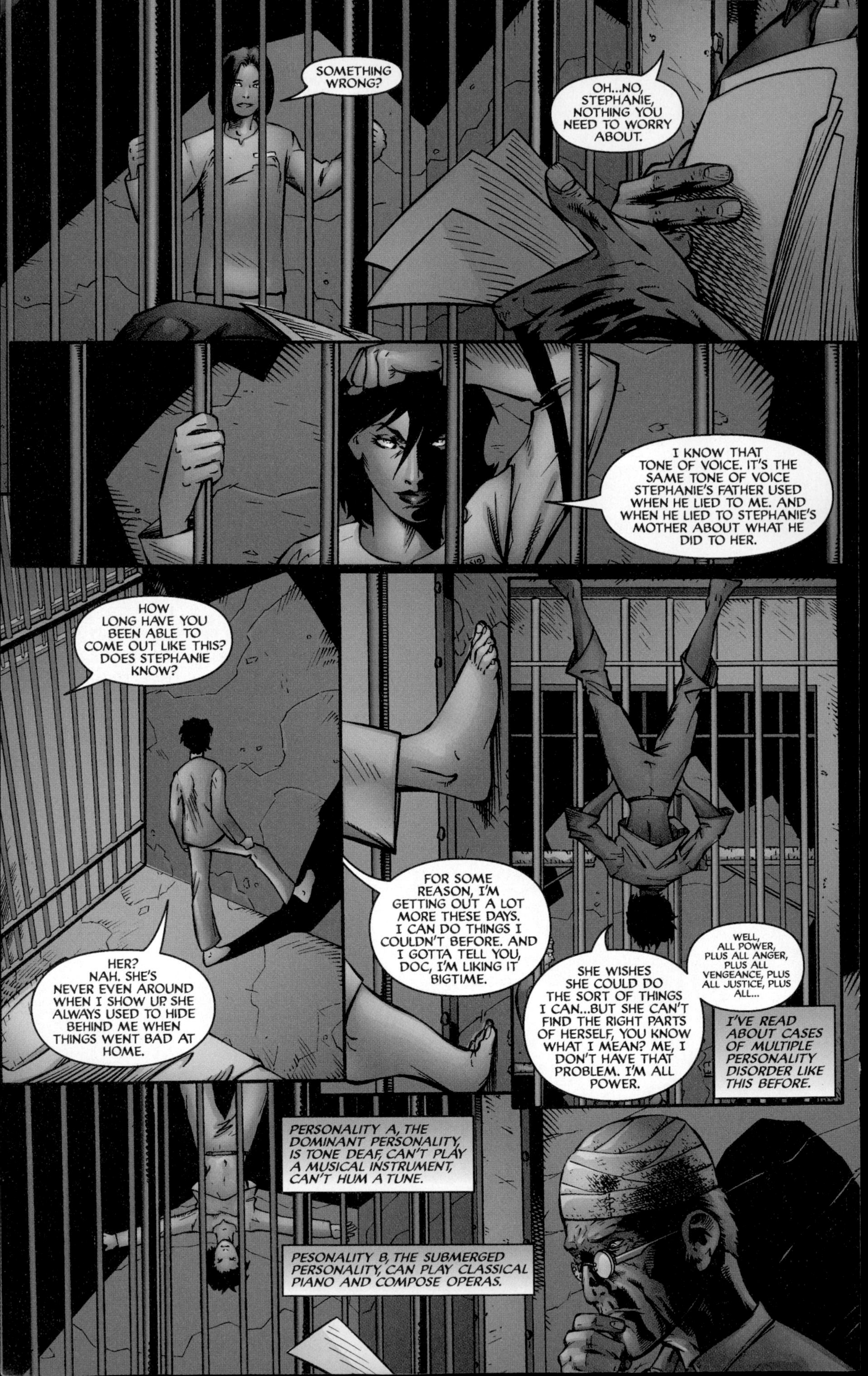

SOMETHING WRONG?
OH...NO, STEPHANIE, NOTHING YOU NEED TO WORRY ABOUT.
I KNOW THAT TONE OF VOICE. IT'S THE SAME TONE OF VOICE STEPHANIE'S FATHER USED WHEN HE LIED TO ME. AND WHEN HE LIED TO STEPHANIE'S MOTHER ABOUT WHAT HE DID TO HER.
HOW LONG HAVE YOU BEEN ABLE TO COME OUT LIKE THIS? DOES STEPHANIE KNOW?
HER? NAH. SHE'S NEVER EVEN AROUND WHEN I SHOW UP. SHE ALWAYS USED TO HIDE BEHIND ME WHEN THINGS WENT BAD AT HOME.
FOR SOME REASON, I'M GETTING OUT A LOT MORE THESE DAYS. I CAN DO THINGS I COULDN'T BEFORE. AND I GOTTA TELL YOU, DOC, I'M LIKING IT BIGTIME.
SHE WISHES SHE COULD DO THE SORT OF THINGS I CAN...BUT SHE CAN'T FIND THE RIGHT PARTS OF HERSELF, YOU KNOW WHAT I MEAN? ME, I DON'T HAVE THAT PROBLEM. I'M ALL POWER.
WELL, ALL POWER, PLUS ALL ANGER, PLUS ALL VENGEANCE, PLUS ALL JUSTICE, PLUS ALL...
I'VE READ ABOUT CASES OF MULTIPLE PERSONALITY DISORDER LIKE THIS BEFORE.
PERSONALITY A, THE DOMINANT PERSONALITY, IS TONE DEAF, CAN'T PLAY A MUSICAL INSTRUMENT, CAN'T HUM A TUNE.
PESONALITY B, THE SUBMERGED PERSONALITY, CAN PLAY CLASSICAL PIANO AND COMPOSE OPERAS.

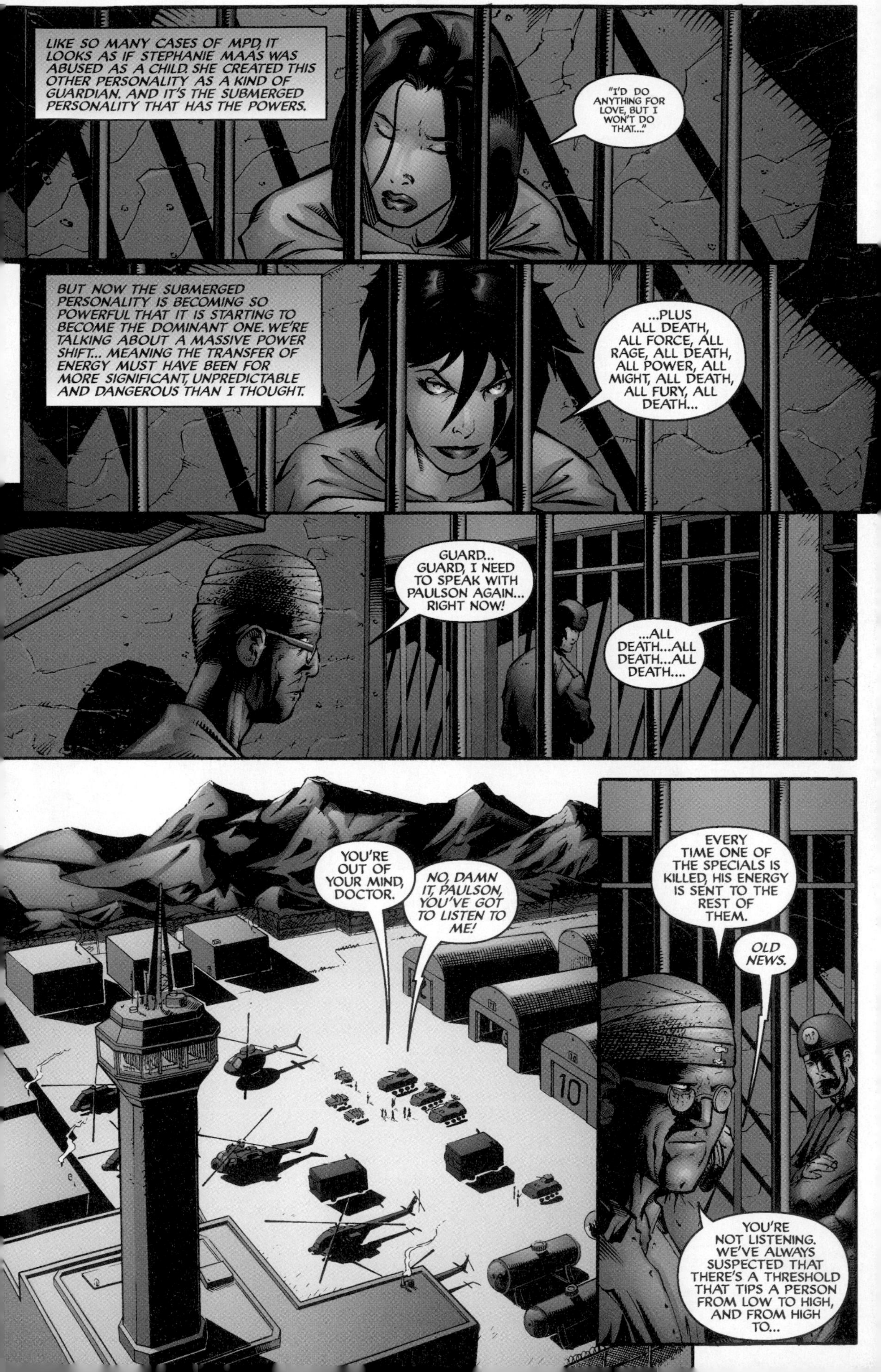
LIKE SO MANY CASES OF MPD, IT LOOKS AS IF STEPHANIE MAAS WAS ABUSED AS A CHILD. SHE CREATED THIS OTHER PERSONALITY AS A KIND OF GUARDIAN. AND IT'S THE SUBMERGED PERSONALITY THAT HAS THE POWERS.
"I'D DO ANYTHING FOR LOVE, BUT I WON'T DO THAT..."
BUT NOW THE SUBMERGED PERSONALITY IS BECOMING SO POWERFUL THAT IT IS STARTING TO BECOME THE DOMINANT ONE. WE'RE TALKING ABOUT A MASSIVE POWER SHIFT... MEANING THE TRANSFER OF ENERGY MUST HAVE BEEN FOR MORE SIGNIFICANT, UNPREDICTABLE AND DANGEROUS THAN I THOUGHT.
...PLUS ALL DEATH, ALL FORCE, ALL RAGE, ALL DEATH, ALL POWER, ALL MIGHT, ALL DEATH, ALL FURY, ALL DEATH...
GUARD... GUARD, I NEED TO SPEAK WITH PAULSON AGAIN... RIGHT NOW!
...ALL DEATH...ALL DEATH...ALL DEATH....
YOU'RE OUT OF YOUR MIND, DOCTOR.
NO, DAMN IT, PAULSON, YOU'VE GOT TO LISTEN TO ME!
EVERY TIME ONE OF THE SPECIALS IS KILLED, HIS ENERGY IS SENT TO THE REST OF THEM.
OLD NEWS.
YOU'RE NOT LISTENING. WE'VE ALWAYS SUSPECTED THAT THERE'S A THRESHOLD THAT TIPS A PERSON FROM LOW TO HIGH, AND FROM HIGH TO...

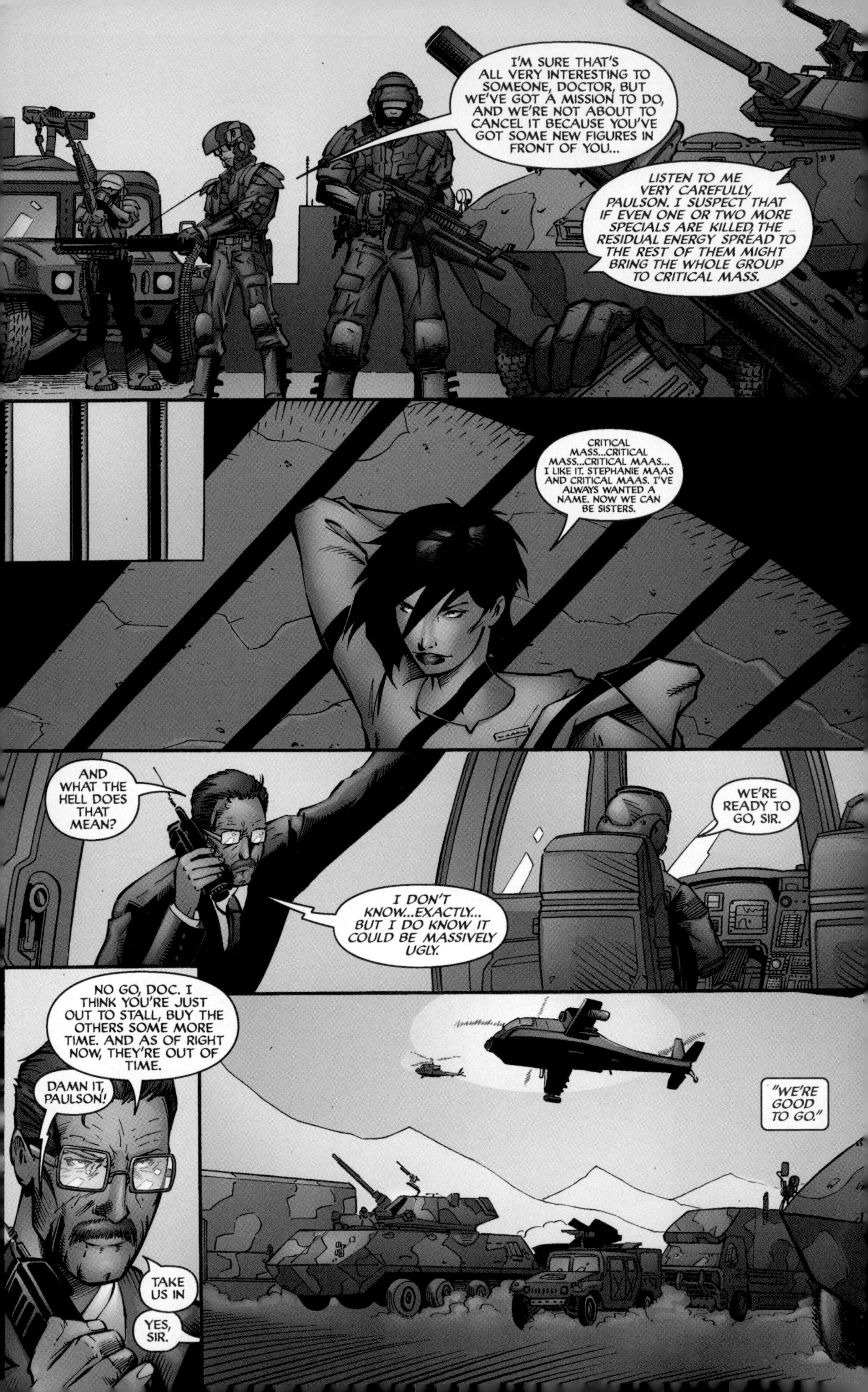
I'M SURE THAT'S ALL VERY INTERESTING TO SOMEONE, DOCTOR, BUT WE'VE GOT A MISSION TO DO, AND WE'RE NOT ABOUT TO CANCEL IT BECAUSE YOU'VE GOT SOME NEW FIGURES IN FRONT OF YOU...
LISTEN TO ME VERY CAREFULLY, PAULSON. I SUSPECT THAT IF EVEN ONE OR TWO MORE SPECIALS ARE KILLED, THE RESIDUAL ENERGY SPREAD TO THE REST OF THEM MIGHT BRING THE WHOLE GROUP TO CRITICAL MASS.
CRITICAL MASS...CRITICAL MASS...CRITICAL MAAS... I LIKE IT. STEPHANIE MAAS AND CRITICAL MAAS. I'VE ALWAYS WANTED A NAME. NOW WE CAN BE SISTERS.
AND WHAT THE HELL DOES THAT MEAN?
WE'RE READY TO GO, SIR.
I DON'T KNOW...EXACTLY... BUT I DO KNOW IT COULD BE MASSIVELY UGLY.
NO GO, DOC. I THINK YOU'RE JUST OUT TO STALL, BUY THE OTHERS SOME MORE TIME. AND AS OF RIGHT NOW, THEY'RE OUT OF TIME.
DAMN IT, PAULSON!
"WE'RE GOOD TO GO."
TAKE US IN
YES, SIR.

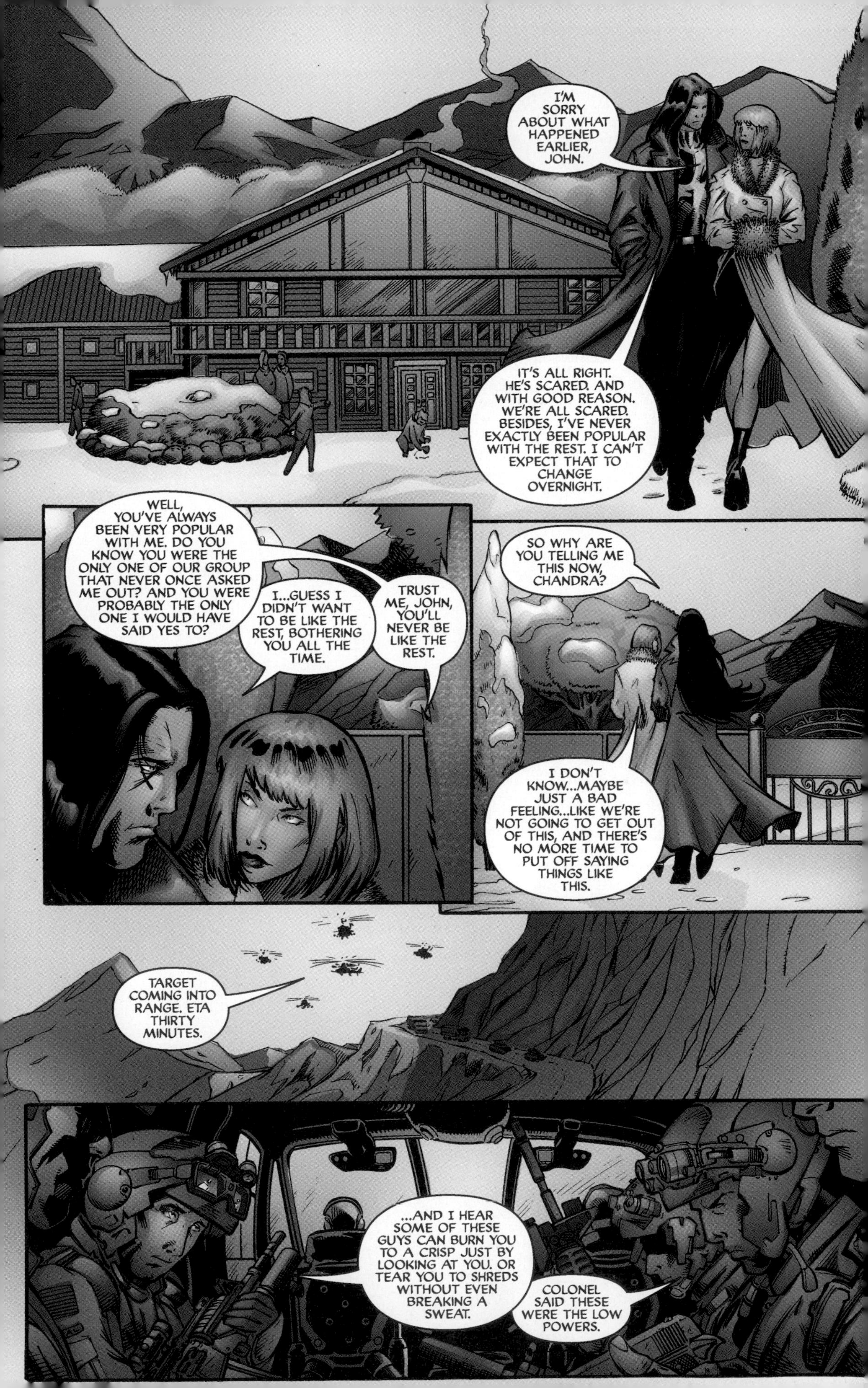
I'M SORRY ABOUT WHAT HAPPENED EARLIER, JOHN.
IT'S ALL RIGHT. HE'S SCARED. AND WITH GOOD REASON. WE'RE ALL SCARED. BESIDES, I'VE NEVER EXACTLY BEEN POPULAR WITH THE REST. I CAN'T EXPECT THAT TO CHANGE OVERNIGHT.
WELL, YOU'VE ALWAYS BEEN VERY POPULAR WITH ME. DO YOU KNOW YOU WERE THE ONLY ONE OF OUR GROUP THAT NEVER ONCE ASKED ME OUT? AND YOU WERE PROBABLY THE ONLY ONE I WOULD HAVE SAID YES TO?
I...GUESS I DIDN'T WANT TO BE LIKE THE REST, BOTHERING YOU ALL THE TIME.
TRUST ME, JOHN, YOU'LL NEVER BE LIKE THE REST.
SO WHY ARE YOU TELLING ME THIS NOW, CHANDRA?
I DON'T KNOW...MAYBE JUST A BAD FEELING...LIKE WE'RE NOT GOING TO GET OUT OF THIS, AND THERE'S NO MORE TIME TO PUT OFF SAYING THINGS LIKE THIS.
TARGET COMING INTO RANGE. ETA THIRTY MINUTES.
...AND I HEAR SOME OF THESE GUYS CAN BURN YOU TO A CRISP JUST BY LOOKING AT YOU. OR TEAR YOU TO SHREDS WITHOUT EVEN BREAKING A SWEAT.
COLONEL SAID THESE WERE THE LOW POWERS.

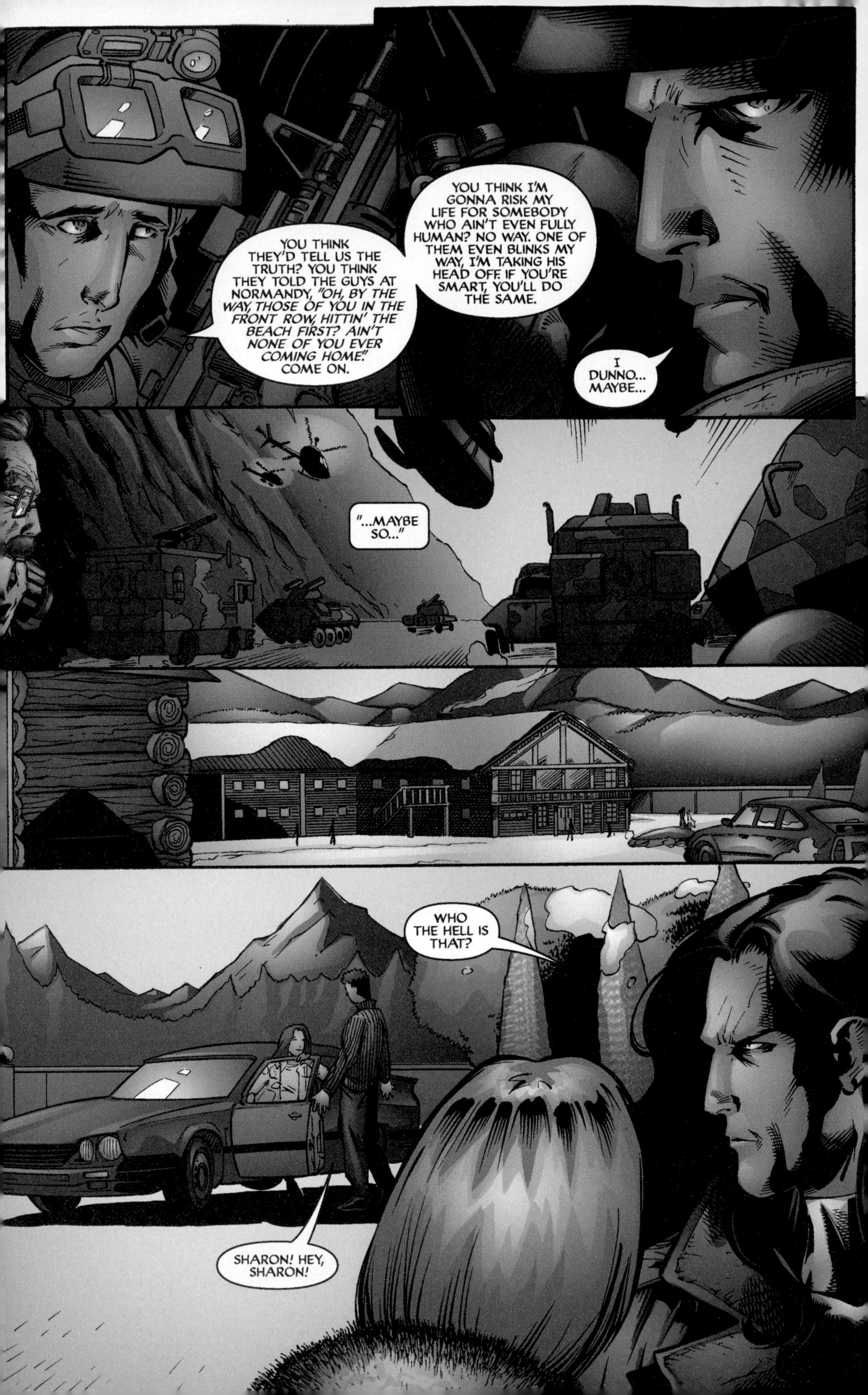
YOU THINK THEY'D TELL US THE TRUTH? YOU THINK THEY TOLD THE GUYS AT NORMANDY, "OH, BY THE WAY, THOSE OF YOU IN THE FRONT ROW, HITTIN' THE BEACH FIRST? AIN'T NONE OF YOU EVER COMING HOME." COME ON.
YOU THINK I'M GONNA RISK MY LIFE FOR SOMEBODY WHO AIN'T EVEN FULLY HUMAN? NO WAY. ONE OF THEM EVEN BLINKS MY WAY, I'M TAKING HIS HEAD OFF. IF YOU'RE SMART, YOU'LL DO THE SAME.
I DUNNO... MAYBE...
"...MAYBE SO..."
WHO THE HELL IS THAT?
SHARON! HEY, SHARON!

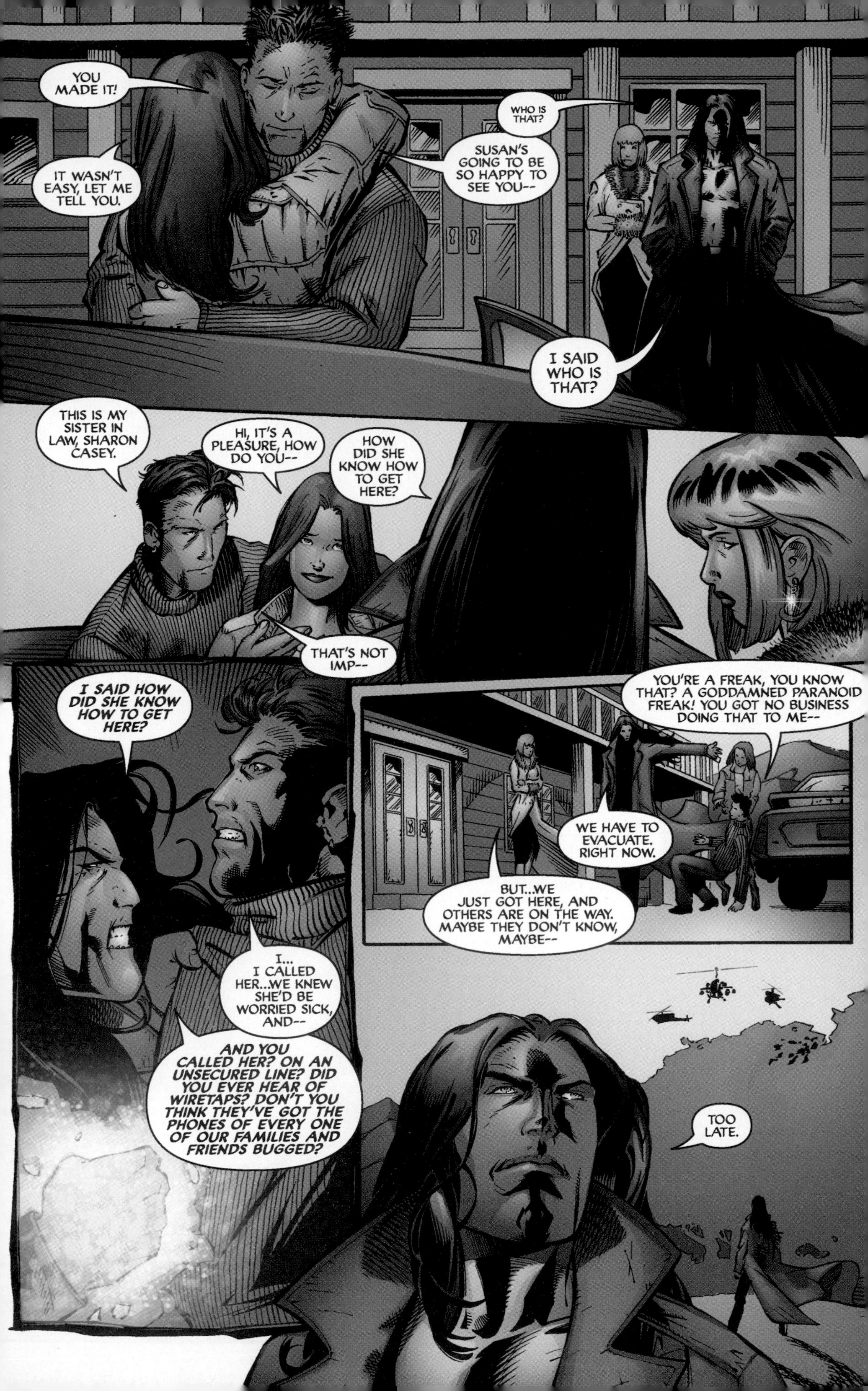
YOU MADE IT!
IT WASN'T EASY, LET ME TELL YOU.
WHO IS THAT?
SUSAN'S GOING TO BE SO HAPPY TO SEE YOU--
I SAID WHO IS THAT?
THIS IS MY SISTER IN LAW, SHARON CASEY.
HI, IT'S A PLEASURE, HOW DO YOU--
HOW DID SHE KNOW HOW TO GET HERE?
THAT'S NOT IMP--
I SAID HOW DID SHE KNOW HOW TO GET HERE?
I... I CALLED HER...WE KNEW SHE'D BE WORRIED SICK, AND--
AND YOU CALLED HER? ON AN UNSECURED LINE? DID YOU EVER HEAR OF WIRETAPS? DON'T YOU THINK THEY'VE GOT THE PHONES OF EVERY ONE OF OUR FAMILIES AND FRIENDS BUGGED?
YOU'RE A FREAK, YOU KNOW THAT? A GODDAMNED PARANOID FREAK! YOU GOT NO BUSINESS DOING THAT TO ME--
WE HAVE TO EVACUATE. RIGHT NOW.
BUT...WE JUST GOT HERE, AND OTHERS ARE ON THE WAY. MAYBE THEY DON'T KNOW, MAYBE--
TOO LATE.

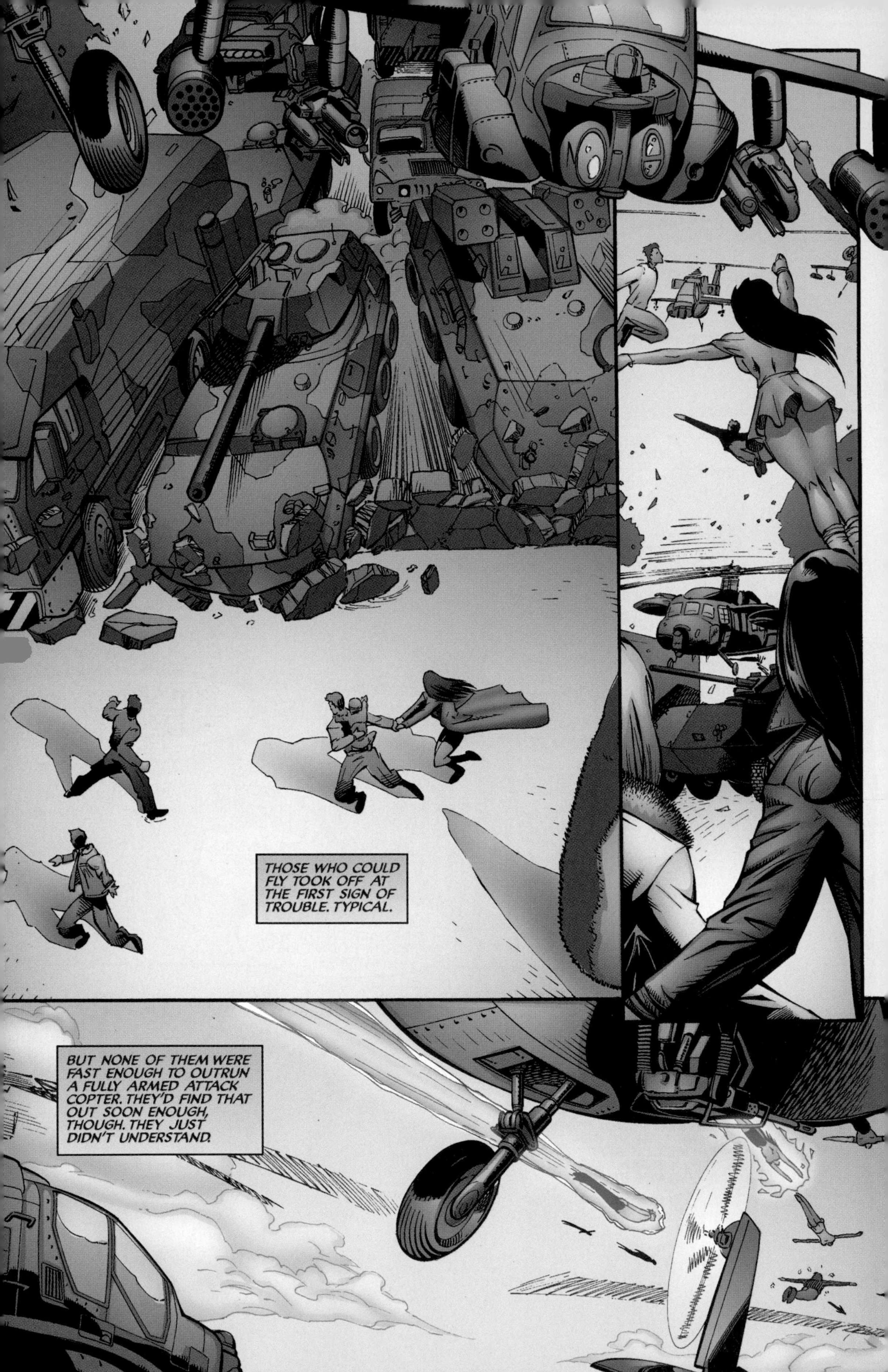
THOSE WHO COULD FLY TOOK OFF AT THE FIRST SIGN OF TROUBLE. TYPICAL.
BUT NONE OF THEM WERE FAST ENOUGH TO OUTRUN A FULLY ARMED ATTACK COPTER. THEY'D FIND THAT OUT SOON ENOUGH, THOUGH. THEY JUST DIDN'T UNDERSTAND.

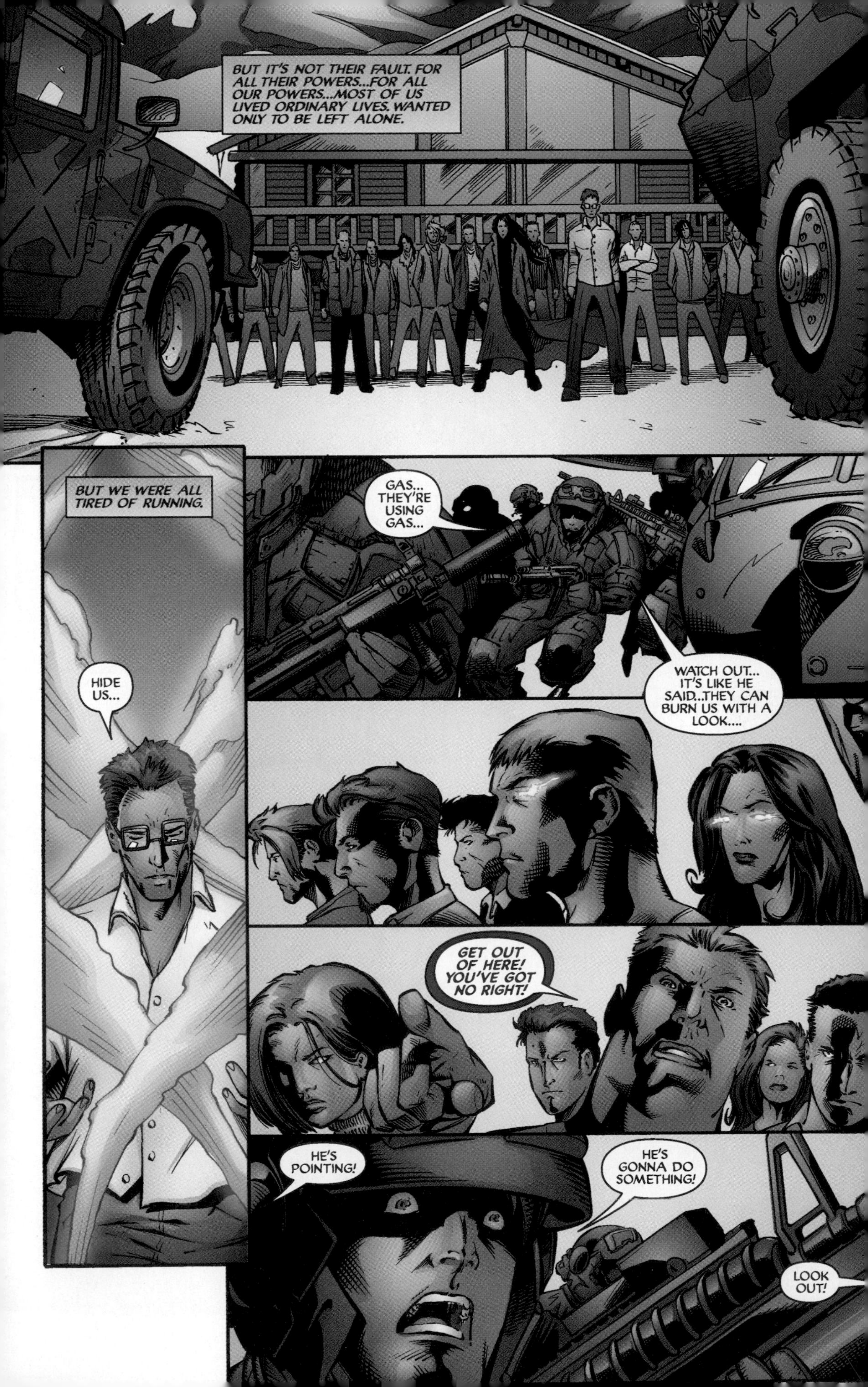
BUT IT'S NOT THEIR FAULT. FOR ALL THEIR POWERS...FOR ALL OUR POWERS...MOST OF US LIVED ORDINARY LIVES. WANTED ONLY TO BE LEFT ALONE.
BUT WE WERE ALL TIRED OF RUNNING.
HIDE US...
GAS... THEY'RE USING GAS...
WATCH OUT... IT'S LIKE HE SAID...THEY CAN BURN US WITH A LOOK....
GET OUT OF HERE! YOU'VE GOT NO RIGHT!
HE'S POINTING!
HE'S GONNA DO SOMETHING!
LOOK OUT!

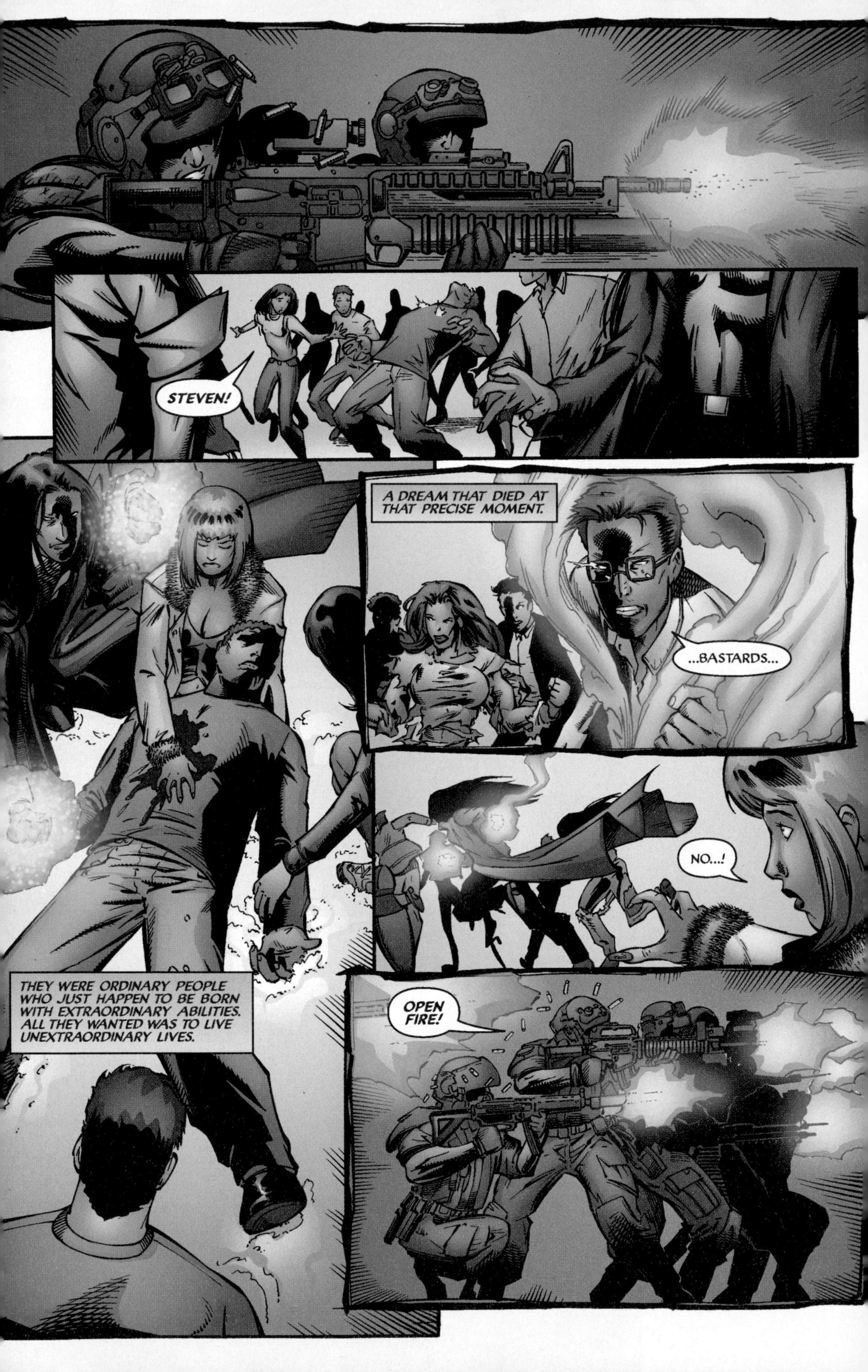
STEVEN!
A DREAM THAT DIED AT THAT PRECISE MOMENT.
...BASTARDS...
NO...!
THEY WERE ORDINARY PEOPLE WHO JUST HAPPEN TO BE BORN WITH EXTRAORDINARY ABILITIES. ALL THEY WANTED WAS TO LIVE UNEXTRAORDINARY LIVES.
OPEN FIRE!

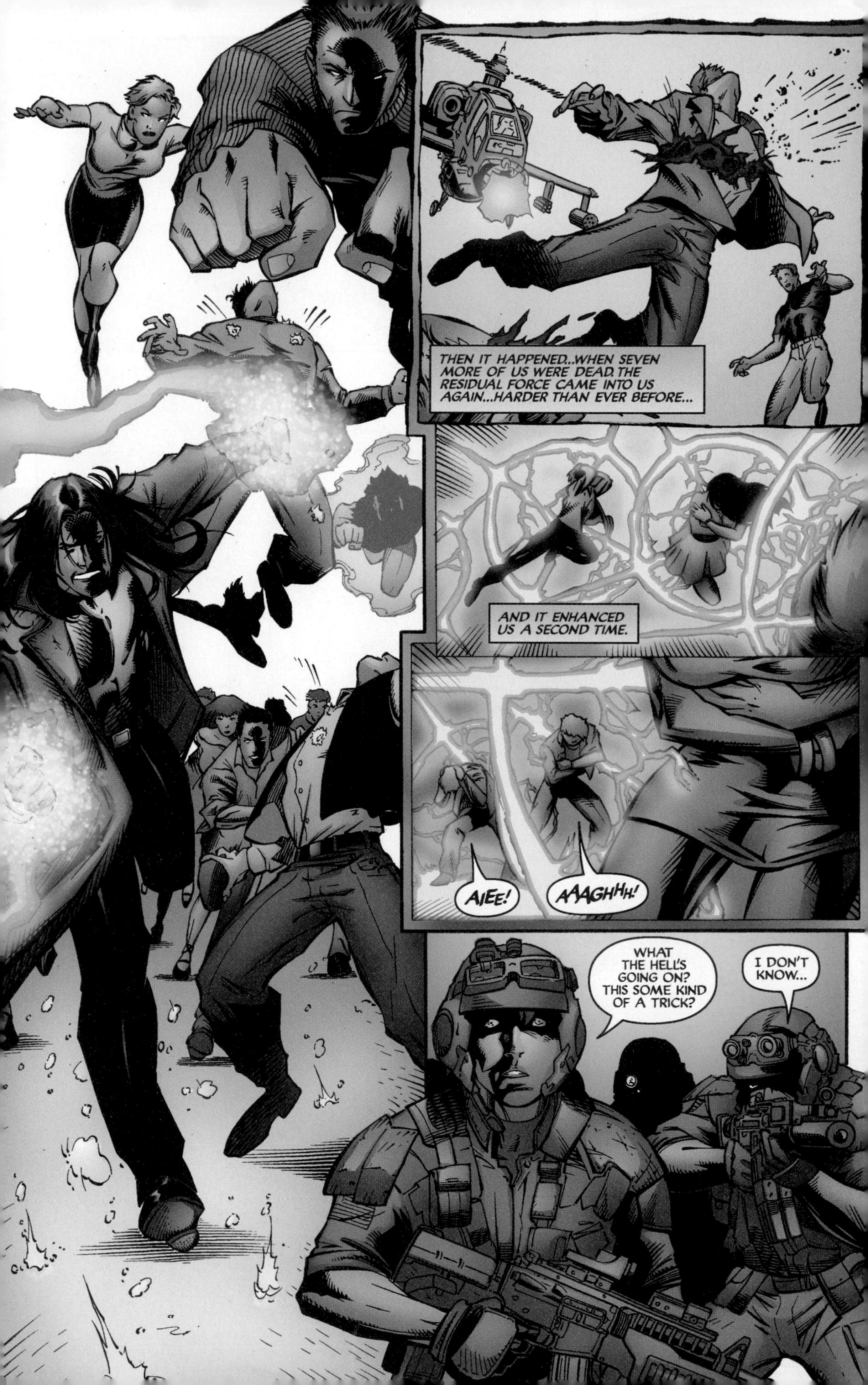
THEN IT HAPPENED...WHEN SEVEN MORE OF US WERE DEAD. THE RESIDUAL FORCE CAME INTO US AGAIN...HARDER THAN EVER BEFORE...
AND IT ENHANCED US A SECOND TIME.
AIEE!
AAAGHHH!
WHAT THE HELL'S GOING ON? THIS SOME KIND OF A TRICK?
I DON'T KNOW...

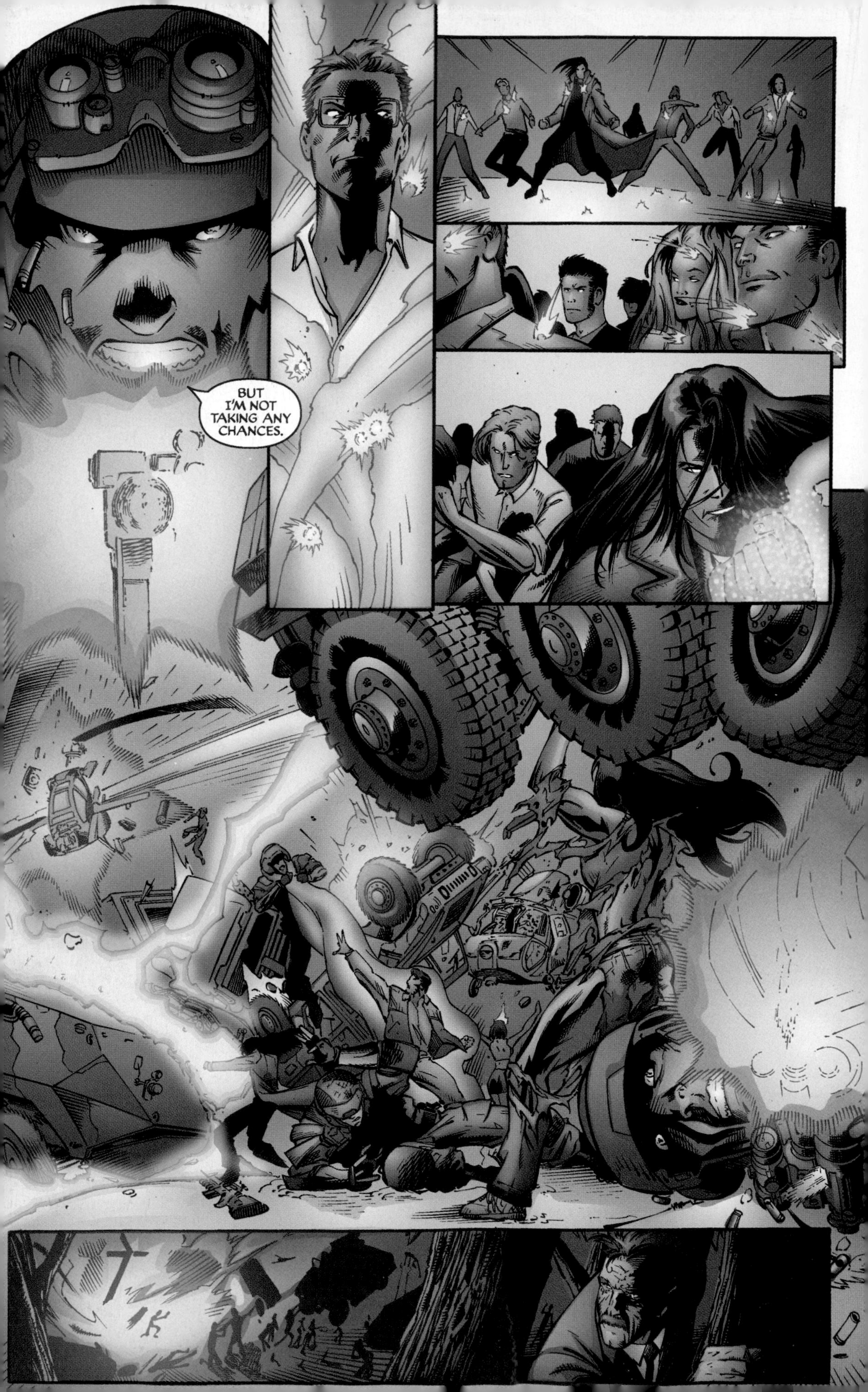
BUT I'M NOT TAKING ANY CHANCES.

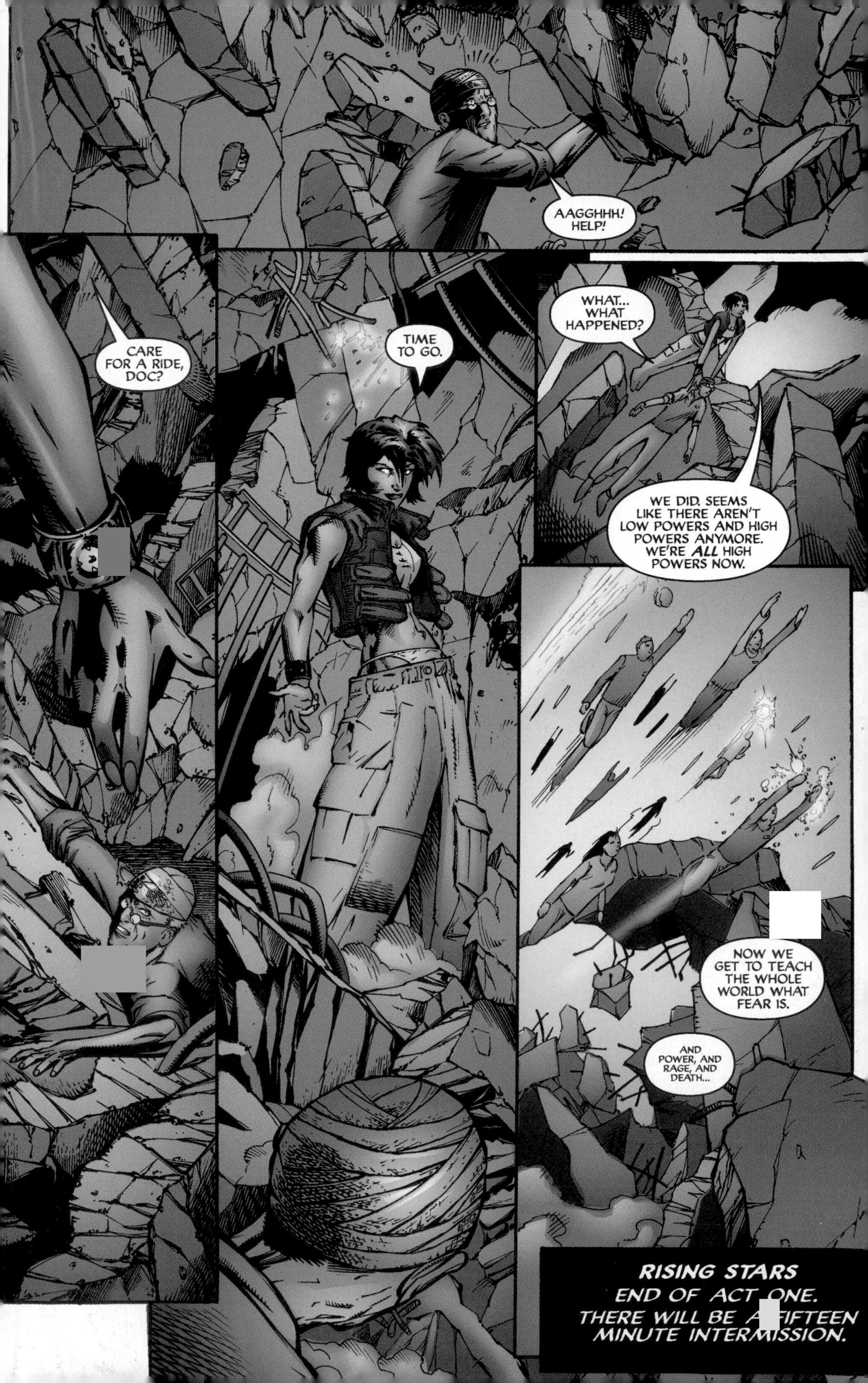
AAGGHHH! HELP!
CARE FOR A RIDE, DOC?
TIME TO GO.
WHAT... WHAT HAPPENED?
WE DID. SEEMS LIKE THERE AREN'T LOW POWERS AND HIGH POWERS ANYMORE. WE'RE ALL HIGH POWERS NOW.
NOW WE GET TO TEACH THE WHOLE WORLD WHAT FEAR IS.
AND POWER, AND RAGE, AND DEATH...
RISING STARS
END OF ACT ONE.
THERE WILL BE A FIFTEEN MINUTE INTERMISSION.

Our kind has never been seen before.
And when the last of us are gone,
will never be seen again.
Because there is a secret behind our creation,
and secrets like this only come around once.

NOT THE END.